lonely planet

Washington, DC

"All you've got to do is decide to go
and the hardest part is over.

So go!"

TONY WHEELER, COFOUNDER – LONELY PLANET

D1115800

Karla Zimmerman
Virginia Maxwell

Contents

Plan Your Trip 4

Explore Washington, DC 52

Understand Washington, DC 237

Survival Guide 267

Washington, DC Maps 292

(left) **Library of Congress p109**

(above) **Spring cherry blossoms (p132) at the Washington Monument p63**

(right) **Washington National Cathedral p188**

Upper Northwest DC p186

Logan Circle, U Street & Columbia Heights p165

Adams Morgan p156

Dupont Circle & Kalorama p143

Georgetown p92

White House Area & Foggy Bottom p76

Downtown & Penn Quarter p128

National Mall p56

Capitol Hill & South DC p104

Northern Virginia p195

Welcome to Washington, DC

The USA's capital teems with iconic monuments, vast museums and the corridors of power, where visionaries and demagogues roam.

Museums & Monuments

There's nothing quite like the Smithsonian Institution, a collection of 19 behemoth, artifact-stuffed museums, many lined up in a row along the Mall. The National Air and Space Museum, National Museum of Natural History, National Museum of African American History and Culture, Reynolds Center for American Art & Portraiture – all here, all free, always.

Alongside the museums, Washington's monuments bear tribute to both the beauty and the horror of years past. They're potent symbols of the American narrative, from the awe-inspiring Lincoln Memorial to the powerful Vietnam Veterans Memorial to the stirring Martin Luther King Jr Memorial.

Arts & Culture

Washington is the showcase of American arts, home to such prestigious venues as the National Theatre, the Kennedy Center and the Folger Theatre. Jazz music has a storied history here. In the early 20th century, locals such as Duke Ellington climbed on stages along U St NW, where atmospheric clubs still operate. The city hosts several adventurous small theaters, like Arena Stage, that put on works by nontraditional writers. Busboys & Poets' open-mike nights provide another outlet for progressive new voices.

Political Life

The president, Congress and the Supreme Court are here, the three pillars of US government. In their orbit float the Pentagon, the State Department, the World Bank and embassies from most corners of the globe. If you hadn't got the idea, *power* is why Washington emits such a palpable buzz.

As a visitor, there's a thrill in seeing the action up close – to walk inside the White House, to sit in the Capitol chamber while senators argue about Arctic drilling, and to drink in a bar alongside congresspeople likely determining your newest tax hike over their single malt Scotch.

History

A lot of history is concentrated within DC's relatively small confines. In a single day, you could gawp at the Declaration of Independence, the real, live parchment with John Hancock's signature scrawled across it at the National Archives; stand where Martin Luther King Jr gave his 'I Have a Dream' speech on the Lincoln Memorial's steps; prowl around the Watergate building that got Nixon into trouble; see the flag that inspired the 'Star Spangled Banner' at the National Museum of American History; and be an arm's length from where Lincoln was assassinated in Ford's Theatre.

ORHAN CAM / SHUTTERSTOCK ©

Why I Love Washington, DC

By Karla Zimmerman, Writer

It begins with the Mall. How sweet is it to have a walkable strip of museums where you can see nuclear missiles, cursed diamonds and exquisite Asian ceramics in cool underground galleries – for free? Further down the path the Lincoln Memorial just kills with its grandness and sweeping view. As a rabid traveler, it thrills me to see all the embassies flying their flags in Dupont and dream of future trips. (I'm coming for you, Kazakhstan. You too, Bulgaria.) And Shaw wins my affection for its neighborhoody beer halls, cafes and groovy murals.

For more about our writers, see p320

Washington, DC's
Top 10

Lincoln Memorial *(p58)*

1 There's something extraordinary about climbing the steps of Abe Lincoln's neo-classical temple, staring into his dignified eyes, and reading about the 'new birth of freedom' in the Gettysburg Address chiseled beside him. Then to stand where Martin Luther King Jr gave his 'Dream' speech and take in the sweeping view – it's a defining DC moment. At dawn, nowhere in the city is as serene and lovely, which is why the Lincoln Memorial is a popular place for proposals.

⊙ *National Mall*

Smithsonian Institution *(p66)*

2 If America was a quirky grandfather, the Smithsonian Institution would be his attic. Rockets, dinosaurs, Rodin sculptures, Tibetan *thangkas* (silk paintings), even the 45-carat Hope Diamond is here. The Smithsonian is actually a collection of 19 museums and they're all free. The National Air and Space, Natural History and African American History and Culture museums are the group's rock stars, while the Freer-Sackler Museums of Asian Art and the Reynolds Center for American Art provide quieter spaces for contemplation.

⊙ *National Mall*

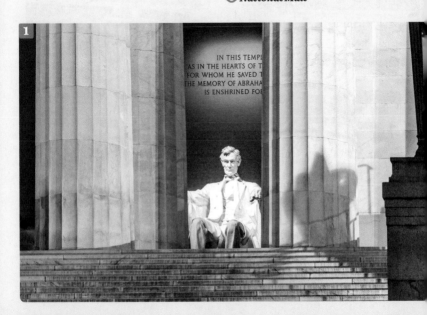

IN THIS TEMPL
AS IN THE HEARTS OF T
FOR WHOM HE SAVED T
THE MEMORY OF ABRAHA
IS ENSHRINED FO

National Gallery of Art *(p61)*

3 It takes two massive buildings at the National Gallery to hold the free-to-see trove of paintings, sculptures and decorative arts from the Middle Ages to the present. The East Building gets the modern stuff: Calder mobiles, Matisse collages, Pollock splatters. The West Building hangs works from earlier eras: El Greco, Monet and North America's only Leonardo da Vinci. Free films and concerts, a sweet cafe with 19 gelato flavors and an adjoining garden studded with whimsical sculptures add to the awesomeness.

⊙ *National Mall*

Capitol Hill *(p104)*

4 City planner Pierre L'Enfant called it a pedestal waiting for a monument. So that's how the Capitol came to sit atop the hill that rises above the city. You're welcome to go inside the mighty, white-domed edifice and count the statues, ogle the frescoes and visit the chambers of the folks who run the country. Afterward, call on the neighbors. The Supreme Court and Library of Congress also reside up here, across the street from the Capitol.

⊙ *Capitol Hill & Southeast DC*

White House *(p78)*

5 Thomas Jefferson groused it was big enough for two emperors, one Pope and the grand Lama, but when you tour the White House you get the feeling – despite all the spectacle – that it really is just a *house,* where a family lives. Admittedly, that family gets to hang out in Jefferson's green dining room and Lincoln's old office where his ghost supposedly roams. If you don't get in (tours require serious pre-planning), the visitors center provides the scoop on presidential pets and favorite foods.

⊙ *White House Area & Foggy Bottom*

Vietnam Veterans Memorial *(p62)*

6 The opposite of DC's white, gleaming marble, this black, low-lying Vietnam memorial cuts into the earth, just as the Vietnam War cut into the national psyche. The monument shows the names of the war's 58,000-plus casualties – listed in the order they died – along a dark, reflective wall. Seeing your own image among the names is meant to bring past and present together. It's a muted but remarkably profound monument, where visitors leave mementos, such as photos of babies and notes ('I wish you could have met him, Dad').

⊙ *National Mall*

National Archives *(p130)*

7 You'll have to elbow your way past all the school groups, but once you reach the front of the rotunda – holy Thomas Jefferson! – you're staring at the real deal Declaration of Independence. There it is, set out in neat cursive on yellowing parchment and signed by John Hancock, Ben Franklin and the rest of the guys. The Constitution unfurls next to it, followed by the Bill of Rights, and it's hard not to be awestruck by the USA's founding documents sitting right there in front of you.

⊙ *Downtown & Penn Quarter*

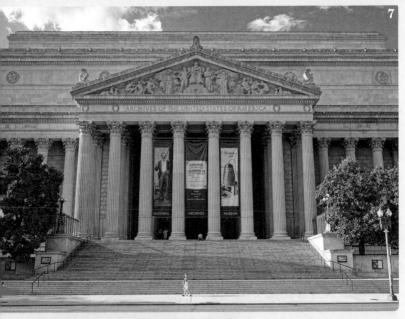

Arlington National Cemetery *(p197)*

8 Soldiers from every war since the Revolution are buried in the 624-acre grounds. Simple white headstones cover the green hills in a seemingly endless procession. Many US leaders and notable civilians are also buried here. An eternal flame flickers over the grave of John F Kennedy. Flowers pile at the marker for the space shuttle *Challenger* crew. Rifle-toting military guards maintain a 24-hour vigil at the Tomb of the Unknown Soldier. Meanwhile, a bugle's lingering notes of 'Taps' hang in the air.

⊙ *Northern Virginia*

Ben's Chili Bowl & U Street Corridor (p171)

9 The U St Corridor has had quite a life. It was the 'Black Broadway' where Duke Ellington got his jazz on in the early 1900s. It was the smoldering epicenter of the 1968 race riots. There was a troubled descent, then a vibrant rebirth as an entertainment district. And Ben's Chili Bowl has stood there through most of it. Despite visits by presidents and movie stars, Ben's remains a real neighborhood spot, with locals downing half-smokes and gossiping over sweet iced tea. It's quintessential DC.

Logan Circle, U Street & Columbia Heights

Washington Monument (p63)

10 Tall, phallic and imbued with shadowy Masonic lore, the 555ft obelisk is DC's tallest structure. Workers set the pyramid on top in 1884 after stacking up some 36,000 blocks of granite and marble over the preceding 36 years. A 70-second elevator ride whisks you to the observation deck at the top for the city's best views. But you'll have to wait until spring 2019 to see them, as the monument is closed until then for structural repairs.

National Mall

What's New

Ivy City

This industrial area of train tracks and warehouses is seeing new life as DC's distillery district. Bourbon, gin and vodka now bubble up from the brick buildings, and hip cocktail lounges and rooftop bars have opened in their wake. (p178)

The Wharf

The city transformed the lonely docks that used to sit along the Southwest Waterfront into a sparkling development of public piers, promenades, concert halls and chic restaurants. (p114)

Michelin Guide

The city earned its culinary stripes when Michelin deemed it worthy of a guide. Reviewers came to town and ate everything in sight before releasing their inaugural list of starred restaurants in 2017. (p29)

Watergate Hotel

The hotel in the infamous Watergate building has undergone a sleek refurbishment that includes a knockout whiskey bar and an eye-popping rooftop lounge with a sky-high ice-skating rink. (p228)

Blagden Alley

This tangle of passageways across from the Convention Center hides several cool bars and restaurants, plus the DC Alley Museum, a group of murals that pay homage to local cultural figures. (p129)

Kreeger Museum

What used to be an appointment-only oddity is now a full-fledged museum open Tuesday through Saturday showing works by Picasso, Van Gogh, Monet and other late 19th-century and early 20th-century masters. (p189)

Navy Yard

A winery and dog-friendly outdoor brewery opened recently, joining heaps of stylish seafood and modern American eateries. Near Nationals Park, this riverfront district continues to get its groove on. (p117)

Audi Field

The freshly built stadium for DC's Major League Soccer team is near the Wharf and Navy Yard, and slings Latin food by celebrity chef José Andrés. (p124)

International Spy Museum

This museum is taking its stash of lipstick-concealed pistols, poison-wielding umbrellas and other secret-agent gear to a fancy new building by L'Enfant Plaza, with twice the space to showcase its wares. (p116)

Hirshhorn Museum

Japanese artist Hiroshi Sugimoto redesigned the lobby into a mod, white, super-cool vision that includes pieces of a 700-year-old Japanese nutmeg tree, Icelandic sculpture and local gelato. (p71)

National Air and Space Museum

The Smithsonian's rock star museum is undergoing a $1 billion overhaul during the next several years, which will freshen current exhibits and add new ones. (p60)

For more recommendations and reviews, see **lonelyplanet.com/washington-dc**

Need to Know

For more information, see Survival Guide (p267)

Currency
US dollar ($)

Language
English

Visas
Generally not required for stays of up to 90 days; check www.travel.state.gov for details.

Money
ATMs widely available. Credit cards accepted at most hotels, restaurants and shops.

Cell Phones
International travelers can use local SIM cards in a smartphone provided it is unlocked. Alternatively, you can buy a cheap US phone and load it up with prepaid minutes.

Time
Eastern Standard Time (GMT/UTC minus five hours)

Tourist Information
Destination DC (202-789-7000; www.washington.org) DC's official tourism site, with the mother lode of online information.

Daily Costs

Budget: Less than $150
➡ Dorm bed: $30–55
➡ Lunchtime specials for food and happy-hour drinks: $15–30
➡ Metro day pass: $14.75
➡ Nationals baseball ticket: $18

Midrange: $150–350
➡ Hotel or B&B double room: $200–350
➡ Dinner in a casual restaurant: $30–55
➡ Bicycle tour: $44
➡ Theater ticket: $40

Top End: More than $350
➡ Luxury-hotel double room: $350+
➡ Dinner at Pineapple and Pearls: $325
➡ Washington National Opera ticket: $100–200

Advance Planning

Three months before Book your hotel, request a White House tour and try for tickets to the African American History and Culture Museum.

One month before Reserve tickets online for the National Archives, United States Holocaust Memorial Museum, Ford's Theatre and Capitol tour.

Two weeks before Reserve must-eat restaurants.

One week before Scan www.washingtoncitypaper.com to check upcoming entertainment and make bookings.

Useful Websites
Destination DC (www.washington.org) Official tourism site packed with sightseeing and event info.

Lonely Planet (www.lonelyplanet.com/usa/washington-dc) Destination information, hotel bookings, traveler forum and more.

Cultural Tourism DC (www.culturaltourismdc.org) Neighborhood-oriented events and DIY tours.

Washingtonian (www.washingtonian.com) Features on dining, entertainment and local luminaries.

WHEN TO GO

Peak season is late March to May. June and July are crowded and hot. August is steamy, but cheap. December is festive.

Washington, DC

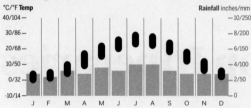

Arriving in Washington, DC

Ronald Reagan Washington National Airport Metro trains (around $2.65) depart every 10 minutes or so between 5am (from 7am weekends) and 11:30pm (to 1am Friday and Saturday); they reach the city center in 20 minutes. A taxi is $19 to $26.

Dulles International Airport The Silver Line Express bus runs every 15 to 20 minutes from Dulles to Wiehle-Reston East Metro between 6am and 10:40pm (from 7:45am weekends). Total time to the city center is 60 to 75 minutes, total cost around $11. A taxi is $62 to $73.

Union Station All trains and many buses arrive at this huge station near the Capitol. There's a Metro stop inside for easy onward transport. Taxis queue outside the main entrance.

For much more on **arrival** see p268

Getting Around

The Metro is the main way to move around the city. Buy a rechargeable SmarTrip card at any Metro station. You must use the card to enter *and* exit station turnstiles.

Metro Fast, frequent, ubiquitous (except during weekend track maintenance). It operates between 5am (from 7am weekends) and 11:30pm (1am on Friday and Saturday). Fares from $2 to $6 depending on distance traveled. A day pass costs $14.75.

DC Circulator bus Useful for the Mall, Georgetown, Adams Morgan and other areas with limited Metro service. Fare is $1.

Bicycle Capital Bikeshare stations are everywhere; a day pass costs $8.

Taxi Relatively easy to find (less so at night), but costly. Ridesharing companies are used more in the District.

For much more on **getting around** see p269

Sleeping

Accommodations will likely be your biggest expense in DC. The best digs are monuments of Victorian and jazz-era opulence. Chain hotels, B&Bs and apartments blanket the cityscape, too. Several hostels are sprinkled around, typically in locations that are a bit far-flung. Boutique hotels abound in the core neighborhoods, as do luxury hotels catering to presidents, prime ministers and heads of state. DC's atmospheric B&Bs (also called guesthouses) are often cheaper than hotels.

Useful Websites

Lonely Planet (www.lonelyplanet.com/usa/washington-dc/hotels) Recommendations and bookings.

Bed & Breakfast DC (www.bedandbreakfastdc.com) For B&Bs and apartments.

WDCA Hotels (www.wdcahotels.com) Discounter that sorts by neighborhood, price or ecofriendliness.

Destination DC (www.washington.org) Options from the tourism office's jam-packed website.

For much more on **sleeping** see p224

Top Itineraries

Day One

National Mall (p56)

 You might as well dive right into the good stuff, and the **Lincoln Memorial** is about as iconically DC as it gets. It's also a convenient starting point, since Abe sits at the far end of the Mall. Next up as you walk east is the powerful **Vietnam Veterans Memorial**. Then comes the **Washington Monument**, which is pretty hard to miss, being DC's tallest structure and all.

> **Lunch** Munch sandwiches by an artsy waterfall at Cascade Café (p75).

National Mall (p56)

After lunch, it's time to explore the **National Museum of African American History and Culture** (assuming you've procured a ticket) or the **National Gallery of Art**. Pick a side: East, for modern; or West, for Impressionists and other classics. Afterward, mosey across the lawn to the **National Air and Space Museum** and gape at the stuff hanging from the ceiling. The missiles and the Wright Brothers' original plane are incomparably cool.

> **Dinner** Hop the Metro to Bistrot du Coin (p149) in Dupont Circle.

Dupont Circle & Kalorama (p143)

Dupont parties in the evening. Sip cocktails at **Bar Charley**, hoist brews with locals at **Board Room** or hit one of the dance clubs.

Day Two

Capitol Hill & South DC (p104)

 Do the government thing this morning. Start in the **Capitol** and tour the statue-cluttered halls. Then walk across the street and up the grand steps to the **Supreme Court**; hopefully you'll get to hear a case argument. The **Library of Congress** and its 500 miles of books blow minds next door.

> **Lunch** Have a burger amid politicos at Old Ebbitt Grill (p86).

White House Area & Foggy Bottom (p76)

Hopefully you planned ahead and booked a **White House** tour. If not, make do at the **White House Visitor Center**. Pop into the **Round Robin** to see if any bigwigs and lobbyists are clinking glasses. Zip over to the **Kennedy Center** to watch the free 6pm show.

> **Dinner** Have French fare at Chez Billy Sud (p97) or pizza at Il Canale (p97).

Georgetown (p92)

After dinner, sink a pint in a friendly pub like the **Tombs**. On warm nights the outdoor cafes and boating action make **Georgetown Waterfront Park** a hot spot. And check if anyone groovy is playing at **Blues Alley**.

Arlington National Cemetery p197

Day Three

Northern Virginia (p195)

 Walking around **Arlington National Cemetery** you can't help but be moved, from the Tomb of the Unknown Soldier's dignified guards to John F Kennedy's eternal flame. One Metro stop south, the **Pentagon** offers another affecting memorial to those who died in the September 11, 2001, attacks.

> **Lunch** Treat yourself at Central Michel Richard (p138) or Rasika (p137).

Downtown & Penn Quarter (p128)

It's an abundance of riches downtown. See the Declaration of Independence at the **National Archives**, and the seat where Lincoln was shot at **Ford's Theatre**. The **Reynolds Center for American Art & Portraiture** hangs sublime paintings. The **Newseum** has the Unabomber's cabin. You'll have to make some hard choices about which sights to visit.

> **Dinner** Seek out Compass Rose (p172) for a romantic global taste-trip.

Logan Circle, U Street & Columbia Heights (p165)

 Mosey around 14th St and U St NW, and there's nightlife galore. Sip beneath the Elizabeth Taylor mural at free-spirited **Dacha Beer Garden**, split your eardrums at the rock-and-roll **Black Cat**, or grab a beer at neighborhood favorite **Right Proper Brewing Co**.

Day Four

Upper Northwest DC (p186)

 If you have kids, get to the **National Zoo**. Even without kids, the zoo entertains thanks to its giant pandas and brainy orangutans. Earmark some quality time for **Washington National Cathedral** and its Darth Vader gargoyle, moon rock and Helen Keller's ashes, among other esoteric offerings.

> **Lunch** 2 Amys (p191) serves excellent thin-crust pizzas, antipasti and craft brews.

Adams Morgan (p156)

Adams Morgan is Washington's party zone, but during the day **Meeps** and **Idle Time Books** provide plenty to do. Plus you're well situated for happy hour at **Songbyrd Record Cafe & Music House**, a cool retro bar.

> **Dinner** Share Mediterranean small plates at Tail Up Goat (p161).

National Mall (p56)

 End in the 'hood where you began your Washington trip, but experience it from a different perspective. Walk along Constitution Ave from east to west. The dramatically lit monuments glow ethereally at night. Climb the steps of the **Lincoln Memorial** and turn around for one last, long fantastic view. That'll do it, until you and DC meet again.

If You Like...

Famous Monuments

Lincoln Memorial Abe Lincoln gazes peacefully across the Mall from his Doric-columned temple. (p58)

Vietnam Veterans Memorial The black wall reflects the names of the Vietnam War's 58,000-plus American casualties. (p62)

Tomb of the Unknown Soldier Military guards maintain a round-the-clock vigil at this crypt in Arlington National Cemetery. (p197)

Martin Luther King Jr Memorial Dr King's 30ft-tall likeness emerges from a mountain of granite. (p71)

Washington Monument The iconic obelisk, DC's tallest structure, offers unparalleled views from the top. (p63)

National WWII Memorial Soaring columns and stirring quotes mark this memorial smack in the Mall's midst. (p72)

Franklin Delano Roosevelt Memorial FDR's sprawling monument is an oasis of alcoves, fountains and contemplative inscriptions. (p70)

Jefferson Memorial Thomas Jefferson's round shrine sits amid a grove of gorgeous cherry trees. (p72)

Not-So-Famous Monuments

Korean War Veterans Memorial The haunting tribute depicts ghostly steel soldiers marching by a wall of etched faces. (p73)

Georgetown Waterfront Park p94

African American Civil War Memorial Rifle-bearing troops who fought in the Union Army are immortalized in bronze. (p167)

George Mason Memorial The statesman who wrote the Bill of Rights' prototype gets his due in flowers and fountains. (p73)

Women's Titanic Memorial The waterside figure honors the men who sacrificed their lives aboard the sinking ship. (p116)

National Japanese American Memorial Two cranes bound with barbed wire represent Japanese Americans held in internment camps during WWII. (p114)

Navy Memorial A large plaza of flags and masts surrounds the lone sailor with his duffel bag. (p135)

Art

National Gallery of Art It takes two massive buildings to hold the rich trove of paintings, sculptures and decorative arts. (p61)

Reynolds Center for American Art & Portraiture Portraits on one side, O'Keeffe, Hopper and more of America's best on the other. (p131)

Phillips Collection Modern art in a house that puts you face-to-face with Renoirs and Rothkos. (p146)

Freer-Sackler Museums of Asian Art Ancient ceramics and temple sculptures spread across two tunnel-connected galleries. (p70)

Hirshhorn Museum Rodin and Brancusi sculptures mingle with Miró and Warhol canvases in this modern-art venue. (p71)

National Museum of Women in the Arts The women show how it's done in a chandeliered mansion downtown. (p135)

National Museum of African Art Eye-popping masks, paintings, sculptures and beaded works brighten the subterranean galleries. (p72)

Dupont Underground Groovy exhibitions held in an abandoned streetcar station beneath Dupont Circle. (p146)

History

National Museum of African American History and Culture A powerful collection with Harriet Tubman's hymnal, Emmett Till's casket and more. (p59)

Ford's Theatre Explore the venue where John Wilkes Booth assassinated Abraham Lincoln. (p134)

National Museum of American History Lincoln's top hat, Washington's sword and a piece of Plymouth Rock are among the stash. (p70)

United States Holocaust Memorial Museum Brutal and impassioned exhibits about the millions murdered by the Nazis. (p108)

Newseum It has the Unabomber's cabin and other artifacts from headline stories. (p134)

Frederick Douglass National Historic Site The statesman's hilltop home impresses almost as much as the man himself. (p114)

African American Civil War Museum It goes beyond the war, following black history through the Civil Rights movement. (p167)

President Lincoln's Cottage Where Abe came to escape the city and jot notes for the Emancipation Proclamation. (p168)

Green Spaces

United States National Arboretum Learn your state tree

For more top Washington, DC's spots, see the following:
- → Eating (p29)
- → Drinking & Nightlife (p36)
- → Entertainment (p40)
- → Shopping (p43)
- → Sports & Activities (p45)

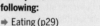

PLAN YOUR TRIP IF YOU LIKE...

amid 450 acres of meadowlands and wooded groves. (p168)

Rock Creek Park It's twice the size of New York's Central Park and wild enough to house coyotes. (p190)

Dumbarton Oaks The Georgetown mansion features sprawling, fountain-dotted gardens; bonus if you visit during spring. (p94)

United States Botanic Garden Exotic flowers bloom in a glassy Mall greenhouse that looks like London's Crystal Palace. (p71)

Theodore Roosevelt Island Car- and bike-free, this Potomac River isle offers woodlands, trails and tranquility. (p199)

Georgetown Waterfront Park Sip an alfresco drink, ogle the yachts and watch rowing teams ply the Potomac. (p94)

East Potomac Park Walk and smell the cherry blossoms in this lovely spot a hop from the Mall. (p116)

Off-the-Beaten-Path Museums

National Postal Museum A whopping stamp collection and poignant old letters lift it beyond its humdrum name. (p275)

Textile Museum The nation's only collection of its kind, with galleries of splendid fabrics and carpets. (p84)

National Museum of Health and Medicine Home to a giant hairball, Lincoln's assassination bullet and other macabre exhibits. (p168)

DEA Museum Showcase of America's old war on drugs, with Nancy Reagan commercials and opium-den relics. (p199)

Anacostia Community Museum This small Smithsonian outpost rotates exhibits on diverse and underserved communities. (p115)

Franciscan Monastery An outdoor collection of re-created holy shrines from around the globe. (p169)

Seeing Politics in Action

Capitol Sit in on committee hearings to see how bills start winding their way toward laws. (p106)

White House The protester-fueled political theater outside the building is where to observe democracy at its finest. (p78)

Round Robin Since 1850 bigwigs and lobbyists have swirled Scotch and cut deals in the gilded bar. (p88)

Le Diplomate Bustling French restaurant where politcos cozy up for coq au vin. (p171)

K Street Traditional avenue where lobbyists have offices and power-lunch meetings. (p83)

Pop-Culture Icons

Watergate Complex The chichi apartment-hotel complex is synonymous with political scandal, thanks to Nixon's wiretaps. (p84)

Lincoln Memorial Steps Where MLK gave his 'dream' speech, and Marian Anderson broke barriers with her singing. (p58)

Washington Monument Tall, phallic and imbued with shadowy lore, it's a frequent target of Hollywood destruction. (p63)

Exorcist Stairs Where demonically possessed characters from *The Exorcist* met an untimely death in Georgetown. (p94)

Ben's Chili Bowl Everyone who's anyone – rock stars, actors, presidents – takes a seat here for the photo op. (p171)

Mayflower Renaissance Hotel J Edgar Hoover famously dined here; John F Kennedy supposedly trysted here. (p227)

Kid-Friendly Activities

National Zoo Bamboo-nibbling pandas, roaring lions, swinging orangutans and many more critters roam the 163 acres. (p189)

National Museum of Natural History Mummies! Henry the giant elephant! Tarantulas feedings! (p70)

National Air and Space Museum It's a blast, with moon rocks, spaceships, starry films and wild simulator rides. (p60)

International Spy Museum Budding James Bonds can crawl through ductwork, peek through vents and find hidden recording devices. (p116)

Discovery Theater Cultural plays, puppet shows and storytelling are all at the Smithsonian children's theater. (p75)

Albert Einstein Memorial Einstein's bemused, chubby bronze likeness is a magnet for climbing kids. (p85)

House Museums

Hillwood Estate, Museum & Gardens Stunning works from Russian and French royal collections, plus pretty gardens. (p189)

Kreeger Museum A 1963 International-style architectural gem stuffed with 20th-century art. (p189)

Carlyle House The grand manor packs historic treasures and teaches about Alexandria's 18th-century gentry. (p200)

Tudor Place Owned by George Washington's step-granddaughter, the mansion features decorative arts from Mount Vernon. (p94)

Woodrow Wilson House See how genteel Washingtonians lived and socialized in this preserved 1920s home on Embassy Row. (p146)

Belmont-Paul Women's Equality National Monument House where women rallied to get the vote, now filled with suffragette artifacts. (p113)

Romantic Spots

Lincoln Memorial At dawn, nowhere is as lovely, which is why it's a popular place for proposals. (p58)

Constitution Gardens The shady grove, small pool and old stone cottage form a hidden oasis on the Mall. (p72)

National Sculpture Garden In summer jazz concerts set the mood; in winter the ice rink gets hearts racing. (p71)

Kennedy Center Terrace Grab a glass of wine and watch the city sparkling in every direction. (p90)

National Arboretum Take your sweetie to the Capital Columns Garden, and it's like walking amid Greek ruins. (p168)

Month By Month

January

January is quiet – unless it's an inauguration year. Then it's madness. Crisp, clear days alternate with gray, frigid days. Every once in a while it will snow, shutting the city down.

★★ Martin Luther King Jr's Birthday

On the third Monday in January and the weekend just prior, the city celebrates MLK's legacy with concerts, films and the recitation of his famous 'I Have a Dream' speech on the Lincoln Memorial steps.

★★ Inauguration Day

Every four years, on January 20, DC is *the* place to be as the new president is sworn in. Dance cards' worth of inaugural balls accompany the peaceful power transition (held in 2021, 2025 etc).

February

The weekend around President's Day (the third Monday) brings crowds, but otherwise it's time for low-season bargains. Several events brighten up the gloomy days.

★★ DC Fashion Week

This five-day event (www. dcfashionweek.org) brings out an array of emerging talent and lesser-known international designers for runway shows and networking parties. Most events are open to the public, though some require tickets. It's also held in September.

March

Cherry-blossom season – DC's tourism apex – ramps up around the 20th, culminating in the famed festival. The trees are gorgeous, but boy, are you gonna pay for it.

★★ St Patrick's Day

Dancers, bagpipers, marching bands and assorted merrymakers share the Irish love along Constitution Ave NW (from 7th to 17th Sts) at this big annual event (www.dcstpatsparade. com). The parade is held on a Sunday, either on or preceding March 17.

★★ Blossom Kite Festival

On the last Saturday of March, the skies near the Washington Monument come alive with color as kite lovers swoop on the Mall. It's part of the National Cherry Blossom Festival.

★★ National Cherry Blossom Festival

The star of DC's annual calendar celebrates spring's arrival with boat rides in the Tidal Basin, evening walks by lantern light, cultural fairs and a parade. The three-week event (p132), from late March to mid-April, also commemorates Japan's gift of 3000 cherry trees in 1912.

April

Cherry-blossom season continues to bring mega-crowds (and prices). The park service determines April 2 as the average 'peak bloom,' so to see the trees at their shimmery pink best, this is the time.

★★ White House Easter Egg Roll

A tradition since 1878, more than 20,000 families from around the US descend on the South Lawn on Easter Monday for storytelling, games, music and dance. The big event is the massive egg hunt (www.whitehouse.gov/eastereggroll), featuring thousands of wooden eggs.

☆ FilmFest DC

Featuring over 70 films from across the globe, this 10-day, midmonth fest (www.filmfestdc.org) showcases new and avant-garde cinema at venues around the city. In addition to film screenings, there are guest appearances by directors and other special events.

May

It rains more in May than other months, but the temperature is comfy. It's a busy time for conventions, school groups and university graduations, so prices bump up and hotels are often full.

☆ Passport DC

Passport DC (www.culturaltourismdc.org) offers the chance to peer inside the city's grandest embassies when they throw open their doors to the public. Embassy tours take place the first and second Saturday of the month; cultural events are ongoing the rest of the month.

🏍 Rolling Thunder Ride for Freedom

In late May, during Memorial Day weekend, more than 500,000 motorcycles rev up and ride from the Pentagon to the National Mall. The bike rally (www.rollingthunder1.com) is a tribute to prisoners of war and those missing in action, as well as a call to

remember the needs of military veterans.

June

June is the end of peak season, as school-group visits start dwindling. Hotel prices are still fairly high. The temperature steams up as the weeks go on.

☆ Capital Pride

Some 250,000 people attend DC's gay pride party (www.capitalpride.org) held in early to mid-June. The parade travels from Dupont Circle to Logan Circle, featuring wild floats and entertainment along the way. There is also a festival and a concert with big-name headliners.

🍴 National Capital Barbecue Battle

Who makes the best barbecue? Teams compete in late June for $40,000 in prizes at this battle (p32). In addition to tender ribs, chicken and sausage, you'll find live bands, cooking demonstrations, celebrity chefs and kiddie toys.

☆ Smithsonian Folklife Festival

For 10 days around Independence Day, this extravaganza (p69) celebrates international and US cultures on the Mall. The fest features folk music, dance, crafts, storytelling and ethnic fare, and it highlights a diverse mix of countries.

July

The days are exceptionally hot and humid, but that doesn't stop lots of vacationers from touring the

DC sights. Temperatures regularly crack 90°F (32°C).

☆ Independence Day

On July 4, huge crowds gather on the Mall to watch marching bands parade and hear the Declaration of Independence read from the National Archives steps. Later, the National Symphony Orchestra plays a concert on the Capitol's steps, followed by megafireworks.

☆ Capital Fringe Festival

The midmonth, three-week festival (www.capfringe.org) offers 500 wild and wacky performances of theater, dance, music, poetry and puppetry, performed by local and international artists at venues around town.

September

The heat breaks. Kids go back to school. Everyone is refreshed after August's congressional break. Hotel rates start to go up again.

☆ National Book Festival

The Library of Congress brings big-name authors, literary events and, of course, books to the Convention Center for a page-packed day. It's the nation's largest reading fest (www.loc.gov/bookfest), and it's all free.

October

October is another banner month with lovely weather and fewer tourists, but business travelers keep

(Below) Independence Day parade
(Bottom) National Cherry Blossom Festival parade p132

VSEVOLOD33 / SHUTTERSTOCK ©

LISSANDRA MELO / SHUTTERSTOCK ©

hotel rates propped up. Daytime temperatures hover near 70°F (21°C).

🏃 Marine Corps Marathon

This popular road race (www.marinemarathon. com) routes through iconic DC scenery on the last Sunday in October. The course winds along the Potomac and takes in Georgetown, the entire length of the Mall, the Tidal Basin and Arlington National Cemetery.

✶✶ High Heel Drag Race

Outrageously dressed divas strut their stuff before large crowds, then line up for a no-holds-barred sprint down 17th St. An informal block party, with more colorful mayhem, ensues. Traditionally held on the Tuesday before Halloween (October 31) in Dupont.

December

'Tis the holiday season, and the city twinkles with good cheer from Zoo Lights to candlelight tours of historic homes to free holiday concerts. As your holiday gift, rates remain reasonable.

✶✶ National Christmas Tree & Menorah Lighting

In early December, the president switches on the lights to the National Christmas Tree (www. thenationaltree.org). Then they, or a member of the administration, does the honors for the National Menorah. Live bands and choral groups play holiday music, which adds to the good cheer.

Like a Local

When in Washington, do as the Washingtonians do. Seek out beer gardens and bountiful happy hours. Make brunch plans and chase down epicurean food trucks. Cheer on the Nationals. Get on your bike. Get in line for late-night chow. Take romantic strolls with your sweetie.

Eastern Market p126

Drinking

Hangouts

Neighborhood bars are all around the city, but the best batch for the local vibe are in Capitol Hill (particularly along H St NE and 8th St SE, aka Barracks Row), Shaw, Logan Circle and Columbia Heights. The hangouts come in many guises: some are watering holes for an older crowd, some are frat-boy-style keg-o-ramas, and some are mod gastropubs with sophisticated drinks and comfort-food menus.

Alfresco

Rooftop terraces, backyard beer gardens, sidewalk patios – alfresco drinking by any name makes local tipplers happy. The relatively temperate climate means Washingtonians have much of the year to head outdoors and hoist their craft libations. Columbia Heights' nighthawk joints, U St's trendy bars, Georgetown's waterfront and the White House Area's hotel bars are all good spots to get out with a glass in hand.

Happy Hour

Work hard, play hard – and that means hitting the bar right after the office. Washington is a big happy-hour town. Practically all bars (and restaurants that double as bars) have some sort of drink and/or food special for a few hours between 4pm and 7pm. Interns and staffers on a budget pile in to take advantage of half-price burgers and two-for-one mojitos and to decompress over the senator's latest appropriations bill. Downtown, Capitol Hill and Dupont Circle see lots of happy-hour action.

Postbar Bites

While DC isn't known as a late-night town, it must be admitted that sometimes citizens do stay out carousing until 2am or so, and then they need something to soak up the booze. Mini-chain Julia's Empanadas (www.juliasempanadas.com) is often there to meet the need. Postpartyers also make their way to Adams Morgan, Dupont Circle or U Street, where establishments like the Diner (p160), Afterwords Cafe (p149) and Busboys & Poets (p172) sling awesome hash in the wee hours.

Eating

Brunch

This meal is taken seriously on weekends, especially Sunday. Meeting up with friends at midday and lingering over bottomless Bloody Marys and a hulking pile of eggs and potatoes is de rigueur. Many restaurants offer boozy specials around Adams Morgan, Dupont Circle and Eastern Market. There are even blogs devoted to the subject. Check out the Bitches Who Brunch (www.bitcheswhobrunch.com).

Food Trucks

Locals love food trucks. They stalk them via Food Truck Fiesta (www.foodtruck fiesta.com) and chase them around Franklin Sq, Farragut Sq, Metro Center and L'Enfant Plaza at lunchtime, then Dupont Circle, Georgetown and Adams Morgan toward evening. New vehicles seem to roll out every week, including trucks by big-name chefs selling everything from Iberico pork sandwiches to gourmet mac 'n' cheese.

Markets

Near Capitol Hill, Eastern Market (p126) is the city's main bazaar and a great place to soak up local flavor. Families shop, browsers browse, friends laugh – oh, and there are good eats (*mmm,* fried oyster sandwiches), too. The time to go is on the weekend, when a lively craft market and an adjoining flea market surround the area.

Hipsters and hipster families make an afternoon of it at Union Market (p174), a sort of chowhound's food court. Vendors sell jerk-chicken empanadas, craft kombucha, French pastries and more that folks nibble at sunlit tables in an urban-cool, renovated warehouse.

Most neighborhoods also have their own farmers market one day per week from May through October. Residents flock to these to buy produce, eggs, cheese, honey and cider from nearby small farms.

Pastimes

Spectator Sports

Washingtonians support a full slate of pro sports teams – the Redskins (football), Nationals (baseball), Wizards (basketball), Capitals (hockey) and DC United (soccer) – and all have rabid fans. The surest way to feel like a local is to catch a Redskins game at a city pub and join in the grumbling when they lose. DC's transients and natives bond over the Nationals too; games are good fun and tickets can be cheap (around $18). Imbibing in one of the outdoor beer gardens around the park is a pregame must.

Biking

The Capital Bikeshare (p270) program prompts many citizens to make short-haul trips on two wheels, and the District's terrific array of long-haul trails brings out droves of weekend cyclists. The 18.5-mile, river-clasping Mount Vernon Trail (p206) is a particular favorite with locals, along with the Capital Crescent Trail (p101) and C&O Canal Towpath (p101). Bike-rental companies make it easy to join the action.

Mall Activities

Yes, tourists throng the Mall, but so do locals. Runners, Ultimate Frisbee teams and volleyball players are among those hanging out on the scrubby green grass.

Odds & Ends

Romantic Places

If you're looking for places that emit a 'kiss me' vibe, follow locals to their favorites. Constitution Gardens, the Lincoln Memorial and the National Sculpture Garden win smooching points on the Mall; being there at sunrise or sunset ups the ante. A Mall stroll at night past the dramatically lit monuments is another sure thing. And what lips can resist their beloved's in the Capitol Columns Garden at the National Arboretum (p168)?

Airplane-Spotting

There are a couple of well-known sites where residents go for fun views of planes taking off and landing. Hains Point (p116), at the southern tip of East Potomac Park in southwest DC, is one with picnicking opportunities. Gravelly Point in Arlington, VA, is another.

For Free

Washington, DC, has a mind-blowing array of freebies. From the Smithsonian Institution's multiple museums, to gratis theater and concerts, to jaunts through the White House and Capitol, you can be entertained for weeks without spending so much as a dime.

Kennedy Center p90

Smithsonian Museums

Top Draws

➡ **National Air and Space Museum** (p60) Rockets, missiles and the Wright brothers' biplane.

➡ **National Museum of Natural History** (p70) Gems, minerals, mummies and a giant squid.

➡ **National Museum of American History** (p70) Everything from the Star Spangled Banner flag to Dorothy's ruby slippers.

➡ **National Museum of African American History and Culture** (p59) Sensational exhibits on subjects ranging from slavery and civil rights fights to sport, music, theater and art.

➡ **National Zoo** (p189) Home to the famed, bamboo-lovin' giant pandas.

Less-Packed Troves

➡ **Reynolds Center for American Art & Portraiture** (p131) Part portrait gallery, part who's who of big-name US artists.

➡ **Freer-Sackler Museums of Asian Art** (p70) Chinese jades, Japanese silk scrolls and smiling Buddhas fill cool, quiet galleries connected by a tunnel.

➡ **National Museum of the American Indian** (p73) Creation stories, costumes, videos and audio recordings from tribes of the Americas.

➡ **Hirshhorn Museum and Sculpture Garden** (p71) Head-scratching, cutting-edge, provocative modern art.

➡ **Steven F Udvar-Hazy Center** (p202) All the space stuff that doesn't fit into the Mall's National Air and Space Museum? It's in giant hangars by Washington Dulles International Airport.

Overlooked Gems

➡ **Renwick Gallery** (p82) Superb collection of American crafts and decorative art pieces.

➡ **National Museum of African Art** (p72) Masks, textiles, paintings, ceramics and ritual objects from sub-Saharan Africa.

➡ **National Postal Museum** (p275) Antique mail planes, historic letters and the world's largest stamp collection.

➡ **Anacostia Community Museum** (p115) Neighborhood outpost with exhibits on diverse and underserved cultures.

Other Free Museums

National Gallery of Art

Its prodigious collection (p61) sprawls through two buildings that display blue-chip works from the Middle Ages to the present.

United States Holocaust Memorial Museum

The museum (p108) haunts with exhibits that show Nazi propaganda films, a rail car used for death-camp transport and survivors telling heartbreaking stories.

Art Museum of the Americas

The hidden gallery (p82) features cool exhibits from its 20th-century collection.

Free Days at Paid Museums

Phillips Collection

The permanent collection (p146), aglow with Renoir, Gauguin, Matisse and other big names, is free every Tuesday through Friday.

National Museum of Women in the Arts

See works by Frida Kahlo, Georgia O'Keeffe and more female artists (p135) for free on the first Sunday each month.

National Museum of Natural History Butterfly Pavilion

The separate-admission area (p70) of fluttering beasties is free on Tuesday.

Government in Action

White House

Unlike many palaces around the globe, the US Presidential Palace (p78), as it was once known, is free to tour. Heck, you might even run into the president.

National Archives

Really – we'd pay to see the Declaration of Independence with John Hancock's, er, John Hancock scrawled across the bottom at the National Archives (p130).

Capitol

Guided excursions through the mighty, white-domed sanctum of Congress (p106), cluttered with busts, statues, frescoes and gardens, cost zilch.

Bureau of Engraving & Printing

Though the tour is about money, it won't be taking any of yours. Watch millions of dollars as they're printed, cut and inspected here (p115).

Library of Congress

The world's largest library (p109) is more than books. It's a museum with 500-year-old world maps, historic photographs, concerts and film screenings – all free.

Show Time

Kennedy Center

The show could star the National Symphony, a gospel group or an Indian dance troupe, but whatever it is, count on it happening at 6pm for free at the Kennedy's Millennium Stage (p90).

Busboys & Poets

OK, the Tuesday-night open mike (p172) costs $5. But that's nothing for the rollicking, two-hour show of seasoned performers, spoken-word rookies and jammin' musicians.

National Theatre

Puppets, magic, ballet and music are all on tap here (p141) for the free, family-oriented Saturday shows at 9:30am and 11am.

Shakespeare Theatre Company

'Free for All' is an annual end-of-summer tradition: the company (p141) picks a Bard classic and performs it gratis for two weeks.

Museum Concerts

The National Gallery of Art (p61) offers free choral and classical concerts on Sunday, which take place in the West Building. It also sponsors Jazz in the Garden (p75) outdoors amid the sculptures from 5pm to 8:30pm on summer Fridays.

KELLY/MOONEY PHOTOGRAPHY / GETTY IMAGES ©

Frederick Douglass National Historic Site p114

History Highlights

Ford's Theatre

The theater (p134) where John Wilkes Booth shot Abraham Lincoln provides free tours exploring what happened that fateful night in April 1865. The basement museum shows artifacts such as the murder weapon. Petersen House, where Lincoln died, sits across the street and is included as part of the ticket.

Frederick Douglass National Historic Site

The hilltop home (p114) of revered abolitionist Frederick Douglass provides a compelling look into his life via original furnishings, books and personal belongings.

Tours

DC by Foot

Knowledgeable guides (p272) working on a tip-only basis share history and lore along routes covering the Mall, Lincoln's assassination and Dupont Circle's ghosts.

Cultural Tourism DC

The tours are DIY using free maps, apps and audio provided by Cultural Tourism DC (www.culturaltourismdc.org). Choose from 17 neighborhood heritage trails; the tours reveal civil rights sites, espionage hot spots and more.

National Public Radio

Wave to your favorite correspondents as you peek into the newsroom and studios of the venerable news organization (p113).

Calamari dish, Central Michel Richard p137

 **Eating**

A homegrown foodie revolution has transformed the once-buttoned-up DC dining scene. Driving it is the bounty of farms at the city's doorstep, along with the booming local economy and influx of worldly younger residents. Small, independent, local-chef-helmed spots now lead the way. And they're doing such a fine job that Michelin deemed the city worthy of its stars.

NEED TO KNOW

Opening Hours
→ **Breakfast** 7am or 8am to 11am

→ **Lunch** 11am or 11:30am to 2:30pm

→ **Dinner** 5pm or 6pm to 10pm Sunday to Thursday, to 11pm or midnight Friday and Saturday.

Price Ranges
The following price ranges represent the cost of a main dish at dinner:

$	under $15
$$	$15–$25
$$$	more than $25

Reservations
→ Make reservations for eateries in the midrange and top-end price bracket, especially on weekends.

→ Apps like OpenTable and Resy can get you a last-minute table.

→ For no-reservations hot spots, get in line an hour before opening time. Make sure your cell phone is charged; once the host takes your name, many restaurants will let you wait elsewhere (ie a nearby bar) and will text when your table is ready.

Tipping
Most people tip between 18% and 20% of the final price of the meal. For takeout, it's polite to drop a few dollars in the tip jar.

Saving Money
Restaurants around downtown, Dupont Circle and Georgetown often have pretheater menus. This generally means a three-course meal for around $35, offered before 6:30pm.

Credit Cards Versus Cash
Almost all restaurants accept credit cards, aside from a smattering of budget places.

Global Influence
Washington, DC, is one of the most diverse, international cities of its size in America, heavily populated by immigrants, expats and diplomats from every country in the

Seafood from Chesapeake Bay

world. People from far away crave the food of home, and so there's a glut of good ethnic eating and international influences around town. Salvadoran, Ethiopian, Vietnamese, French, Spanish, West African – they've all become Washingtonian.

Local Bounty
The city's unique geography puts it between two of the best food-production areas in America: Chesapeake Bay and the Virginia Piedmont. From the former come crabs, oysters and rockfish; the latter provides game, pork, wine and peanuts. Chefs take advantage of this delicious abundance, and it has led to lofty accolades: the prestigious Michelin Guide added DC to its roster, releasing its first list of star-rated local restaurants in 2017.

Southern Influence
Keep in mind that DC also occupies the fault line between two of America's greatest culinary regions: the Northeast and the South. The South, in particular, exerts a tremendous pull. The city offers heaps of soul food and its high-class incarnations, so get ready to loosen the belt for plates of fried chicken, catfish, collard greens, sweet-potato hash and butter-smothered grits – all washed down with sweet iced tea, of course.

Half-Smokes
DC's claim to native culinary fame is the half-smoke, a bigger, coarser, spicier and

Above: Ramen dish, Daikaya p136

Right: Food trucks, National Mall p74

ROB CRANDALL / SHUTTERSTOCK ©

National Capital Barbecue Battle festival

DC by Foot (p272) Among the company's many free, themed walking tours are food-oriented jaunts around Eastern Market, Georgetown and U St. You also can download the tours from the website and do them as a self-guided walk.

Festivals

DC Restaurant Week (www.ramw.org/restaurantweek) For seven days in late January, 200 eateries – including many big-name restaurants – serve affordable, three-course, fixed-price meals.

National Capital Barbecue Battle (www.bbqdc.com; Penn Quarter; tickets $15; ☉June) This meaty battle takes place during a late June weekend downtown, with bands and celebrity chefs.

Taste of DC (www.thetasteofdc.org; $10) More than 65 restaurants sell mini portions of their wares during a mid-October weekend. Includes the Ben's Chili Bowl Eating Championship. Check the website for location.

Eat Streets

➡ **14th St NW (Logan Circle)** DC's most happening road: an explosion of hot-chef bites and bars.

➡ **18th St NW (Adams Morgan)** Korean, Indian, Thai, Ethiopian, Japanese and Latin mash-up, plus late-night snacks.

➡ **8th St SE (Capitol Hill)** Known as Barracks Row, it's the locals' favorite for welcoming comfort-food spots.

➡ **H St NE (Capitol Hill)** Hip strip of pie cafes, noodle shops and gastropubs.

➡ **Upshur St (Petworth)** Block of cozy, casual *Bon Appetit*–beloved eateries and cocktail bars.

➡ **11th St NW (Columbia Heights)** Ever-growing scene of hipster cafes, edgy gastropubs and all-the-rage foodie nooks.

Local Blogs & Foodie Websites

Eater DC (www.dc.eater.com) News and reviews on the local dining scene.

Bitches Who Brunch (www.bitcheswhobrunch.com) These 'bitches' have been at it for a while.

Young & Hungry (www.washingtoncitypaper.com/food/young-hungry) Blog about local food trends and culture.

Hungry Lobbyist (http://hungrylobbyist.com) Restaurant reviews, chef interviews and event info by a group of locals.

better version of the hot dog. There's little agreement on where the name comes from. But there is general consensus as to what goes on a half-smoke: chili, mustard and chopped onions.

Food Trucks

As in most other US cities, the food-truck frenzy has hit Washington. Empanadas, chocolate pie, crab cakes, cupcakes – you name it and there's a truck driving around selling it out the window. Trucks generally prowl office-worker-rich hot spots like Farragut Sq, Franklin Sq, Metro Center and L'Enfant Plaza around lunchtime, and then Dupont Circle, Georgetown and Adams Morgan toward evening. Food Truck Fiesta (www.foodtruckfiesta.com) tracks their real-time locations.

Tours

DC Metro Food Tours (p272) These walking tours explore various neighborhoods, stopping for multiple bites along the way. Offerings include Capitol Hill, U St, Little Ethiopia, Georgetown and Alexandria, VA.

Eating by Neighborhood

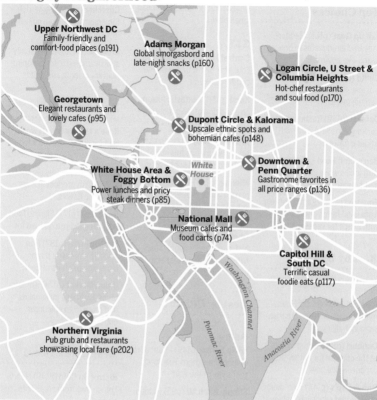

Upper Northwest DC
Family-friendly and comfort-food places (p191)

Adams Morgan
Global smorgasbord and late-night snacks (p160)

Logan Circle, U Street & Columbia Heights
Hot-chef restaurants and soul food (p170)

Georgetown
Elegant restaurants and lovely cafes (p95)

Dupont Circle & Kalorama
Upscale ethnic spots and bohemian cafes (p148)

White House Area & Foggy Bottom
Power lunches and pricy steak dinners (p85)

White House

Downtown & Penn Quarter
Gastronome favorites in all price ranges (p136)

National Mall
Museum cafes and food carts (p74)

Capitol Hill & South DC
Terrific casual foodie eats (p117)

Northern Virginia
Pub grub and restaurants showcasing local fare (p202)

Washington Channel

Potomac River

Anacostia River

Supper Clubs

Underground supper clubs come and go in DC. Some are hoity-toity, but others offer great value if you're an adventurous eater and don't mind hanging out with strangers around a communal table.

Meal Tribes (www.mealtribes.com) The group puts together potluck dinners in participants' homes to foster community and the sharing of ideas. There are usually a couple of gatherings per month. They're free, but you need to bring a dish

everyone can eat. Around six to 10 people take part, most in their 20s and 30s. Sign up online to get news about upcoming events.

Underground Kitchen (www.theunderground kitchen.org) It gives members access to a one-night-only, five- to seven-course dinner (per person $150) by a well-known chef at a pop-up location. Only 25 to 40 people get a ticket, so you need to keep your eyes on the sparse schedule and act fast.

Lonely Planet's Top Choices

Tail Up Goat (p161) Mediterranean shared plates in breezy, island-like environs.

ChiKo (p117) Foodie-beloved Chinese-Korean fusion with bargain prices.

Dabney (p139) Rustic room cooking up overlooked mid-Atlantic flavors.

Ben's Chili Bowl (p171) Gossip with locals while downing a half-smoke.

Equinox (p87) Sourced entirely from local farms and waters, with heaps for vegetarians.

Best by Budget

$

A Baked Joint (p138) House-made bread cushions creative sandwich fillings.

Donburi (p160) Fifteen seats at the counter for authentic Japanese rice bowls.

Bub & Pop's (p148) Fine-dining chef turned sandwich fashioner who makes his own condiments.

Woodward Takeout Food (p86) Hot spot near the White House for epicurean sandwiches and the daily doughnut.

Toki Underground (p117) Belly-warming ramen noodles on hip H St NE.

$$

Compass Rose (p172) Like a secret garden offering street foods from around the globe.

Ambar (p125) Buzzy spot for lamb salami, roasted eggplant and more Balkan dishes.

Mintwood Place (p161) Twinkling room for escargot hush puppies and other French-American mash-ups.

Zaytinya (p137) Bustling, glass-walled room for Mediterranean small plates.

$$$

Central Michel Richard (p137) Four-star bistro that redefines comfort food.

Komi (p150) Fantastic fusion fare and one of DC's most dazzling dining experiences.

Kinship (p140) Roast chicken takes the prize at this sociable, Michelin-starred spot.

Minibar (p138) Twelve-seat restaurant to experience José Andrés' molecular gastronomy.

Chez Billy Sud (p97) Charming bistro with duck confit, *steak frites* (steak and fries) and mustachioed servers.

Best by Cuisine

Asian

Little Serow (p149) Multicourse dinner of northern Thai food that's worth the wait.

Simply Banh Mi (p95) Hidden cafe to gobble Vietnamese pho and lemongrass pork sandwiches.

Tiger Fork (p139) Bright, clamorous room for Hong Kong–style snacks, noodles and cocktails.

Southern US

Georgia Brown's (p88) High-end, okra-dotted fare from the Carolina and Georgia Lowcountry.

Hitching Post (p182) Fried chicken and catfish with the neighbors in Petworth.

Oohh's & Aahh's (p173) No-frills joint where locals go for collard greens and hummingbird cake.

Ethiopian

Chercher (p171) Veggie-rich Ethiopian stews in an colorful town house.

Ethiopic (p120) An unusually stylish ambience for scooping platters of lamb and lentils.

Best for Foodies

Rose's Luxury (p120) Worth the wait for worldly comfort food and awesomely friendly service.

Himitsu (p182) Tiny eatery in Petworth producing huge Japanese flavors.

Bad Saint (p173) Filipino food you'll be glad you queued for.

Timber Pizza (p182) *Bon Appetit*–approved pizzas alongside pitchers of beer.

Union Market (p174) Korean tacos, Burmese milkshakes and more from epicurean entrepreneurs.

Best Like a Local

Bistrot du Coin (p149) Hearty French fare from *steak frites* to mussels.

Duke's Grocery (p149) Cozy gastropub where the chalkboard menu changes daily.

Maple (p181) Tiny Columbia Heights spot for rich pastas and housemade limoncello.

Best for Romance

Masseria (p174) The outdoor patio under twinkling lights sets the mood.

Estadio (p170) Inventive tapas in a low-lit, date-night space.

Le Grenier (p120) Wine, escargot and a cozy Left Bank vibe equal amour.

Martin's Tavern (p97) Sit in the booth where JFK proposed to Jackie in Georgetown.

Best Brunch

Ted's Bulletin (p120) Sink into a retro booth for beer biscuits and housemade pop tarts.

Tabard Inn Restaurant (p150) Poached eggs, whipped-cream doughnuts and oysters in English-manor environs.

Perry's (p161) The drag-queen brunch packs the place every Sunday.

Best Late Night

Diner (p160) Stuffed pancakes at 4am never tasted so good.

Afterwords Cafe (p149) Browse the stacks and feed your face at this night-owl bookstore-bistro combo.

Busboys & Poets (p172) Progressive cafe dishing vegetarian and Southern eats into the night.

Julia's Empanadas (p161) The local chain fries plump, meat-filled turnovers into the wee hours.

Best Vegetarian

Shouk (p138) Bright-tiled eatery for vegan Israeli street food.

Rasika (p137) Avant-garde Indian food served in a mod Jaipur palace.

Amsterdam Falafelshop (p160) Fried chickpea patties with DIY toppings.

Sticky Fingers (p173) Retro vegan bakery that also makes meat-free burgers, burritos and breakfasts.

Best Politician-Spotting

Old Ebbitt Grill (p86) Play spot-the-senator while slurping an oyster.

Le Diplomate (p171) DC's political glitterati flock here for a Parisian-style night out.

Cafe Milano (p98) Famed place to twirl spaghetti and spy big shots in Georgetown.

Best Solo Dining

District Commons (p86) The tavern's happening bar welcomes one and all for nouveau comfort food.

Daikaya (p136) Walk-in ramen-noodle spot full of small, secluded tables.

Jaleo (p137) José Andrés's tapas eatery makes you feel part of the festive crowd.

Macon (p193) Creative blend of French and Southern US fare, best consumed at the 20-seat bar.

Best Sweets

Bread Furst (p191) James Beard Award–winning baker selling baguettes and pastries that'll make you moan.

Baked & Wired (p95) This sunny cafe serves DC's biggest, bestest cupcakes.

Un Je Ne Sais Quoi (p148) Vintage French pastries piled high with meringue and ganache.

Dolcezza (p148) Spoon into offbeat flavors like strawberry tarragon.

Best Seafood

Fiola Mare (p97) Georgetown's sceney, river-view hot spot delivers the goods with an Italian twist.

Maine Avenue Fish Market (p119) Shrimp, crabs and oysters fried, broiled or steamed wharfside.

Hank's Oyster Bar (p150) Bivalves and playful cocktails in a breezy ambience.

Salt Line (p120) Navy Yard favorite for regional oysters and beers with river views.

Best Pizza

Comet Ping Pong (p191) Creative pies served amid Ping-Pong tables and with the occasional band.

Il Canale (p97) Authentic Neapolitan style in a Georgetown town house.

Seventh Hill Pizza (p120) Addictive pie joint with offbeat ingredients and killer crust.

2 Amys (p191) The pizzas emerging from the oven can barely keep up with neighborhood masses.

THE WASHINGTON POST / GETTY IMAGES ©

Bluejacket Brewery p121

🍷 Drinking & Nightlife

When Andrew Jackson swore the oath of office in 1800, the self-proclaimed populist dispensed with pomp and circumstance and, quite literally, threw a raging kegger. Folks got so gone they started looting art from the White House. The historical lesson: DC loves a drink, and these days it enjoys said tipples in many incarnations besides executive-mansion-trashing throwdowns.

Beer

The city is serious about beer. It even brews much of its own delicious stuff. That trend started in 2009, when DC Brau became the District's first brewery to launch in more than 50 years. Several more beer makers followed. As you drink around town, keep an eye out for local concoctions from 3 Stars, Atlas Brew Works, Hellbender and Lost Rhino (from Northern Virginia).

TASTING ROOMS & BEER GARDENS

Many breweries have no-frills tasting rooms where you can get pints or growlers of the house beers, and they usually offer free tours on Saturday. DC Brau (p179) and Atlas Brew Works (p178) are heady ones to sample. The city also has a handful of brewpubs, such as Right Proper Brewing Co (p175) and Bluejacket Brewery (p121), where you can slurp the wares in a more refined ambience and get a meal.

Beer gardens are popular, especially in Shaw, Columbia Heights, Petworth and the H St Corridor. Dacha Beer Garden (p175), Bardo Brewing (p122) and DC Reynolds (p182) are exemplars of the genre.

TOURS

Visit three to four breweries by van with DC
Brew Tours (p272). Routes vary but could
include DC Brau, Atlas, Capital City and
Port City, among others. Five-hour jaunts
feature tastings of 15-plus beers and a light
meal. The 3½-hour tour forgoes the meal
and pares down the brewery tally. Depar-
ture is from downtown by the Reynolds
Center. Tours go daily, at various times.

FESTIVALS

Savor (www.savorcraftbeer.com; Penn Quarter;
tickets $135; ☉June) The National Building
Museum hosts this two-day fest in early June,
described as the 'prom of the beer world.' Sip
from around 90 breweries and nosh on small plates
that pair with the beers.

Brew at the Zoo (www.nationalzoo.si.edu;
tickets $65) The National Zoo fundraiser in mid-
July brings out 70 breweries, including many small
ones from Virginia that you don't often see in DC.

Snallygaster (www.snallygasterdc.com; tickets
$35) Beloved by beer geeks, this outdoor fest held
next to Nationals Park features a terrific selection
of 400 brews (some quite rare), dance punk bands
and food trucks. Held on a Saturday in mid- to late
September.

Cocktails

The craft-cocktail craze is in full swing.
Mixologists do their thing using small-batch
liqueurs, freshly squeezed juices and hand-
chipped ice. It may sound pretentious, but
most of the bars are actually pretty cool.

And get this: DC has an official cocktail
– the Rickey. It's a mix of bourbon or gin,
lime juice and soda water served over ice.
Drinkers describe it as air-conditioning
in a glass, as it's perfect on a hot summer
day. It was invented in 1883 at a downtown
(now defunct) bar popular with politicos
and journalists. Colonel Joseph K Rickey, a
Democratic lobbyist known to toss back a
drink or 10 at the venue, lent his name to
it. Columbia Room (p140), Tryst (p160) and
Room 11 (p180) make good Rickeys.

Wine

Virginia ranks sixth in number of wineries
among US states, and many of the local
varietals make their way to DC's tables.
Particularly notable is the Virginia viognier,
an exotic white grape that becomes a lightly
fruity wine that pairs well with seafood.
Blue Duck Tavern (p150) and Marcel's

NEED TO KNOW

Opening Hours

➡ **Bars** 5pm to 1am or 2am weekdays,
3am on weekends.

➡ **Nightclubs** 9pm to 1am or 2am
weekdays, 3am on weekends; often
closed Monday through Wednesday

Taxes

Drink tax is 10%.

Tipping

Tip 15% to 20% per round, or a minimum
per drink of $1 for standard drinks, $2 for
specialty cocktails.

Door Policies

➡ The drinking age is 21 years. Take
your driver's license or passport out at
night: you will be asked for ID.

➡ No dress code typically, though some
clubs require closed-toe shoes and
long pants, and occasionally no jeans
or hats.

Resources & Websites

➡ **Washington City Paper** (www.
washingtoncitypaper.com) Alternative
publication with entertainment
coverage.

➡ **DC Beer** (www.dcbeer.com) Info and
events on the local craft-brew scene.

➡ **Washington Blade** (www.washington
blade.com) Gay and lesbian happenings.

➡ **On Tap** (www.ontaponline.com)
Nightlife and entertainment listings.

➡ **Brightest Young Things** (www.
brightestyoungthings.com) Web
magazine of cultural and clubby
events for 20-somethings.

(p88) both have robust lists of Virginia
wines. Several wineries can be visited on a
day trip from DC.

Coffee

DC has been getting its caffeine on. Local
mini-chains such as Filter (p153) and Peregrine Espresso (p123) use beans from small-
batch roasters and get hard-core with their
brewing techniques. Peregrine pays the
knowledge forward by offering DIY brewing classes. Petworth's Qualia Coffee (p177)

Drinking & Nightlife by Neighborhood

Upper Northwest DC
Quiet, with a neighborhood feel (p193)

Adams Morgan
Raucous dive bars and youthful guzzling spots (p162)

Logan Circle, U Street & Columbia Heights
DC's club, brewery and patio hot spot (p175)

Georgetown
European-style cafes and cozy pubs (p98)

Dupont Circle & Kalorama
Cocktail lounges, raunchy bars, dance clubs (p150)

Downtown & Penn Quarter
Sports bars and hidden cocktail dens (p140)

White House Area & Foggy Bottom
Wheeler-dealer hotel bars (p88)

White House

Capitol Hill & South DC
Friendly taverns and awesomely offbeat bars (p121)

Northern Virginia
Elegant cocktail dens and gas-lamp pubs (p204)

Washington Channel

Potomac River

Washington Channel

Anacostia River

roasts its own beans and offers bimonthly tasting sessions. Compass Coffee (p141) is a local, fast-growing roaster. The city's Ethiopian community shows how it's done too: Sidamo Coffee & Tea (p122) is one of several family-run shops that roasts beans and puts on traditional Ethiopian coffee ceremonies.

Clubs

Washington's club scene is pretty casual. Dupont Circle and U St host much of the action. Some places have a dress code that requires closed-toe shoes and long pants, and occasionally no jeans or hats, but usually you can come as you are. Many bars that are low-key drinking holes during the week turn clubby on weekends when they bring in DJs.

Happy Hour

Washington is a big happy-hour town. Practically all bars have some sort of drink and/or food special for a few hours between 4pm and 7pm. This is particularly welcome at restaurants that double as bars – which many do – because often they'll sell affordable, small-plate versions of menu items during happy hour.

Lonely Planet's Top Choices

Right Proper Brewing Co (p175) Housemade ales flow in Duke Ellington's old pool hall.

Copycat Co (p121) Fizzy cocktails in welcoming, opium-den environs.

Off the Record (p88) Where Very Important People drink martinis, steps from the White House.

Round Robin (p88) Since 1850 bigwigs and lobbyists have swirled drinks and cut deals in the gilded bar.

Atlas Brew Works (p178) No-frills Ivy City taproom that hosts a welcoming crew of beer buffs.

Best Beer

Bluejacket Brewery (p121) Genre-spanning suds made on-site, from sour blonds to barley wines.

Churchkey (p175) The hulking menu has 500 different beers, including 50 craft brews on tap.

Right Proper Brewing Co Brookland Production House (p178) Gape at the eye-popping chalk mural while drinking pale ales and wheat ales.

City Tap House (p140) Lodge-like gastropub with 40 taps and upscale pub grub.

Best Cocktails

Columbia Room (p140) Swirl exquisite drinks in the Punch Garden or Spirits Library.

Bar Charley (p151) Friendly Dupont spot that mixes the gingery Suffering Bastard in vintage glassware.

Hank's Cocktail Bar (p182) Playful beverages in a modern-meets-medieval room.

Best Wine

Primrose (p178) French wines in a cafe that feels straight out of the Left Bank.

Dabney Cellar (p140) Cozy underground room for reds, whites and oyster nibbles.

Ruta del Vino (p182) Comfy Petworth gathering place for wines from Latin America.

District Winery (p122) Sleek Navy Yard spot to sip and soak up river views.

Best Coffee

The Coffee Bar (p175) Beloved neighborhood cafe where folks hang out all day.

Sidamo Coffee & Tea (p122) Ethiopian family-run spot with traditional coffee ceremonies and organic beans.

Qualia Coffee (p177) Java heads get jacked up over this shop with tasting sessions.

Grace Street Coffee (p98) Hip Georgetown spot that roasts its own beans and makes its own syrups.

Best Like a Local

Board Room (p151) Knock back draft beers and crush your opponent at Battleship, Operation and other games.

Songbyrd Record Cafe & Music House (p162) Gulp coffee or beer upstairs, then hear indie bands in the basement.

Tombs (p98) Drink and think at Georgetown University's favorite watering hole.

Dacha Beer Garden (p175) German brews in glass boots make their way around the picnic tables.

Best Clubs

U Street Music Hall (p175) Casual, DJ-owned spot to get your dance on.

Flash (p177) Deep house, techno and dubstep DJs spin in the intimate upstairs room.

18th Street Lounge (p151) Sexy young things groove in a Dupont mansion.

Best Gay & Lesbian

Larry's Lounge (p151) Neighborhood tavern that's perfect for people-watching and stiff drinks.

JR's (p153) Dupont pub where a young, well-dressed crowd kicks back and sings show tunes.

Nellie's (p175) Drinkers amass for sports-tuned TVs and the sweet roof deck.

Best Rooftop Decks

Top of the Gate (p88) Sweet bar atop the Watergate Hotel with lovely breezes and Potomac views.

Marvin (p177) A banging roof deck brings out the U St crowd.

Jack Rose Dining Saloon (p162) The retractable roof means weather won't spoil your whiskey.

Best Dives

Tune Inn (p121) Ah, beer swilled under mounted deer heads.

Dan's Cafe (p162) It's like an evil Elks Club, with massive pours of booze.

Raven (p177) Locals, lovers, neon and the finest jukebox in Washington.

Indiana Pacers score against the Washington Wizards at Capital One Arena p142

 # Entertainment

From the evening-wear elegance of the Kennedy Center to punk stripping the paint off at an H St club, the nation's capital has an enviable slate of performances. It caters to Shakespeare, jazz, rock, classical-music and poetry-slam fans particularly well. Best of all, many shows are free.

Music

JAZZ

Washington's jazz affair started in the early 20th century, when U St NW was known as Black Broadway for its many music theaters. Relics from that era, such as the Howard Theatre (p179), still host sweet notes.

ROCK

DC's rock scene thrives, and the city is a great place to catch a show. Clubs like the Black Cat (p179) are typical: intimate, something indie-cool always going on, and nights of DJ music in the mix.

CLASSICAL

The Kennedy Center (p90) is the hub for symphony, opera and other classical fare. But for all its high-falutin' ways, it's also surprisingly accessible to the masses, with free performances nightly at 6pm.

MILITARY

Military music is big here. The Marine Corps, Air Force, Army and Navy bands alternate performing at 8pm most weeknights on the Capitol's steps and at the Mall's Sylvan Theater (p75) in summer.

Theater

Washington has many adventurous small stages and multifaceted arts centers that do intriguing work. Keep an eye out for Woolly Mammoth (p141), Atlas (p124) and Studio (p181) theaters.

Spoken Word

DC has hundreds of author readings, poetry slams, story slams and open-mike nights. Busboys & Poets (p139) anchors the scene.

Spectator Sports

The football-playing Redskins are the most watched team, love 'em or hate 'em. The other ties that bind are the Capitals on ice; the Wizards pro basketball team; DC United, one of Major League Soccer's most popular and successful clubs; and the Nationals, with their shiny baseball stadium and 'Racing Presidents' tradition. The Howard Bisons, Georgetown Hoyas and other university teams have rabid student-body fans.

Entertainment by Neighborhood

➡ **National Mall** (p75) Free jazz in the sculpture garden.

➡ **White House Area & Foggy Bottom** (p90) The Kennedy Center runs the show, with performances nightly.

➡ **Georgetown** (p100) Dizzy Gillespie's old stomping grounds are the main draw.

➡ **Capitol Hill & South DC** (p123) Rock, Shakespeare and avant-garde theater make this 'hood top of the heap.

➡ **Downtown & Penn Quarter** (p141) The majority of theaters, from opulent to comic to experimental, are concentrated here.

➡ **Dupont Circle & Kalorama** (p154) Improv, Jewish theater and artsy chamber music play.

➡ **Adams Morgan** (p163) Rowdy live music, deep reggae and cozy jazz fill the nights.

➡ **Logan Circle, U Street & Columbia Heights** (p179) Splendid mix of jazz venues, thrashing rock clubs and poetry slams.

➡ **Upper Northwest DC** (p193) A groovy cinema, French culture and literary events are on tap.

➡ **Northern Virginia** (p205) Fiddlin' music halls and jazzy lounges make it worth the trip.

NEED TO KNOW

Ticket Discounters

➡ **Gold Star** (www.goldstar.com/washington-dc) National broker that sells discounted tickets (up to 50% off) to local performances.

➡ **TodayTix** (www.todaytix.com) Mobile app that sells discounted and full-price last-minute tickets.

Other Money-Saving Strategies

➡ Many theaters offer deep discounts to patrons aged 18 to 30 years, including the Kennedy Center via its MyTix program (www.kennedy-center.org/offers/mytix).

➡ Many theaters offer cheap, day-of tickets that go on sale 30 minutes (Arena Stage, Studio Theatre) to two hours (Woolly Mammoth) before showtime.

Pro Teams

For all spectator sports, buy tickets direct from the team's website or stadium box office, or via StubHub (www.stubhub.com).

➡ **DC United** (www.dcunited.com) Major League Soccer, MLS

➡ **Washington Capitals** (www.nhl.com/capitals) National Hockey League, MHL

➡ **Washington Nationals** (www.mlb.com/nationals) Major League Baseball, MLB

➡ **Washington Redskins** (www.redskins.com) National Football League, NFL

➡ **Washington Wizards** (www.nba.com/wizards) National Basketball Association, NBA

Resources

➡ **Destination DC** (www.washington.org/calendar) Full events listings.

➡ **Culture Capital** (www.culturecapital.com) Arts-specific listings.

➡ **Pink Line Project** (www.pinklineproject.com) Weekly newsletter about the coolest cultural things to do in DC.

Lonely Planet's Top Choices

Kennedy Center (p90) DC's performing-arts king of the hill is home to the symphony, opera and more.

Black Cat (p179) Intimate, beer-splattered stalwart of DC's rock and indie scene.

Woolly Mammoth Theatre Company (p141) Experimental theater that puts on edgy original works.

Busboys & Poets (p172) Nerve center for open-mike poetry readings and story slams.

9:30 Club (p179) Where the Franz Ferdinand and Yo La Tengo–type bands of the world come to rock.

Best Rock, Funk & Blues

Anthem (p123) Sweet new venue that lets you get close to your musical heroes.

Rock & Roll Hotel (p123) A down-and-dirty club offering thrashing rock, but also hip-hop, punk and metal.

Hamilton (p90) Alt-rock and funk bands plug in a stone's throw from the White House.

Madam's Organ (p163) Prepare for yee-hawin' wild times in Adams Morgan's bluesy hot spot.

DC9 (p181) Up-and-coming local bands beat it at this snug, tri-level venue.

Best Jazz

Blues Alley (p100) This sophisticated icon has been bringing in top names since Dizzy Gillespie's day.

Jazz in the Garden (p75) Tune in amid whimsical artworks in the National Sculpture Garden.

Howard Theatre (p179) Historic venue where Ella Fitzgerald once sang, now home to big-name touring acts.

Twins Jazz (p179) Small, red-walled jazz enthusiasts' gathering spot on U St.

Mr Henry's (p122) Pub that hosts snappy local bands, vocalists and poets.

Best Theater

Shakespeare Theatre Company (p141) The nation's top troupe does the Bard proud.

Studio Theatre (p181) Award-winning venue for contemporary plays, known for its powerhouse premieres.

Arena Stage (p123) Vast venue focusing on American works, especially African American stories.

Atlas Performing Arts Center (p124) Four theaters in art deco environs for avant-garde performances.

Best Spectator Sports

Nationals Park (p123) Cheap tickets, the Racing Presidents, and hip eats and drinks make for a fun evening.

Audi Field (p124) Big tailgating scene, Latin American food and crazy-cheering fans in DC's new soccer stadium.

Capital One Arena (p142) The Capitals fight hard at hockey, and the Wizards shoot some mean hoops here.

FedEx Field (p170) Die-hard fans flock to games despite the arena's middle-of-nowhere location.

Best For Free

Kennedy Center (p90) The Millennium Stage hosts a free music or dance performance daily at 6pm.

Library of Congress (p109) Events daily, from swing bands to documentary films to poetry lectures.

Shakespeare Theatre Company (p141) Each August the troupe puts on a Bard classic gratis.

Best World & Folk Music

Birchmere (p205) Mural-splashed music hall for folk, country, R&B and even the odd burlesque show.

Bukom Cafe (p163) Join the West African crowd getting its groove on to reggae beats.

La Maison Francaise (p194) Concerts that showcase the music of France.

Best Cinema

E Street Cinema (p142) Downtown theater where neighborhood urbanites drink craft beer and watch indie movies.

Avalon Theatre (p193) Much-loved cinema that shows indie and mainstream films and hosts family events.

Arlington Cinema & Drafthouse (p205) Art-house and Hollywood films to go with your beer.

Shopping

Shopping in DC means many things, from browsing funky antique shops to perusing rare titles at secondhand booksellers. Temptations abound for lovers of vinyl, vintage wares, and one-of-a-kind jewelry, art and handicrafts. And, of course, that Abe Lincoln pencil sharpener and Uncle Sam bobblehead you've been wanting await...

Specialties

No surprise: politically oriented souvenirs are Washington's specialty, from stars-and-stripes boxer shorts to rubber Nixon masks to White House snow globes. Museum shops contain iconic gifts like stuffed pandas from the National Zoo and balsa-wood airplanes from the National Air and Space Museum, as well as more unusual items like weavings from indigenous tribes at the National Museum of the American Indian and Kenyan handicrafts from the National Museum of African Art.

Fashion

Don't be fooled by all the blue suits and khakis you see those government people wearing. This is a city where you'll find an assortment of funky vintage shops, fashion-forward boutiques, couture-loving consignment stores and specialty shops dealing in African robes, hats, lingerie, urban gear and stylish footwear.

Markets

Eastern Market (p126), near Capitol Hill, is the city's main bazaar. It's a splendid place to pick up fresh fruits, vegetables and other edible items. The time to go is on the weekends, when a lively craft market and an adjoining flea market surround the area. Union Market (p174), northeast in the NoMa neighborhood, is an old warehouse converted to a mod court of artisanal oils, smoked meats, herbed cheeses and microbrews. It has become quite the hot spot since opening in 2012.

Shopping by Neighborhood

➜ **National Mall** (p74) It's all about museum shops.

➜ **White House Area & Foggy Bottom** (p91) Gems hide in office buildings, but mostly souvenir shops dot the streets.

➜ **Georgetown** (p100) DC's top corridor for upscale brand-name stores is also peppered with antique shops.

➜ **Capitol Hill & South DC** (p124) Eastern Market is the core, along with bookstores and homewares shops.

➜ **Downtown & Penn Quarter** (p142) The CityCenter sparkles with swank shops, while museum shops add character.

➜ **Dupont Circle & Kalorama** (p155) A big, quirky variety of bookstores, hats, homewares and artsy stuff.

➜ **Adams Morgan** (p163) Indie record shops, doorknob shops, bong shops and ethnic handicrafts scatter along 18th St.

➜ **Logan Circle, U Street & Columbia Heights** (p183) Distinctive antiques and homewares line 14th and U Sts; big-box retailers throng the Columbia Heights Metro.

➜ **Upper Northwest DC** (p194) Lots of family-friendly shops, plus a famed bookstore; malls toward Friendship Heights.

➜ **Northern Virginia** (p206) Galleries in Alexandria; malls in Arlington and beyond.

NEED TO KNOW

Opening Hours

➡ **Malls** 10am to 8pm or 9pm Monday to Saturday, 11am to 6pm Sunday.

➡ **Shops** 10am to 7pm Monday to Saturday, noon to 6pm Sunday.

Taxes

Sales tax is 5.75% in DC, 6% in both Virginia and Maryland.

Websites

➡ **Washingtonian** (www. washingtonian.com) Up-scale lifestyle magazine covering chic shops.

➡ **Spicy Candy** (www. spicycandydc.com) Blog covering style, beauty and cocktails around DC.

➡ **DC Fashion Fool** (www.dcfashionfool. com) Men's fashion and lifestyle blog.

Lonely Planet's Top Choices

Miss Pixie's (p183) A trove of timeworn curiosities to sort through.

National Archives Shop (p142) For when you need a Declaration-inscribed ruler or John Adams stuffed toy.

Capitol Hill Books (p124) So many volumes that they're even for sale in the bathroom.

Torpedo Factory Art Center (p206) Three floors of artists' studios fill an old munitions factory.

Eastern Market (p126) Butcher, baker and blue-crab maker on weekdays, plus artisans and farmers on weekends.

Flea Market (p126) Weekend browsing spot for cool art, furniture, clothing, global wares and bric-a-brac.

Best Souvenirs

White House Gifts (p91) Presidential golf balls, T-shirts, snow globes: a quintessential spot for goofy DC trinkets.

National Building Museum Shop (p142) Puzzles of the Metro system, LEGO models of the Capitol and hip architecture stuff.

Library of Congress Shop (p109) Socks decorated with Thomas Jefferson quotes, cherry-blossom journals and other gifts for bookworms.

White House Historical Association Museum Shop (p91) Sells the president's official ornaments, artwork and classy tchotchkes.

Best Books

Kramerbooks (p155) New books on the shelves, hearty food in the cafe, happening into the wee hours.

Second Story Books (p155) Antiquarian books and old sheet music, plus cheap sidewalk bins to rummage in.

Politics and Prose Bookstore (p194) Iconic, brain-food bookstore that hosts readings, cultural events and a comfy cafe.

Idle Time Books (p163) Great political and history stacks among the three creaky floors of used tomes.

Best Antiques

Book Hill (p93) Galleries, interior-design stores and antique shops all in a row in Georgetown.

Brass Knob (p163) Salvaged lamps, mirrors, mantelpieces and heaps of doorknobs from old buildings.

Good Wood (p183) Mid-century armoires, vintage tables, elegant old lamps and more.

Best Arts & Crafts

Shop Made in DC (p155) Illustrated city maps, George Washington woodblock prints and other wares by local makers.

Indian Craft Shop (p91) High-quality pottery, fetish carvings and beadwork by the USA's tribal groups.

Woven History (p126) Emporium of Silk Road crafts, carpets and tapestries.

Best Fashion

Meeps (p163) Cowboy shirts, Jackie O sunglasses and magnificent duds from past eras.

CityCenterDC (p142) Glittery boutiques galore fill this shopping oasis.

Fia's Fabulous Finds (p183) Well-curated, gently used, brand-name clothes for women.

Best Homewares

Cady's Alley (p100) Tucked-away Georgetown lane of interior-design boutiques.

Tabletop (p155) Dupont shop selling design-savvy room decor and kitchen items.

Hill's Kitchen (p126) Groovy pots, pans, whisks and US state-shaped cookie cutters.

Sports & Activities

DC residents are active types, and the city provides a surprising amount of parkland for everyone to play in. Miles of trails crisscross the area, offering top-notch hiking and cycling opportunities. Meanwhile, the Potomac and Anacostia Rivers cut through the District and provide loads of paddling possibilities. It's easy to get outside and take advantage of it all.

Cycling

DC has a savvy and ever-growing cycling population. The Capital Bikeshare (p270) program helps facilitate it. The network has 3700-plus bicycles at some 440 stations scattered around the region, including many that fringe the Mall. The flat green landscape is a great place to start rolling, and from there you can wheel onward to the Tidal Basin and beyond.

Acres of parkland along the Potomac River also make for great bike touring around DC. The miles and miles of off-road bike paths up the ante. Areas with sweet trails include Georgetown, Upper Northwest DC and Northern Virginia.

Hiking & Running

Everyone runs on the Mall. Rock Creek Park has 15 miles of unpaved trails. A good map is *Map N: Trails in the Rock Creek Park Area,* published by the Potomac Appalachian Trail Club (www.patc.net). Better yet, join the welcoming District Running Collective (www.districtrunningcollective.com) on their Wednesday group run through the city.

Paddling

Kayaks and canoes cruise the waters of both the Potomac River and the Anacostia River. Convenient boathouses that rent vessels are in Georgetown, the Navy Yard, the Wharf and Upper Northwest DC. Staff at these facilities provide instruction if you need it.

Sports & Activities by Neighborhood

➡ **National Mall** (p75) Join the locals tossing Frisbees, jogging and otherwise recreating.

➡ **Georgetown** (p101) Top 'hood for cycling trails and paddling options.

➡ **Capitol Hill & South DC** (p126) Kayak and bicycle rentals and tours.

➡ **Downtown & Penn Quarter** (p142) Pro basketball and hockey.

➡ **Logan Circle, U Street & Columbia Heights** (p183) Golf and far-flung natural areas for hikes.

➡ **Upper Northwest DC** (p194) Horseback riding and sweet trails in Rock Creek Park.

➡ **Northern Virginia** (p206) Laced with hiking and biking paths like Mount Vernon Trail.

NEED TO KNOW

Opening Hours

Most parks are open from sunrise to sunset.

Recreational Leagues

➡ **DC Bocce League** (www.dcbocce.com) Lawn bowling league with the motto 'Our balls are hard-er.'

➡ **DC Kickball** (http://dckickball.org) League for the soccer-meets-baseball activity.

Websites

➡ **Bike Washington** (http://bikewashington.org) Trail information.

➡ **Running Report** (www.runwashington.com) Information on races and training.

➡ **DC Front Runners** (www.dcfrontrunners.org) Club for LGBT runners and walkers.

Lonely Planet's Top Choices

National Mall (p57) Nothing inspires a run like this big green lawn studded with monuments.

Mount Vernon Trail (p206) Ride to George Washington's estate past Arlington Cemetery, airplanes, marshes and birds.

Rock Creek Park Trails (p190) Amazingly wild paths for cycling and hiking crisscross a stone's throw from civilization.

Best Cycling

C&O Canal Towpath (p101) Bucolic trail a few steps from Georgetown's shopping frenzy.

Capital Crescent Trail (p101) Converted railbed that runs by Potomac River outlooks and woodsy scenes.

Big Wheel Bikes (p270) Convenient rental shop near three ace cycling trails.

Capital Bikeshare (p270) Stations around the city rent two-wheelers for quick trips.

Best Golf

East Potomac Park Golf Course (p127) Eighteen holes plus a driving range, mini-golf course and foot golf.

Langston Golf Course (p127) Holes that fringe the National Arboretum and Anacostia River.

Rock Creek Golf Course (p183) Eighteen holes over hills surrounded by woods.

Best Guided Jaunts

Key Bridge Boathouse (p101) Paddle by monuments on twilight kayaking tours.

Bike & Roll (p272) The nighttime cycling rides around the illuminated Mall impress.

DC by Foot (p272) Excellent pay-what-you-want walks by theme or by neighborhood.

Best Walking & Running

Georgetown Waterfront Park (p94) Riverside path to watch yachts and take a break at outdoor cafes.

Theodore Roosevelt Island (p199) The Potomac River isle has shoreline boardwalks and trails through tranquil woodlands.

East Potomac Park (p116) A 5-mile paved loop offers airplane-spotting, fishing holes and cherry blossoms.

Dumbarton Oaks Park (p95) Escape the crowds on wooded, bridge-crossed trails.

Anacostia Riverwalk Trail (p127) Amble along the waterway by Nationals Park and the Navy Yard.

Best Paddling

Key Bridge Boathouse (p101) Rents canoes, kayaks and stand up paddleboards for Potomac River gliding.

Tidal Basin Boathouse (p75) Easy-breezy paddleboats offer sweet views of the Martin Luther King and Jefferson memorials.

Thompson Boat Center (p101) Georgetown hot spot for canoes, kayaks and rowing classes, plus bicycles for landlubbers.

Ballpark Boathouse (p127) Float along the Anacostia River, then enjoy postpaddle refreshments in the Navy Yard 'hood.

National Museum of Natural History p70

◉ With Kids

Washington bursts with kid-friendly attractions. Not only do they hold the nation's best collection of dinosaur bones, rockets and one-of-a-kind historical artifacts, but just about everything is free. Another bonus: green space surrounds all the sights, so young ones can burn off energy to their hearts' content.

Kid-Friendly Museums

National Zoo (p189) Pandas play, orangutans swing and lions roar at DC's top family attraction.

National Museum of Natural History (p70) The mummified kitty, *Tyrannosaurus rex* skull and tarantula feedings generate big squeals.

National Air and Space Museum (p60) Touch moon rocks, look up at rockets and walk through space capsules in the Mall's most popular museum.

National Museum of American History (p70) Gawp at the Star-Spangled Banner flag, George Washington's sword and a 23-room doll house.

Newseum (p134) Junior journalists report 'live from the White House' via the TV studio – and get the take-home video to prove it.

National Gallery of Art (p61) Stay busy with activity booklets and a ride on the underground walkway; don't forget to pick up the kids' audioguide to see highlights.

International Spy Museum (p116) Kids get to become secret agents and identify disguises, find hidden cameras and go on GPS-driven scavenger hunts.

Museum sleepovers Who doesn't want to spend the night in a sleeping bag beneath a 50ft whale? The Smithsonian offers sleepovers at its Natural History and American History museums, as well as at the Air and Space Udvar-Hazy annex in Virginia. See www.smithsoniansleepovers.org for details.

NEED TO KNOW

Advance Reservations

Some sights – including the International Spy Museum (p116), National Archives (p130), Washington Monument (p63), Ford's Theatre (p142) and the Capitol (p106) – allow you to make advance reservations for a small fee. During peak season (late March through August), it pays to go online and do so up to a month prior if you want to avoid lengthy queues.

Resources

➡ **Family Guide Booklets** Most museums provide booklets with activities kids can do on-site; ask at the information desk.

➡ **DC Cool Kids** (www.washington.org/family-friendly) Features activity guides, insider tips from local youngsters on things to do, and museum info.

➡ **Discounts** The Newseum (p134) and International Spy Museum (p116) run money-saving promotions on their websites. The ticket broker Goldstar (www.goldstar.com/washington-dc) often has half-price tickets.

Outdoor Activities

Georgetown Waterfront Park (p94) It has fountains to splash in, a labyrinth to curlicue around and boats to watch (or hop aboard for a sightseeing ride).

Carousel (p72) Take a spin on the old-fashioned merry-go-round on the Mall.

Tidal Basin Boathouse (p75) For a gentle jaunt, rent a paddleboat and glide out past the Jefferson Memorial.

Attractions Out of Town

A couple of popular attractions lie beyond the city limits:

Glen Echo Park (☑301-634-2222; www.glenechopark.org; 7300 MacArthur Blvd, Glen Echo, MD; ☺6am-1am) This beautiful park 9 miles northwest of downtown has a huge retro **carousel** (per ride $1.25, operating May through September) and excellent children's shows by

two resident troupes: the Puppet Company and Adventure Theatre MTC.

Six Flags America (☑301-249-1500; www.sixflags.com/america; 13710 Central Ave. Upper Marlboro; ☺May-Oct, hours vary; adult/child $70/50;) The park offers a full array of roller coasters and tamer kiddie rides. It's located about 15 miles east of downtown DC in Maryland.

Mount Vernon (p209) George Washington's home in Virginia is always a crowd-pleaser. Youngsters can pet the horses and other animals at the Pioneer Farm (open April through October) and dress up like Martha Washington in the Reynolds Museum and Education Center.

National Harbor (www.nationalharbor.com) An enormous Ferris wheel, public art to climb on, and free outdoor movies and concerts make National Harbor a fun family destination, especially if you travel by water taxi across the Potomac, from DC to its site in Maryland.

Children's Theater

National Theatre (p141) Free performances, from puppet shows to tap dancers, take place on Saturday mornings at this elegant, and some say haunted, theater.

Discovery Theater (p75) The Smithsonian's kids' theater features cultural plays and storytelling.

Glen Echo Park Two theater companies are based at this park just over the border in Maryland. The **Puppet Company** (☑301-634-5380; www.thepuppetco.org; tickets $12; ☺Thu-Sun) specializes in puppet shows putting on classics such as *Beauty and the Beast* every Thursday through Sunday. Also here is **Adventure Theatre MTC** (☑301-634-2270; www.adventuretheatre-mtc.org; tickets $19.50), which has been around for more than 65 years and stages musicals based on children's books.

Tours

Bike & Roll (p270) Among the company's many offerings is an all-ages, 4-mile cycling tour that zips around the Mall and Tidal Basin. Children's bikes are provided.

DC by Foot (p272) This operation offers pay-what-you-want walking tours. While it's not specifically geared to kids, it is popular with families. The Mall tour takes about two hours and covers a mile; the route is stroller friendly.

Kids by Neighborhood

Upper Northwest DC
National Zoo, National Cathedral and parks (p186)

Logan Circle, U Street & Columbia Heights
Far-flung National Arboretum and nature sites (p165)

Georgetown
Parkland and riverfront paths (p92)

White House Area & Foggy Bottom
Kennedy Center and White House (p76)

White House

Downtown & Penn Quarter
National Archives, Newseum, art and theater (p128)

National Mall
Slew of museums and green space (p56)

Capitol Hill & South DC
Eastern Market and play areas (p104)

Washington Channel

Potomac River

Anacostia River

Rainy-Day Options

Catch an IMAX The Smithsonian has two IMAX theaters on the Mall: one in the National Museum of Natural History (p70), and the other in the National Air and Space Museum (p60). The latter also holds the Einstein Planetarium. Schedules are amalgamated at www.si.edu/imax.

Rise & Rhyme The activist cafe chain Busboys & Poets hosts a weekly morning storytelling and performance series for children age five and under. The 90-minute events (per child $5) take place at B&P's various locations around town. Check www.busboysandpoets.com/events/info/rise-rhyme for the schedule.

Boogie Babes This program (www.facebook.com/boogiebabesdc) gets the preschool-age crowd rockin' with interactive musical performances at Eastern Market every Thursday at 10:30am (per child $6). It also travels to other venues on occasion; check the website for locations.

Eat Streets for Kids

➡ **Mall** The National Museum of the American Indian's Mitsitam Native Foods Cafe (p75) provides unique options. The National Gallery of Art's Cascade Café (p75) has pizza, pasta and a gelato bar. Or there's the old standby McDonald's in the National Air and Space Museum.

➡ **7th and 8th Sts NE** 7th St has Eastern Market (p126) for sandwiches and picnic supplies, plus cafes and gelaterias; next door 8th St has fast-food chains, bakeries and kid-friendly restaurants like Ted's Bulletin (p120).

➡ **7th St NW** In Penn Quarter leading north from the National Archives, this street and its environs have quite a few kid-friendly burger and pizza places.

➡ **Zoo area** The areas north and south of the Connecticut Ave entrance have heaps of restaurants, such as Lebanese Taverna (p193).

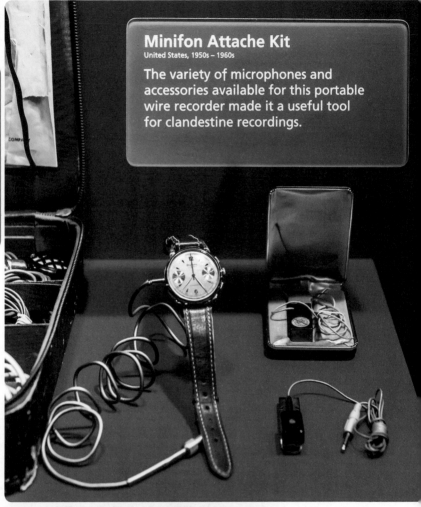

Minifon Attache Kit
United States, 1950s – 1960s

The variety of microphones and
accessories available for this portable
wire recorder made it a useful tool
for clandestine recordings.

Above: International Spy Museum p116

Left: National Museum of American
History p70

JON HICKS / GETTY IMAGES ©

Lonely Planet's Top Choices

National Zoo (p189) Perfect for kids big and little, with exhibits ranging from the huge (13,000lb elephants) to the tiny (twig catfish).

National Museum of Natural History (p70) Its collections reflect the natural world and form the foundation for scientific discovery.

National Air and Space Museum (p60) Name the historic aircraft or spacecraft and it's here amid the two-floor spread of awesomeness.

National Museum of American History (p70) With an array of cultural artifacts shown in a bright and interactive way.

Best Restaurants for Kids

Comet Ping Pong (p191) Heaps of fun playing Ping-Pong while waiting for awesome pizza.

Ted's Bulletin (p120) Retro spot serving smiley-face pancakes and peanut-butter-and-jelly sandwiches.

Diner (p160) Cartoons for kids, booze for parents, 24-hour service and American food classics for all.

Good Stuff Eatery (p119) Terrific burgers and milkshakes made with sustainable ingredients.

Best Shopping for Kids

International Spy Museum (p116) The shop carries everything from mustache disguises to voice-changing gadgets.

Barstons Child's Play (p194) Fun toys plus a daily storytime.

Tugooh Toys (p100) Wood blocks, ecofriendly stuffed animals and educational games line the shelves.

National Air and Space Museum (p60) The only place to buy astronaut ice cream and a kid-sized NASA spacesuit.

Best Lodging for Kids

Embassy Suites Washington DC (p234) Big rooms, an indoor pool and evening wine for mom and dad.

Kimpton Hotel Monaco DC (p231) Cribs, safety kits and toys for children, plus a convenient downtown location.

Omni Shoreham Hotel (p236) Treats kids right with milk, cookies, toys and games a stone's throw from the zoo.

Explore Washington, DC

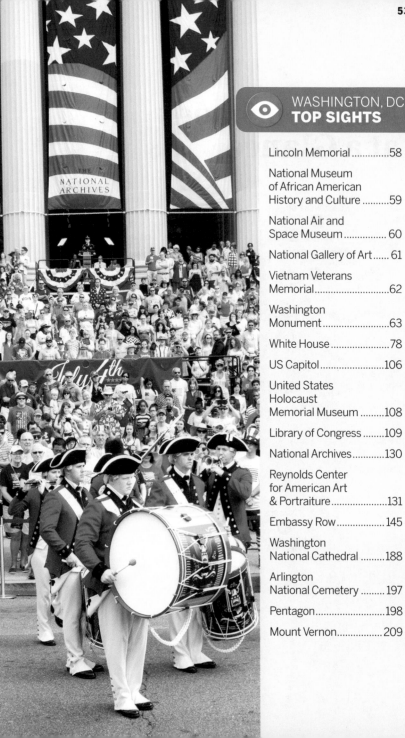

WASHINGTON, DC'S TOP SIGHTS

Neighborhoods at a Glance

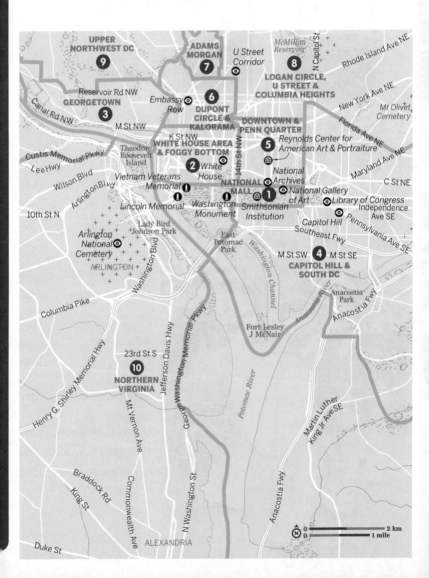

UPPER NORTHWEST DC 9

ADAMS MORGAN 7

U Street Corridor

McMillan Reservoir

N Capitol St

Rhode Island Ave NE

LOGAN CIRCLE, U STREET & COLUMBIA HEIGHTS 8

Reservoir Rd NW

GEORGETOWN 3

Embassy Row

DUPONT CIRCLE & KALORAMA 6

New York Ave NE

Mt Olivet Cemetery

Canal Rd NW

M St NW

K St NW

DOWNTOWN & PENN QUARTER 5

Florida Ave NE

Custis Memorial Pkwy

Theodore Roosevelt Island

WHITE HOUSE AREA & FOGGY BOTTOM

14th St NW

Reynolds Center for American Art & Portraiture

Maryland Ave NE

Lee Hwy

Wilson Blvd

Vietnam Veterans Memorial

White House 2

National Archives

C St NE

Arlington Blvd

Lincoln Memorial

Washington Monument

NATIONAL MALL 1

Smithsonian Institution

National Gallery of Art

Library of Congress

Independence Ave SE

10th St N

Lady Bird Johnson Park

Capitol Hill

Pennsylvania Ave SE

Arlington National Cemetery

East Potomac Park

Southeast Fwy

ARLINGTON

Washington Channel

M St SW 4 M St SE

CAPITOL HILL & SOUTH DC

Washington Blvd

Anacostia River

Columbia Pike

Anacostia Park

Anacostia Fwy

Fort Lesley J McNair

Jefferson Davis Hwy

George Washington Memorial Pkwy

23rd St S

10 **NORTHERN VIRGINIA**

Potomac River

Henry G Shirley Memorial Hwy

Mt Vernon Ave

Martin Luther King Jr Ave SE

Braddock Rd

King St

Commonwealth Ave

N Washington St

Anacostia Fwy

Duke St

ALEXANDRIA

N

2 km
1 mile

❶ National Mall p56

The National Mall is a monument-studded park edged by the magnificent Smithsonian museums. It's a must-visit destination that provides days – if not weeks – of enjoyment and edification for visitors.

❷ White House Area & Foggy Bottom p76

The White House, aka the president's pad, is likely to take your breath away the first time you see it. The surrounding streets are equally impressive, with a bustle that comes courtesy of this neighborhood's role as America's center of bureaucratic and political business.

❸ Georgetown p92

Georgetown is DC's most aristocratic neighborhood, home to elite university students, ivory-tower academics and diplomats. Chichi brand-name shops, dark-wood pubs and upscale restaurants line the streets. Lovely parks and gardens color the edges.

❹ Capitol Hill & South DC p104

The city's geographic and legislative heart surprises by being mostly a row-house–lined residential neighborhood. The vast area holds top sights such as the Capitol, Library of Congress and Holocaust Memorial Museum, but creaky bookshops and cozy pubs also thrive here. The areas around Eastern Market and H St NE are locals' hubs, with good-time restaurants and nightlife.

❺ Downtown & Penn Quarter p128

Penn Quarter forms around Pennsylvania Ave as it runs between the White House and the Capitol. Downtown extends north beyond it. Major sights include the National Archives, the Reynolds Center for American Art & Portraiture and Ford's Theatre. This is also DC's entertainment district and convention hub, so the place bustles day and night.

❻ Dupont Circle & Kalorama p143

Dupont offers flashy new restaurants, hip bars, cafe society and cool bookstores. It's also the heart of the city's LGBT community. It used to be where turn-of-the-20th-century millionaires lived. Today those mansions hold DC's greatest concentration of embassies. Kalorama sits in the northwest corner and ups the regal quotient.

❼ Adams Morgan p156

Adams Morgan has long been Washington's fun, nightlife-driven party zone. It's also a global village of sorts. The result today is a raucous mash-up centered on 18th St NW. Vintage boutiques, record shops and ethnic eats poke up between thumping bars and a growing number of stylish spots for gastronomes.

❽ Logan Circle, U Street & Columbia Heights p165

This neighborhood covers a lot of ground. Logan Circle stars with hot restaurants and stylish bars amid stately old manors. Historic U St has been reborn as a jazzy arts and entertainment district. Columbia Heights booms with Latino immigrants and hipsters. Onward, Northeast DC is a stretch of prosperous residential blocks holding some great far-flung sights.

❾ Upper Northwest DC p186

The leafy lanes and winding boulevards of Upper Northwest DC have long been the place for well-to-do Washingtonians to settle down. Three popular parks offer opportunities for hiking, cycling and horseback riding. Two impressive museums – the Kreeger and Hillwood Estate – are among DC's most underrated sights.

❿ Northern Virginia p195

Arlington has the solemn National Cemetery and imposing Pentagon. Alexandria is a posh collection of historic house museums, cobblestoned streets, outdoor cafes and a waterfront promenade. Nature areas and trails fringe both towns.

National Mall

Neighborhood Top Five

1 **Lincoln Memorial** (p58) Climbing the steps, staring into Abe's stony eyes, reading his Gettysburg Address chiseled in the wall and then standing where Martin Luther King Jr gave his 'I Have a Dream' speech.

2 **National Museum of African American History and Culture** (p59)

Learning about the diverse African American experience and how it has helped shape the nation.

3 **National Air and Space Museum** (p60) Marveling at the graceful design and technological innovation apparent in the craft that have transported humans into the sky and space.

4 **National Gallery of Art** (p61) Gazing at hundreds of masterpieces housed in two cleverly connected buildings.

5 **Vietnam Veterans Memorial** (p62) Reflecting on the sea of names etched into this evocative piece of architecture.

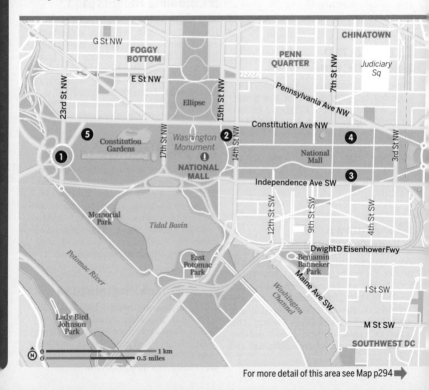

For more detail of this area see Map p294 ➡

Explore the National Mall

With so many monuments and museums to see (for free!), you could spend your entire trip on the National Mall. It's easy to lose a full day to the National Gallery of Art, the National Museum of African American History and Culture or the Air and Space Museum, and many of the other museums also deserve multiple-hour visits.

Whatever places you decide to explore, be prepared to walk. The main row of sights, from the Smithsonian museums west to the Lincoln Memorial, is about 2 miles tip to tip. The DC Circulator National Mall bus route stops by many of the hot spots, but you'll still end up hoofing it quite a bit. Eating and drinking options are thin on the ground beyond the museum cafes. And while the monuments are beautiful at night, there's not much going on after hours – consider starting early at the memorials, which are open 24/7, commencing your museum-going at 10am, when the Smithsonian venues open, and then heading to another neighbourhood at night.

Local Life

➡ **Early to Rise** Many locals say the best cherry blossom viewing is from the Franklin Delano Roosevelt Memorial (p70) at sunrise.

➡ **Rest Area** Head to the pretty and peaceful Enid A Haupt Garden (p71) behind the Smithsonion Castle to read, picnic or meditate.

➡ **Nighttime Stroll** Don't overlook visiting the Mall at night. A walk along Constitution Ave past the dramatically lit monuments is incredibly atmospheric (and safe).

Getting There & Away

➡ **Metro** Smithsonian (Orange, Silver, Blue Lines) and L'Enfant Plaza (Orange, Silver, Blue, Green and Yellow Lines) for most sights; Foggy Bottom-GWU (Orange, Silver, Blue Lines) for the Lincoln and Vietnam Memorials – though they're about a mile walk from the station.

➡ **Bus** The DC Circulator National Mall bus goes from Union Station around the Mall and Tidal Basin, with stops at main sights.

➡ **Bicycle** Several Capital Bikeshare stations fringe the Mall.

Lonely Planet's Top Tip

The Mall is lacking in eating and drinking choices. The best option is to head to the cafes in the National Museum of African American History and Culture, National Museum of the American Indian, or the National Gallery of Art Sculpture Garden at the start of the lunch period to score a table and have first dibs at the dishes in the bains-marie.

⊙ Best Museums

➡ National Museum of African American History and Culture (p59)
➡ National Air and Space Museum (p60)
➡ National Gallery of Art (p61)
➡ Freer-Sackler Museums of Asian Art (p70)
➡ National Museum of Natural History (p70)

 For reviews, see p70.

⊙ Best Gardens

➡ National Gallery of Art Sculpture Garden (p71)
➡ United States Botanic Garden (p71)
➡ Enid A Haupt Garden (p71)
➡ Hirshhorn Sculpture Garden (p71)

For reviews, see p70.

🔒 Best Shopping

➡ National Gallery of Art (p61)
➡ National Museum of the American Indian (p73)
➡ National Museum of African Art (p72)

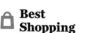 For reviews, see p74.

⊙ TOP SIGHT
LINCOLN MEMORIAL

In a city of icons, the monument for the nation's 16th president stands out in the crowd. Maybe it's the classicism evoked by the Greek temple design, or the stony dignity of Lincoln's gaze. Whatever the lure, a visit here while looking out over the Reflecting Pool is a defining DC moment.

The Columns
Plans for a monument to Abraham Lincoln began in 1867 – two years after his assassination – but construction didn't begin until 1914. Henry Bacon designed the memorial to resemble a Doric temple, with 36 columns to represent the 36 states in Lincoln's union.

The Statue & Words
Carvers used 28 blocks of marble to fashion the seated figure. Lincoln's face and hands are particularly realistic, since they are based on castings done when he was president. The words of his Gettysburg Address and Second Inaugural speech flank the statue on the north and south walls, along with murals depicting his principles. Look for symbolic images of freedom, liberty and unity, among others.

MLK Marker
From the get-go, the Lincoln Memorial became a symbol of the Civil Rights movement. Most famously, Martin Luther King Jr gave his 'I Have a Dream' speech here in 1963. An engraving of King's words marks the spot where he stood. It's on the landing 18 steps from the top, and is usually where everyone is gathered, snapping photos of the awesome view out over the Mall.

DON'T MISS
➡ Martin Luther King's 'Dream' speech marker
➡ Gettysburg Address text
➡ Lincoln's Second Inauguration Address text

PRACTICALITIES
➡ Map p294, A2
➡ www.nps.gov/linc
➡ 2 Lincoln Memorial Circle NW
➡ ⊙24hr
➡ 🚌Circulator, Ⓜ Orange, Silver, Blue Line to Foggy Bottom-GWU

TOP SIGHT
NATIONAL MUSEUM OF AFRICAN AMERICAN HISTORY AND CULTURE

Museums don't get much better than this. Opened in 2016, this magnificently curated and presented museum explores African American life, culture and history through artifacts, interactive exhibitions, installations and shared experiences.

Slavery & Freedom Exhibit
Start your tour on the subterranean C3 level, which utilizes interpretive panels, audiovisual presentations and a scattering of artifacts to recount its narrative of injustice, cruelty and the beginning of hope. Exhibits include a timber slave cabin from a South Carolina plantation.

Segregation Exhibits
On the C2 level are a handful of exhibits that enable visitors to gain an inkling of what daily life was like for African Americans in the first half of the 20th century, including stools from a segregated Woolworth's lunch counter at Greensboro North Carolina, site of a 1960 sit-in that led to the company removing its policy of racial segregation. Also here is a segregated Pullman Palace passenger car that ran along the Southern Railway route during the infamous Jim Crow era.

A Changing America
The narrative of oppression really starts to recalibrate in the exhibit A Changing America. Tracing the creation and growth of the modern civil rights movement in America, the artifact-rich C1 floor highlights developments since 1968, including the Black Arts Movement, the Black Panthers and the election of Barak Obama as president.

Leveling the Playing Field
African American athletes have long excelled in sports, both in the so-called 'Negro Leagues' formed in the era of segregation and in the subsequent decades, when sport becomes synonymous with power and big business. Baseball, football, basketball, boxing and tennis take center court (and field) in this 3rd-floor exhibit, with loads of audiovisual presentations and artifacts on show.

Musical Crossroads
This fabulous exhibition in the culture galleries on the fourth floor celebrates the contribution that African Americans have made to the global musical scene. See Chuck Berry's 1973 fine-engine-red Cadillac Eldorado, Dinah Washington's fur stole, Louis Armstrong's Selmer trumpet, Little Richard's sequinned jacket, Cab Calloway's tuxedo and much, much more.

DON'T MISS

➡ Slavery and Freedom gallery
➡ Musical Crossroads gallery
➡ Segregation exhibits
➡ A Changing America exhibit
➡ Leveling the Playing Field exhibit

TOP TIP

➡ This museum is very popular, and daily visitor numbers are capped; it's best to book online months in advance or try for one of the same-day tickets released online at 6:30am daily.

PRACTICALITIES

➡ Map p294, D2
➡ ☏844-750-3012
➡ www.nmaahc.si.edu
➡ 1400 Constitution Ave NW
➡ admission free
➡ ⊙10am-5:30pm
➡ 🚻
➡ 🚌Circulator, ⓂOrange, Silver, Blue Line to Smithsonian or Federal Triangle

NATIONAL AIR AND SPACE MUSEUM

The Air and Space Museum is among the Smithsonian's biggest crowd-pullers. Families flock here to view the mind-blowing array of planes, rockets and other contraptions – and all of it is as rousing for adults as kids. Name the historic aircraft or spacecraft, and it's bound to be on one of the museum's two chock-a-block floors.

The museum's entrance hall makes a grand impression. Walk in the Mall-side entrance and look up: Chuck Yeager's sound-barrier-breaking Bell X-1 and Charles Lindbergh's transatlantic-crossing *Spirit of St Louis* hang from the ceiling. Nuclear missiles and rockets rise up from the floor.

On the second floor, the Wright Brothers get their own gallery, and its centerpiece is the 1903 biplane they built and flew at Kitty Hawk, North Carolina in 1903. That's right: the world's first airplane is here. Nearby, Amelia Earhart's natty red Lockheed 5B Vega shines in the Pioneers of Flight gallery.

Skylab was America's first space station, launched in 1973. The orbital workshop was its largest component, and was where the astronauts lived. Crews of three stayed aboard for up to three months. Walk through to see the shower, exercise bicycle and other cramped quarters. It's part of the Space Race exhibition (1st floor).

The Lockheed Martin Imax Theater screens a rotating list of films throughout the day. Shows at the Albert Einstein Planetarium send viewers hurtling through space on tours of the universe. Buy your tickets as soon as you arrive, or on the museum website before you visit.

DON'T MISS

➡ Lindbergh's *Spirit of St Louis*

➡ Wright Brothers' original airplane

➡ Amelia Earhart's plane

➡ Skylab Orbital Workshop

➡ Chuck Yeager's Bell X-1

PRACTICALITIES

➡ Map p294, F2

➡ ☎ 202-633-2214

➡ www.airandspace.si.edu

➡ cnr 6th St & Independence Ave SW

➡ admission free

➡ ⏱ 10am-5:30pm

➡ 👫

➡ 🚌 Circulator, Ⓜ Orange, Silver, Blue, Green, Yellow Line to L'Enfant Plaza

⊙ TOP SIGHT
NATIONAL GALLERY OF ART

Affiliated with but not a part of the Smithsonian, the two connected buildings of the National Gallery of Art are home to an extraordinary collection of art spanning the Middle Ages to the present. It's one of America's greatest cultural institutions.

West Building

The original neoclassical building, known as the West Building, exhibits primarily European works from the Middle Ages to the early 20th century. You could spend days wandering through the trove in this wing alone. The National Gallery is the only art museum in the western hemisphere displaying a Leonardo da Vinci (*Ginevra di' Benci,* in the 13th- to 16th-century Italian galleries) and there are also huge galleries devoted to French, Spanish, Dutch, German, Flemish, British and American art. Impressionist and Postimpressionist fans should make a beeline for galleries 80 to 93, where all the big-name brushmen hang. There are entire rooms filled with examples of Cézanne's rough-hewn paintwork (as in *Houses in Provence: The Riaux Valley near L'Estaque*), Van Gogh's vivid swirls (*Green Wheat Fields, Auvers*), Monet's fleeting light (*two Rouen Cathedral* studies) and Renoir's saturated color (*Girl with a Watering Can*).

East Building

Across 4th St NW, the angular East Building, designed by IM Pei, holds modern and contemporary art. Highlights include Alexander Calder's stunning mobile *Untitled*, commissioned especially for this building, which swings over the atrium; Picasso's *Family of Saltimbanques;* Henri Matisse's *Open Window, Collioure,* and Jackson Pollock's *Number 1, 1950* (*Lavender Mist*).

Cafe & Subterranean Walkway

To get between the two buildings, jump on the trippy, twinkling, moving sidewalk that connects them underground. It's a work of art itself, titled *Multiverse,* by Leo Villareal. The Cascade Cafe buzzes with patrons at the walkway's west end.

Concerts & Film Screenings

The gallery's documentary and avant-garde film program takes place several times a month in the East Building auditorium. Free classical concerts fill the air on Sundays in the West Building's West Garden Court and jazz concerts are held in the sculpture garden in summer. Check www.nga.gov/calendar for details of all events.

DON'T MISS

➡ 13th- to 16th-century Italian galleries
➡ Pollock and Picasso works in the East Building
➡ 19th-century French (Impressionist) galleries
➡ Leo Villareal's *Multiverse* walkway

TOP TIPS

➡ If you're short on time, take the free, multilanguage 'Director's Tour' audioguide, which introduces the gallery's highlights. It's available from a desk near the main entrance.
➡ Ask about the dedicated audioguide and tours for kids.

PRACTICALITIES

➡ Map p294, F2
➡ ☎202-737-4215
➡ www.nga.gov
➡ Constitution Ave NW, btwn 3rd & 7th Sts
➡ admission free
➡ ⊙10am-5pm Mon-Sat, 11am-6pm Sun
➡ ♿
➡ ▣Circulator, Ⓜ Green, Yellow Line to Archives

TOP SIGHT
VIETNAM VETERANS MEMORIAL

A black granite 'V' cuts into the Mall, just as the war it memorializes cut into the national psyche. The monument eschews mixing conflict with glory. Instead, it quietly records the names of service personnel killed or missing in action in Vietnam, honoring those who gave their lives and explaining, in stark architectural language, the true price paid in war.

The Design

Maya Lin, a 21-year-old Yale architecture student, designed the memorial following a nationwide competition in 1981. The 'V' is comprised of two walls of polished granite that meet in the center at a 10ft peak, then taper to a height of 8in. The mirror-like surface lets visitors see their own reflection among the names of the dead, bringing past and present together.

Order of Names

The wall lists soldiers' names chronologically according to the date they died (and alphabetically within each day). The list starts at the monument's vertex on panel 1E on July 8, 1959. It moves day by day to the end of the eastern wall at panel 70E, then starts again at panel 70W at the western wall's end. It returns to the vertex on May 15, 1975, where the war's beginning and end meet in symbolic closure. There are more than 58,000 names; new ones are added sporadically due to clerical errors in record keeping. Rank is not provided on the wall, and privates share space with majors.

Diamonds & Plus Signs

A diamond next to the name indicates 'killed, body recovered.' A plus sign indicates 'missing and unaccounted for.' There are approximately 1200 of the latter. If a soldier returns alive, a circle is inscribed around the plus sign. To date, no circles appear.

Reaction & Nearby Sculptures

In 1984, vocal critics of Maya Lin's design insisted that a more traditional sculpture be added to the monument. Frederick Hart's bronze Three Servicemen Memorial depicts three soldiers – one white, one African American and one Latino – who seem to be gazing upon the nearby sea of names. The tree-ringed Vietnam Women's Memorial, showing female soldiers aiding a fallen combatant, is also nearby.

DON'T MISS

➡ Your reflection in the wall

➡ Symbols beside the names

TOP TIPS

➡ Paper indices at each end of the wall let you look up individual names and get their panel location. Or you can look electronically via the Vietnam Veterans Memorial Fund (www.vvmf.org/Wall-of-Faces), which also provides photos and further info on each name.

➡ If you have questions, national park rangers are on-site from 10am to 10pm.

PRACTICALITIES

➡ Map p294, B2

➡ www.nps.gov/vive

➡ 5 Henry Bacon Dr NW

➡ ⊗24hr

➡ 🚌Circulator, ⓂOrange, Silver, Blue Line to Foggy Bottom-GWU

TOP SIGHT
WASHINGTON MONUMENT

Rising on the Mall like an exclamation point, this 555ft obelisk embodies the awe and respect the nation felt for George Washington, the USA's first president and founding father. The monument is DC's loftiest structure, and by federal law no local building can reach above it. Alas, it is closed until spring 2019 for repairs.

Mismatched Marble

Construction began in 1848, but a lack of funds during the Civil War grounded the monument at 156ft. President Ulysses S Grant got the ball rolling again in 1876.

There was a problem, though. The original marble was drawn from a quarry in Maryland, but the source dried up during the construction delay. Contractors had to turn to Massachusetts for the rest of the rock. If you look closely, there is a visible delineation in color where the old and new marble meet about a third of the way up (the bottom is a bit lighter).

Pyramid Topper

In December 1884 workers heaved a 3300lb marble capstone on the monument and topped it off with a 9in pyramid of cast aluminum. At the time, aluminum was rare and expensive. Before the shiny novelty went to Washington, the designers displayed the pyramid in the window of Tiffany's in New York City.

The monument was the culmination of some 36,000 stacked blocks of granite and marble, weighing 81,120 tons. The 'Father of his Country' had his due.

Observation Deck & Memorial Stones

Inside the monument, an elevator takes you to the sky-high observation deck that provides grand city vistas. There are also exhibits that explain how the Washington Monument was the world's tallest structure until the Eiffel Tower surpassed it. And how in August 2011 an earthquake rattled the monument, causing structural damage. It took 33 months and $15 million to fix.

On the way back down, the elevator slows so you can glimpse some of the 195 memorial stones that decorate the shaft's interior. Various states, cities and patriotic societies purchased them as part of the monument's initial construction. There's even one from the Pope.

Sadly, the elevator went kaput in the summer of 2016. Funds are in hand to undertake renovations, but the monument won't be ready to host visitors again until spring 2019.

Lines & Tickets

When the monument reopens, you'll need a ticket to get in. Same-day passes for a timed entrance are available at the **kiosk** (Map p294) by the monument. During peak season it's a good idea to reserve tickets in advance by phone (☏877-444-6777) or online (www.recreation.gov) for a small fee. And don't despair if you look online and see that tickets are sold out; there are still 1000 more available each day to be given out at the kiosk. Rangers advise getting there by 7:30am in peak season, and 9am in the off season to snag day-of tickets.

DON'T MISS

➡ Change in color a third of the way up
➡ Inscribed stones inside
➡ Views from the top

PRACTICALITIES

➡ Map p294, D2
➡ www.nps.gov/wamo
➡ 2 15th St NW
➡ admission free
➡ 🚌Circulator, Ⓜ Orange, Silver, Blue Line to Smithsonian

National Mall

A DAY TOUR

Folks often call the Mall 'America's Front Yard,' and that's a pretty good analogy. It is indeed a lawn, unfurling scrubby green grass from the Capitol west to the Lincoln Memorial. It's also America's great public space, where citizens come to protest their government, go for scenic runs and connect with the nation's most cherished ideals writ large in stone, landscaping, monuments and memorials.

You can sample quite a bit in a day, but it'll b full one that requires roughly 4 miles of walk

Start at the ❶ **Vietnam Veterans Memori** then head counterclockwise around the Ma swooping in on the ❷ **Lincoln Memorial,** ❸ **Martin Luther King Jr Memorial** and ❹ **Washington Monument.** You can also pause for the cause of the Korean War and WWII, among other monuments that dot th Mall's western portion.

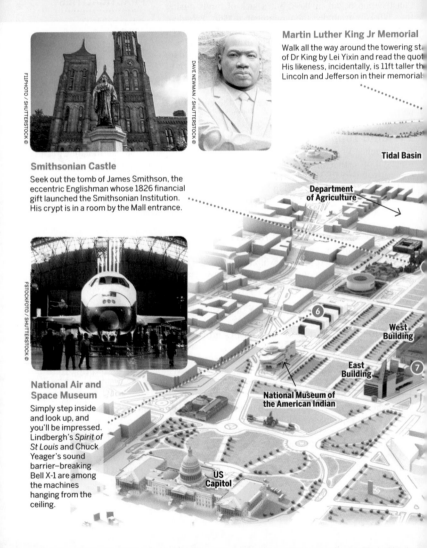

Martin Luther King Jr Memorial

Walk all the way around the towering sta of Dr King by Lei Yixin and read the quot His likeness, incidentally, is 11ft taller th Lincoln and Jefferson in their memorial

Tidal Basin

Department of Agriculture

Smithsonian Castle

Seek out the tomb of James Smithson, the eccentric Englishman whose 1826 financial gift launched the Smithsonian Institution. His crypt is in a room by the Mall entrance.

West Building

East Building

National Museum of the American Indian

National Air and Space Museum

Simply step inside and look up, and you'll be impressed. Lindbergh's *Spirit of St Louis* and Chuck Yeager's sound barrier–breaking Bell X-1 are among the machines hanging from the ceiling.

US Capitol

FJJPHOTO / SHUTTERSTOCK ©

DAVE NEWMAN / SHUTTERSTOCK ©

FSTOCKFOTO / SHUTTERSTOCK ©

Then it's onward to the museums, all fabulous and all free. Begin at the ❺ Smithsonian Castle to get your bearings – and to say thanks to the guy making all this awesomeness possible – and commence browsing through the ❻ National Air & Space Museum, ❼ National Gallery of Art & National Sculpture Garden and ❽ National Museum of African American History and Culture.

TOP TIPS

Start early, especially in summer. You'll avoid the crowds, but more importantly you'll avoid the blazing heat. Try to finish with the monuments and be in the air-conditioned museums by 10:30am. Also, consider bringing snacks, since the only food available is from scattered cart vendors and museum cafes.

Lincoln Memorial

Commune with Abe in his chair, then head down the steps to the marker where Martin Luther King Jr gave his 'Dream' speech. The view of the Reflecting Pool and Washington Monument is one of DC's best.

ADAM PARENT / SHUTTERSTOCK ©

Korean War Veterans Memorial

National WWII Memorial

National Museum of American History

National Museum of Natural History

National Sculpture Garden

Vietnam Veterans Memorial

Check the symbol that's beside each name. A diamond indicates 'killed, body recovered.' A plus sign indicates 'missing and unaccounted for.' There are approximately 1200 of the latter.

Washington Monument

As you approach the obelisk, look a third of the way up. See how it's slightly lighter in color at the bottom? Builders had to use different marble after the first source dried up.

National Museum of African American History and Culture

Feel the power at newest Smithsonian museum, where artifacts include Harriet Tubman's hymnal, Emmett Till's casket, a segregated lunch counter and Michael Jordan's sneakers. The building's design is based on a three-tiered Yoruban crown.

National Gallery of Art & National Sculpture Garden

Beeline to Gallery 6 (West Building) and ogle the Western Hemisphere's only Leonardo da Vinci painting. Outdoors, amble amid whimsical sculptures by Miró, Calder and Lichtenstein. Also check out IM Pei's design of the East Building.

RARRARORRO / SHUTTERSTOCK ©

The Smithsonian Institution

It's not a single place, as commonly thought. Rather, the Smithsonian Institution consists of 19 museums, the National Zoo and nine research facilities. Most are in DC, but others are further afield in the US and abroad. And to think it all started with a gift from an eccentric anti-monarchist Englishman...

Mr Smithson's Gift

The whole story began with James Smithson, a British scientist who never set foot in the USA, let alone Washington, DC. He died in 1829 with a provision in his will to found 'at Washington, under the name of the Smithsonian Institution, an establishment for the increase and diffusion of knowledge.' Actually, that was the backup plan. The money first went to his nephew Henry, but Henry died a few years after Smithson, without heirs. So the 'institution' clause kicked in, and $508,318 arrived in Washington for the task.

The US government promptly ignored the amazing gift. Various senators grumbled it was undignified for America to accept such presents, particularly from an unknown foreigner. Anti-British sentiment informed some of this debate: the 1814 British torching of Washington remained fresh in many American minds. Finally, though, Congress accepted the money and began constructing the Smithsonian Institution in 1846.

Mysterious Motive

So who was Smithson? He was the illegitimate son of the Duke of Northumberland. A mineralogist by trade and a shrewd investor by evidence (his donation was a fortune for its time), Smithson was well educated and wealthy by any measure. But his motivations for

SMITHSONIAN'S DC ROSTER

- National Air and Space Museum
- National Museum of Natural History
- National Museum of American History
- National Museum of African American History and Culture
- National Zoo
- National Air and Space Museum Steven F Udvar-Hazy Center (annex)
- Reynolds Center for American Art & Portraiture (two museums)
- National Museum of the American Indian
- Smithsonian Castle
- Hirshhorn Museum and Sculpture Garden
- Renwick Gallery
- National Postal Museum
- Freer-Sackler Museums of Asian Art (two museums)
- National Museum of African Art
- Anacostia Community Museum
- S Dillon Ripley Center
- Arts & Industries Building (closed indefinitely)

1. Smithsonian Castle p73 2. Gemstones and minerals at the National Museum of Natural History p70

bequeathing so much money to the USA, as opposed to his native Britain, remain a mystery. Some say he was an anti-monarchist who took a particular shine to the American Republic. He may have just loved learning.

Smithson was 64 years old when he died in Genoa, Italy, and was buried there, until Alexander Graham Bell – in his role as Smithsonian regent – collected his remains and brought them to Washington in 1904. Today Smithson is entombed in the Smithsonian Castle on the Mall.

The Smithsonian Today

Smithson's gift morphed into a vast vault of treasures. The Smithsonian holds approximately 155 million artworks, scientific specimens, artifacts and other objects, of which less than 2% are on display at any given time. The collection sprawls across 19 museums – 10 on the Mall, seven others around DC and two in New York City (the American Indian Museum Heye Center and Cooper Hewitt Design Museum). The Smithsonian also operates the National Zoo. There is no

entry fee for any of the venues. They're all free, always.

The institution needs (and is receiving) some expensive upkeep, and it continues to expand. It's been suggested the museums start charging for admission, but the powers that be won't hear of it. They argue fees would hinder Smithson's original goal of spreading knowledge. So the quest for financing keeps on. The Smithsonian is about 60% federally funded. In 2017 Congress appropriated $863 million to the institution. The rest of the budget comes from private sources such as corporations, foundations and individuals.

Research Centers

In addition to museums, the Smithsonian holds nine research centers under its umbrella, and they're scattered all over the place. They include the Archives of American Art (in DC and NYC), Astrophysical Observatory (Cambridge, MA), Conservation Biology Institute (Front Royal, VA), Environmental Research Center (Edgewater, MD), Marine Station (Fort Pierce, FL), Museum Conservation Institute (Suitland, MD), Smithsonian Archives (DC),

1. National Air and Space Museum p60 2. National Zoo p189

Smithsonian Libraries (DC, NY, MA and Panama) and Tropical Research Institute (Panama). The Astrophysical Observatory, Environmental Research Center and Marine Station have public programs, and the Museum Conservation Institute offers artifact appraisals and instruction on antique restoration to the community. But for the most part the research centers are for scholarly endeavors.

Record Label

Yes, the institution even has its own record label. Smithsonian Folkways documents folk music, spoken word and sounds from around the world. It's an incredible enterprise that preserves everything from civil-rights protesters' songs in Selma, AL, to 1940s Dixieland jazz to Comanche flute music to Norwegian lullabies. This branch of the Smithsonian also puts on the annual Folklife Festival (www.festival.si.edu), a 10-day music and cultural bash on the Mall in late June and early July.

Odds & Ends

Of the Smithsonian's roughly 155 million specimens and artifacts, 145 million belong to the National Museum of Natural History (p70). You can look up just about anything – anything – in the 13.3 million digital records available through the Smithsonian Collections Search Center (http://collections.si.edu/search).

HIGHLIGHTS OF THE SMITHSONIAN

➡ Hope Diamond (National Museum of Natural History)

➡ Star-Spangled Banner flag (National Museum of American History)

➡ 1903 Wright Brothers flyer (National Air and Space Museum)

➡ Abraham Lincoln's top hat (National Museum of American History)

➡ Dorothy's ruby slippers (National Museum of American History)

➡ Enola Gay bomber (National Air and Space Museum Udvar-Hazy Center)

➡ Giant pandas (National Zoo)

 SIGHTS

LINCOLN MEMORIAL　MONUMENT
See p58.

**NATIONAL MUSEUM OF
AFRICAN AMERICAN
HISTORY AND CULTURE**　MUSEUM
See p59.

**NATIONAL AIR AND
SPACE MUSEUM**　MUSEUM
See p60.

NATIONAL GALLERY OF ART　MUSEUM
See p61.

**VIETNAM VETERANS
MEMORIAL**　MONUMENT
See p62.

WASHINGTON MONUMENT　MONUMENT
See p63.

**FREER-SACKLER MUSEUMS
OF ASIAN ART**　MUSEUM
Map p294 (☎202-633-1000; www.asia.si.edu; 1050 Independence Ave SW; ◷10am-5:30pm; ⓺Circulator, ⓂOrange, Silver, Blue Line to Smithsonian) FREE This is a lovely spot in which to while away a Washington afternoon. Japanese silk scrolls, smiling Buddhas, rare Islamic manuscripts and Chinese jades are exhibited in cool, quiet galleries in two galleries connected by an underground tunnel. The Freer also houses works by American painter James Whistler, including five *Nocturnes*. Don't miss the extraordinarily beautiful blue-and-gold Peacock Room on its ground floor, designed by Whistler in 1876-77 as an exotic showcase for a shipping magnate's collection of Chinese porcelain.

Like all Smithsonian institutions, the venues host free lectures, concerts and film screenings, though the ones here typically have an Asian bent; the website has the schedule.

**NATIONAL MUSEUM
OF NATURAL HISTORY**　MUSEUM
Map p294 (☎202-663-1000; www.natural history.si.edu; cnr 10th St & Constitution Ave NW; ◷10am-5:30pm, to 7:30pm some days; ⓺; ⓺Circulator, ⓂOrange, Silver, Blue Line to Smithsonian or Federal Triangle) FREE Arguably the most popular of the Smithsonian museums, so crowds are pretty much guaranteed. Wave to Henry, the elephant who guards the rotunda, then zip to the 2nd floor's Hope Diamond, a 45.52-carat bauble that is said to have cursed its owners, which included Marie Antoinette. The beloved dinosaur hall is under renovation until 2019, but the giant squid (1st floor, Ocean Hall), live butterfly pavilion and tarantula feedings provide the thrills at this kid-packed venue.

Adults will find lots to love here too: Easter Island heads (lobby at the Constitution Ave entrance), mummies (second floor), ground-floor halls devoted to mammals and oceans, and a vibrant temporary exhibition program.

The butterfly pavilion has a separate admission fee (adult/child two to 12 years $7.50/6.50); it's free on Tuesdays.

On select days, usually in spring and summer, the museum extends its hours and stays open until 7:30pm.

**NATIONAL MUSEUM
OF AMERICAN HISTORY**　MUSEUM
Map p294 (☎202-663-1000; www.american history.si.edu; cnr 14th St & Constitution Ave NW; ◷10am-5:30pm, to 7:30pm some days; ⓺; ⓺Circulator, ⓂOrange, Silver, Blue Line to Smithsonian or Federal Triangle) FREE Containing all kinds of artifacts of the American experience, this museum has as its centerpiece the flag that flew over Baltimore's Fort McHenry during the War of 1812 – the same flag that inspired Francis Scott Key to pen 'The Star-Spangled Banner' (it's on the entry level). Other highlights include Julia Child's kitchen (1st floor, east wing) and 'The First Ladies' costume exhibit on the 3rd floor. New exhibits include 'American Culture' and 'On with the Show' on the 3rd floor.

On select days, usually in spring and summer, the museum extends its hours and stays open until 7:30pm. To do the collection justice, take a volunteer-led guided tour of its highlights or hire an audioguide ($6).

There are two on-site places to eat: a cafe serving fast-food staples and the LeRoy Neiman Jazz Cafe, which specialises in New Orleans cuisine.

**FRANKLIN DELANO
ROOSEVELT MEMORIAL**　MONUMENT
Map p294 (www.nps.gov/frde; 400 W Basin Dr SW; ◷24hr; ⓺Circulator, ⓂOrange, Silver, Blue Line to Smithsonian) The 7.5-acre memorial pays tribute to the longest-serving president in US history. Visitors are taken through four red-granite areas that narrate FDR's time in office, from the Depression

to the New Deal to WWII. The story is told through statuary and inscriptions, punctuated with fountains and peaceful alcoves. It's especially pretty at night, when the marble shimmers in the glossy stillness of the Tidal Basin.

The irony is, FDR didn't want a grand memorial. Instead, he requested a modest stone slab (p135) by the Archives building. DC honored that request too.

MARTIN LUTHER
KING JR MEMORIAL   MONUMENT

Map p294 (www.nps.gov/mlkm; 1850 W Basin Dr SW; ⊙24hr; 🚊Circulator, MOrange, Silver, Blue Line to Smithsonian) Opened in 2011, this was the first Mall memorial to honor an African American. Sculptor Lei Yixin carved the piece, which is reminiscent in concept and style to the Mount Rushmore memorial. Besides Dr King's striking, 30ft-tall image, known as the Stone of Hope, there are two blocks of granite behind him that represent the Mountain of Despair. A wall inscribed with King's powerful quotes about democracy, justice and peace flanks the piece.

King's statue, incidentally, is 11ft taller than those of Lincoln and Jefferson in their nearby memorials.

NATIONAL GALLERY
OF ART SCULPTURE GARDEN   GARDENS

Map p294 (www.nga.gov; cnr Constitution Ave NW & 7th St NW; ⊙10am-5pm Mon-Sat, 11am-6pm Sun, extended hours summer & mid-Nov–mid-Mar; 🚻; 🚊Circulator, MGreen, Yellow Line to Archives) FREE The National Gallery of Art's 6-acre garden is studded with whimsical sculptures such as Roy Lichtenstein's *House* (1974), a giant Claes Oldenburg typewriter eraser (1998) and Roxy Paine's *Graft* (2008-09), a stainless steel tree.. They are scattered around a fountain – a great place to dip your feet in summer. From mid-November to mid-March the fountain is transformed into an ice rink (p75), and the garden stays open a bit later. The garden's Pavilion Cafe (p74) is a popular breakfast and lunch stop.

From May to August, the garden hosts free evening jazz concerts on Fridays between 5pm and 8:30pm.

HIRSHHORN MUSEUM   MUSEUM

Map p294 (📞202-633-1000; www.hirshhorn. si.edu; cnr 7th St & Independence Ave SW; ⊙10am-5:30pm; 🚻; 🚊Circulator, MOrange, Silver, Blue, Green, Yellow Line to L'Enfant Plaza) FREE The Smithsonian's cylindrical art museum shows works from modernism's early days to today's most cutting-edge practitioners. Exhibitions of works drawn from the museum's extensive collection are offered alongside curated shows of work by prominent contemporary artists. Visitors can relax in the third-floor sitting area, which has couches, floor-to-ceiling windows and a balcony offering Mall views. A lobby redesign by Japanese artist Hiroshi Sugimoto opened in 2018, and includes Dolcezza at Hirshhorn (p75), a gelato and coffee bar.

There are free 45-minute guided tours at 12.30pm and 3.30pm daily.

HIRSHHORN
SCULPTURE GARDEN   GARDENS

Map p294 (Jefferson Dr SW; ⊙7:30am-sunset; 🚊Circulator, ML'Enfant Plaza) Works by Rodin, Arp, Moore, Miró and de Kooning are among those on show in this sunken sculpture garden opposite the Hirshhorn's main museum. The site is in need of some TLC – many of the works are looking dated and the garden itself is nowhere near as attractive or welcoming as the National Gallery of Art's sculpture garden across the mall.

UNITED STATES
BOTANIC GARDEN   GARDENS

Map p294 (📞202-225-8333; www.usbg.gov; 100 Maryland Ave SW; ⊙10am-5pm; 🚻; 🚊Circulator, MOrange, Silver, Blue Line to Federal Center SW) FREE Built to resemble London's Crystal Palace, this garden's iron-and-glass greenhouse provides a beautiful setting to view orchids, ferns and cacti. When you're done with those, seek out the so-called 'Corpse Flower' *Amorphophallus titanum,* whose name translates to 'giant misshapen penis' and whose erratic blooms smell like rotting flesh. Mmm! Alas, it only blooms every three to five years and it's not on show during its hibernation.

A rose garden, butterfly garden and water garden fill the landscape just outside the building. Bartholdi Park (p113), a showcase of sustainable and accessible landscape design, is located on a traffic island behind the garden.

ENID A HAUPT GARDEN   GARDENS

Map p294 (www.gardens.si.edu; 12 Independence Ave SW; ⊙dawn-dusk; 🚻; 🚊Circulator, MOrange, Silver, Blue Line to Smithsonian) FREE The lovely green space behind the Smithsonian Castle is actually a rooftop garden, with three peaceful sections: a Moon Gate garden inspired by a 15th-century Chinese temple, a Victorian-style parterre garden and a Moorish-style garden with a mosaic fountain modelled after those in the Alhambra in Granada, Spain. Shaded benches and tables dot the grounds, making this urban oasis a perfect picnic location.

JEFFERSON MEMORIAL   MONUMENT

Map p294 (www.nps.gov/thje; 900 Ohio Dr SW; ⏰24hr; 🚌Circulator, Ⓜ️Orange, Silver, Blue Line to Smithsonian) Set on the south bank of the Tidal Basin amid the cherry trees, this memorial honors the third US president, political philosopher, drafter of the Declaration of Independence and founder of the University of Virginia. Designed by John Russell Pope to resemble Jefferson's library at the university, the rounded monument was initially derided by critics as 'the Jefferson Muffin.' Inside is a 19ft bronze likeness, and excerpts from Jefferson's writings are etched into the walls.

NATIONAL MUSEUM
OF AFRICAN ART   MUSEUM

Map p294 (www.nmafa.si.edu; 950 Independence Ave SW; ⏰10am-5:30pm; ♿; 🚌Circulator, Ⓜ️Orange, Silver, Blue Line to Smithsonian) FREE Enter the museum's ground-level pavilion through the Enid A Haupt Garden (p71), then descend into the dim underground exhibit space. Devoted to ancient and modern sub-Saharan African art, the quiet galleries display wooden masks, beaded textiles, ceramics, fetish dolls and other examples of the region's visual traditions. Intentionally or not, there's a definite West African focus with lots of traditional art from Nigeria, Benin and Cameroon.

One-hour guided highlights tours are usually available at 10.30am a few days per week – check the events schedule for details. African dance troupes, theater companies and multimedia artists frequently stage shows here. An underground tunnel connects to the Sackler Gallery.

TIDAL BASIN   WATERFRONT

Map p294 (www.nps.gov/articles/dctidalbasin. htm; 🚌Circulator, Ⓜ️Orange, Silver, Blue Line to Smithsonian) The 2-mile stroll around this constructed inlet incorporates the Franklin Delano Roosevelt (p70) and Thomas Jefferson (p72) memorials as well as the Floral Library. It's a lovely way to spend a couple of hours – just watch out for low-hanging tree branches near the FDR memorial. During the National Cherry Blossom Festival, the city's annual spring rejuvenation, the basin bursts into a pink-and-white floral collage. Rent a paddleboat from the boathouse (p75) to get out on the water.

CONSTITUTION GARDENS   GARDENS

Map p294 (www.nps.gov/coga; Constitution Ave NW; ⏰24hr; 🚌Circulator, Ⓜ️Orange, Silver, Blue Line to Foggy Bottom-GWU) FREE Constitution Gardens is a bit of a locals' secret. Quiet, shady and serene, it's a reminder of the size of the Mall – how can such isolation exist amid so many tourists? Here's the simple layout: a copse of trees set off by a small kidney-shaped pool, punctuated with a tiny island holding the Signers' Memorial, a stone platform honoring those who signed the Declaration of Independence.

If you're in need of a romantic getaway, the 'kiss me' vibes don't get much better than this spot at sunset. The gardens are undergoing renovations to add a cafe, ice-skating facilities and more amenities, to be completed over the next few years.

SIGNERS' MEMORIAL   MEMORIAL

Map p294 (⏰24hr; 🚌Circulator, Ⓜ️Orange, Silver, Blue Line to Smithsonian) Honoring those 56 visionary men who signed the Declaration of Independence, this memorial in Constitution Garden shows how diverse this group of signers was (it included lawyers, physicians, ironmasters, merchants, farmers, clergymen, writers and surveyors). Located on a little island and accessed via a walkway, it's a a great spot for rest and contemplation.

CAROUSEL   LANDMARK

Map p294 ($3.50; ⏰10am-6pm; ♿; 🚌Circulator, Ⓜ️Orange, Silver, Blue Line to Smithsonian) Kids love taking a ride on this musical merry-go-round with its 58 brightly painted horses. It's on the Mall by the Smithsonian Castle.

NATIONAL WWII MEMORIAL   MONUMENT

Map p294 (www.nps.gov/wwii; 17th St SW; ⏰24hr; 🚌Circulator, Ⓜ️Orange, Silver, Blue Line to Smithsonian) Dedicated in 2004, this grandiose memorial honors the 16 million US soldiers who served in WWII. Groups of veterans regularly come here to pay their respects to the 400,000 Americans who died as a result of the conflict. The plaza's dual arches symbolize victory in the Atlantic and Pacific theaters, and the 56 surrounding pillars represent each US state and territory.

The Freedom Wall is studded with 4048 hand-sculpted gold stars, one for every 100 Americans who lost their lives in the war (the stars are replicas of those worn by mothers who lost their sons in the fighting). Bas-relief panels depict both combat and the mobilization of the home front. Beside the memorial to the south there is an information **kiosk** (Map p294) where you can look through the registry of war veterans.

KOREAN WAR
VETERANS MEMORIAL   MONUMENT
Map p294 (www.nps.gov/kwvm; 10 Daniel French Dr SW; ⊘24hr; ⬜Circulator, ⓂOrange, Silver, Blue Line to Foggy Bottom-GWU) Nineteen steel soldiers wander through clumps of juniper past a wall bearing images of the 'Forgotten War' that assemble, in the distance, into a panorama of the Korean mountains. The memorial is best visited at night, when the sculpted patrol – representing all races and combat branches that served in the war – takes on a phantom cast. In winter, when snow folds over the infantry's field coats, the impact is especially powerful.

NATIONAL MUSEUM
OF THE AMERICAN INDIAN   MUSEUM
Map p294 (☎202-663-1000; www.americanindian.si.edu; cnr 4th St & Independence Ave SW; ⊘10am-5:30pm; ⬤; ⬜Circulator, ⓂOrange, Silver, Blue, Green, Yellow Line to L'Enfant Plaza) FREE Ensconced in an architecturally notable building clad in honey-colored limestone, this museum offers cultural artifacts, video and audio recordings related to the indigenous people of the Americas. Sadly, navigation of the exhibits is confusing on both a curatorial and physical level. The focus on didactic panels at the expense of interpretative labels for artifacts is also problematic. The 'Our Universes' gallery (on Level 4) about Native American beliefs and creation stories is one of the more interesting exhibits.

The museum offers storytelling, percussion workshops and lots of other family programming. The ground-floor Mitsitam Native Foods Cafe (p75) is one of the Mall's most-popular dining options.

SMITHSONIAN CASTLE   NOTABLE BUILDING
Map p294 (☎202-633-1000; www.si.edu; 1000 Jefferson Dr SW; ⊘8:30am-5:30pm; ⬜Circulator, ⓂOrange, Silver, Blue Line to Smithsonian) James Renwick designed this turreted, red-sandstone fairy-tale in 1855. Today the castle houses the Smithsonian Visitors Center, which makes a good first stop on the Mall. Inside you'll find history exhibits, multilingual touch-screen displays, a staffed information desk, free maps, a cafe – and the tomb of James Smithson, the institution's founder. His crypt lies inside a little room by the main entrance off the Mall.

REFLECTING POOL   MONUMENT
Map p294 (⬜Circulator, ⓂOrange, Silver, Blue Line to Foggy Bottom-GWU) Henry Bacon, who designed the Lincoln Memorial, also conceived the iconic Reflecting Pool, modeling it after the canals at Versailles and Fontainebleau. The 0.3-mile-long pond holds 6.75 million gallons of water that circulate in from the nearby Tidal Basin.

CAPITOL REFLECTING POOL   POND
Map p294 (Capitol grounds; ⬜Circulator, ⓂOrange, Silver, Blue Line to Federal Center SW) At the base of Capitol Hill, this pool echoes the larger, rectangular Reflecting Pool by the Lincoln Memorial at the other end of the Mall. The Capitol Pool actually caps the I-395 freeway, which dips under the Mall here.

DISTRICT OF COLUMBIA
WAR MEMORIAL   MONUMENT
Map p294 (www.nps.gov/nr/feature/places/14000388.htm; West Potomac Park, off Independence Ave; ⊘24hr; ⬜Circulator, ⓂOrange, Silver, Blue Line to Foggy Bottom-GWU) This small Greek-Revival bandstand and monument was constructed in 1931. It commemorates local soldiers killed in WWI, making it the only local District memorial on the Mall. Twelve Doric 22ft-high marble columns support the circular structure; inside are the names of the 26,000 Washingtonians who served in the war and the 499 DC soldiers killed in action.

GEORGE MASON MEMORIAL   MONUMENT
Map p294 (www.nps.gov/gemm; cnr Ohio Dr & E Basin Dr SW; ⊘24hr; ⬜Circulator, ⓂOrange, Silver, Blue Line to Smithsonian) This little oasis of flowers and fountains honors the famed statesman and author of the Commonwealth of Virginia Declaration of Rights (a forerunner to the US Bill of Rights). Wendy M Ross' bronze sculpture of Mason sits (literally; his legs are crossed and the man looks eminently relaxed) on a marble bench

SHOPPING THE NATIONAL MALL

The Mall's museums all have shops where you'll unearth rare finds. Amazonian art-work, West African handicrafts and surreal space food are just a few things on offer.

National Gallery of Art (p61) Boasts several shops, including a huge one lining the underground corridor linking the East and West Buildings. You'll find framed and unframed reproductions of the museum's best-known works, greeting cards, jewelry, creative games and activities for kids, and loads of books.

National Museum of the American Indian (p73) The smaller 1st-floor shop sells pottery, artwork and jewelry made by tribes from across the Americas. The busier store upstairs has books, crafts and native-themed souvenirs (dream catchers, Mola purses, replica arrowheads).

National Museum of African Art (p72) This is a great gift-buying spot with African textiles, baskets, musical instruments and dolls. Be sure to check out the exquisite jewelry and wood-carved boxes.

National Air and Space Museum (p60) The three-floor emporium offers books, toys, kites, posters, model aircraft and such iconic DC souvenirs as freeze-dried astronaut ice cream. The shop even has child-size space suits, complete with official NASA patches.

National Museum of Natural History (p70) It has four different specialty shops, including a ground-floor store devoted to toys, stuffed dinosaurs and East Asian–themed items (origami sets, silk purses, kimonos). Outside the Geology Hall, the gem store sells fine and costume jewelry, vases, bowls, candleholders and a variety of unpolished stones.

Freer-Sackler Museums of Asian Art (p70) The Sackler side features Asian art posters and limited-edition prints, exotic jewelry and world crafts. The Freer side stocks antique ceramics from Asia, plus unique prints, scarves, bags and Eastern music.

National Museum of American History (p70) Replica souvenirs (brass binoculars, lanterns, wooden model ships) plus books and DVDs on all aspects of American cul-ture and history fill the shelves.

under a pretty covered arcade. His wise words against slavery and in support of human rights are incised in the bench.

EATING

The Mall has always been a bit of a food desert. The National Park Service operates a handful of kiosks that sell cold drinks, sandwiches and ice creams, and food trucks congregate on Constitution Ave behind the National Museum of African American History and Culture, on Independence Ave SW behind the National Museum of the American Indian, and on 7th St SW near the Hirshhorn Museum.

SWEET HOME CAFÉ   AMERICAN $
Map p294 (✆202-633-6174; www.nmaahc. si.edu/visit/sweet-home-cafe; 1400 Constitution Ave NW, National Museum of African American History & Culture; mains $14-19; ◷10am-5pm; ☐Circulator, ⓜOrange, Silver, Blue Line to Smithsonian or Federal Triangle) The well-regarded cafeteria at the National Museum of African American History and Culture (p59) is divided into four stations based on the compass. Think buttermilk fried chicken from the South, oyster pan roast from the north, pan-fried trout from the west and catfish po'boys from Louisiana. It's solely for museum patrons.

PAVILION CAFE   CAFE $
Map p294 (✆202-289-3361; www.pavilioncafe. com; cnr Constitution Ave & 7th St NW; sand-wiches $10-12, salads $11-13; ◷10am-4pm Mon-Sat, 11am-5pm Sun, with seasonal late openings; ☐Circulator, ⓜGreen, Yellow Line to Archives) A pocket of Paris secreted on the edge of the National Gallery of Art's Sculpture Garden, this cafeteria is housed in a glass

pavilion whose design was inspired by the metro signs designed by Art Nouveau master, Hector Guimard. Head here to enjoy a salad, sandwich or pastry accompanied by tea, coffee or glass of wine.

CASCADE CAFÉ   CAFE $

Map p294 (☑202-842-6679; www.nga.gov/visit/cafes/cascade-cafe.html; East Bldg, National Gallery of Art, concourse; sandwiches $7-13.50; ⊙11am-3pm Mon-Sat, to 4pm Sun; ☕; ☐Circulator, ⓂGreen, Yellow Line to Archives) Located at the juncture of the National Gallery's two wings, the Cascade offers views of just that: a shimmering, IM Pei–designed artificial waterfall. The cafeteria-style restaurant is divided into different stations where you pick up a tray and choose from pizza, pasta, sandwiches, barbecue and salads. The adjoining espresso bar serves coffee and pastries, as well as gelato.

DOLCEZZA AT HIRSHHORN   CAFE $

Map p294 (www.dolcezzagelato.com; Hirshhorn Museum; gelato $4, pastries $2-7; ⊙8am-5pm Mon-Fri, from 10am Sat & Sun; ☎) Located in the recently unveiled Hiroshi Sugimoto–designed lobby of the Hirshhorn Museum (p71), this branch of the popular chain serves handmade gelato, specialty espresso drinks, tea, chai and gourmet pastries.

MITSITAM NATIVE
FOODS CAFE   NATIVE AMERICAN $$

Map p294 (www.mitsitamcafe.com; cnr 4th St & Independence Ave SW, National Museum of the American Indian; mains $12-22; ⊙11am-5pm, reduced hours in winter; ☐Circulator, ⓂOrange, Silver, Blue, Green, Yellow Line to L'Enfant Plaza) Certainly the most unique food on the Mall, Mitsitam introduces visitors to the Native American cuisine of five different regions, including the Northwest coast (think cedar-planked wild salmon), Great Plains (buffalo chili) and northern woodlands (maple-brined turkey and wild rice). There are also fast-food staples including tacos, *totopos* (corn tortilla chips) and burgers. It's a cafeteria-style set-up.

⭐ ENTERTAINMENT

JAZZ IN THE GARDEN   LIVE MUSIC

Map p294 (☑202-842-6941; www.nga.gov/jazz; cnr Constitution Ave & 7th St NW; ⊙5-8:30pm Fri late May-late Aug; ☐Circulator, ⓂGreen, Yellow Line to Archives) FREE Lots of locals show up for these free outdoor jazz, blues and world-music concerts at the National Gallery of Art Sculpture Garden (p71). Bring a blanket and picnic food, and supplement with beverages from the on-site Pavilion Cafe.

DISCOVERY THEATER   THEATER

Map p294 (☑202-633-8700; www.discovery theater.org; 1100 Jefferson Dr SW, Ripley Center; tickets $6; ☕; ☐Circulator, ⓂOrange, Silver, Blue Line to Smithsonian) In the basement of the Ripley Center, the Smithsonian's Discovery Theater stages delightful puppet shows and other live educational performances for children aged two to 11 years.

SYLVAN THEATER   THEATER

Map p294 (cnr 15th St & Independence Ave SW; ☐Circulator, ⓂSmithsonian) The open-air Sylvan Theater, a stone's throw southeast of the Washington Monument, hosts a variety of performances. The summer evening military band concerts (usually at 8pm) draw big crowds.

🏃 SPORTS & ACTIVITIES

TIDAL BASIN BOATHOUSE   BOATING

Map p294 (☑202-479-2426; www.boatingindc.com/boathouses/tidal-basin; 1501 Maine Ave SW; 2-/4-person boat rental $18/30; ⊙10am-6pm mid-Mar–Sep; ☐Circulator, ⓂOrange, Silver, Blue Line to Smithsonian) Rents paddleboats to take out on the Tidal Basin. Make sure you bring a camera as there are great views from the water.

ICE RINK   ICE SKATING

Map p294 (www.nga.gov/visit/ice-rink.html; cnr Constitution Ave NW & 7th St NW; adult/child 12yr & under $9/8, skate rental $3.50; ⊙10am-9pm Mon-Thu, to 11pm Fri, 11am-11pm Sat, 11am-9pm Sun mid-Nov–mid-Mar; ☐Circulator, ⓂGreen, Yellow Line to Archives) In winter, the fountain at the National Sculpture Garden is transformed into a popular ice rink.

NATIONAL MALL ENTERTAINMENT

White House Area & Foggy Bottom

Neighborhood Top Five

1 **White House** (p78) Wandering through ornately decorated reception rooms, viewing portraits of presidents and their wives, and perhaps bumping into Lincoln's ghost roaming the halls at the president's official abode.

2 **Round Robin** (p88) Knocking back a Scotch or mint julep at one of America's most famous hotel bars.

3 **Kennedy Center** (p90) Watching a free performance any night of the week at this massive cultural center on the banks of the Potomac River.

4 **Textile Museum** (p84) Browsing themed exhibitions showcasing

exquisite fabrics and weavings from across the globe.

5 **Old Ebbitt Grill** (p86) Playing spot-the-politician while slurping oysters and sipping cocktails at this boisterous tavern near the White House.

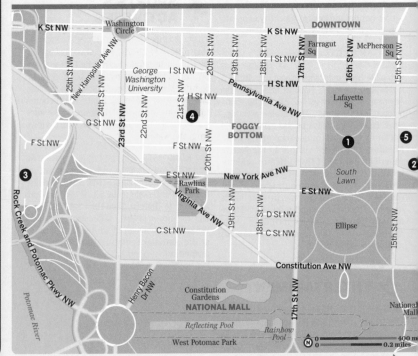

For more detail of this area see Map p296 ➡

Explore White House Area & Foggy Bottom

By day the streets near the White House hum with the comings and goings of office workers, diplomats, lobbyists, tourists and bureaucrats. You'll need at least a full day to do this part of town justice, and should aim to explore by foot. Start outside the White House and then explore the surrounding streets, admiring the architecture, visiting museums and popping into a government building or two.

From there, head west of the White House area to Foggy Bottom, a neighborhood that derives its name from its low-lying geography, which serves as a catchment for Potomac mists. This enclave is synonymous with the State Department, World Bank, International Monetary Fund (IMF) and other hefty institutions. George Washington University (GWU) infuses it with a bit of youthful energy, the modernist monolith of the Watergate complex gives it architectural heft and the world-renowned Kennedy Center supplies it with liberal doses of culture and a smidge of nightlife.

Come evening, there's an exodus of office workers and the streets quieten. You could stay and mingle with DC powerbrokers over a cocktail in one of the hotel bars, enjoy a meal in one of the fine-dining restaurants, or elbow up to a tavern counter alongside GWU students. If these options don't tickle your fancy, consider catching a free early show on the Millennnium Stage at the Kennedy Center before taking a short riverside stroll into ever-busy Georgetown for dinner.

Local Life

→ **Cheap Eats** Source economical fare in this neighborhood of expensive power-player dining by following office workers to the food trucks parked on local streets.

→ **Romantic Drink** The terrace at the Kennedy Center (p90) unfurls fantastic views where sharp-dressed Washingtonians enjoy a romantic cocktail.

→ **Smell the Roses** Students and workers looking for a green respite grab a bench in rosebush-strewn University Yard (p85).

Getting There & Away

→ **Metro** The Orange, Silver and Blue Lines run in tandem here. Get off at Federal Triangle or McPherson Sq for the White House; Farragut West for the Renwick and other museums; and Foggy Bottom-GWU for the university and Kennedy Center.

→ **Bus** A free shuttle runs every 15 minutes between the Foggy Bottom-GWU Metro station and the Kennedy Center.

Lonely Planet's Top Tip

Plan ahead! To visit the White House you need to make a tour request 21 days to three months in advance. For the best chance of success, do it three months beforehand. You also need to book in advance to take tours of the Department of the Interior and the State Department – two weeks ahead of your visit for the former, and 90 days for the latter.

 ### Best Places to Eat

→ Equinox (p87)

→ Sichuan Pavilion (p86)

→ Old Ebbitt Grill (p86)

→ Woodward Takeout Food (p86)

For reviews, see p85.

Best Places to Drink

→ Top of the Gate (p88)

→ Round Robin (p88)

→ Off the Record (p88)

→ Le Bar (p90)

For reviews, see p88.

Best Shopping

→ The Indian Craft Shop (p91)

→ Renwick Gallery Store (p91)

→ White House Gifts (p91)

→ White House Historical Association Museum Shop (p91)

For reviews, see p91.

WHITE HOUSE AREA & FOGGY BOTTOM

TOP SIGHT
WHITE HOUSE

The White House is a home as well as a symbol. It stuns visitors with its sense of pomp and circumstance, yet it also charms with little traces left behind by those who have lived here before, which includes every US president since John Adams. Icon of the American presidency? Yeah. But it's also someone's home.

The Building

George Washington picked the site for the White House in 1791. Pierre L'Enfant was the initial architect, but he was fired for insubordination. Washington held a national competition to find a new designer. Irish-born architect James Hoban won.

Hoban's idea was to make the building simple and conservative, so as not to seem royal, in keeping with the new country's principles. He modeled the neoclassical-style manor on Leinster House, a mid-18th-century duke's villa in Dublin that still stands and is now used by Ireland's Parliament.

The 'President's House' was built (and partially rebuilt) in stages between 1792 and 1829. Legend has it that after the British burned the building in the War of 1812, the house was restored and painted white to cover the smoke marks, and people began to call it the White House. That's not true – it had been white almost from the get-go – but it makes a nice story. Hoban, incidentally, was hired to supervise the rebuilding. It was a big job, as all that remained were the exterior walls and interior brickwork.

Presidential Rooms

The White House has 132 rooms and 35 bathrooms. This includes 412 doors, 147 windows, 28 fireplaces, eight staircases and three elevators (for those who are counting).

DON'T MISS

➜ View across South Lawn

➜ View across North Lawn

➜ James Hoban's neoclassical design

➜ Visitor-center exhibits

PRACTICALITIES

➜ Map p296, F5

➜ ☏202-456-2322

➜ www.whitehouse.gov

➜ 1600 Pennsylvania Ave NW

➜ admission free

➜ ⊙tours 7:30-11:30am Tue-Thu, to 1:30pm Fri & Sat

➜ ⓂOrange, Silver, Blue Line to Federal Triangle or McPherson Sq

The Residence is in the middle, flanked by the East and West Wings. In general, the West Wing is the business side, and the East Wing is the social side. So the Situation Room – a 5000-sq-ft complex staffed 24/7 to monitor national and world intelligence information – is in the west. The Cabinet Room is there too, with its huge mahogany table around which the cabinet secretaries sit to discuss business with the president. The East Wing holds the first lady's office, the social secretary's office, and the Graphics and Calligraphy Office (though tour participants don't see any of these).

The Residence has three main levels: the Ground Floor, State Floor and Second Floor. The Ground and State floors have rooms used for official entertaining and ceremonial functions (many of which you see on the tour). The Second Floor holds the private living quarters of the president and family.

Tours

Tours are free, but they have to be arranged in advance. Americans must apply via one of their state's members of Congress; non-Americans must ask their country's embassy in DC for assistance – in reality, there's only a slim chance that the embassy will be able to help source tickets. Applications are taken from 21 days to three months in advance; the earlier you request during this time frame the better. Don't take it personally if you don't get accepted. Capacity is limited, and often official events take precedence over public tours. If you do get in, the self-guided walk-through takes about 30 minutes.

Visitor Center

Getting inside the White House can be difficult, so the **visitor center** (Map p296; ☏202-208-1631; www.nps.gov/whho; 1450 Pennsylvania Ave NW; ⊗7:30am-4pm; ⓂOrange, Silver, Blue Lines to Federal Triangle) FREE is your backup plan. Housed in the splendiferous 1932 Patent Search Room of the Department of Commerce Building, it has plenty of artifacts, anecdote-packed information panels and informative multimedia exhibits, including a presentation on the history and lives of the presidential families and an interactive touch-screen tour of the White House. It's obviously not the same as seeing the real deal firsthand, but the center does do its job very well, giving good history sprinkled with great anecdotes on presidential spouses, kids, pets and dinner preferences (betcha didn't know President Garfield liked squirrel soup!). The gift shop is excellent if you're looking for classy souvenirs.

BEST PHOTO OPPORTUNITIES

Want to snap a selfie with a White House backdrop? You have two options. First head to Pennsylvania Ave, past the peace activists who are always there, for photos across the North Lawn. This view shows the triangular north portico and main driveway. Then walk to E St NW for pictures with a South Lawn background. The view here focuses on the rounded south portico and distant flowery gardens. Alas, there's a security barrier between you and the White House fence, so you won't be getting any unfettered close-ups.

PERSONAL TOUCHES

Presidents have customized the property over time. Franklin Roosevelt added a pool; Truman gutted the whole place (and simply discarded many of its historical features – today's rooms are replicas); Jacqueline Kennedy brought back antique furnishings and historic details; Nixon added a bowling alley; Carter installed solar roof panels, which Reagan then removed; Clinton added a jogging track; and George W Bush included a T-ball field.

White House

A PRESIDENTIAL TOUR

The most striking thing about the White House is how much it feels like a house. A 55,000-sq-ft house, but still a real one where a family lives. If you're lucky enough to get inside on a public tour, you'll see several rooms in the main residence, each rich in presidential lore: this is where Thomas Jefferson ate; Abe Lincoln's coffin stood over there...

The walk-through is self-guided and starts at the visitor entrance by the White House's southeast gate. From there you pass by the ❶ Library, Vermeil Room and China Room, all on the ground floor (they're roped off, so you don't actually go in). Next you go up a flight of stairs to the State Floor and continue on through the ❷ East Room, Green Room, ❸ Blue Room, Red Room and ❹ State Dining Room. Unlike the floor below, you can enter these rooms. The Secret Service guys standing guard everywhere are ace at answering questions – really.

The White House's 2nd and 3rd floors, as well as the east and west wings, are off-limits. So you won't get to see two of the most famous rooms – the ❺ Lincoln Bedroom and the ❻ Oval Office – but you'll feel their aura.

You depart from the building's front (north) side. Before leaving the neighborhood, swing over to 15th St NW and stroll south to E St NW. Turn right and walk along the South Lawn, and you'll have a photo-ready ❼ view of the house you just visited.

State Dining Room
Residence, State Floor
Imagine inviting over 130 of your closest kings, prime ministers and movie stars for a little poached lobster. The fireplace mantel's quote is from a letter John Adams wrote in 1800.

DANITA DELIMONT / GETTY IMAGES ©

West Wing

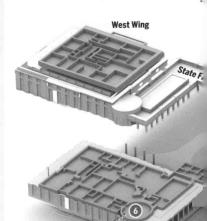

State F

❻

Oval Office
West Wing, Ground Floor
Suppose you were allowed into the west wing. You'd see the Oval Office, the president's official workspace. Each president has changed it to suit their taste, even designing the carpet.

BARRY WINKER / GETTY IMAGES ©

East Room
Residence, State Floor
Admire the White House's largest room, used for ceremonies and press conferences. Lincoln, Kennedy and five other presidents have lain in state here. Note how gilded eagles hold up the piano.

Blue Room
Residence, State Floor

Pretend the president is receiving you here, as he does other guests. Fifth prez James Monroe bought the gilded French Empire decor. Eighth prez Martin Van Buren painted the room blue.

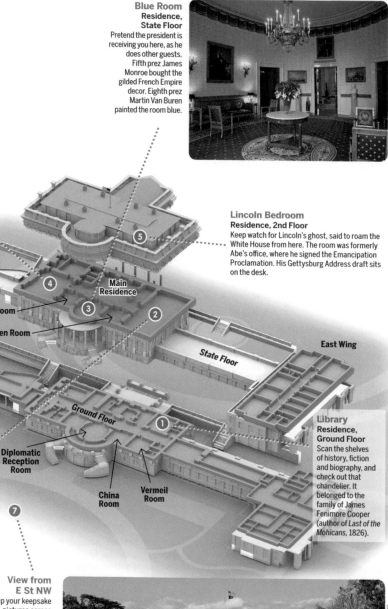

BARRY WINKER / GETTY IMAGES ©

Lincoln Bedroom
Residence, 2nd Floor

Keep watch for Lincoln's ghost, said to roam the White House from here. The room was formerly Abe's office, where he signed the Emancipation Proclamation. His Gettysburg Address draft sits on the desk.

Main Residence

Room

een Room

State Floor

East Wing

Ground Floor

Library
Residence, Ground Floor

Scan the shelves of history, fiction and biography, and check out that chandelier. It belonged to the family of James Fenimore Cooper (author of *Last of the Mohicans*, 1826).

Diplomatic Reception Room

China Room

Vermeil Room

View from E St NW

ap your keepsake pictures across the South Lawn. ecognize the view? 's commonly used he backdrop to TV news reports.

ROBERT CICCHETTI / SHUTTERSTOCK ©

⊙ SIGHTS

⊙ White House Area

WHITE HOUSE   LANDMARK
See p78.

RENWICK GALLERY   MUSEUM
Map p296 (☑202-633-7970; www.renwick. americanart.si.edu; 1661 Pennsylvania Ave NW; ⊙10am-5:30pm; MOrange, Silver, Blue Line to Farragut West) FREE Part of the Smithsonian group, the Renwick Gallery is set in a stately 1859 mansion. Its two upstairs galleries showcase exhibits of modern and contemporary American crafts and decorative art pieces that are drawn from the American Art Museum's permanent collection and occasionally change. Most straddle the line between utilitarian and artistic, with more than a dash of whimsy thrown in. The Grand Salon and rear downstairs gallery host temporary site-specific installations.The gallery's gift shop is full of tempting items.

ELLIPSE   PARK
Map p296 (Constitution Ave, btwn 15th & 17th Sts NW; MOrange, Silver, Blue Line to Federal Triangle) The expansive, oval-shaped park on the White House (p78)'s south side is known as the Ellipse. It's studded with a random collection of monuments, such as the Zero Milestone (the marker for highway distances all across the country) and the Second Division Memorial. It also hosts parades and public events such as the lighting of the national Christmas tree.

DAUGHTERS OF THE AMERICAN REVOLUTION MUSEUM   MUSEUM
Map p296 (DAR Museum; ☑202-879-3220; www. dar.org/museum; 1776 D St NW; ⊙9:30am-4pm Mon-Fri, 9am-5pm Sat; MOrange, Silver, Blue Line to Farragut West) FREE This neoclassical behemoth is supposedly the largest complex of buildings in the world owned exclusively by women. They own the entire city block! Enter from D St to reach its museum, where you'll find two galleries and a series of 'Period Rooms' furnished to reflect how Americans decorated their houses between the late 17th century and early 20th centuries. Guided tours of the rooms are offered from 10am to 2:30pm Monday to Friday and from 9am to 5pm on Saturday.

If the DAR's name sounds familiar, it's possibly because in 1939 the ladies barred African American contralto Marian Anderson from singing at its hall. Anderson then performed her famous civil rights concert on the Lincoln Memorial's steps. The DAR eventually changed its policies and mended fences with Anderson.

DECATUR HOUSE   HISTORIC BUILDING
Map p296 (www.whitehousehistory.org/events/ tour-the-historic-decatur-house; 1610 H St NW; ⊙11am-2pm Mon; MOrange, Silver, Blue Line to Farragut West) FREE Designed in 1818 by Benjamin Latrobe for naval hero Stephen Decatur and his wife Susan, this brick building holds the honor of being the first and last house on Lafayette Sq to be occupied as a private residence. It's also one of the few urban residences in the US retaining slave quarters (in this case built in 1836). The White House Historical Association runs one-hour free guided tours of the house at 11am, 12:30pm and 2pm on Mondays.

ART MUSEUM OF THE AMERICAS   MUSEUM
Map p296 (☑202-370-0147; www.museum.oas. org; 201 18th St NW; suggested donation $5; ⊙10am-5pm Tue-Sun; MOrange, Silver, Blue Line to Farragut West, Federal Triangle) The Organization of American States operates this small art museum in a separate building on its property. It features changing exhibits of modern and contemporary paintings and photography from Latin America and the Caribbean. It's well worth popping in, though you'll likely be the only one there walking across the creaky floors to examine the often politically charged works.

DEPARTMENT OF THE INTERIOR MUSEUM   MUSEUM
Map p296 (☑202-208-4743; www.doi.gov/ interiormuseum; 1849 C St NW; ⊙8:30am-4:30pm Mon-Fri; MOrange, Silver, Blue Line to Farragut West) FREE Responsible for managing the nation's natural resources, the Department of the Interior operates this small museum to educate the public about its current goals and programs, but the major drawcard here is the building itself, which contains tremendous New Deal murals from the 1930s and 1940s, as well as 26 photographic murals by Ansel Adams, plus panels by Maynard Dixon and Allan Houser. Bring photo ID to enter the building.

It's possible to view most of the murals on your own as you walk through the structure, but the best way to see them is on a guided tour. These hour-long jaunts are offered at 2pm Tuesday and Thursday; call to make a reservation two weeks in advance (though staff can sometimes do it with less notice).

LAFAYETTE SQUARE   SQUARE

Map p296 (Pennsylvania Ave NW, btwn 15th & 17th Sts NW; Ⓜ Orange, Silver, Blue Line to Farragut West, McPherson Sq) The land north of 1600 Pennsylvania Ave was originally deeded as part of the White House grounds. However, in 1804 President Thomas Jefferson decided to divide the plot and give half back to the public in the form of a park, now known as Lafayette Sq. A statue of Andrew Jackson astride a horse holds court in the center, while the statues anchoring the four corners are all of foreign-born revolutionary leaders, a nice reminder that non-American freedom fighters helped ensure American independence.

In the southeast corner check out the likeness of the Marquis de Lafayette, a revolutionary war general by the age of 19. Although Lafayette was branded a traitor in his native France following the war, he was consistently lauded in the young America. In the northeast corner is a memorial to Tadeusz Kościusko, a Polish soldier and prominent engineer in Washington's army. The sculpture is one of the more in-your-face ones in town: Kościusko towers over an angry imperial eagle killing a snake atop a globe, and an inscription at the base, taken from Scottish poet Thomas Campbell, reads: 'And Freedom shrieked as Kosciusko fell!'

OCTAGON MUSEUM   MUSEUM

Map p296 (☏202-626-7439; www.architects foundation.org/octagon-museum; 1799 New York Ave NW; ◷1-4pm Thu-Sat; Ⓜ Orange, Silver, Blue Line to Farragut West) FREE Designed by William Thornton (the Capitol's first architect) in 1800 for one of the largest slave-owners in the state of Virginia, this minimally furnished house museum occupies a symmetrically winged structure designed to fit an odd triangular lot. Its unusual floorplan and clearly delineated spaces for servants and homeowners are curious but there's not much else here to attract visitors.

BLAIR HOUSE   HISTORIC BUILDING

Map p296 (1651 Pennsylvania Ave NW; ◷closed to public; Ⓜ Orange, Silver, Blue Line to Farragut West) Together, the 1824 Blair House and adjoining 1858 Lee House have functioned as part of the official presidential guesthouse

ℹ SHORTCUT TO GEORGETOWN

Head down F St NW (between the Kennedy Center and Watergate Complex) toward the river. Veer right a bit and you'll see a crosswalk that goes over Rock Creek Pkwy. That leads to a path that runs alongside the water. Follow it north – you'll likely be sharing it with several joggers and cyclists – and in a half mile you're in Georgetown's Waterfront Park.

complex since 1943, when Eleanor Roosevelt got tired of tripping over dignitaries in the White House. Plaques note that this is where Robert E Lee declined command of the Union Army when the Civil War erupted, and also where a bodyguard was killed while protecting President Truman from a 1950 assassination attempt by pro-independence militants from Puerto Rico.

LEE HOUSE   HISTORIC BUILDING

Map p296 (1653 Pennsylvania Ave NW; Ⓜ Orange, Silver, Blue Line to Farragut West) Attached to Blair House as part of the official accommodations for the President's overnight guests, this building was built for Robert E Lee's cousin in 1858.

ST JOHN'S CHURCH   CHURCH

Map p296 (☏202-347-8766; www.stjohns-dc.org; 1525 H St NW; ◷9am-3pm Wed-Mon, from 11am Tue; Ⓜ Orange, Silver, Blue Line to McPherson Sq) St John's isn't DC's most imposing church, but it is arguably its most important. That's because it's the 'Church of the Presidents' – every president since Madison has attended services here at least once, and pew 54 is permanently reserved for the incumbent of the White House. Services take place at 7:45am, 9am and 11am on Sunday, and there's a concert performance on the first Wednesday of the month at 12:10pm.

K STREET   AREA

Map p296 (Ⓜ Orange, Silver, Blue Line to Farragut North, McPherson Sq) The descriptors 'K St' and 'lobbyist' have practically become synonymous since the 1990s. This is where high-powered lawyers, consultants and, of course, lobbyists bark into their smartphones and enjoy expensive lunches. Come nightfall, the same power set comes back with hair considerably slicked and/or flattened to drink expensive cocktails while surrounded by the sort of people who swoon over everything we've just described.

MCPHERSON SQUARE   SQUARE
Map p296 (MOrange, Silver, Blue Line to McPherson Sq) Named for Civil War general James B McPherson, who once commanded the Army of Tennessee, this square sports an 1876 statue of McPherson on his horse. Homeless people often cluster here.

⊙ Foggy Bottom

TEXTILE MUSEUM   MUSEUM
Map p296 (202-994-5200; www.museum.gwu. edu; 701 21st St NW; suggested donation $8, children free; ⊙11am-5pm Mon & Fri, to 7pm Wed & Thu, 10am-5pm Sat, 1-5pm Sun; MOrange, Silver, Blue Line to Foggy Bottom-GWU) This gem is the country's only textile museum. Galleries spread over two floors hold exquisite fabrics and carpets. Exhibits revolve around a theme – say Asian textiles depicting dragons or Kuba cloth from the Democratic Republic of the Congo – and rotate a few times a year. Bonus: the museum shares space with George Washington University's Washingtonia trove of historic maps, drawings and ephemera.

The museum is old (founded in 1925) but the building is new (opened in early 2015). The collection also includes rare kimonos, pre-Columbian weaving, American quilts and Ottoman embroidery. Accompanying wall commentary explains how the textiles mirror the social, spiritual, economic and aesthetic values of the societies that made them.

WATERGATE COMPLEX   NOTABLE BUILDING
Map p296 (2600 Virginia Ave NW; MOrange, Silver, Blue Line to Foggy Bottom-GWU) Designed by Italian architect Luigi Moretti and DC-based landscape architect Boris Timchenko and constructed between 1963 and 1971, this five-building curvilinear riverfront complex encompasses apartments, fountains, terraces, boutiques, the recently refurbished Watergate Hotel (p228), and the office towers that made 'Watergate' a byword for political scandal after it broke that President Nixon's 'plumbers' had bugged the headquarters of the 1972 Democratic National Committee here. Though now acknowledged as an architectural masterpiece, the Watergate was derisively refered to as 'Antipasto on the Potomac' on its opening in 1971. The first large-scale mixed-use development in DC, it lost its lustre as a residential and commercial address after the scandal, but in recent years has edged back into fashion.

STATE DEPARTMENT   NOTABLE BUILDING
Map p296 (US Department of State; 202-647-3241; https://diplomaticrooms.state.gov/tours/; 2201 C St NW; ⊙tours 9:30am, 10:30am & 2:45pm Mon-Fri; MOrange, Silver, Blue Line to Foggy Bottom-GWU) FREE The headquarters of the American diplomatic corps is a forbidding, well-guarded edifice – modernist, monolithic and unfriendly. In stark contrast are the elegant, grand diplomatic reception rooms, where Cabinet members and the Secretary of State entertain visiting potentates amid ornate 18th-century American art and antiques. Tours of the rooms are by reservation only; telephone or go to the website at least 90 days beforehand to request a spot. Bring photo ID to the tour.

NATIONAL ACADEMY
OF SCIENCES   NOTABLE BUILDING
Map p296 (NAS; 202-334-2000; www.cpnas. org; 2101 Constitution Ave NW; ⊙9am-5pm Mon-Fri; MOrange, Silver, Blue Line to Foggy Bottom-GWU) Made up of approximately 2000 members, including almost 200 Nobel Prize winners, these are the folks the government hits up for scientific advice (whether the government listens to them or not is, as you may have guessed, entirely up to the government). Inside, the NAS displays its impressive permanent art collection and hosts temporary art exhibitions, lectures and films. Download the useful Visitors Guide from the website before heading here and be sure to bring photo ID.

ST MARY'S
EPISCOPAL CHURCH   CHURCH
Map p296 (202-333-3985; www.stmarys foggybottom.org; 728 23rd St NW; ⊙Holy Eucharist 12.10pm Wed & 10am Sun; MOrange, Silver, Blue Line to Foggy Bottom-GWU) Built in 1887, St Mary's was home to the first black Episcopal congregation in DC, which was established in 1867. James Renwick, designer of the Smithsonian Castle, created the beautiful redbrick building especially for the congregation. Above the altar are French-made stained-glass windows that depict, among others, the African bishop and martyr St Cyprian. The church's Tiffany-designed Stanton window depicts an angel holding an orb of peace.

GEORGE WASHINGTON UNIVERSITY

UNIVERSITY

Map p296 (www.gwu.edu; 800 21st St NW; Ⓜ Orange, Silver, Blue Line to Foggy Bottom-GWU) Known as 'G-dub' or 'GW,' this university has been a bedrock of Washington identity since its founding in 1821. Besides shaping much of the American political landscape, GW has shaped the capital itself, buying up town houses on such a scale that it is now the city's second-biggest landowner after the federal government. Its list of famous alumni is mighty impressive, and includes Edgar Hoover, Jacqueline Kennedy Onassis, John Foster Dulles, J William Fulbright, Colin Powell, Bob Woodward and Elizabeth Warren. The university is spread over several blocks between F, 20th and 24th Sts and Pennsylvania Ave in Foggy Bottom. The best bit of the campus is **University Yard** (H St NW), between G, H, 20th and 21st Sts, where Colonial-revival buildings flank a green park bedecked with roses and a statue of – who else? – George Washington.

ALBERT EINSTEIN MEMORIAL

SCULPTURE

Map p296 (2101 Constitution Ave NW; Ⓜ Orange, Silver, Blue Line to Foggy Bottom-GWU) The grounds in front of the National Academy of Sciences feature DC's most huggable monument: Robert Berks' bronze 1978 statue of Albert Einstein. The larger-than-life, sandal-shod, chubby bronze reclines on a bench, while little kids crawl all over him and frolic on a granite 'star map' dais depicting the heavens that his theories reshaped for humanity.

FEDERAL RESERVE

NOTABLE BUILDING

Map p296 (☎202-452-3324; www.federalreserve.gov; 20th St NW, btwn C St & Constitution Ave; Ⓜ Orange, Silver, Blue Line to Farragut West) FREE 'The Fed,' is the Olympus of the Gods of the American Economy. Housed in a monolithic white building that closely resembles a Soviet ministry, it is largely off-limits to members of the public, with access to the building and its notable art collection limited to college students and adults with a research interest in the Federal Reserve.

EATING

As you might guess, this is high-end eating territory, the pinnacle of the power-lunch and show-off-dinner school of sartorial activity. With all that said,

---

PECULIAR PRESIDENTIAL PETS

Though the current incumbent of the White House and his family have yet to invite a pet to share their presidential abode, many previous presidents did so. Remember Bo and Sunny Obama, the Portuguese water dogs? Or Barney the terrier, Socks the cat and Buddy the labrador? These are only a few of the many animals that have lived at the White House:

Billy the pygmy hippo In 1927 rubber-maker Harvey Firestone brought Billy all the way from Liberia for Calvin Coolidge, who, for the record, already owned a wallaby, a duiker (a kind of African antelope) and a raccoon. Billy ended up in the National Zoo when (contrary to his species name) he got too big for the White House.

The Adams alligators Let's say you're the Marquis de Lafayette and you want to get a present for John Quincy Adams, the kind of guy who likes to go swimming, naked, in the Potomac every morning. How about: two alligators! In the 1820s, Adams, skinny-dipping badass that he was, happily housed the two reptiles in the White House bathtub.

Pauline Wayne the cow William Taft let Pauline, a Holstein gift from a Wisconsin Senator, graze the front lawn of the White House from 1909 to 1913, during his term. The trade-off? Pauline provided milk for the first family during Taft's last three years in office.

Josiah the badger All of the above animals were thoughtful presents to sitting presidents. Josiah, on the other hand, was apparently a furry assassination attempt. In 1903, a girl in Kansas threw ornery Josiah directly at Theodore Roosevelt. Roosevelt, the kind of guy who hunted lions and charged fortified positions like San Juan hill on foot, ended up taking the little guy back to Washington.

you usually get what you pay for – there's too much competition around for local chefs to rest lazily on their laurels.

★ WOODWARD TAKEOUT FOOD
AMERICAN $

Map p296 (202-347-5355; www.woodward table.com; 1426 H St NW; sandwiches $6-12; 7:30am-2:30pm Mon-Fri; Orange, Silver, Blue Line to McPherson Sq) Woodward Takeout is the small, mostly carryout adjunct to the popular Woodward Table restaurant. Jump in the line with all of the office workers to order a gourmet lunch sandwich, pizza slice, pasta or salad. Breakfast is busy too, with egg-laden sandwiches on crumbly biscuits, salted chocolate croissants and a daily doughnut. A smattering of close-set bar tables provide seating. You can preorder via the website and save some waiting time.

G STREET FOOD
INTERNATIONAL $

Map p296 (202-842-8484; www.gstreetfood. com; 1030 15th St NW; sandwiches $9-11; 7am-4pm Mon-Fri; ; Orange, Silver, Blue Line to McPherson Sq) Regulars can't get enough of the culinary snapshots of global street food offered at G Street. Sandwiches are the main focus, and range from banh mi to falafel, katsu to Italian sub. Gluten-free and vegetarian options abound, and sandwich alternatives include satays, curries and quesadillas.

BREADLINE
SANDWICHES $

Map p296 (202-822-8900; www.breadline. com; 1751 Pennsylvania Ave NW; sandwiches $7-9, salads $8-10; 7am-5:30pm Mon-Fri; Orange, Silver, Blue Line to Farragut West) 'Food is ammunition – don't waste it!' commands a WWII-era poster on the wall of Breadline, a polished bakery and sandwich shop. Come here for a good, cheap lunch alongside local office workers. It'll probably be crowded, and with reason. The fresh sandwiches – stacked with, say, Italian sausage or barbecued vegetables on ciabatta bread – are delicious, as are the salads.

★ SICHUAN PAVILION
CHINESE $$

Map p296 (202-466-7790; www.sichuan-pavilion.com; 1814 K St NW; mains lunch $10-18, dinner mains $12-35; 11:30am-9:30pm; Orange, Silver, Blue Line to Farragut West) Many Chinese come to this few-frills restaurant to feast on fiery, aromatic Sichuan classics. Around the world, piquant Sichuan (or Szechuan) cuisine is often toned down for Western customers, but these guys keep it real for all their clientele, Asian or not. Menu highlights include fried string beans and the *ma-po tofu* laden with fermented black beans and fiery peppercorns.

★ OLD EBBITT GRILL
AMERICAN $$

Map p296 (202-347-4800; www.ebbitt.com; 675 15th St NW; mains $18-32; 7:30am-1am Mon-Fri, from 8:30am Sat & Sun, happy hour 3-6pm & 11pm-1am; Red, Orange, Silver, Blue Line to Metro Center) Established in DC in 1856, this legendary tavern has occupied prime real estate near the White House since 1983. Political players and tourists pack into the wood-paneled interior, where thick burgers, succulent steaks and jumbo lump crab cakes are rotated out almost as quickly as the clientele. Pop in for a cocktail and oysters during happy hour.

Presidents Ulysses S Grant, Andrew Johnson, Grover Cleveland, Theodore Roosevelt and Warren Harding are said to have imbibed at the original boarding house, DC's first saloon, which was located near Chinatown. According to legend, the animal heads over the bar were bagged by Teddy Roosevelt himself.

DISTRICT COMMONS
INTERNATIONAL $$

Map p296 (202-587-8277; www.district commonsdc.com; 2200 Pennsylvania Ave NW; flatbreads $13, mains $17-29; 11:30am-10pm Mon-Thu, to 11pm Fri, 11am-11pm Sat, to 9pm Sun; Orange, Silver, Blue Line to Foggy Bottom-GWU) Washington Circle's best-known tavern/bistro has sleek surrounds, friendly but harried staff and extensive food and drink menus. The main drawcard is the hopping bar, where drinkers sit alongside diners enjoying choices from the kitchen (steaks, burgers, pastas), raw bar and open-hearth oven. The formidable beer list includes 99 choices.

SOI 38
THAI $$

Map p296 (202-558-9215; www.soi38dc.com; 2101 L Street NW; mains lunch $12-19, dinner $16-19; 11am-10pm; Orange, Silver, Blue Line to Foggy Bottom-GWU, Red Line to Dupont Circle) Street-food dishes are the focus at this Thai restaurant, but there are also plenty of classic salads, curries and stir-fries on the menu. Named after the district and night market of the same name in Bangkok, (home turf for the restaurant's owners), this place is considerably more upmarket than Bangkok's famous street-food stands, but offers a similarly rewarding eating experience. Enter from 21st St NW.

WOODWARD TABLE
INTERNATIONAL **$$**

Map p296 (☏202-347-5353; www.woodward table.com; 1426 H St NW; pizzas $17-20, mains $19-23; ⏰11:30am-10:30pm; ☑; Ⓜ Orange, Silver, Blue Line to McPherson Sq) A classic French-brasserie ambience characterizes this welcoming restaurant next to the excellent Woodward Takeout Food. The menu is comprehensive – everything from shrimp and grits to duck confit, spiced fish and *steak frites* (steak and fries) – and there's an excellent wine and bar list.

BOMBAY CLUB
INDIAN **$$**

Map p296 (☏202-659-3727; www.bombayclubdc. com; 815 Connecticut Ave NW; mains $18-28; ⏰11:30am-2:30pm & 5:30-10:30pm Mon-Fri, 5:30-11pm Sat, 11:30am-2:30pm & 5:30-9:30pm Sun; ☑; Ⓜ Orange, Silver, Blue Line to Farragut West) No bad sitar music or heat-lamp-warmed buffets here; Bombay Club cooks eclectic, modern Indian fare. The wild-boar curry intrigues, duck kebabs are punchy with ginger-chili heat, and the fenugreek-laced lobster curry explodes with flavor. Sit inside where ceiling fans swirl lazily and piano tinklings fill the air, or outside on the breezy patio. Vegetarians have several options.

FOUNDING FARMERS
AMERICAN **$$**

Map p296 (☏202-822-8783; www.wearefounding farmers.com; 1924 Pennsylvania Ave NW; breakfast dishes $6-15, mains $12-37; ⏰7am-10pm Mon, to 11pm Tue-Thu, to midnight Fri, 9am-midnight Sat, to 10pm Sun; ☑; Ⓜ Orange, Silver, Blue Line to Foggy Bottom-GWU or Farragut West) ⬙ The philosophy here is laudable: majority owned by farmers, this attractive restaurant in the IMF building aspires to serve contemporary American fare made with fresh and sustainable produce that is grown with care. Sadly, the execution of dishes lets the side down, with food being rushed out of the kitchen without sufficient attention being given to taste or presentation.

★EQUINOX
MODERN AMERICAN **$$$**

Map p296 (☏202-331-8118; www.equinox restaurant.com; 818 Connecticut Ave NW; mains $31-38; ⏰11:30am-2pm & 5:30-9pm Mon-Fri, 5:30-10:30pm Sat, to 9pm Sun; ☑; Ⓜ Orange, Silver, Blue Line to Farragut West) ⬙ Chef Todd Gray has long eschewed imported ingredients in favor of meat, fish, fowl, vegeta-

bles and fruit sourced from farms in the Shenandoah Valley and Chesapeake Bay, and the food served at this stylish restaurant is a delectable testament to his enlightened approach. Dishes are seasonal and up to 50% plant-based (Sunday brunch is 100% plant-based). Love it.

MIRABELLE
FRENCH **$$$**

Map p296 (☏202-506-3833; www.mirabelledc. com; 900 16th St NW; mains lunch $28-30, dinner $43-46; ⏰11:30am-2pm & 5:30-9:30pm Mon-Fri, 5:30-9:30pm Sat & Sun; Ⓜ Orange, Silver, Blue Line to Farragut West) This *très élégant* modern brasserie is a particularly good choice at lunch, when the outdoor terrace and airy dining room are lovely spaces in which to enjoy modern takes on classic French dishes. We particularly love the decadent dessert trolley and the wine list, which is replete with top French drops.

OVAL ROOM
AMERICAN **$$$**

Map p296 (☏202-463-8700; www.ovalroom.com; 800 Connecticut Ave NW; mains lunch $16-28, dinner $29-38; ⏰11:30am-2:30pm & 5:30-10pm Mon-Fri, 5:30-10:30pm Sat; Ⓜ Orange, Silver, Blue Line to Farragut West) DC powerbrokers and those who aspire to influence them are regulars at this upmarket restaurant near Lafayette Sq. Contemporary American dishes grounded in classic French techniques are the main draw, most of which feature fish and meat (vegetarians may like to steer clear). The $20 bar menu at lunch offers two courses and a glass of wine and is exceptional value.

PRIME RIB
STEAK **$$$**

Map p296 (☏202-466-8811; www.theprimerib. com; 2020 K St NW; mains $25-59; ⏰11:30am-3pm & 5-10pm Mon-Thu, to 10:30pm Fri & Sat; Ⓜ Orange, Silver, Blue Line to Foggy Bottom-GWU) Many DC restaurants serve up fussy and faddish fare. Not the Prime Rib. Excuse a bit of stereotyping, but power is still best exemplified by sitting in a dark-wood dining room cutting deals over huge hunks of seared cow, stepping outside for a cigar (damned smoking ban) then returning for a cognac. Regulars swear by the daily specials ($24 to $30).

The waitstaff, clad in tuxedos, dress the part, and you'd better too – that means ties and jackets at dinner, gentlemen. The food lives up to the atmosphere; while this place may not be cutting edge, that doesn't mean it isn't good at what it does.

GEORGIA BROWN'S SOUTHERN US $$$

Map p296 (202-393-4499; www.gbrowns. com; 950 15th St NW; mains $21-37; 11:30am-10pm Mon-Thu, to 11pm Fri & Sat, 10am-4pm & 5:30-10pm Sun; Orange, Silver, Blue Line to McPherson Sq) Georgia Brown's treats the humble ingredients of the American South (shrimp, okra, red rice, grits and sausage) with the respect great French chefs give their provincial dishes. The result is high-class cuisine from the Carolina and Georgia Lowcountry served in a welcoming and attractive interior. The Sunday buffet Jazz brunch (adult/child five to 12 years $45/22) is particularly popular – book ahead.

MARCEL'S FRENCH $$$

Map p296 (202-296-1166; www.marcelsdc.com; 2401 Pennsylvania Ave NW; 3-/7-course menus $115/165; 5-10pm Mon-Thu, to 11pm Fri & Sat, 11:30-2:30 & 5-9:30pm Sun; Orange, Silver, Blue Line to Foggy Bottom-GWU) Chef Robert Wiedmaier stays true to classic French techniques while adding contemporary ingredient embellishments. This imparts a certain *je ne sais quoi* to his daily-changing menu, making dining here extremely enjoyable. Menu options include a four-course vegetarian menu ($85) and a three-course pretheater menu ($85) with complimentary limousine service to the Kennedy Center at the meal's end.

OCCIDENTAL GRILL STEAK $$$

Map p296 (202-783-1475; www.occidentaldc.com; 1475 Pennsylvania Ave NW; mains lunch $16-29, dinner $25-49; 10am-11pm Mon-Sat, 11am-9pm Sun; Orange, Silver, Blue Line to Metro Center) This DC institution is practically wallpapered with mug shots of congress-people and other political celebs who have dined here through the years. And although the Occidental isn't the nerve center it once was, plenty of bigwigs still roll up their pin-stripes to dive into its hamburgers (lunch only), salads, steaks and seafood. It also hosts a popular happy hour (4pm to 7pm weekdays).

KAZ SUSHI BISTRO JAPANESE $$$

Map p296 (202-530-5500; www.kazsushi.com; 1915 I St NW; lunch specials $16.50, mains $22-36; 11:30am-2pm Mon-Fri, 5:30-10pm Mon-Sat; Orange, Silver, Blue Line to Farragut West) Here, chef Kaz Okochi and his three sushi chefs offer a large choice of nigiri sushi, sashimi, hand rolls and seafood-dominated small plates. The food is fresh and flavorful, although its execution lacks finesse, and the restaurant interior is worn but comfortable. Lunch bentos and sushi platters offer good value.

DRINKING & NIGHTLIFE

College kids, bureaucrats, lobbyists, journalists and theater-goers coexist in this neighborhood, and there are multiple drinking dens geared towards each group; many of these can be found on K St.

⭐ TOP OF THE GATE ROOFTOP BAR

Map p296 (www.thewatergatehotel.com/dine-and-drink/top-of-the-gate; 2650 Virginia Ave NW, Watergate Hotel, Foggy Bottom; ice skating adult/child 5-12 $20/10; 5pm-midnight Sun-Thu, to 1am Fri & Sat summer, 5-10pm Wed-Fri, 1-10pm Sat & Sun winter; Red Line to Foggy Bottom-GWU) The downstairs whiskey bar at the plush Watergate Hotel is impressive, but it pales in comparison with the hotel's rooftop bar and lounge, which offers ice skating in winter, blissfully balmy river breezes in summer and spectacular views all year round.

⭐ ROUND ROBIN BAR

Map p296 (202-628-9100; http://washington.intercontinental.com/food-drink/round-robin-bar; 1401 Pennsylvania Ave NW, Willard InterContinental Hotel; noon-1am Mon-Sat, to midnight Sun; Red, Orange, Silver, Blue Line to Metro Center) Dispensing drinks since 1850, the bar at the Willard hotel is one of DC's most famous watering holes. The small, circular space is done up in Gilded Age accents, all dark wood walls, marble bar and velvet curtains, and while it's touristy, you'll still see officials here likely determining your latest tax hike over a mint julep or single malt Scotch.

The bar claims to be the place where the mint julep was introduced to DC courtesy of planter and statesman Henry Clay.

⭐ OFF THE RECORD BAR

Map p296 (202-638-6600; www.hayadams.com/dining/off-the-record; 800 16th St NW, Hay-Adams Hotel; 11:30am-midnight Sun-Thu, to 12:30am Fri & Sat; Orange, Silver, Blue Line to McPherson Sq) Table seating, an open fire in winter and a discrete basement location in one of the city's most prestigious hotels,

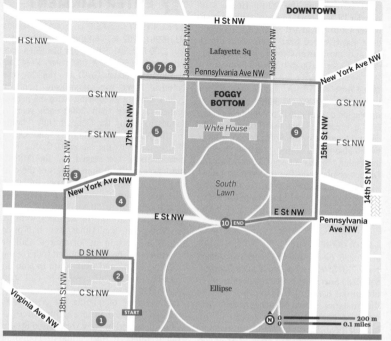

Neighborhood Walk
Architecture of Power

START ORGANIZATION OF AMERICAN STATES
END WHITE HOUSE SOUTH LAWN
LENGTH 2 MILES; 1½ HOURS

Start at the ❶ **Organization of American States** (☎202-370-5000; www.oas.org; 17th St NW), a frieze-clad marble palazzo built in 1910. Stroll up to D St NW to the headquarters of the ❷ **Daughters of the American Revolution** (p82). It's a great example of neoclassical architecture; go inside for a peek at the 'Period Rooms' in its museum; furnished to reflect how Americans decorated their houses between the late 17th century and early 20th century.

On to the ❸ **Octagon Museum** (p83), a curiously shaped 1800 Federal-style mansion where President James Madison lived after the British burned Washington. Past the beaux-arts ❹ **Corcoran School of the Arts & Design** (☎202-994-1700; www.corcoran.gwu.edu; 500 17th St NW), built in 1869 for a wealthy art collector. At the corner of 17th St NW and Pennsylvania Ave NW, the ❺ **Eisenhower Building** is done up with

all the baroque flair of the late 19th century. Currently the building is used as an office wing of the executive branch. Walk north on 17th St NW and veer east onto Pennsylvania Ave NW.

A cluster of interesting buildings is on your left: these include the ❻ **Renwick Gallery** (p82), housed in a recently renovated Second Empire–style 1859 mansion; ❼ **Lee House** (p83), built for Robert E Lee's cousin in 1858; and ❽ **Blair House** (p83), built for a surgeon general of the US Army in 1824. The latter two now form part of the official presidential guesthouse. Continue toward 15th St NW and veer south toward the ❾ **Treasury Building**. It took a while to find a site to house this, and legend has it President Andrew Jackson, ticked off by foot-dragging, stood on the current spot and yelled, 'Build it here!' As a result, Pierre L'Enfant's planned clear line of sight between the White House and the Capitol was ruined. Last stop: E St NW, for the quintessential view of the city's most famous building, the White House (p78) from the ❿ **South Lawn**.

right across from the White House – no wonder DC's important people submerge to be seen and not heard (as the tagline goes) here. Experienced bartenders swirl martinis and manhattans for the suit-wearing crowd. Enter through the hotel lobby.

★ LE BAR
BAR

Map p296 (☏202-730-8800; www.sofitel-washington-dc.com; 806 15th St NW, Sofitel Lafayette Sq; ◷8am-midnight; ⓜMcPherson Sq) The central location of the Sofitel's corner bar – which also serves coffee – ensures that it is a popular rendezvous spot for tourists and DC power-players. After undergoing a renovation in early 2018, the bar is also one of the most stylish drinking dens in town. The outdoor patio is wonderful on spring and summer nights.

LA COLOMBE
CAFE

Map p296 (☏202-846-6823; www.lacolombe.com; 1710 I St NW; ◷7am-7pm Mon-Fri, 9am-4pm Sat & Sun) Specialist coffee roasters aren't as ubiquitous here in DC as in other cities, so the existence of five branches of this well-regarded chain is to be celebrated. This branch near Farragut Sq has a team of young baristas who are good at their job, and it also sells excellent pastries (the cinnamon scrolls are particularly delicious).

POV
LOUNGE

Map p296 (☏202-661-2419; www.povrooftop.com; 515 15th St NW, W Hotel Washington; ◷11am-midnight Sun-Thu, to 2am Fri & Sat; ⓜOrange, Silver, Blue Line to Metro Center) It's all about the view at POV, which sits atop the W Hotel Washington. The sky terrace imparts terrific vistas over the White House, and is particularly spectacular at sunset. Open-air in summer, sheathed in plastic in the cooler months, it's popular with a young and chichi crowd who congregate for pricey cocktails and to see and be seen.

FROGGY BOTTOM PUB
BAR

Map p296 (www.froggybottompub.com; 2021 K St NW; ◷11am-midnight Mon-Sat, happy hours 4-7pm & 11pm-close; ⓜOrange, Silver, Blue Line to Foggy Bottom-GWU) This popular GWU hangout attracts students with its happy hours, pub grub (burgers $9 to $11, pizzas $13 to $17), a frat-boy-esque atmosphere and the sort of shot specials that make you want to down a lot of hard alcohol very quickly. As you might have guessed, things can get messy, but in a good, all-American college kinda way.

☆ ENTERTAINMENT

★ KENNEDY CENTER
PERFORMING ARTS

Map p296 (☏202-467-4600; www.kennedy-center.org; 2700 F St NW; ◷box office 10am-9pm Mon-Sat, noon-9pm Sun; 🚌♿; ⓜOrange, Silver, Blue Line to Foggy Bottom-GWU) Overlooking the Potomac River, the magnificent Kennedy Center hosts a staggering array of performances – more than 2000 each year in venues including the Concert Hall – home to the National Symphony – and Opera House, home to the National Opera. Free performances are staged on the Millennium Stage daily at 6pm as part of the center's 'Performing Arts for Everyone' initiative.

Reduced-rate tickets are available for people aged 18 to 30 via the MyTix program; details are on the Kennedy website. Students can sometimes get half-price tickets for certain performances. Call or visit the box office. Free guided tours of the building are offered from 10am to 5pm on weekdays, to 1pm on weekends; call ☏202-416-8340 for more information.

At the time of writing the center was undergoing an expansion, adding three pavilions designed by New York–based Steven Holl Architects to the original 1971 building designed by Edward Durell Stone. These will house a performance space, rehearsal spaces, classrooms and a lecture hall. A new cafe, outdoor video wall and walkway connecting the center with the river are also planned.

A free shuttle bus runs to and from the Metro station every 15 minutes from 10am (noon on Sunday) to 11:30pm.

HAMILTON
LIVE MUSIC

Map p296 (☏202-787-1000; www.thehamiltondc.com; 600 14th St NW; ⓜRed, Orange, Silver, Blue Line to Metro Center) There's lots on offer here. On the ground floor there's a popular restaurant and three bars, one of which offers free live music most Thursday, Friday and Saturday nights. In the basement is Hamilton LIVE, a 700-person club that genre-jumps from funk to blues to alt-rock with pickers. Bands play most nights of the week; check the website for details.

WASHINGTON BALLET
PERFORMING ARTS

Map p296 (☏202-362-3606; www.washingtonballet.org; 2700 F St NW, Kennedy Center; ⓜOrange, Silver, Blue Line to Foggy Bottom-GWU) The Washington Ballet hasn't been known for many groundbreaking productions, although its reputation is beginning to change as it explores the work of younger choreographers. The troupe stages its performances at venues including the Kennedy Center and THEARC (p115) in Southeast DC.

WASHINGTON NATIONAL OPERA
PERFORMING ARTS

Map p296 (www.kennedy-center.org/wno; 2700 F St NW, Kennedy Center; Ⓜ Orange, Silver, Blue Line to Foggy Bottom-GWU) The Washington Opera is based at the Kennedy Center and puts on a varied showcase throughout the year. Plácido Domingo helmed the company until 2011, when he stepped down after 15 years for Francesca Zambello.

NATIONAL SYMPHONY ORCHESTRA
PERFORMING ARTS

Map p296 (www.kennedy-center.org/nso; 2700 F St NW, Kennedy Center; Ⓜ Orange, Silver, Blue Line to Foggy Bottom-GWU) This is the affiliate orchestra of the Kennedy Center and one of the best chamber symphonies in the nation.

SHOPPING

WHITE HOUSE GIFTS
GIFTS & SOUVENIRS

Map p296 (☑202-737-9500; www.whitehousegifts.com; 701 15th St NW; ⊘8am-9pm Mon-Sat, 9am-8pm Sun; Ⓜ Red, Orange, Silver, Blue Line to Metro Center) Though not to be confused with the official White House gift shop (p91) (in the White House Visitor Center), this store sells official souvenirs alongside less-orthodox offerings. So while you can still find the certified White House Christmas ornament among the stock, you'll also see caricature Trump bottle openers and the Political Inaction Figures paper-doll set.

THE INDIAN CRAFT SHOP
ARTS & CRAFTS

Map p296 (☑202-208-4056; www.indiancraftshop.com; 1849 C St NW, Dept of Interior; ⊘8:30am-4:30pm Mon-Fri; Ⓜ Orange, Silver, Blue Line to Farragut West) Representing more than 45 tribal groups in the US, this compact shop sells basketry, weavings, pottery, beadwork, sand paintings and fetish carvings made by Native Americans. The high-quality pieces don't come cheap. The shop is hidden inside the Department of the Interior; show photo ID to enter the building.

RENWICK GALLERY STORE
GIFTS & SOUVENIRS

Map p296 (☑202-633-6856; www.renwick.americanart.si.edu; 1661 Pennsylvania Ave NW; ⊘10am-5pm; Ⓜ Orange, Silver, Blue Line to Farragut West) The Renwick Gallery (p82) has one of DC's best museum shops. Handmade textiles and hand-dyed silks are available, as is glasswork, woodwork and unique jewelry, much of it rather affordable. The excellent choice of books includes how-to manuals on jewelry- and fabric-making, ceramics, glassblowing and cabinetry, many appropriate for kids.

WHITE HOUSE HISTORICAL ASSOCIATION MUSEUM SHOP
GIFTS & SOUVENIRS

Map p296 (http://shop.whitehousehistory.org; 1450 Pennsylvania Ave NW; ⊘7:30am-4pm; Ⓜ Orange, Silver, Blue Line to Federal Triangle) Located inside the White House Visitor Center, this is the spot to get White House–branded mementos such as the official Christmas ornament, White House tea towels or First Ladies mug.

AMERICAN INSTITUTE OF ARCHITECTS BOOKSTORE
BOOKS

Map p296 (1735 New York Ave NW; ⊘9am-5pm Mon-Fri; Ⓜ Orange, Silver, Blue Line to Farragut West) Architecture buffs are in good company in this small specialty shop, which stocks the latest architecture and design titles and periodicals. For the classic overview on the city's iconic buildings, pick up the AIA *Guide to the Architecture of Washington, DC* by Martin Moeller, Jr.

W CURTIS DRAPER TOBACCONIST
CIGARS

Map p296 (☑202-638-2555; www.wcurtisdraper.com; 699 15th St NW; ⊘9:30am-6:30pm Mon-Fri, 10am-4pm Sat; Ⓜ Red, Orange, Silver, Blue Line to Metro Center) Follow your nose into W Curtis Draper, which has been selling cigars to politicos since 1887. Staff are friendly and helpful to stogie-smoking newbies.

Georgetown

Neighborhood Top Five

1 **Dumbarton Oaks** (p94) Meandering the ponds, pools and terraced formal gardens outside, then heading inside to peruse El Greco art, pre-Columbian ceramics and the library of centuries-old books.

2 **C&O Canal Towpath** (p101) Escaping the concrete jungle by walking or cycling a bit of the bucolic path, perhaps going far enough to see wooden bridges and vintage lock houses.

3 **Georgetown Waterfront Park** (p94) Sipping an alfresco drink, admiring the yachts and watching rowing teams skim the Potomac.

4 **Key Bridge Boathouse** (p101) Paddling past DC's stony monuments on a sunset tour.

5 **Martin's Tavern** (p97) Swirling a cocktail and forking into a crab cake in the same room where JFK proposed to Jackie.

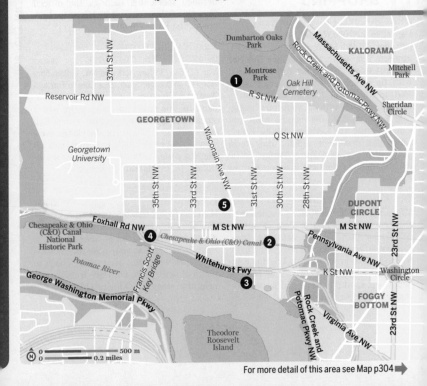

For more detail of this area see Map p304 ➡

Explore Georgetown

You'll want to spend at least a half-day nosing around Georgetown, and shoppers, history buffs and outdoor enthusiasts could easily do a full day. M St NW is a good place to start. It's the neighborhood's main vein, jam-packed with stylish brand stores, cupcake shops and sleek restaurants. Head north if you're a fan of grand house museums, alluring gardens and historic cemeteries. Several sights fill a pocket between Q and R Sts NW, edged by Wisconsin Ave NW, which itself is home to historic taverns and antique shops. Head south of M St for cycling trails, waterfront park strolls and Potomac River kayak rentals.

As Washington's oldest neighborhood, founded in 1751, the area draws plenty of tourists who come to walk its cobbled streets and admire its Federal-style architecture. But Georgetown University students and many diplomats also call the area home, so there's a lived-in feel to it too. Daytime is the best time to visit, but nighttime has its perks too, when you can dine in chic restaurants (keep an eye out for DC glitterati) and linger over drinks in cozy pubs.

Local Life

➤ **Book Hill** A Paris-like row of art galleries, interior-design stores and antique shops slope down the 1600 block of Wisconsin Ave (between Q St and R St NW). The area is called Book Hill, and when Georgetowners need Chinese lacquered chests or lavender linen-drawer liners for their home, it's their one-stop shop.

➤ **Tombs Trivia** University folks get psyched for Trivia Night at the Tombs (p98), held on various Tuesdays.

➤ **Party at the Waterfront** On warm nights the outdoor cafes and boating action make Georgetown Waterfront Park (p94) the neighborhood hot spot.

➤ **Walk in the Woods** For a peaceful jaunt, it'll likely be you and the occasional runner or dog walker on the forested paths in Dumbarton Oaks Park (p95).

Getting There & Away

➤ **Metro** The Foggy Bottom-GWU stop (Orange, Silver, Blue Lines) is a 0.75-mile walk from M St's edge.

➤ **Bus** The DC Circulator's Dupont–Georgetown–Rosslyn line runs from the Dupont Circle Metro station (south entrance), with stops along M St. The Union Station–Georgetown line runs via K St and Wisconsin Ave.

➤ **Boat** Water taxis glide between Georgetown's dock (p272) – near 31st and K Sts – and the Wharf in Southwest DC, with onward links to Alexandria, VA.

➤ **Walk** A half-mile riverside path connects Georgetown Waterfront Park to the Kennedy Center.

Lonely Planet's Top Tip

Georgetown is a terrific cycling spot. Two top trails are the C&O Canal Towpath (p101), which is flat, wide, forested and scenic; and the Capital Crescent Trail (p101), a paved path built on an old railroad bed that provides beautiful lookouts over the Potomac River. The neighborhood has several bike-rental shops that make it easy to get rolling.

GEORGETOWN

Best Parks & Gardens

➤ Dumbarton Oaks (p94)
➤ Georgetown Waterfront Park (p94)
➤ Tudor Place (p94)
➤ Dumbarton Oaks Park (p95)

For reviews, see p94.➡

Best Places to Eat

➤ Baked & Wired (p95)
➤ Simply Banh Mi (p95)
➤ Fiola Mare (p97)
➤ Il Canale (p97)
➤ Chez Billy Sud (p97)

For reviews, see p95.➡

Best Places to Drink

➤ Tombs (p98)
➤ Ching Ching Cha (p98)
➤ Grace Street Coffee (p98)
➤ Sovereign (p100)

For reviews, see p98.➡

◉ SIGHTS

★ DUMBARTON OAKS GARDENS, MUSEUM

Map p302 (📞202-339-6401; www.doaks.org; 1703 32nd St NW; museum free, gardens adult/child $10/5; ⊘museum 11:30am-5:30pm Tue-Sun, gardens 2-6pm; 🚌Circulator) The mansion's 10 acres of enchanting formal gardens are straight out of a storybook. In springtime the blooms – including heaps of cherry blossoms – are stunning. The mansion itself is worth a walk-through to see exquisite Byzantine and pre-Columbian art (including El Greco's *The Visitation*) and the fascinating library of rare books that date as far back as 1491.

In 1944 diplomatic meetings took place here that laid the groundwork for the UN. The trustees of Harvard University operate the house, so Harvard students, faculty and staff get in for free. From November to mid-March the gardens are free to all (and they close at 5pm). The garden entrance is at R and 31st Sts NW.

GEORGETOWN WATERFRONT PARK PARK

Map p302 (www.georgetownwaterfrontpark. org; Water St NW, btwn 30th St & Key Bridge; 🚻; 🚌Circulator) This park is a favorite with couples on first dates, families on an evening stroll and power players showing off their yachts. Benches dot the way, where you can sit and watch the rowing teams out on the Potomac River. Alfresco restaurants cluster near the harbor at 31st St NW. They ring a terraced plaza filled with fountains (which become an ice rink in winter). The docks are also here for boats that ply the Potomac to Alexandria, VA, and Capitol Hill's Wharf.

The park covers 10 riverside acres, extending from 30th St west to the Key Bridge. Kids splash in the fountains at Wisconsin Ave's foot. At 33rd St there's a labyrinth in the grass; walk the circles and see if you feel more connected to the universe.

EXORCIST STAIRS FILM LOCATION

Map p302 (3600 Prospect St NW; 🚌Circulator) The steep set of stairs dropping down to M St is a popular track for joggers, but more famously it's the spot where demonically possessed Father Karras tumbles to his death in horror-film classic *The Exorcist* (1973). Come on foggy nights, when the stone steps really are creepy as hell.

TUDOR PLACE MUSEUM

Map p302 (📞202-965-0400; www.tudorplace. org; 1644 31st St NW; 1hr house tour adult/child $10/3, self-guided garden tour $3; ⊘10am-4pm Tue-Sat, from noon Sun, closed Jan; 🚌Circulator) This 1816 neoclassical mansion was owned by Thomas Peter and Martha Custis Peter, the granddaughter of Martha Washington. Today the manor functions as a small museum, featuring furnishings and artwork from Mount Vernon, which give a good insight into American decorative arts. The grand, 5-acre gardens bloom with roses, lilies, poplar trees and exotic palms.

GEORGETOWN UNIVERSITY UNIVERSITY

Map p302 (📞202-687-0100; www.georgetown. edu; cnr 37th & O Sts NW; 🚌Circulator) Georgetown is one of the nation's top universities, with a student body that's equally hardworking and hard-partying. Founded in 1789, it was America's first Roman Catholic university. Notable Hoya (derived from

---

THE C&O CANAL TOWPATH: A HISTORY (WITH MULES)

When work began on the C&O in 1828, the canal was considered an engineering marvel. Unfortunately, by the time it was completed in 1850, the waterway was already obsolete, rendered out of date by the railroad. Nonetheless, the C&O remained in operation for 74 years until a series of floods closed it in 1924.

Mules typically were the 'engines' of the canal boats, pulling them along the water from the roadside. The 1000lb creatures were sturdier and cheaper than horses. Some mules worked on the C&O for more than 20 years.

After the canal closed, it almost became a highway but for the efforts of Supreme Court judge William Douglas, one of the court's most committed civil libertarians and environmentalists. He felt the towpath should be set aside for future generations, and to prove his point he organized a creative publicity stunt. In March 1954 Douglas led a group on an eight-day hike from Cumberland, MD, to Georgetown along the path. The ploy worked: press coverage of the hike was positive, as was the public reaction, and the towpath became a national park.

the Latin *hoya saxa*, 'what rocks') alumni include Bill Clinton, as well as many international royals and heads of state. Near the campus' east gate, medieval-looking Healy Hall impresses with its tall, Hogwartsesque clock tower. Pretty Dalghren Chapel and its quiet courtyard hide behind it.

DUMBARTON OAKS PARK
PARK

Map p302 (www.dopark.org; Lovers' Lane; ⊙sunrise-sunset; ⛟Circulator) Next door to Dumbarton Oaks (p94) garden, Dumbarton Oaks Park was once part of the estate but is now a public woodland beloved by joggers and dog walkers. Access it via Lovers' Lane (a paved path 200ft east of R and 31st Sts) and enter a world of forested trails, quaint stone bridges, mini waterfalls and deer-filled meadows.

OAK HILL CEMETERY
CEMETERY

Map p302 (☎202-337-2835; www.oakhill cemeterydc.org; 3001 R St NW; ⊙9am-4:30pm Mon-Fri, 11am-4pm Sat, 1-4pm Sun; ⛟Circulator) This 24-acre, obelisk-studded cemetery contains winding walks and 19th-century gravestones set into the hillsides of Rock Creek. It's a fantastic spot for a quiet walk, especially in spring, when it seems like every wildflower in existence blooms on the grounds. James Renwick designed the lovely gatehouse and charming gneiss chapel.

The 2017 publication of *Lincoln in the Bardo*, George Saunders' bestselling novel, has sparked renewed interest in the cemetery. Literary fans come to seek out the Carroll family mausoleum, which temporarily held the casket of Willie Lincoln, Abraham Lincoln's young son who died of typhoid in 1862. In the book, the grief-stricken president visits the crypt and holds Willie's body (which supposedly happened in real life), as the cemetery's residents rise up to watch and deal with their own anguish. The cemetery office has a map with the vault's location. If you've read the book, the setting is quite evocative.

DUMBARTON HOUSE
MUSEUM

Map p302 (☎202-337-2288; www.dumbarton house.org; 2715 Q St NW; adult/child $10/free; ⊙10am-3pm Tue-Sun, closed Jan; ⛟Circulator) Often confused with Dumbarton Oaks (the mansion and gardens), Dumbarton House is a modest Federal-style historic home, constructed by a wealthy family in 1799. Now it's run by the National Society of the Colonial Dames of America, who have their headquarters here. The focus isn't just the house – chockablock with antique china, silver, furnishings, gowns and books – but also quaint customs of the era, like passing round the chamber pot after formal dinners so gentlemen could have a group pee.

Visiting on the weekend for a 45-minute guided tour (held at 10:30am and 1:30pm Saturday and Sunday) provides the biggest bang for the buck; it's best to reserve online in advance (there's no fee). The landscaped grounds offer a pleasant browse. They're open from sunrise to sunset and are free to walk through.

✖️ EATING

⭐ BAKED & WIRED
BAKERY $

Map p302 (☎703-663-8727; www.bakedand wired.com; 1052 Thomas Jefferson St NW; baked goods $3-6; ⊙7am-8pm Mon-Thu, to 9pm Fri, 8am-9pm Sat, to 8pm Sun; ⛟Circulator) This cheery cafe whips up beautifully made coffees, bacon cheddar buttermilk biscuits and enormous cupcakes (like the banana and peanut-butter-frosted Elvis). It's a fine spot to join university students and cyclists coming off the nearby trails for a sugar buzz. When the weather permits, patrons take their treats outside to the adjacent grassy area by the C&O Canal.

Inside, head to the right for coffee drinks and stay left for the sweet treats.

⭐ SIMPLY BANH MI
VIETNAMESE $

Map p302 (☎202-333-5726; www.simplybanh midc.com; 1624 Wisconsin Ave NW; mains $7-10; ⊙11am-7pm Tue-Sun; ✍️; ⛟Circulator) There's nothing fancy about the small, below-street-level space, and the compact menu sticks mostly to sandwiches and bubble tea. But the brother-sister owners know how to take a crusty baguette, stuff it with delicious lemongrass pork or other meat (or tofu), and make your day. They're super-attentive to quality and customer needs (vegan, gluten-free etc). They also ladle out a couple of types of pho (noodle soup).

PIE SISTERS
BAKERY $

Map p302 (☎202-338-7437; www.piesisters.com; 3423 M St NW; slices $5-6; ⊙11am-7pm Tue-Sun; ⛟Circulator) The neighbors can't help but stop in to see what the Pie Sisters have cooling on the rack. Chocolate cream and jumbleberry tempt among the sweet wares,

AFRICAN AMERICAN GEORGETOWN

Three sites recall the history of Georgetown's 19th-century free black community, who lived in an area known as Herring Hill (located south of P St between Rock Creek Park and 31st St NW).

Mt Zion United Methodist Church (Map p302; ☑202-234-0148; www.mtzionumcdc. org; 1334 29th St NW; ☺10am-2pm Sun, by appt Mon-Sat) Founded in 1816, the church is DC's oldest black congregation. Its original site, on 27th St NW, was a stop on the Underground Railroad. A fire later forced the church to move to its present building, completed in 1884.

Mt Zion Cemetery (Map p302; near intersection 27th & Q Sts NW; ☺sunrise-sunset) The crumbling graveyard dates from the early 1800s. It takes its name from Mt Zion United Methodist Church, which used to be located beside the site. Toppled, overgrown headstones scatter in a forlorn patch of trees, marking the graves of some 1000 African American residents. During the mid-1800s, slaves escaping from the South hid in a vault on the grounds.

Female Union Band Society Cemetery (Map p302; near intersection 27th & Q Sts NW; ☺sunrise-sunset) Founded in 1842 by a society of free black women who pledged to help one another in sickness and in death, this graveyard was originally adjacent to Mt Zion Cemetery, but it has since been absorbed by it, so now it's all one site.

To reach the cemeteries, look for the 'No Outlet' road leading in just west of the building at 2531 Q St NW (and just east of Dumbarton House's gate).

while chicken pot pie and pork barbecue pie waft savory goodness. The sweet ones come in bite-size and cupcake-size versions, but go for a full slice for best results. A smattering of tables let you fork in immediately.

PIZZERIA PARADISO   PIZZA $

Map p302 (☑202-337-1245; www.eatyourpizza. com; 3282 M St NW; 9in pizzas $12-15; ☺11:30am-10pm Mon-Thu, to 11pm Fri & Sat, noon-10pm Sun; ▣Circulator) Casual Paradiso serves wood-oven Neapolitan-style pizzas with scrumptious toppings to crowds of hungry patrons. The pizza crust is perfect: light, crisp and a little flaky. There's great people-watching from the big plate-glass windows and popular happy hours. A fine beer and ale selection heightens the appeal. Bonus: the restaurant's lower level holds an arcade with pinball, shuffleboard and classic video games. It has a separate entrance via the alley that runs behind the building.

PATISSERIE POUPON   CAFE $

Map p302 (☑202-342-3248; www.patisserie poupon.net; 1645 Wisconsin Ave NW; baked goods $3-5, mains $8-14; ☺8:30am-6pm Tue-Fri, 8am-5:30pm Sat, to 4pm Sun; ▣Circulator) The society ladies know where to replenish mid–shopping spree: Patisserie Poupon. Join them in nibbling almond croissants, macarons or a niçoise salad at one of the little cafe's tables. Once the French-press coffee and *chocolat chaud* (hot chocolate) arrive, it's easy to linger.

GEORGETOWN CUPCAKE   BAKERY $

Map p302 (☑202-333-8448; www.georgetown cupcake.com; 3301 M St NW; cupcakes $3.50; ☺10am-9pm Mon-Sat, to 8pm Sun; ▣Circulator) Here's what's going to happen: you'll be walking down M St and will see a gigantic line spilling out of a small shop: moms with kids, preppy students and ladies-who-lunch types. Shouts of 'They have salted caramel!', 'I'm getting the lava fudge!' will fill the air. You won't be able to resist and will fall in behind them.

Honestly, we don't think these are the best cupcakes in town. That honor belongs to nearby Baked & Wired (p95). That said, the shop does make a damn fine cake.

SWEETGREEN   HEALTH FOOD $

Map p302 (☑202-838-4300; www.sweetgreen. com; 1044 Wisconsin Ave NW; mains $9-12; ☺10:30am-10pm; ☑; ▣Circulator) ✿ Georgetown's two-story branch of the uberhealthy salad and frozen-yogurt maker is the chain's largest. Order your whopping bowl of curry-yogurt-sauced roast chicken and greens (or other equally wholesome dish) at the counter, then take it to a rustic-chic table indoors or outdoors on the patio.

⭐ IL CANALE ITALIAN $$

Map p302 (☎202-337-4444; www.ilcanale.com; 1063 31st St NW; mains $18-25; ⊙11am-10:30pm Mon-Thu, to 11pm Fri & Sat, to 10pm Sun; ☷Circulator) Real-deal Neapolitan pizza emerges from the real-deal, Italian wood-fired oven in Il Canale's bouncy town-house digs. It's casual and low-cost for Georgetown, which is why families, couples and groups of friends pile in at all hours. The calamari, lasagna, pastas and cannoli are all crowd-pleasers.

MARTIN'S TAVERN AMERICAN $$

Map p302 (☎202-333-7370; www.martins tavern.com; 1264 Wisconsin Ave NW; mains $18-34; ⊙11am-1:30am Mon-Thu, to 2:30am Fri, 9am-2:30am Sat, 8am-1:30am Sun; ☷Circulator) John F Kennedy proposed to Jackie in booth three at Georgetown's oldest saloon, and if you're thinking of popping the question there today, the attentive waitstaff keep the champagne chilled for that very reason. With an old-English country scene, including the requisite fox-and-hound hunting prints on the wall, this DC institution serves unfussy classics like thick burgers, crab cakes and icy-cold beers.

FARMERS FISHERS BAKERS AMERICAN $$

Map p302 (☎202-298-8783; www.farmers fishersbakers.com; 3000 K St NW, Washington Harbour; mains $15-29; ⊙7:30-10pm Mon-Wed, to 11pm Thu, to midnight Fri, 9am-midnight Sat, to 10pm Sun; ☷Circulator) The folksy cow above the front door might tip you off. Or the larder-designed corner lined with farm-canned goods. This eco-chic restaurant on the Georgetown waterfront (sibling to acclaimed Founding Farmers, p87) is all about paying homage to Americana – the menu roams from honey pot-fried chicken to jambalaya. And everything is fresh, fresh, fresh. The patio remains open year-round.

KOTOBUKI JAPANESE $$

(☎202-625-9080; www.kotobukidc.com; 4822 MacArthur Blvd NW, 2nd fl; mains $22-29; ⊙noon-2:30pm Mon-Sat, 5-9:30pm Mon-Thu & Sun, to 10:30pm Fri & Sat; ☷D5 or D6) Kotobuki is one of DC's better spots for sushi, thanks to its excellent platters (at around $16 for a lunch and $26 for a dinner platter); its tucked-away location, which adds a feeling of discovery; and its oh-so-Japanese interior, all stripped-down aesthetic overlaid by running cursive kanji script on the walls. No reservations, but usually there's not much of a wait.

The modest restaurant is located on the building's 2nd floor, above another Japanese restaurant.

⭐ FIOLA MARE SEAFOOD $$$

Map p302 (☎202-628-0065; www.fiolamaredc. com; 3050 K St NW, Washington Harbour; mains $28-54; ⊙5-10pm Mon, 11:30am-2:30pm & 5-10pm Tue-Fri, 11:30am-2pm & 5-10:30pm Sat, 11am-2pm & 5-10pm Sun; ☷Circulator) Fiola Mare delivers the chichi Georgetown experience. It flies in fresh fish and crustaceans from Maine to Tasmania daily. The yacht-bobbling river view rocks. The see-and-be-seen multitudes are here. It's DC at its luxe best. Try it at lunchtime on a weekday, when $20 or so gets you an Italian-style seafood main and a drink in the bar area. Make reservations.

It also offers a popular pretheater menu (three courses for $45) from 5pm to 6:30pm Tuesday through Sunday.

⭐ CHEZ BILLY SUD FRENCH $$$

Map p302 (☎202-965-2606; www.chezbillysud. com; 1039 31st St NW; mains $25-38; ⊙5-10pm Mon, 11:30am-2pm & 5-10pm Tue-Thu, 11:30am-2pm & 5-11pm Fri, 11am-2pm & 5-11pm Sat, 11am-2pm & 5-10pm Sun; ☷Circulator) An endearing little bistro tucked away on a residential block, Billy's mint-green walls, gilt mirrors and wee marble bar exude laid-back elegance. Mustachioed servers bring baskets of warm bread to the white-linen-clothed tables, along with crackling pork and pistachio sausage, golden trout, tuna niçoise salad and plump cream puffs.

Lots of fine wine swirls in glasses, with more flowing at Billy's sister wine bar across the courtyard.

MAKOTO JAPANESE $$$

(☎202-298-6866; www.sakedokoromakoto.com; 4822 MacArthur Blvd NW, 1st fl; 8-course set menu $135; ⊙6:30-8:30pm Tue-Thu, to 9:30pm Fri, 6-9:30pm Sun; ☷D5 or D6) Makoto is simply and classically....*Japanese*. The napkins look like origami. The wasabi is fresh grated. You leave your shoes at the door. And the food – a chef's-choice tasting menu – is exquisite, with dishes such as fava-bean-encrusted halibut and shrimp with cherry-blossom-leaf sauce. There's no mucking about: this is traditional stuff prepared with the height of focus and technique.

The restaurant is tiny, with barely 30 seats, and you must reserve in advance. Note there's a business-casual dress code (no athletic gear allowed). Another, less expensive Japanese restaurant sits on the upper floor.

LA CHAUMIÈRE
FRENCH $$$

Map p302 (☏202-338-1784; www.lachaumiere dc.com; 2813 M St NW; mains $23-34; ⏱11:30am-2:30pm Mon-Fri, 5:30-10:30pm Mon-Sat; ☐Circulator) There are artists and there are craftspeople, and La Chaumière's kitchen seems to fall into the second category. This isn't a bad thing; there's no fooling around with funny envelope-pushing here, just very good, classic French food prepared in an intimate dining room that screams 'expensive date.' This is hearty, stick-to-your-ribs stuff straight from the terroir: duck breast, beef medallions, calf brains – things that are long- and slow-braised with love. The central stone fireplace adds to the warmth.

1789
AMERICAN $$$

Map p302 (☏202-965-1789; www.1789 restaurant.com; 1226 36th St NW; mains $30-48; ⏱6-10pm Mon-Thu, to 11pm Fri, 5:30-11pm Sat, to 10pm Sun; ☐Circulator) This place was one of the first high-end purveyors of 'rustic New American' fare, so if you're going to try local ingredients sexed up with provincial flair (think Shenandoah Valley beef with wild-mushroom bread pudding), this is the spot to indulge. The menu is ever changing. Most diners opt for the tasting menu of four ($83), five ($95) or six courses ($107). Political bigwigs often sup in the cozy, colonial room. While there's no longer a jacket requirement, the majority of folks still look sharp.

CAFE MILANO
ITALIAN $$$

Map p302 (☏202-333-6183; www.cafemilano. com; 3251 Prospect St NW; mains $25-55; ⏱11:30am-11pm Mon & Tue, to midnight Wed-Sat, 11am-11pm Sun; ☐Circulator) Milano has been reeling in the political glitterati and besotted Georgetown couples for years with its executions of northern Italian favorites. Be prepared to pay for the European-chic ambience and celebrity-spotting. The pastas get the biggest praise, especially the ones prepared tableside.

BLACKSALT
SEAFOOD $$$

(☏202-342-9101; www.blacksaltrestaurant. com; 4883 MacArthur Blvd NW; mains $36-40; ⏱11:30am-2:30pm & 5:30-9:30pm Mon-Thu, to 10pm Fri & Sat, to 9pm Sun; ☐D5 or D6) There are many who claim BlackSalt – located in the rich, residential Palisades neighborhood – serves the best seafood in the city. The chef always seems to find new flavors, delving into whatever culinary pleasure one can ratchet out of a sole, skate or soft-shell crab. Smoky, buttery, minty: the shifting, innovative menu is typically spot on. Five- and seven-course tasting menus ($80/110) are also available. If you can't get enough, BlackSalt doubles as a fish market, overflowing with fresh, organic sea creatures for cooking at home.

🍷 DRINKING & NIGHTLIFE

★TOMBS
PUB

Map p302 (☏202-337-6668; www.tombs.com; 1226 36th St NW; ⏱11:30am-1:30am Mon-Thu, to 2:30am Fri & Sat, 9:30am-1:30am Sun; ☐Circulator) Every college of a certain pedigree has 'that' bar – the one where faculty and students alike sip pints under athletic regalia of the old school. The Tombs is Georgetown's contribution to the genre. If it looks familiar, think back to the '80s: the subterranean pub was one of the settings for the film St Elmo's Fire. The close-set tables buzz on various Tuesdays for Trivia Night shenanigans; check the website for the schedule.

★CHING CHING CHA
TEAHOUSE

Map p302 (☏202-333-8288; www.chingching cha.com; 1063 Wisconsin Ave NW; ⏱11am-8pm Thu-Mon; ☐Circulator) Airy, Zen-like Ching Ching Cha is a world away from the shopping mayhem of M St. Stop in for a leisurely pot of rare tea (it brews more than 70 varieties) and snacks such as steamed dumplings, coconut tarts, or a 'tea meal,' with three little dishes along the lines of green squash and miso salmon.

★GRACE STREET COFFEE
COFFEE

Map p302 (☏202-470-1331; www.gracestcoffee. com; 3210 Grace St NW; ⏱7am-5pm Mon-Thu, to 6pm Fri-Sun; ☐Circulator) This little shop roasts its own beans and makes its own syrups, and then morphs them into exquisite coffee drinks. It's in a mini food hall that shares space with a juice bar and top-notch sandwich shop (called Sundevich, which specializes in creations named after global

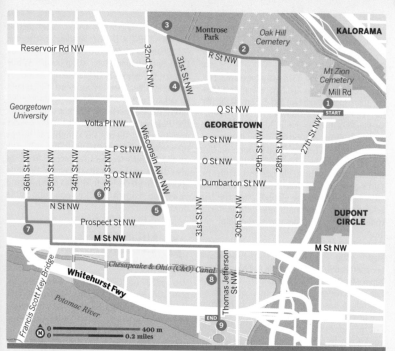

🏃 Neighborhood Walk
Genteel Georgetown

START MT ZION CEMETERY
END GEORGETOWN WATERFRONT PARK
LENGTH 3 MILES; THREE HOURS

If ever a neighborhood were prime for ambling, it's Georgetown, in all its leafy, filigreed-manor glory. African American ❶ **Mt Zion Cemetery** (p96), near the intersection of 27th and Q Sts NW, dates from the early 1800s. A nearby church was a stop on the Underground Railroad, and it hid escaping slaves in a vault in the cemetery.

The entrance to ❷ **Oak Hill Cemetery** (p95) is a few blocks away at 30th and R Sts NW. Stroll the obelisk-studded grounds and look for gravesites of prominent Washingtonians such as Edwin Stanton (Lincoln's war secretary). Up the road, ❸ **Dumbarton Oaks** (p94) offers exquisite Byzantine art inside and sprawling, fountain-dotted gardens outside. The blooms in springtime are stunning.

George Washington's step-granddaughter Martha Custis Peter owned ❹ **Tudor Place** (p94), the neoclassical mansion at 1644 31st St NW. It has some of George's furnishings from Mount Vernon on show and pretty landscaped grounds.

Head over to Wisconsin Ave NW, and stop in at ❺ **Martin's Tavern** (p97), where John F Kennedy proposed to Jackie. Walk west along N St NW and you'll pass several Federal-style town houses in the 3300 block. JFK and Jackie lived at ❻ **3307 N St** between 1958 and 1961, when they left for the White House.

At the corner of 36th and Prospect Sts NW, stare down the ❼ **Exorcist Stairs** (p94), which featured in the 1973 horror film *The Exorcist*. Joggers use the steep steps by day, but at night they're legitimately creepy. Go down to M St NW, popping in to whatever boutiques and high-end chain stores your wallet permits. At Thomas Jefferson St turn right and sniff your way to ❽ **Baked & Wired** (p95) to replenish with a monster cupcake and fine coffee. From there you can stroll down to ❾ **Georgetown Waterfront Park** (p94) to watch the boats and other action along the Potomac River.

cities, like the chicken-and-avocado Lima and the Gruyère-and-ham Paris). Lots of hip locals relax over a cup here.

★ SOVEREIGN   BAR

Map p302 (☑202-774-5875; www.thesovereigndc. com; 1206 Wisconsin Ave NW; ⊙5pm-1am Mon-Fri, 11am-3pm & 5pm-1am Sat & Sun; ☐Circulator) The Sovereign takes its Belgian theme seriously. All of the beers here – 50 on tap and 300 more in bottles – are Belgian or Belgian-style. The top floor is done up like an old Flemish beer hall, with long wooden tables and stag's-head chandeliers, while the 1st floor is more modern. Mussels and rabbit stew help soak up the alcohol. Note the bar is set back from the road; follow the lanterns that lead along the alleyway to the door.

CAFE BONAPARTE   CAFE

Map p302 (☑202-333-8830; www.cafe bonaparte.com; 1522 Wisconsin Ave NW; ⊙9am-10pm Mon-Thu & Sun, to 11pm Fri, 10am-11pm Sat; ☐Circulator) This jewel-box cafe feels as though it has been plucked straight from the streets of Paris. Come to sip a café au lait or a glass of sparkling wine. Hopefully you're not in a hurry, because service can be slow. *Frites* (fries), crêpes and chocolate tortes emerge from the kitchen for those in need of a nosh.

KAFE LEOPOLD   CAFE

Map p302 (☑202-965-6005; www.kafeleopolds. com; 3315 Cady's Alley NW; ⊙8am-10pm Sun-Tue, to 11pm Wed & Thu, to midnight Fri & Sat; ☐Circulator) Leopold serves full meals, but it shines most as a European-vibed spot for coffee and German and Austrian wines. Sip at one of the umbrella-shaded tables that spill out into the courtyard. Banana rum macarons, five-layer hazelnut cake and chocolatey Sacher torte entice from the glass case. Service can be lackluster, though it doesn't seem to deter the crowds.

J PAUL'S   PUB

Map p302 (☑202-333-3450; www.jpaulsdc.com; 3218 M St NW; ⊙11:30am-midnight Mon-Wed, to 2am Thu & Fri, 10:30am-2am Sat, to midnight Sun; ☐Circulator) Politicians, lobbyists, students and other locals belly up at J Paul's to knock beers back and enjoy great burgers, steaks, ribs and seared salmon. Join the group at the long mahogany shotgun bar, especially during happy hour, when there are deals on oysters and other menu items.

SEQUOIA   BAR

Map p302 (☑202-944-4200; www.sequoia dc.com; 3000 K St NW, Washington Harbour; ⊙11:30am-10pm Mon-Thu, to 11pm Fri, 10am-11pm Sat, to 10pm Sun; ☐Circulator) While snazzy, cavernous Sequoia is known mostly as a restaurant, we recommend it as a spot to get an alfresco drink. Umbrella-shaded tables pack a cascading terrace overlooking the Potomac, and though it's a bit cheesy and touristy, there's no denying it jumps on steamy summer nights. Sip and soak up the swanky Georgetown scene. You can also drink at the bar inside, where Sequoia sports a fresh design in shades of white and Valentine red, with funky neon tube lights buzzing overhead.

☆ ENTERTAINMENT

BLUES ALLEY   JAZZ

Map p302 (☑202-337-4141; www.bluesalley. com; 1073 Wisconsin Ave NW; tickets from $20; ⊙shows 8pm & 10pm; ☐Circulator) Greats like Dizzy Gillespie and Sarah Vaughan played this venerable club back in the day. The talent remains just as sterling now, and the setting just as sophisticated. Reserve a ticket in advance if a big name is making music. Enter through the alley just off M St, south of Wisconsin Ave. There's a $12 food or beverage minimum purchase requirement once you're seated.

SHOPPING

TUGOOH TOYS   TOYS

Map p302 (☑202-338-9476; www.tugoohtoys. com; 1355 Wisconsin Ave NW; ⊙11am-5pm Mon-Thu, to 6pm Fri, 10am-6pm Sat, to 5pm Sun; ☐Circulator) If you've ever been nostalgic for the great wooden toys of childhood, this hip wonderland has the goods with clever modern touches. Lots of ecofriendly playthings (ie cuddly animals made with high-quality organic cotton) and educational games stack the shelves, too.

CADY'S ALLEY   HOMEWARES

Map p302 (www.cadysalley.com; 3314 M St NW; ⊙8am-6pm Mon-Sat, from noon Sun; ☐Circulator) Not a store per se, Cady's Alley is a small cobblestone lane lined with ubercool (and often expensive) clothing and interior-design boutiques selling everything from little black dresses to concept furniture. It runs parallel to M St NW, between 33rd and 34th Sts NW; you can enter off M St.

OLIVER DUNN, MOSS & CO
ANTIQUES

Map p302 (☑202-338-7410; 1657 Wisconsin Ave NW; ☺11am-5pm Tue-Sat; ⛟Circulator) The lengthy name comes from two businesses under one roof. Located in a cute row house in the thick of Book Hill, this spot spreads posh linens, Scandinavian textiles, French signs and concrete garden ornaments through six rooms and into the backyard.

RELISH
CLOTHING

Map p302 (☑202-333-5343; www.relishdc.com; 3312 Cady's Alley NW; ☺10am-6pm Mon-Sat; ⛟Circulator) Set on Cady's Alley, Relish sells high-end fashion for the ladies. The two-level store boasts top-name labels and indie designers alike, including pieces by Marni, Dries van Noten and Nicole Farhi. Shoes, bags and accessories all make nice eye candy.

SPORTS & ACTIVITIES

C&O CANAL TOWPATH
CYCLING

Map p302 (www.nps.gov/choh; 1057 Thomas Jefferson St NW; ⛟Circulator) The shaded hiking-cycling path – part of a larger national historic park – runs alongside a waterway built in the mid-1800s to transport goods all the way to West Virginia. Step on at Jefferson St for a lovely green escape from the crowd. Note the canal and environs are being restored and enhanced over the next several years, so you might run into construction along the way; check the latest updates before setting off.

In its entirety, the gravel path runs for 185 miles from Georgetown to Cumberland, MD. Lots of cyclists do the 14-mile ride from Georgetown to Great Falls, MD. The tree-lined route goes over atmospheric wooden bridges and past waterwheels and old lock houses. It's mostly flat, punctuated by occasional small hills. The park's website and Bike Washington (http://bikewashington.org) have trail maps.

KEY BRIDGE BOATHOUSE
WATER SPORTS

Map p302 (☑202-337-9642; www.boatingindc.com/boathouses/key-bridge-boathouse; 3500 Water St NW; ☺hours vary mid-Apr–Oct; ⛟Circulator) Located beneath the Key Bridge, the boathouse rents canoes, kayaks and stand up paddleboards (prices start at $16 per hour). In summer it also offers guided, 90-minute kayak trips ($45 per person) that glide past the Lincoln Memorial as the sun sets. If you have a bike, the boathouse is a mere few steps from the Capital Crescent Trail.

CAPITAL CRESCENT TRAIL
CYCLING

Map p302 (www.cctrail.org; Water St; ⛟Circulator) Stretching between Georgetown and Bethesda, MD, the constantly evolving Capital Crescent Trail is a fabulous (and very popular) jogging and biking route. Built on an abandoned railroad bed, the 11-mile trail is paved and is a great leisurely day trip. It has beautiful lookouts over the Potomac River, and winds through woodsy areas and upscale neighborhoods.

In Georgetown, the trail begins under the Key Bridge on Water St (which is what K St becomes as it moves west along the waterfront); the trailhead is clearly marked. In Bethesda, it starts at the Wisconsin Ave Tunnel, on Wisconsin Ave just south of Old Georgetown Rd (it's clearly marked here too, and accessible from Bethesda Metro station). The trail also links up with the C&O Canal Towpath and trails through Rock Creek Park.

BIG WHEEL BIKES
CYCLING

Map p302 (☑202-337-0254; www.bigwheelbikes.com; 1034 33rd St NW; per 3hr/day $21/35; ☺11am-7pm Tue-Fri, 10am-6pm Sat & Sun; ⛟Circulator) Big Wheel has a wide variety of two-wheelers to rent, and you can spin onto the C&O Canal Towpath practically from the front door. Staff members also provide the lowdown on the nearby Capital Crescent Trail and Mount Vernon Trail (p206). There's a three-hour minimum with rentals. For an extra $10 you can keep your bike overnight.

THOMPSON BOAT CENTER
WATER SPORTS

Map p302 (☑202-337-9642; www.boatingindc.com/boathouses/thompson-boat-center; 2900 Virginia Ave NW; ☺hours vary mid-Apr–Oct; ⛟Circulator) At the Georgetown waterfront's eastern edge, Thompson Boat Center rents canoes and kayaks (prices start at $16 per hour) and offers rowing classes. This is also a convenient place to rent bicycles (from $11 per hour).

THE WASHINGTON POST / GETTY IMAGES ©

1. Martin's Tavern p97
John F Kennedy proposed to Jacqueline Bouvier in this booth at Georgeotown's oldest saloon.

2. Row houses p259
Federal-style buildings still dominate the contemporary domestic architecture here.

3. Georgetown University p94
One of the nation's top universities.

4. Georgetown Waterfront Park p94
Covering 10 acres along the Potomac River, it is popular year-round.

Capitol Hill & South DC

Neighborhood Top Five

1 **US Capitol** (p106) Counting the statues, ogling the frescoes, eating the bean soup and visiting the chambers of the guys and gals who run the country under the big white dome.

2 **United States Holocaust Memorial Museum** (p108) Immersing yourself in the good and bad sides of human nature.

3 **Library of Congress** (p109) Being wowed by the sheer volume of, well, volumes, then discovering ancient maps and cartoons in the exhibition rooms.

4 **Supreme Court** (p112) Listening in on case arguments and watching Ruth Bader Ginsburg, Sonia Sotomayor and the other black-robed justices in action.

5 **Nationals Park** (p123) Catching a baseball game and getting your photo taken with a giant-headed Abe Lincoln or Tom Jefferson after the famous 'racing presidents' contest.

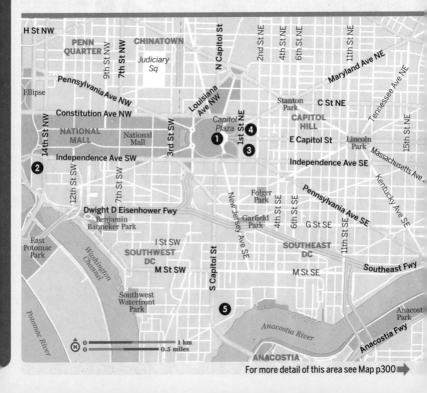

For more detail of this area see Map p300 ⇒

Explore Capitol Hill & South DC

This area is quite large, and you'll need at least a day to experience the highlights. The focal point is the big domed Capitol (p106), which sits atop Capitol Hill and across a plaza from the almost-as-regal Supreme Court (p112) and Library of Congress (p109). The three are touristy top draws, best visited in the morning.

The US Holocaust Memorial Museum (p108) and money-churning Bureau of Engraving & Printing (p115) are other prime sights. They're in Southwest DC, a little sliver of spillover from the Mall. It's generating big buzz these days thanks to the Wharf (p114), a new waterfront complex of chic restaurants, shops and entertainment venues, along with playful parks and boat-laden piers. Likewise, in farther-flung Southeast DC, the Nationals' stadium (p123) has sparked development of a mod riverside park and exciting zone of eats and drinks at the Navy Yard. Frederick Douglass' historic home (p114) lies across the water in hardscrabble Anacostia. Either area – Southwest or Southeast – can easily occupy an afternoon.

For evening festivities, linger at the Wharf or Navy Yard, or move on to H St NE (near Union Station) or 8th St SE (near Eastern Market). Both roads are rockin' local favorites, densely packed with hip bars and eateries. If you're in the area during the weekend, a morning visit to Eastern Market (p126) is a must.

Local Life

➡ **Beer and Bean Bags** The cornhole (aka bean bag toss) games get fierce at Bardo Brewing (p122), an alfresco beer garden set under a bridge by the river.

➡ **Jazz Party** Wednesday's jazz jam at Mr Henry's (p122) brings a rotating cast of DC musicians, vocalists, tap dancers and poets.

➡ **All-Day Pretzels** Breakfast, lunch or dinner, the Pretzel Bakery (p119) bakes warm ones.

Getting There & Away

➡ **Metro** Union Station (Red Line), Capitol South (Orange, Silver and Blue), Eastern Market (Orange, Silver and Blue) and Navy Yard (Green) are the main stations. The Wharf is equidistant from L'Enfant Plaza (Orange, Silver, Blue, Yellow and Green) and Waterfront (Green).

➡ **Bus** The free Southwest Shuttle runs between L'Enfant Plaza Metro station, the Wharf and the Mall.

➡ **Streetcar** DC's free new line zips along H St from Union Station to 15th St. Catch it behind Union Station.

➡ **Boat** Water taxis glide from the **Wharf Transit Pier** (Map p300; 950 Wharf St SW, Transit Pier; Ⓜ Orange, Silver, Blue, Yellow, Green Lines to L'Enfant Plaza or Green Line to Waterfront) to Georgetown and Alexandria, VA. One-way fares start at adult/child $12/8.40; it's a 25-minute ride.

Lonely Planet's Top Tip

During peak season (late March through June), it pays to plan ahead for certain sights, given the crowds and potential sell-out of tickets. The US Capitol lets you reserve tours online for free. The US Holocaust Memorial Museum lets you reserve tickets for a $1 fee. The Bureau of Engraving & Printing doesn't take bookings, so show up at 8am to get a ticket. For the Marines' drill parade, book online starting March 1.

◉ **Best Underrated Sights**

➡ National Postal Museum (p112)

➡ Frederick Douglass National Historic Site (p114)

➡ Belmont-Paul Women's Equality National Monument (p113)

For reviews, see p112.

✕ **Best Places to Eat**

➡ ChiKo (p117)

➡ Rose's Luxury (p120)

➡ Ambar (p125)

➡ Toki Underground (p117)

➡ Ethiopic (p120)

For reviews, see p117.

🍷 **Best Places to Drink**

➡ Copycat Co (p121)

➡ Tune Inn (p121)

➡ Bluejacket Brewery (p121)

➡ Granville Moore's (p121)

➡ Little Miss Whiskey's Golden Dollar (p122)

➡ Bardo Brewing (p122)

For reviews, see p121.

◉ TOP SIGHT
US CAPITOL

The political center of the US government and geographic heart of the District, the US Capitol sits atop a high hill overlooking the National Mall and the wide avenues flaring out to the city beyond. The towering 288ft cast-iron dome, ornate fountains and marble Roman pillars set on sweeping lawns scream: 'This is DC.'

Background & History

Since 1800, the Capitol is where the legislative branch of the US government – ie Congress – has met. The lower House of Representatives (435 members) and upper Senate (100 members) meet respectively in the south and north wings of the building.

Pierre L'Enfant chose the site for the Capitol in his original 1791 city plans; construction began in 1793. George Washington laid the cornerstone, anointing it with wine and oil in Masonic style. In 1814, midway through construction, the British marched into DC and burnt the Capitol (and much of the city) to the ground. The destruction tempted people to abandon Washington altogether, but the government finally rebuilt both city and structure. In 1855 the iron dome (weighing nine million pounds) was designed, replacing a smaller one; the House and Senate wings were added in 1857. The final touch, the 19ft *Statue of Freedom* sculpture, was placed atop the dome in 1863.

Visiting the Building

The **Capitol Visitor Center** (Map p300) sits below the East Plaza and is where all visits begin. Tours are free, but you need a ticket. Get one at the information desk, or reserve online

DON'T MISS

➡ Constantino Brumidi frieze around rotunda

➡ *Freedom* sculpture atop dome

➡ Hall of Statues

➡ Summerhouse

➡ Military bands playing on Capitol steps

PRACTICALITIES

➡ Map p300, D3

➡ ☏202-226-8000

➡ www.visitthecapitol.gov

➡ 1st St NE & E Capitol St

➡ admission free

➡ ⊙8:30am-4:30pm Mon-Sat

➡ Ⓜ Orange, Silver, Blue Line to Capitol South

in advance (there's no fee). It's a good idea to make reservations between March and August.

The hour-long jaunt starts with a cheesy film where you'll hear a lot about 'E Pluribus Unum' (Out of Many, One) and how the US government works. Then staff members lead you to the good stuff.

Inside the halls and ornate chambers you really get a feel for the power-playing side of DC. The centerpiece of the Capitol is the magnificent Rotunda (the area under the dome). It's 96ft in diameter and 180ft high. A Constantino Brumidi frieze around the rim replays more than 400 years of American history. Look up into the eye of the dome for the *Apotheosis of Washington,* an allegorical fresco by Brumidi.

The Capitol also contains sculptures of two famous residents per state. Many of these are found in the Hall of Statues. You might recognize likenesses of George Washington (Virginia) and Ronald Reagan (California), less so Uriah Milton Rose (Arkansas). After the tour, swing by the Exhibition Hall and check out the plaster model for the *Statue of Freedom* that crowns the dome.

Note you cannot bring any food or drinks inside the building. Security staff will make you get rid of them before entering.

Capitol Grounds

The Capitol's sweeping lawns owe their charm to famed landscape architect Frederick Law Olmsted, who also designed New York City's Central Park. During the Civil War, soldiers camped in Capitol halls and stomped around its lawns. In 1874, spring cleaning was in order: Olmsted added lush greenery and majestic terraces, creating an elegant landscape that gave rise to more than 4000 trees from all 50 states and many countries. Northwest of the Capitol is the charming 1879 Summerhouse, a redbrick hexagon with black-iron gates and an interior well. This is where women, back in the day, came to stay cool in their big hoop dresses during the warmer months.

At the base of Capitol Hill, the Capitol Reflecting Pool (p73) echoes the larger Reflecting Pool by the Lincoln Memorial at the Mall's western end. The Capitol Pool actually caps the I-395 freeway, which dips under the Mall here. The ornate Ulysses S Grant Memorial dominates the pool's eastern side, showing the general in horseback action.

VISITING THE HOUSE & SENATE FLOORS

To watch Congress in session, you need a separate pass. US citizens must get one from their representative or senator; foreign visitors should take their passports to the House and Senate Appointment Desks on the upper level. Congressional committee hearings are more interesting if you care about what's being debated; check for a schedule, locations and to see if they're open to the public (they often are) at www.house.gov and www.senate.gov. Prepare to go through rigid security; you'll have to store most of your belongings before entering the chambers.

BANDS

The Army, Navy, Marine Corps and Air Force bands take turns performing on the steps of the Capitol on weekdays (except Thursday) June through August. Look for them at 8pm on the West Front.

TOP SIGHT
UNITED STATES HOLOCAUST MEMORIAL MUSEUM

For a deep understanding of the Holocaust, this harrowing museum is a must-see. It gives visitors the identity card of a single Holocaust victim, whose story gets revealed as you plunge into a past marked by ghettos, rail cars and death camps. It also shows the flip side of human nature, documenting the risks many citizens took to help the persecuted.

Design
James Ingo Freed designed the extraordinary building in 1993, and its stark facade and steel-and-glass interior echo the death camps themselves. Look up at the skylight in the Hall of Witness when you enter the building. Many survivors say this reminds them of the sky above the camps. For them it was symbolic: the only thing the Nazis couldn't control.

Permanent Exhibit
The permanent exhibit presents the Holocaust's history chronologically from 1933 to 1945. Galleries span three floors and use more than 900 artifacts, 70 video monitors, historic film footage and eyewitness testimonies.

Start on the 4th floor, which is titled 'Nazi Assault' and covers the period between 1933 and 1939. Watch propaganda videos of Hitler, Goebbels and others, and learn how the Nazis used modern techniques such as video to craft their message and sway citizens.

The 3rd floor is 'The Final Solution,' covering the period between 1940 and 1945. Here you'll see a rail car used to transport people to the camps, a wooden bunk bed from Auschwitz and a harrowing scale model of Crematorium II at Auschwitz. There's also a listening room where you can hear recordings of people speaking about their experiences in the camps.

The 2nd floor is the 'Last Chapter,' where old film footage shows the camps' liberation, and videos flicker across screens illuminating individual survivors telling their stories.

Hall of Remembrance & Wexner Center
As you exit the permanent exhibit, you come out into the candlelit Hall of Remembrance, a sanctuary for quiet reflection. The Wexner Center is likewise on this floor, featuring exhibits on other genocides around the world. The museum is a major advocate against, and information clearing-house on, current acts of genocide such as those in Darfur. Here's something you'll learn: the word genocide didn't exist until 1944. That's when Raphael Lemkin, a Jewish refugee from Poland, coined it to describe what was happening in German-occupied Europe.

Entry Tickets
Same-day passes to view the permanent exhibit are required March through August, available at the pass desk on the 1st floor. The passes allow entrance at a designated time. Arrive early because they do run out. Better yet, reserve tickets in advance via the museum's website for a $1 surcharge.

DON'T MISS
➡ Hall of Remembrance
➡ Skylight in the Hall of Witness
➡ Propaganda videos
➡ Survivor testimonies
➡ Wexner Center

PRACTICALITIES
➡ Map p300, A3
➡ ☎202-488-0400
➡ www.ushmm.org
➡ 100 Raoul Wallenberg Pl SW
➡ admission free
➡ ⏱10am-5:20pm, extended hours Apr–mid-Jun
➡ ☐Circulator, ⓂOrange, Silver, Blue Line to Smithsonian

The world's largest library, with 164 million books, manuscripts, maps, photos, films and other items, awes in both scope and design. A browse through turns up everything from Thomas Jefferson's dusty tomes to 500-year-old maps to Revolutionary War cartoons.

The library spreads through three buildings. The centerpiece is the 1897 Jefferson Building, where you can wander around the spectacular Great Hall, done up in stained glass, marble sculptures and mosaics of mythical characters. Multimedia kiosks provide details on all of it.

Pick up a map at the entrance, which will take you to top draws such as the Gutenberg Bible (c 1455) on the 1st floor. The 2nd floor holds Thomas Jefferson's round library – or to be more precise – a reconstruction of it, though several of the books are really his. It was Jefferson's personal collection of 6487 volumes that formed the library's foundation. Also on the 2nd floor are the Waldseemuller World Map from 1507 (the first to show America) and the overlook into the Main Reading Room. Guides lead free hour-long tours from the ground floor information desk at 10:30am, 11:30am, 12:30pm, 1:30pm, 2:30pm and 3:30pm that take in the highlights.

A groovy underground tunnel runs from the Jefferson Building to the **Madison Building** (⊘8:30am-9:30pm Mon-Fri, to 5pm Sat) FREE, where the Madison Cafe hides on the 6th floor and offers swell views of the city. Room 140 is where staff members issue library cards to anyone who wants to do research. The **Adams Building** (120 2nd St SE; ⊘8:30am-4:30pm Mon-Sat) FREE is the third part of the complex. It's used mostly by researchers. Check www.loc.gov/loc/events for the day of your visit. The library puts on free lectures, concerts and films throughout its multibuilding complex regularly.

DON'T MISS

➡ Great Hall

➡ 1507 Waldseemuller World Map

➡ Main Reading Room overlook

➡ Thomas Jefferson's library

➡ Gutenberg Bible

PRACTICALITIES

➡ Map p300, E3

➡ ☏202-707-8000

➡ www.loc.gov

➡ 101 Independence Ave SE

➡ admission free

➡ ⊘8:30am-4:30pm Mon-Sat

➡ Ⓜ Orange, Silver, Blue Line to Capitol South

1. Dome, US Capitol p106
The *Apotheosis of Washington*, in the dome, is an allegorical fresco by Constantino Brumidi.

2. United States Holocaust Memorial Museum p108
The permanent exhibit presents the Holocaust's history chronologically from 1933 to 1945.

3. Union Station p113
Detail of the statue of Columbus at the front of Union Station.

4. Supreme Court p112
The highest court in the United States.

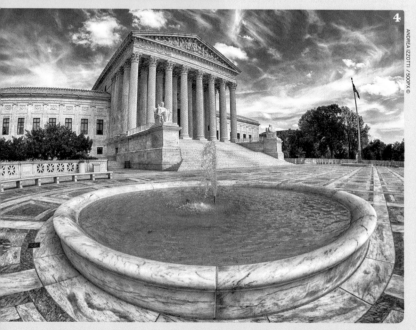

◉ SIGHTS

◉ Capitol Hill

US CAPITOL LANDMARK
See p106.

HOLOCAUST MUSEUM MUSEUM
See p108.

LIBRARY OF CONGRESS LIBRARY
See p109.

SUPREME COURT LANDMARK
Map p300 (📞202-479-3030; www.supremecourt.gov; 11st St NE; ⏱9am-4:30pm Mon-Fri; Ⓜ Orange, Silver, Blue Line to Capitol South) **FREE** The highest court in the USA sits in a pseudo-Greek temple protected by 13,000lb bronze doors. Arrive early to watch arguments (periodic Monday through Wednesday October to April). You can visit the permanent exhibits and the building's five-story, marble-and-bronze, spiral staircase year-round. On days when court is not in session you can also hear lectures (every hour on the half-hour) in the courtroom. When departing, be sure to exit via the doors that lead to the regal front steps.

To attend arguments, lines form out front by the court steps starting at 8am. There are usually two queues: one for people who wish to sit through the entire argument, and another for people who want to observe the court in session for 10 to 15 minutes. Bring quarters to use for lockers; you're not allowed to take anything into the courtroom.

When the building was erected in 1935, some justices felt it was too large and didn't properly reflect the subdued influence of the nine justices within. The neoclassical design was meant to evoke a Greek temple. The seated figures in front of the building represent the female Contemplation of Justice and the male Guardian of Law; panels on the front doors depict the history of jurisprudence. The interior grand corridor and Great Hall are no less impressive. Downstairs is an exhibit on the history of the court. Friezes within the courtroom also depict legal history and heroes.

NATIONAL POSTAL MUSEUM MUSEUM
Map p300 (📞202-633-5555; www.postalmuseum.si.edu; 2 Massachusetts Ave NE; ⏱10am-5:30pm; 👶; Ⓜ Red Line to Union Station) **FREE** The Smithsonian-run Postal Museum is way cooler than you might think. Level 1 has exhibits on postal history from the Pony Express to modern times, where you'll see antique mail planes and touching old letters from soldiers and pioneers. Level 2 holds the world's largest stamp collection. Join the stamp geeks pulling out drawers and snapping photos of the world's rarest stamps (the Ben Franklin Z Grill!), or start your own collection, choosing from among thousands of free international stamps (Guyana, Congo, Cambodia...).

The museum is kid-friendly and hosts story times and card-making workshops. It also has a stamp shop where you can browse the catalog of oddball US Postal Service stamps and have the 'philatelic clerk' (excellent job title) fetch your selection. Many of the stamps are hot off the press and aren't available elsewhere.

FOLGER SHAKESPEARE LIBRARY LIBRARY
Map p300 (📞202-544-4600; www.folger.edu; 201 E Capitol St; ⏱10am-5pm Mon-Sat, noon-5pm Sun; Ⓜ Orange, Silver, Blue Line to Capitol South) **FREE** Bard-o-philes will be all aflutter here, as the library holds the largest collection of old Billy's works in the world. Stroll through the Great Hall to see Elizabethan artifacts, paintings, etchings and manuscripts. The highlight is a rare First Folio that you can peek at. Pop into the evocative on-site theater (p123), a replica of the Elizabethan Globe Theatre; it's worth returning in the evening to catch a show.

The centerpiece, however, is the library's reading rooms, closed to all but scholars, except on Shakespeare's birthday (April 23) and during weekend tours (noon to 1pm Saturday and 1pm to 2pm Sunday; book online in advance). Here you'll find most of the library's most valued Elizabethan artifacts, paintings, etchings and manuscripts. The Shakespeare bust on the east end wall is one of only two approved likenesses.

Docents also give hour-long tours (11am, 1pm and 3pm Monday through Saturday,

---

ℹ STREET ADDRESSES

In Capitol Hill, different streets in close proximity can have the same letter, depending on whether they are north or south of E Capitol St (ie A St NE is just two blocks north of A St SE). Pay attention to the directional (NE or SE) to avoid confusion.

noon and 3pm Sunday) of the building and exhibitions; no reservations are required for those. An Elizabethan garden, full of flowers and herbs cultivated during Shakespeare's time, blooms on the building's eastern end.

The Folger building itself is notable for being the most prominent example of the modernist-classical hybrid movement that swept Washington, DC, during the Great Depression. Jokingly referred to as 'Stark Deco,' it tends to inspire strong feelings: lovers say it elegantly pays homage to Greek classicism and 20th-century modernism, while haters say it ruins both styles.

BELMONT-PAUL WOMEN'S EQUALITY NATIONAL MONUMENT
HISTORIC SITE

Map p300 (☑202-546-1210; www.nps.gov/bepa; 144 Constitution Ave NE; ⊙9am-5pm Wed-Sun; MRed Line to Union Station) FREE This brick house, only steps from the US Capitol, may not look like much, but throughout the 20th century it was ground zero for women fighting for their rights. Multimillionaire socialite and suffragist Alva Belmont helped purchase the house in 1929 for the National Woman's Party. Activist Alice Paul lived here for 43 years, spearheading rallies and demonstrations. Designated a national monument in 2016 – the only one dedicated to women's history – it's now a house museum filled with fascinating artifacts celebrating women's historical achievements.

National park rangers give tours, or you can explore the two floors of displays on your own. The little gift shop sells feminist books and suffragette-focused souvenirs. The entrance is on 2nd St, next to the Hart Senate Office Building. As an interesting historical aside, Robert Sewall built the original two-story brick house in 1799. He later rented it to Albert Gallatin, secretary of the treasury, who likely wrote the Louisiana Purchase agreement here.

UNION STATION
LANDMARK

Map p300 (☑202-289-1908; www.unionstation dc.com; 50 Massachusetts Ave NE; ⊙24hr; MRed Line to Union Station) DC's main rail and bus hub, a 1907 beaux-arts beauty designed by Daniel Burnham, is an eye popper. The Grand Concourse is patterned after the Roman Baths of Diocletian and is awash in marble and gold filigree. Besides being an architectural gem, the station features an arcade of beyond-the-norm shops and fast-food restaurants. At the time of research, scaffolding covered various parts of the interior. Renovations to polish, expand and modernize the facility are due for completion in late 2020.

More than 90,000 visitors pass through the busy station daily. When walking around the main hall, take a moment to check out the legionnaire statues atop the arches that span the entrances and exits. Although shields are strategically placed across their waists, the guys' man-bits are visible. They are supposed to be anatomically correct, but rumor holds that only one was built that way.

NATIONAL PUBLIC RADIO
NOTABLE BUILDING

(☑202-513-2000; http://tours.npr.org; 1111 N Capitol St NE; ⊙tours 11am Mon-Fri; MRed Line to NoMa) FREE Fans of *Morning Edition* and *All Things Considered* can see where the magic happens at National Public Radio's eco-friendly headquarters. Hour-long tours peek into the newsroom and high-tech production studio. The guides – usually former employees – entertain with insider stories. Reservations required. The on-site shop sells nifty gifts such as the Nina Totin' bag (named for longtime reporter Nina Totenberg).

BARTHOLDI PARK
GARDENS

Map p300 (cnr 1st St SW & Independence Ave SW; ⊙sunrise-sunset; ◻Circulator, MOrange, Silver, Blue Line to Federal Center) FREE Beautifying a traffic island at the rear of the United States Botanic Garden, this modest showcase of sustainable and accessible landscape design has at its centerpiece the bronze-coated, cast-iron *Fountain of Light and Water* (1876) by Frédéric Auguste Bartholdi, creator of the Statue of Liberty. Benches, rocking chairs and tables dot the grounds. It's a sweet little refuge where you can escape the Mall crowds.

TAFT MEMORIAL CARILLON
MONUMENT

Map p300 (Constitution Ave NW, btwn New Jersey Ave & 1st St NW; ⊙24hr; MRed Line to Union Station) What is that chiming you hear every hour and quarter-hour? It's the 27 bells of the Taft Memorial Carillon, built to honor Senator Robert A Taft from Ohio in 1959. The 100ft marble tower is part of the Capitol grounds.

CAPITOL HILL & SOUTH DC SIGHTS

NATIONAL JAPANESE
AMERICAN MEMORIAL   MONUMENT

Map p300 (www.njamemorial.org; btwn Louisiana Ave, New Jersey Ave & D St NW; ⊘24hr; MRed Line to Union Station) Tucked back from the road and providing a peaceful sanctuary, the memorial centers on a statue of two cranes bound with barbed wire. During WWII, some 120,000 Japanese Americans were held in internment camps as suspected 'enemy aliens.' Even as this discrimination occurred under government mandate, hundreds of their relatives enrolled in the all–Japanese American 442nd Infantry Regiment, which went on to become the war's most decorated American combat unit. The memorial honors both the soldiers and interred civilians.

LINCOLN PARK   PARK

Map p300 (E Capitol St, btwn 11th & 13th Sts NE; ⊘5am-midnight; MOrange, Silver, Blue Line to Eastern Market) Lincoln Park is the lively center of Capitol Hill's east end. Joggers and stroller-pushing families zip past the **Emancipation Memorial** (Map p300; near E Capitol St & 12th St NE), a statue of a chained slave kneeling at Lincoln's feet. Freed black slaves raised the funds to erect it in 1876, but the slave's supplicant position makes it DC's most bizarrely uncomfortable monument. Across the park, the **Mary McLeod Bethune Memorial** (Map p300; near E Capitol St & 13th St NE) is DC's first statue of a black woman. Bethune was an educator and founder of the National Council of Negro Women.

⊙ Southeast DC

FREDERICK DOUGLASS
NATIONAL HISTORIC SITE   HISTORIC SITE

(📞202-426-5961; www.nps.gov/frdo; 1411 W St SE; ⊘9am-5pm Apr-Oct, to 4:30pm Nov-Mar; MGreen Line to Anacostia then B2 bus) FREE Escaped slave, abolitionist, author and statesman Frederick Douglass occupied this beautifully sited hilltop house from 1878 until his death in 1895. Original furnishings, books, photographs and other personal belongings paint a compelling portrait of both the private and public life of this great man. Keep an eye out for his wire-rim eyeglasses on his roll-top desk. Visits into the home – aka Cedar Hill – are by guided tour only.

Tour times are 9am, 12:15pm, 1:15pm, 3pm and 3:30pm (plus 4pm from April to October). It's best to reserve a ticket online (for a $1.50 fee, at www.recreation.gov) at least a day in advance, though unreserved tickets are available at the site's visitor center on a first-come basis.

The B2 bus runs from the Metro station to a stop right in front of Cedar Hill. However, you can't catch the return bus from the house. Instead, walk three blocks north to Good Hope Rd and get the B2 bus to the Metro there.

YARDS PARK   PARK

Map p300 (www.capitolriverfront.org/yards-park; 355 Water St SE; ⊘7am-2hr past sunset; MGreen Line to Navy Yard) The riverside green space is just down the road from the Nationals'

THE WHARF

The Southwest Waterfront has long been home to the Maine Avenue Fish Market (p119), but the area was otherwise unremarkable – until the Wharf shot up. The huge complex of restaurants, hotels, entertainment venues, parks and piers officially opened in late 2017, and now it buzzes.

The public piers are the niftiest bits. The Transit Pier has a winter ice rink, summer mini-golf course and small outdoor stage for free concerts. The Georgetown water taxi departs from here, hence the name. The District Pier is the longest dock, jutting well out into the Washington Channel and hosting a big stage for festivals. The Recreation Pier makes for a fine stroll with its benches, swinging seats and boathouse for kayak and paddleboard rentals.

Loads of eateries sit waterside, including branches of Shake Shack (p137), Taylor Gourmet (p119), Hank's Oyster Bar (p150) and Dolcezza (p148). Swanky new spots seem to open weekly. The Anthem (p123) and Pearl Street Warehouse (p124) are fab venues for live music. Politics and Prose (p126) brings the books. And more is on the way, as you'll see from the ongoing construction that will add to the Wharf for the next several years.

stadium. There are shaded tables by the water, a wooden boardwalk, fountains you can splash in and a funky modernist bridge that looks like a giant, open-faced plastic straw. Free concerts take place on summer Fridays at 6:30pm. Several restaurants and bars at the park's edge ensure you won't go hungry or thirsty.

MARINE BARRACKS   NOTABLE BUILDING

Map p300; www.barracks.marines.mil/Parades/General-Information; cnr 8th & I Sts SE; ⊘parade 8:45pm Fri May-Aug; MOrange, Silver, Blue Line to Eastern Market) FREE The 'Eighth and Eye Marines' are on largely ceremonial duty at the nation's oldest Marine Corps post. Most famously, this is the home barracks of the Marine Corps Band, once headed by John Philip Sousa, king of the military march, who was born nearby at 636 G St SE. On Friday evenings in summer the 1¼-hour ceremonial drill parade featuring the band, drum and bugle corps and silent drill team draws crowds. Reserve online as early as possible; tickets become available March 1.

You can also show up for general admission at 8pm when they distribute any unclaimed tickets. In addition, the band performs on summer Tuesdays at 7pm at the Marine Corps War Memorial by Arlington National Cemetery; no reservations are required for that one.

ANACOSTIA COMMUNITY MUSEUM   MUSEUM

(☎202-633-4820; www.anacostia.si.edu; 1901 Fort Pl SE; ⊘10am-5pm; MGreen Line to Anacostia then bus W2 or W3) FREE This Smithsonian museum has rotating exhibitions on the experience of diverse and underserved communities in the USA. They typically focus on art (quilts of a certain region; landscape paintings by an overlooked artist) or history (the first black baseball teams in the area; a slave family's story). The museum also serves as a community hall for the surrounding neighborhood of Anacostia. Call ahead, since it often closes between installations.

You'll likely have the place to yourself, as this is the Smithsonian's least-visited museum. It's not the easiest to reach by public transport. From the Metro station, take the 'Local' exit to Howard Rd and transfer to the W2 or W3 bus. The W2 runs during rush hours, the W3 every 30 minutes. A car (there's free parking) or rideshare works best to get here.

THEARC   ARTS CENTER

(☎202-889-5901; www.thearcdc.org; 1901 Mississippi Ave SE; ⊘11am-7pm Mon-Fri, 10am-2pm Sat; MGreen Line to Southern Ave) FREE The Town Hall Education, Arts and Recreation Campus (THEARC) has been a cornerstone for community redevelopment in River East and Far Southeast. A multipurpose community center, arts education campus and performance space, the sleek building was the first one of its kind in what was then a neglected area of town. If you want a sense of the pulse of contemporary African American DC, catch a show or see one of the center's frequent special exhibitions.

THEARC is about a half-mile from the closest Metro; it's easiest to drive here.

11TH STREET BRIDGE PARK   PARK

Map p300 (www.bridgepark.org; 11th St SE & riverfront; MGreen Line to Navy Yard) FREE It won't come to fruition until late 2019 or so, but keep an eye on the space at 11th St SE and the Anacostia River. The city is converting the piers from an old bridge into a mod park that will span the water, linking the prosperous Navy Yard district to the neglected Anacostia neighborhood. Play spaces, public art, urban agriculture and kayak and canoe launches will all be part of the $45-million project.

⊙ Southwest DC

UNITED STATES HOLOCAUST MEMORIAL MUSEUM   MUSEUM
See p108.

BUREAU OF ENGRAVING & PRINTING   LANDMARK

Map p294 (☎202-874-2330; www.moneyfactory.gov; cnr 14th & C Sts SW; ⊘9-10:45am, 12:30-3:45pm & 5-6pm Mon-Fri Mar-Aug, reduced hours Sep-Feb; Circulator, MOrange, Silver, Blue Line to Smithsonian) FREE Cha-ching! The nation's paper currency is designed and printed here. Guides lead 40-minute tours during which you peer down onto the work floor where millions of dollars roll off the presses and get cut (by guillotine!). It's actually a pretty dry jaunt; don't expect exciting visuals or snappy dialogue. In peak season (March to August), timed entry tickets are required. Get in line early at the **ticket kiosk** (Map p294; Raoul Wallenberg Pl/15th St; ⊘from 8am Mar-Aug; Circulator, MOrange,

Silver, Blue Lines to Smithsonian). It opens at 8am. Tickets are often gone by 10am.

During non-peak season (September through February), no tickets are required and you can come in through the main entrance at 14th and C Sts; tours take place every 15 minutes from 9am to 10:45am and from 12:30pm to 2pm.

The building is expected to undergo structural renovations starting in late 2018; tours will continue to run, but there may be tweaks to the scheduled times, so call or check the website before heading out.

INTERNATIONAL SPY MUSEUM   MUSEUM

Map p300 (☏202-393-7798; www.spymuseum.org; 955 L'Enfant Plaza SW; adult/child $23/15; ⊙9am-7pm mid-Apr–mid-Aug, 10am-6pm rest of year; 🚻; ⓂBlue, Orange, Silver Line to L'Enfant Plaza Station) One of DC's most popular museums, the International Spy Museum is flashy, over the top, and probably guilty of overtly glamming up a life of intelligence-gathering. But who cares? You basically want to see Q's lab, and that's what the Spy Museum feels like. Check out James Bond's tricked-out Aston Martin, the KGB's lipstick-concealed pistol and more. Kids go crazy for this spot, but be warned: lines form long and early. Ease the wait somewhat by reserving online.

There are all kinds of artifacts and interactive displays, and guests are invited to play the role of a secret agent by adopting a cover at the start of their visit. You can try to identify disguises, listen to bugs and spot hidden cameras throughout the museum. A lot of the exhibits are historical in nature, focusing on the Cold War in particular (a re-creation of the tunnel under the Berlin Wall is an eerie winner). The museum also offers several tours, such as 'Spy in the City' ($15), a sort of GPS-driven scavenger hunt across DC. The museum moved to its new digs at L'Enfant Plaza in fall 2018.

EAST POTOMAC PARK   PARK

Map p300 (Ohio Dr SW; ⓂOrange, Silver, Blue Line to Smithsonian) Although only a stone's throw from the National Mall, for tourists, East Potomac Park may as well be in Siberia. The pleasant, green, cherry-blossom-lined expanse is a lovely spot for walking, fishing and general gamboling. Cyclists flock to the scenic 5-mile loop that Ohio Dr

makes as it zips around the park's circumference. The East Potomac Park golf course lies at the center.

The park sits on a finger of land that extends southward from the Tidal Basin into the Potomac River. On foot, you can access it by following trails that lead from the Thomas Jefferson Memorial under the bridges. If you drive out this way, you can park on the shoulder of Ohio Dr.

HAINS POINT   AREA

(East Potomac Park; ⓂOrange, Silver, Blue Line to Smithsonian) The southern tip of East Potomac Park that juts out into the river is called Hains Point. Lots of folks come here to picnic, and the spot provides great views of the planes taking off from nearby Reagan National Airport.

MUSEUM OF THE BIBLE   MUSEUM

Map p300 (☏855-554-5300; www.museumofthebible.org; 400 4th St SW; suggested donation $15; ⊙10am-5pm; ⓂOrange, Silver, Blue Line to Federal Center SW) Opened in 2017, the museum spans six floors with exhibits on the history and impact of the Bible. It has scholarly displays, like those on the 4th floor, where ancient Torah scrolls, a 1200-year-old Jewish prayer book and heaps of bibles through the ages are encased. It's also a bit like a theme park – at the 3rd floor's World of Jesus exhibit, live people re-enact scenes from Jesus' time, and a flashy multimedia walk takes you through Old Testament stories.

There's also a restaurant, theater and changing exhibitions where you might see religious art or Vatican artifacts. While the museum states it is nonsectarian, there's a conservative Christian tint to it.

Admission is by donation, but you need a ticket to enter. Get one at the ticket desk. The entrance is at 4th and D Sts SW.

WOMEN'S TITANIC MEMORIAL   MEMORIAL

Map p300 (waterfront & P St SW; ⓂGreen Line to Waterfront) The red-granite memorial honors the men who died aboard the sinking ship. It was paid for by a group of women (hence the name) who wanted to commemorate the heroes who stood aside to let women and children go first in the lifeboats. The statue's outstretched arms look a lot like Kate Winslet's pose in the 1997 film *Titanic,* but the sculptor carved it in 1931.

CONGRESSIONAL CEMETERY: FAMOUS TOMBS & HAPPY DOGS

It is jarring the first time you see a dachshund lower its haunches and poo right next to a tombstone. Some people say it's disrespectful. Others say the dogs saved Washington, DC's **Congressional Cemetery** (Map p300; ☎202-543-0539; www. congressionalcemetery.org; 1801 E St SE; ⊙sunrise-sunset; ⓂOrange, Silver, Blue Lines to Potomac Ave) FREE.

Founded in 1807, the burial ground had become a forlorn place of crack deals and toppled monuments by the 1990s. But then a group of locals had an idea: turn the graveyard into a members-only dog park, and use the fees to restore the site.

It's now a lovely spot to ramble, and the cemetery has done a fab job documenting the dead. Pick up maps at the entrance (at 18th and E Sts) to find famed civil rights heroes, global explorers, beer brewers, War of 1812 officers, and loads of other people you should know. Favorite spirits to seek out:

➡ Mathew Brady: The Civil War photographer is known as the father of photo-journalism. He took the picture of Lincoln that's now on the $5 bill.

➡ Belva Lockwood: Ran for US president in 1884 as the Equal Rights Party's candidate, and yes, she was aware women didn't have voting rights at the time. She still got 4000 votes.

➡ J Edgar Hoover: The infamous FBI director has a grave that's surrounded by a fence and faces DC's jail.

Just watch out for loping black labs, stick-chasing Yorkies and other members of the K9 Corps patrolling the stony rows. Incidentally, there's a year-long waiting list to join the pack.

AMERICAN VETERANS DISABLED FOR LIFE MEMORIAL
MEMORIAL

Map p300 (www.avdlm.org; 150 Washington Ave SW; ⓂOrange, Silver, Blue Line to Federal Center SW) Oddly situated in a triangular plaza between drab federal buildings and busy roadways, this subtle memorial opened in late 2014. It's dedicated to the more than four million US soldiers who have returned home with life-changing disabilities. It features a still, star-shaped fountain, glass-etched walls and benches for contemplation.

✖ EATING

Hip, upscale eateries have colonized the neighborhood, especially along Pennsylvania Ave, Barracks Row (especially 8th St SE, near the Marine Barracks) and around the Navy Yard and Wharf. H St NE, east of Union Station, has seen lots of action. The formerly beat-up area continues to transform with scads of fun, offbeat restaurants and bars stretching from 4th to 14th Sts NE.

★CHIKO
ASIAN $

Map p300 (☎202-558-9934; www.chikodc.com; 423 8th St SE; mains $9-18; ⊙5-11pm Mon-Thu, to midnight Fri & Sat, to 10pm Su; ⓂOrange, Silver, Blue Line to Eastern Market) ChiKo stands for Chinese and Korean, and it fuses the cuisine with low-key style. Dishes such as pork and kimchi potstickers and chilled acorn noodles wow the foodie masses: it's highbrow fare at a budget price. The restaurant is fast-casual in set up: order at the counter, then try to score one of the handful of picnic tables in the fluorescent-lit room.

Another option is to reserve a seat at the back counter and do a $50 tasting menu; you'll have to plan well ahead to book it.

★TOKI UNDERGROUND
ASIAN $

Map p300 (☎202-388-3086; www.toki underground.com; 1234 H St NE; mains $13-15; ⊙11:30am-2:30pm & 5-10pm Mon-Thu, to midnight Fri & Sat; ⓂRed Line to Union Station then streetcar) Spicy ramen noodles and dumplings sum up wee Toki's menu. Steaming pots obscure the busy chefs, while diners slurp and sigh contentedly. The eatery takes limited reservations, so there's typically a wait. Use the opportunity to explore

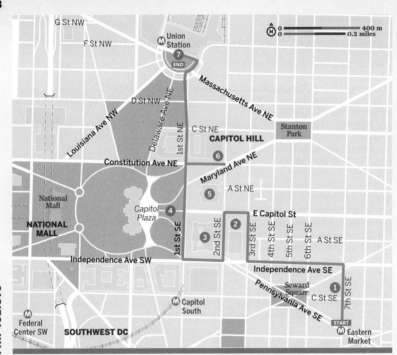

🚶 Neighborhood Walk
Cap Hill Crawl

START EASTERN MARKET METRO
END UNION STATION
LENGTH 2 MILES; THREE TO FOUR HOURS

Start by fueling up at ①**Eastern Market** (p126), a short distance north of the Eastern Market Metro station. This is the true heart of Capitol Hill: a neighborhood hangout, a covered bazaar and just a great place to soak up local flavor.

Walk west on Independence Ave SE toward the Capitol Dome, which is pretty hard to miss. At 3rd St SE, detour a couple of blocks north to the ②**Folger Shakespeare Library** (p112). The building, jokingly referred to as 'Stark Deco,' holds the world's largest collection of Shakespeare's works, along with cool exhibits. Get ready for a literary comparison, because our next stop is the ③**Library of Congress** (p109). Pop in for an excellent guided tour of the impressive building.

Now go underground into the ④**Capitol Visitor Center** (p106). You can easily spend two or more hours here learning about the seat of the legislative branch of government (ie Congress). Across the street the government's judiciary branch, the ⑤**Supreme Court** (p112), rises up in Greek temple–esque splendor. If you happen to stumble upon the day of an interesting case, you may find that your tour comes to an abrupt, albeit serendipitous end – watching verbal arguments conducted in front of the nine justices is an opportunity you shouldn't pass up.

Make another detour to the museum at the ⑥**Belmont-Paul Women's Equality National Monument** (p113), home base of the National Woman's Party since 1929, and 43-year residence of the party's legendary founder, suffragette Alice Paul. US women: she's why you can vote.

Return to 1st St NE and head north until you get to ⑦**Union Station** (p113). This is one of the masterpieces of the early-20th-century beaux-arts movement, patterned after the Roman Baths of Diocletian. We like to think even an emperor would be awed by the sights just traversed.

the surrounding bars; Toki will text when your table is ready. The restaurant isn't signposted; look for the Pug bar, and Toki is above it.

The only reservations accepted are for weekday lunch times and from 5pm to 6pm for dinner.

MAINE AVENUE FISH MARKET   SEAFOOD $
Map p300 (1100 Maine Ave SW; mains $7-13; ⊙8am-9pm; Ⓜ Orange, Silver, Blue, Yellow, Green Line to L'Enfant Plaza) The pungent, open-air Maine Avenue Fish Market is a local landmark. No-nonsense vendors sell fish, crabs, oysters and other seafood so fresh it's almost still flopping. They'll kill, strip, shell, gut, fry or broil your selection, which you can take to the waterfront benches and eat blissfully (mind the seagulls!).

The surrounding area – aka the Wharf (p114) – is being heavily redeveloped with shiny condos, offices and retailers. The market, too, is getting some renovations (more seating, a plaza for entertainment, a new oyster house), but overall it's slated to retain its salty ambience.

DANGEROUSLY DELICIOUS PIES   AMERICAN $
Map p300 (☑202-398-7437; www.dangerous piesdc.com; 1339 H St NE; slices $6.50-8.50; ⊙9am-midnight Mon, 11am-midnight Tue-Thu, 9am-3:30am Fri & Sat, 9am-10pm Sun; ☑; Ⓜ Red Line to Union Station then streetcar) The eponymous wares come in both sweet and savory varieties, which means you can – without shame – make a meal of pie. Pull up a chair in the red-walled, rock-and-roll art-filled room and scan the chalkboard for options like vegan vegetable pie, SMOG (steak-mushroom-onion-Gruyere) pie and the mega-rich, cookie-infused Baltimore Bomb. Bonus: they serve alcohol to go with the flaky goodness.

GOOD STUFF EATERY   BURGERS $
Map p300 (☑202-543-8222; www.goodstuff eatery.com; 303 Pennsylvania Ave SE; burgers $7-9; ⊙11am-10pm Mon-Sat; ☑; Ⓜ Orange, Silver, Blue Line to Capitol South or Eastern Market) 🍴 Spike Mendelsohn (of *Top Chef* TV fame) is the cook behind Good Stuff, a popular burgers-shakes-and-fries spot. You can top off fries at the 'dipping bar' of various sauces, and the toasted-marshmallow milkshake comes with an honest-to-god toasted marshmallow. The ambience is that of a fast-food joint,

and seats are at a premium weekend nights, when Cap Hill youth descend on the place.

JIMMY T'S   DINER $
Map p300 (☑202-546-3646; 501 E Capitol St; mains $6-10; ⊙6:30am-3pm Tue-Fri, from 8am Sat & Sun; ☑; Ⓜ Orange, Silver, Blue Line to Capitol South or Eastern Market) Jimmy's is a neighborhood joint of the old school, where folks come in with their dogs, cram in to read the *Post,* have a burger or a coffee or an omelet (breakfast all day, by the way) and basically be themselves. If you're hungover on Sunday and in Cap Hill, come here for a greasy cure. Cash only.

PRETZEL BAKERY   BAKERY $
Map p300 (☑202-450-6067; www.thepretzel bakery.com; 257 15th St SE; items $2.50-8; ⊙7am-6pm Mon-Fri, 8am-5pm Sat & Sun; Ⓜ Orange, Silver, Blue Line to Potomac Ave) Who doesn't adore soft pretzels warm from the oven? Get a mustard or gooey cheese dip to enhance the experience, along with coffee, beer or basil lemonade. This little spot is a neighborhood favorite, especially in the morning when locals line up for the revered cheddar-bacon-egg breakfast sandwich (on a pretzel bun, of course).

Prefer sweet to savory? The glazed pretzel with warm, melted Nutella inside will do the trick. Order at the counter, then enjoy at the umbrella-shaded benches on the patio.

PITANGO GELATO   GELATO $
Map p300 (☑202-701-6222; www.pitango gelato.com; 660 Pennsylvania Ave SE; gelato $5-7; ⊙noon-9pm Mon-Thu, 11am-10pm Fri, 11am-9pm Sat & Sun, closed Mon winter; Ⓜ Orange, Silver, Blue Line to Eastern Market) The DC mini-chain scoops terrific all-natural gelato, but the sorbet is the standout. Fruity flavors made from Haitian mangoes, white grapefruits and Bosc pears from a nearby farm explode on the tongue. Staff are very sweet (pun!) about letting you try lots of samples.

TAYLOR GOURMET   DELI $
Map p300 (☑202-684-7001; www.taylorgourmet. com; 1116 H St NE; sandwiches $8-13; ⊙11am-9pm Sun-Thu, to 3:30am Fri & Sat; Ⓜ Red Line to Union Station then streetcar) When you just need a good sandwich, Taylor has got you covered. You can walk out of here with a foot of excellent anything between two pieces of Italian seeded bread. We race here

for the Race Street – turkey, prosciutto, pesto and mozzarella. Several other branches of the local chain dot the DC area.

★ ETHIOPIC
ETHIOPIAN $$

Map p300 (☏202-675-2066; www.ethiopic restaurant.com; 401 H St NE; mains $14-20; ⊙5-10pm Tue-Thu, from noon Fri-Sun; ✍; Ⓜ Red Line to Union Station) In a city with no shortage of Ethiopian joints, Ethiopic stands above the rest thanks to its warm, stylish ambience. Top marks go to the various *wats* (stews) and the signature *tibs* (sautéed meat and veg), derived from tender lamb that has sat in a bath of herbs and hot spices. Vegans get lots of love here too.

TED'S BULLETIN
AMERICAN $$

Map p300 (☏202-544-8337; www.tedsbulletin capitolhill.com; 505 8th St SE; mains $12-20; ⊙7am-10:30pm Sun-Thu, to 11:30pm Fri & Sat; ✍; Ⓜ Orange, Silver, Blue Line to Eastern Market) Plop into a booth in the art-deco-meets-diner ambience, and loosen the belt. Beer biscuits and sausage gravy for breakfast, meatloaf with ketchup glaze for dinner and other hipster spins on comfort foods hit the table. You've got to admire a place that lets you substitute pop tarts for toast. Breakfast is available all day and pulls big crowds on weekends.

MONTMARTRE
FRENCH $$

Map p300 (☏202-544-1244; www.montmartre dc.com; 327 7th St SE; mains $20-30; ⊙11:30am-2:30pm & 5:30-10pm Tue-Fri, 10:30am-3pm & 5:30-10:30pm Sat, 10:30am-3pm & 5:30-9pm Sun; Ⓜ Orange, Silver, Blue Line to Eastern Market) Montmartre is the place French expats take their friends to give them a taste of home. Great wines, very fine steak, silky homemade pâté and delightful desserts emerge from clanging pans in the kitchen. The cozy space is cluttered in a *maman's*-dining-room kinda way, and the overall vibe is much more neighborhood spot than highbrow restaurant.

SEVENTH HILL PIZZA
PIZZA $$

Map p300 (☏202-544-1911; www.montmartredc. com/seventhhill; 327 7th St SE; pizzas $11-17; ⊙11:30am-2:30pm & 5-10pm Tue-Fri, 11:30am-10pm Sat, noon-9pm Sun; Ⓜ Orange, Silver, Blue Line to Eastern Market) It's just blistered, thin-crust pizza, but it's soooo addictive. Each pie is named for a local street or park, like the 'Potomac Ave,' topped with Felino salami and arugula, or the 'Maryland Ave' with egg, pesto and pecorino. Seventh Hill is the

sibling of genial Montmartre (p120) next door, and some of the French wines find their way over to accompany the pizzas.

LE GRENIER
FRENCH $$

Map p300 (☏202-544-4999; www.legrenierdc. com; 502 H St NE; mains $19-27; ⊙5-10pm Tue-Thu, 5-11pm Fri, 11am-11pm Sat, 11am-10pm Sun; Ⓜ Red Line to Union Station) This romantic French bistro, set in an exposed-brick row house and spread over two floors, checks all the boxes: buttery escargot, rich cheese plates, great wines, vintage Left Bank ambience. Order a sparkling aperitif, a saucy mushroom crepe or the beef bourguignon and pretend you're across the Atlantic.

SALT LINE
SEAFOOD $$

Map p300 (☏202-506-2368; www.thesaltline. com; 79 Potomac Ave SE; mains $18-30; ⊙5-10pm Sun-Thu, 11am-3pm & 5-10:30pm Fri & Sat; Ⓜ Green Line to Navy Yard) With lovely river views and a buzzy crowd, Salt Line is a Navy Yard hot spot, especially during Nats games. Take a seat inside amid modern nautical decor, or outside at the open-air bar and commence slurping regional oysters and top-notch draft beers, or maybe a lobster roll and twisted Cape Cod cocktail. It's pricey, but you're paying for the seaside vibe.

MARKET LUNCH
AMERICAN $$

Map p300 (☏202-547-8444; www.marketlunch dc.com; 225 7th St SE; mains $9-22; ⊙7:30am-2:30pm Tue-Fri, 8am-3pm Sat, 9am-3pm Sun; Ⓜ Orange, Silver, Blue Line to Eastern Market) The popular food stall sits smack in the middle of Eastern Market. The ingredients are local and fresh, plucked from surrounding vendors. The fried-oyster sandwich is a lunchtime favorite, while the blueberry-buckwheat pancakes slay for breakfast. Eat at the long communal table or outside at the picnic tables. Cash only.

★ ROSE'S LUXURY
AMERICAN $$$

Map p300 (☏202-580-8889; www.rosesluxury. com; 717 8th St SE; small plates $13-16, family-style plates $28-36; ⊙5-10pm Mon-Sat; Ⓜ Orange, Silver, Blue Line to Eastern Market) Michelin-starred Rose's is one of DC's most buzzed-about eateries. Crowds fork into worldly Southern comfort food as twinkling lights glow overhead and candles flicker around the industrial, half-finished room. Rose's doesn't take reservations, but ordering your meal at the upstairs bar can save time (and the cocktails are delicious).

The pork sausage, habanero and lychee salad wow, as does the staff, which has an uncanny knack for treating everyone right. Rose's is the rare place that lives up to its hype. The line starts forming by 4:30pm.

PINEAPPLE AND PEARLS   AMERICAN $$$

Map p300 (☑202-595-7375; www.pineappleand pearls.com; 715 8th St SE; tasting menu $225-325; ☺seatings 5pm & 8pm Tue-Fri & occasional Sat; ⓂOrange, Silver, Blues Line to Eastern Market) Local celeb chef Aaron Silverman operates this kicky restaurant that has a pair of Michelin stars and features a 12-course tasting menu of wild takes on comfort foods. He is often around and explaining the dishes – maybe a sweetbread-stuffed chicken wing, or potato ice cream with chocolate and fried chestnuts. Reservations open online at 10am Monday for dates five weeks in advance. Seating at the bar sans drinks puts you at the low end of the price range. Seating in the dining room and at the chef's counter with drink pairings is most expensive. The fee covers tax and tip.

If you can't score a reservation, Silverman's other restaurant – Rose's Luxury (no reservations, but likely a line) – sits next door.

BEUCHERT'S SALOON   AMERICAN $$$

Map p300 (☑202-733-1384; www.beucherts saloon.com; 623 Pennsylvania Ave SE; small plates $9-19; ☺5:30-10pm Mon, 11am-2:30pm & 5:30-10pm Tue-Thu & Sun, 11am-2:30pm & 5:30-11pm Fri & Sat; ⓂOrange, Silver, Blue Line to Eastern Market) Beuchert's has an old-timey, hipster vibe with antique wallpaper and sweet cocktails. It takes the locally sourced concept seriously, and everyone who works at the restaurant also has to work on the owner's farm in Maryland, where the chicken, eggs and vegetables come from. The playful dishes span cardamom-braised cabbage to horseradish egg custard to pork and sweet-potato dumplings. It's all lovely.

DRINKING & NIGHTLIFE

The boozing atmosphere on Capitol Hill, still very much a residential neighborhood, is one of those cozy pubs where policy talk gives way to Redskins predictions in the NFL. H St NE is a funky contrast to the Hill's red-brick conviviality. **The Navy Yard area around Nats Park has hip breweries and a winery.**

★COPYCAT CO   COCKTAIL BAR

Map p300 (☑202-241-1952; www.copycat company.com; 1110 H St NE; ☺5pm-2am Sun-Thu, to 3am Fri & Sat; ⓂRed Line to Union Station then streetcar) When you walk into Copycat it feels like a Chinese fast-food restaurant. That's because it is (sort of) on the 1st floor, where Chinese street-food nibbles are available. The fizzy drinks and egg-white-topped cocktails fill glasses upstairs, in the dimly lit, speakeasy-meets-opium-den-vibed bar. Staff are unassuming and gracious in helping newbies figure out what they want from the lengthy menu.

★TUNE INN   BAR

Map p300 (☑202-543-2725; 331 Pennsylvania Ave SE; ☺8am-2am Sun-Thu, to 3am Fri & Sat; ⓂOrange, Silver, Blue Line to Capitol South or Eastern Market) Tune Inn has been helping the thirsty since 1947. Mounted deer heads stare from the wall and watch over old-timers knocking back Budweisers at the bar. Meanwhile, Hill staffers, off-duty cops and other locals scarf greasy-spoon grub and all-day breakfasts in the vinyl-backed booths. How do you know when you're in a first-rate dive? When your beer-and-shot combo glows under the dim light of an antler chandelier.

★BLUEJACKET BREWERY   BREWERY

Map p300 (☑202-524-4862; www.bluejacketdc. com; 300 Tingey St SE; ☺11am-1am Sun-Thu, to 2am Fri & Sat; ⓂGreen Line to Navy Yard) Beer-lovers' heads will explode in Bluejacket. Pull up a stool at the mod-industrial bar, gaze at the silvery tanks bubbling up the ambitious brews, then make the hard decision about which of the 20 tap beers you want to try. A dry-hopped kolsch? Sweet-spiced stout? A cask-aged farmhouse ale? Four-ounce tasting pours help with decision-making.

★GRANVILLE MOORE'S   PUB

Map p300 (☑202-399-2546; www.granville moores.com; 1238 H St NE; ☺5pm-midnight Mon-Thu, 5pm-1am Fri, 11am-1am Sat, 11am-midnight Sun; ⓂRed Line to Union Station then streetcar) Besides being one of DC's best places to grab frites and a steak sandwich, Granville Moore's has an extensive Belgian beer menu that should satisfy any fan of low-country boozing. With its raw, wooden fixtures and walls that look as if they were made from

CAPITOL HILL & SOUTH DC DRINKING & NIGHTLIFE

daub and mud, the interior resembles a medieval barracks. The fireside setting is ideal on a winter's eve.

★ LITTLE MISS WHISKEY'S GOLDEN DOLLAR
BAR

Map p300 (www.littlemisswhiskeys.com; 1104 H St NE; ⊙5pm-2am Sun-Thu, to 3am Fri & Sat; Ⓜ Red Line to Union Station then streetcar) If Alice had returned from Wonderland so traumatized by her near beheading that she needed a stiff drink, we imagine she'd pop down to Little Miss Whiskey's. She'd love the whimsical-meets-dark-nightmares decor. And she'd probably have fun with the club kids partying on the upstairs dancefloor on weekends. She'd also adore the weirdly fantastic back patio.

The excellent beer and whiskey menu and savvy staff make this feel like a bartender's bar.

★ BARDO BREWING
BEER GARDEN

Map p300 (www.facebook.com/bardobrewing; 25 Potomac Ave SE; ⊙5pm-midnight Mon-Fri, from 1pm Sat & Sun, closed Nov-early Mar; Ⓜ Green Line to Navy Yard) Sprawled by the river in the shadow of Nationals Park, Bardo feels post-apocalyptic. Silver fermentation tanks rise from the dirt, dogs lope around rusted shipping containers, and a wire fence encircles it all. It rarely feels crowded (because it's huge), and almost always is relaxed with bearded types hobnobbing over beers. The suds tend toward brawny stouts and India Pale Ales.

The setting is exceptional, though the beers can be hit or miss. Food trucks often swing by. If there's an afternoon Nats game, Bardo opens two hours prior.

MR HENRY'S
PUB

Map p300 (⌕202-546-8412; www.mrhenrysdc. com; 601 Pennsylvania Ave SE; ⊙11:15am-midnight Mon-Fri, from 10am Sat & Sun; Ⓜ Orange, Silver, Blue Line to Eastern Market) Lots of regulars hang out at this pub, a scruffy, Victorianesque cornerstone that some call the Cheers of Capitol Hill, which has been around for 50-plus years. The upstairs room hosts live music Wednesday through Saturday, mostly jazz; a $15 minimum applies Friday and Saturday, $12 the other nights. Wednesday's Jazz Jam is worth the trip.

SIDAMO COFFEE & TEA
CAFE

Map p300 (⌕202-548-0081; www.sidamo coffeeandtea.com; 417 H St NE; ⊙7am-7pm Mon-Fri, 8am-6pm Sat, 8am-5pm Sun; 🛜; Ⓜ Red Line to Union Station) Owned by an Ethiopian family, Sidamo offers excellent, organic African coffee, tasty and strong as hell. There's friendly staff and that just-right bohemian atmosphere. You can use the wi-fi and smell the beans roasting and write books while blustery days go by. On Sunday at 2pm, the family puts on a free Ethiopian coffee ceremony; all customers are invited to participate.

DISTRICT WINERY
WINERY

Map p300 (⌕202-484-9210; www.districtwinery. com; 385 Water St SE; ⊙11:30am-10pm Mon-Thu, 11:30am-10:30pm Fri, 11am-10:30pm Sat, 11am-9pm Sun; Ⓜ Green Line to Navy Yard) Is the wine made here world class? No. But the space is really cool. It's enormous, with steel tanks fermenting the juice in back, and a clean-lined, blond wood, Scandinavian-looking room in front. Light streams in floor-to-ceiling windows, which provide ace views

H STREET CORRIDOR

H St NE rolls out several blocks of awesomeness east of Union Station. Cool coffee houses, fun bars, pie cafes, noodle shops, rock halls and more stack up all the way to 14th St. Most cluster between 4th and 6th Sts, and between 11th and 14th Sts.

The road was once one of Washington's major shopping strips. That was before the race riots of 1968, which gutted the area. It has had a comeback in recent years, thanks to a profusion of creative businesses. The Atlas Performing Arts Center (p124) was one of the leaders of the charge, which is why the area is sometimes referred to as the Atlas District.

H St rocks hardest at night. By day it's a bit deserted and edgy. The district's long-awaited streetcars have helped energize the scene. They clang from Union Station past all the H St hot spots. Check www.dcstreetcar.com for route info. Otherwise, the corridor is about a 25-minute walk from Union Station.

of the river. The outdoor patio beckons in summer. It's a swell Navy Yard spot for a glass or two.

There's a tasting bar in back; expect a wait on weekends. The front room is also a restaurant that serves modern American dishes.

H STREET COUNTRY CLUB BAR

Map p300 (☎202-399-4722; www.hstcountry club.com; 1335 H St NE; ⊙4pm-1am Mon-Thu, 4pm-3am Fri, 11:30am-3am Sat, 11:30am-1am Sun; Ⓜ Red Line to Union Station then streetcar) The Country Club is three levels of great. The bottom floor is packed with pool tables, skeeball and shuffleboard, while the upper floor contains its own minigolf course ($9 to play) done up to resemble a small-scale Washington. You putt-putt past a trio of Lego lobbyists, through Beltway traffic snarls and past a King Kong–clad Washington monument. A rooftop deck sits on top.

The whole vibe of the place just facilitates a relaxed atmosphere where it's very easy to strike up conversations with locals – if you're shy and new to town, we'd highly recommend joining the Country Club.

PEREGRINE ESPRESSO COFFEE

Map p300 (☎202-629-4381; www.peregrine espresso.com; 660 Pennsylvania Ave SE; ⊙7am-8pm Mon-Sat, 8am-8pm Sun; 🛜; Ⓜ Orange, Silver, Blue Line to Eastern Market) The local mini-chain wins lots of 'best coffee' awards, and locals agree it's the real caffeinated deal. Join the laptop pack and sip your foam art in the sleek interior or on the outdoor patio.

☆ ENTERTAINMENT

★ **NATIONALS PARK** STADIUM

Map p300 (☎202-675-6287; www.mlb.com/ nationals; 1500 S Capitol St SE; 🛜; Ⓜ Green Line to Navy Yard) The major-league Washington Nationals play baseball at this spiffy stadium beside the Anacostia River. Don't miss the mid-fourth-inning 'Racing Presidents' – an odd foot race between giant-headed caricatures of George Washington, Abraham Lincoln, Thomas Jefferson and Teddy Roosevelt. Hip bars and eateries and playful green spaces surround the ballpark, and more keep coming as the area gentrifies.

Catch a game if you can. The Nats act as a strong social glue among DC's transients

and natives. And tickets can be cheap, starting at around $18.

ANTHEM CONCERT VENUE

Map p300 (☎202-888-0020; www.theanthemdc. com; 901 Wharf St SW; ⊙box office noon-7pm; Ⓜ Orange, Silver, Blue, Yellow, Green Line to L'Enfant Plaza or Green Line to Waterfront) The Anthem opened in 2017 and has quickly become one of DC's best live-music venues. The 6000-capacity hall books acts from Judas Priest to Lorde to Big Sean, though rock is the mainstay genre. Most tickets are general admission to stand on the floor. Get in line early on show day, and you could be front row for your favorite band.

ROCK & ROLL HOTEL LIVE MUSIC

Map p300 (☎202-388-7625; www.rockandroll hoteldc.com; 1353 H St NE; Ⓜ Red Line to Union Station then streetcar) The R&R Hotel is a great, grotty spot to catch rockin' live sets from the likes of Thurston Moore, St Vincent and the Dead Kennedys. Don't let the name fool you; the venue hosts all kinds of genres besides rock, from Afrofunk to indie, punk and hip hop, too. It only holds 400 people, so you're always close to the action.

The building was once a funeral parlor, and some say it's haunted by lingering spirits.

ARENA STAGE THEATER

Map p300 (☎202-554-9066; www.arenastage. org; 1101 6th St SW; tickets from $55; Ⓜ Green Line to Waterfront) The mod, glassy Arena Stage is the second-largest performing-arts complex in Washington after the Kennedy Center. The three theaters inside (including a theater-in-the-round) are top venues for traditional and experimental works, especially American classics, premieres of new plays and contemporary stories. Arena Stage was the city's first racially integrated theater and has continued its progressive tradition through performances addressing African American history.

FOLGER THEATRE THEATER

Map p300 (☎202-544-7077; www.folger.edu/ folger-theatre; 201 E Capitol St; tickets from $30; Ⓜ Orange, Silver, Blue Line to Capitol South) The 250-seat, Renaissance-style theater attached to the Folger Shakespeare Library stages classic and modern interpretations of the bard's plays, as well as new works inspired by Shakespeare. Literary readings (including the PEN/Faulkner series) and great programs for children are also all part of the venue's repertoire.

With its three-tiered wooden balconies, half-timbered facade and sky canopy, the theater evokes an inn courtyard, where troupes often staged plays in Shakespeare's day.

AUDI FIELD
SOCCER

Map p300 (☎202-587-5000; www.dcunited.com; 1711 1st St SW; Ⓜ Green Line to Navy Yard) Multiple-time Major League Soccer champions DC United play March through October at shiny new Audi Field, opening mid-2018. Tickets start at around $30. The team's fans are legendarily loud and diehard, and there's a raucous pre-game tailgating scene.

ATLAS PERFORMING
ARTS CENTER
PERFORMING ARTS

Map p300 (☎202-399-7993; www.atlasarts. org; 1333 H St NE; tickets $15-35; ⊗box office 1-6pm Mon-Fri; Ⓜ Red Line to Union Station then streetcar) All kinds of indie goodness get performed at the art-deco Atlas, from operettas to innovative new plays, ethnic dance shows and cabaret music. Four theaters inside host the goings on. The lobby cafe provides drinks and puts on a free concert series of its own.

PEARL STREET WAREHOUSE
LIVE MUSIC

Map p300 (☎202-380-9620; www.pearlstreet warehouse.com; 33 Pearl St SW; ⊗8:30am-1am Tue & Wed, to 2am Thu-Sat, to midnight Sun; Ⓜ Orange, Silver, Blue, Yellow, Green Line to L'Enfant Plaza or Green Line to Waterfront) This small Wharf venue has a rootsy feel, like it could be set in Austin or Nashville. Blues, country and rock bands take the stage, including the occasional big name. Tickets typically cost between $10 and $20. The attached diner serves breakfast, burgers and beer.

🔒 SHOPPING

⭐ CAPITOL HILL BOOKS
BOOKS

Map p300 (☎202-544-1621; www.capitol hillbooks-dc.com; 657 C St SE; ⊗11:30am-6pm Mon-Fri, from 9am Sat & Sun; Ⓜ Orange, Silver, Blue Line to Eastern Market) A trove of secondhand awesomeness, this shop has so many books staff have to double-stack them on the shelves. Superb notes by the cantankerous clerks help guide your selection. Cat-

🏃 Local Life
A Local's Day
on Capitol Hill

Pretend you're a resident of one of the brownstone homes along the red-brick sidewalks and shop for seafood at Eastern Market or browse the Flea Market's curios. Have breakfast anytime in a dive bar, then stop by the rambling, double-stacked bookshop. Share small plates and drinks with friends, and wave to neighbors at the riverside park.

❶ The Dive Bar: Tune Inn
Tune Inn (p121) has been around for decades and is where the neighborhood's older residents come to down beers. The mounted deer heads and antler chandelier set the mood, as greasy-spoon grub and all-day breakfasts get gobbled in the vinyl-backed booths.

❷ Capitol Hill Books
Rambling Capitol Hill Books has so many used tomes they're stacked two deep on the shelves. They're even stacked in the bathroom. Floors creak and classical music plays as neighborhood bibliophiles sift through the whopping selection.

❸ Eastern Market
Eastern Market (p126) is the true heart of Capitol Hill. Vendors selling baked goods, cheeses, meats, seafood and produce fill the covered arcade. It's not that large... until the weekend, when artisans and farmers join the fun and the market spills onto the street.

❹ Flea Market Finds
On weekends the Flea Market (p126) sets up in the street adjacent to Eastern Market, doubling the browsing acreage. Vendors sell art, antiques, furniture, maps, prints, global wares, clothing and curios. Sunday is the busier day, with more stalls.

❺ Street Art at the Fridge
First you have to find the **Fridge** (Map p300; ☎202-664-4151; www.instagram.com/ thefridgedc; 516½ 8th St SE, rear alley; ⊗1-7pm Thu & Fri, noon-7pm Sat, noon-5pm Sun; Ⓜ Orange, Silver, Blue Lines to Eastern Market) FREE, a friendly gallery specializing in street art. Follow the murals into the alley

Capitol Hill Books

across 8th St from Ambar restaurant. The Fridge's opening times can be erratic, but at least you'll see lots of cool paintings en route.

⑥ Meet Friends at Ambar

Ambar (Map p300; ☎202-813-3039; www.ambarrestaurant.com; 523 8th St SE; small plates $7-13; ⊙11am-2pm & 4-10pm Mon-Thu, to 11pm Fri, 10am-11pm Sat, 10am-10pm Sun; Ⓜ Orange, Silver, Blue Lines to Eastern Market) buzzes, especially at happy hour, when the convivial restaurant slings heaps of small plates. Roasted pepper and eggplant, lamb salami, brandy-soaked mussels – tables of friends share intriguing Balkan dishes (alongside drinks, of course).

⑦ Dinner at Rose's Luxury

Locals line up for shabby-chic Rose's Luxury (p120), which offers a small, changing menu of 10 or so plates a day. The pork sausage, habanero and lychee salad is the salty-sweet dish on everyone's lips.

⑧ River Views at Yards Park

Lovely Yards Park (p114) is a sculpted public space with a wooden board-walk, excellent river views, a funky modernist bridge and a mini tidal pool that is popular with neighborhood families on summer evenings.

egories are, er, unconventional, including 'Hinduism and Bobby Knight' and 'Sideshows and Carnivals.' The section on US presidents is huge (Chester Arthur books! An entire shelf of Truman books!).

Bookworms will find vintage cookbooks and mystery novels in abundance. Be sure to check the table outside for any freebies on offer.

EASTERN MARKET
MARKET

Map p300 (202-698-5253; www.eastern market-dc.org; 225 7th St SE; 7am-7pm Tue-Fri, to 6pm Sat, 9am-5pm Sun; Orange, Silver, Blue Line to Eastern Market) One of the icons of Capitol Hill, this roofed bazaar sprawls with delectable chow and good cheer, especially on the weekend. Built in 1873, it is the last of the 19th-century covered markets that once supplied DC's food. The South Hall has a bakery, a dairy, a fishmonger, butchers, flower vendors, and fruit and vegetable sellers.

The Market Lunch (p120) stall sells prepared foods and is a crowd favorite for its oyster sandwiches and blueberry-buckwheat pancakes.

Come the weekend, the market grows massively in size. Artisans and farmers bring their wares and set up outside. Besides fresh apples, peppers, eggplants and other produce, you can pick up handmade soaps, colorful pottery, painted ceramics and unusual jewelry. A flea market also joins the fun, plunking more booths along 7th St and adding antiques, clothing and global goods to the browsing acreage. The scene basically becomes a big street fair.

FLEA MARKET
MARKET

Map p300 (www.easternmarket.net; 7th St SE, btwn C St & Penn Ave; 10am-5pm Sat & Sun; Orange, Silver, Blue Line to Eastern Market) On weekends an outdoor flea market sets up on a two-block stretch of 7th St SE, adjacent to Eastern Market. Vendors sell all kinds of cool art, antiques, furniture, maps, prints, global wares, clothing, crafts and curios. Sunday is the bigger day, with more stalls.

REI WASHINGTON DC FLAGSHIP STORE
SPORTS & OUTDOORS

(202-543-2040; www.rei.com/stores/ washington-dc.html; 201 M St NE; 10am-9pm Mon-Sat, 11am-7pm Sun; Red Line to NoMa-Gallaudet U) Who says Washington isn't an adventure city? This 51,000-sq-ft building in the revitalizing NoMa neighborhood – outdoor retailer REI's fifth flagship store – proves it. Peruse an enormous array of outdoor gear and clothing, sign up for a guided local hike, attend a navigation-skills event, or simply sip coffee at the in-house cafe (or around the outdoor fire pit).

POLITICS AND PROSE
BOOKS

Map p300 (202-488-3867; www.politics-prose.com/wharf; 70 District Sq SW; 10am-10pm; Orange, Silver, Blue, Yellow, Green Line to L'Enfant Plaza or Green Line to Waterfront) A small branch of the venerable independent bookshop in Northwest DC, the Wharf Politics and Prose has in-the-know staff, literary readings and lots of love for local authors.

WOVEN HISTORY
ARTS & CRAFTS

Map p300 (202-543-1705; www.woven history.com; 315 7th St SE; 10am-6pm Tue-Sun; Orange, Silver, Blue Line to Eastern Market) It's as if a Silk Road caravan got lost and pitched up near the Eastern Market. The lovely emporium is stuffed with crafts, carpets and tapestries from across Central Asia, Tibet and Mongolia. Unlike a lot of stores of this genre, Woven History feels more like an authentic tented bazaar than a hippie hangout.

HILL'S KITCHEN
HOMEWARES

Map p300 (202-543-1997; www.hillskitchen. com; 713 D St SE; 10am-6pm Tue-Sat, to 5pm Sun; Orange, Silver, Blue Line to Eastern Market) A great variety of spices, cookbooks, whisks, cast-iron pans and other colorful kitchenwares stuff this 1884 townhouse near Eastern Market. Behold the cookie cutters that come in the shape of every US state. The proprietor is welcoming to cooks both pro and novice.

SPORTS & ACTIVITIES

BIKE & ROLL
CYCLING

Map p300 (202-842-2453; www.bikeandrolldc. com; 955 L'Enfant Plaza SW; tours adult/child from $44/34; 9am-8pm, reduced hours spring & fall, closed early Dec–mid-Mar; Orange, Silver, Blue, Yellow, Green Line to L'Enfant Plaza) This branch of the bike-rental company (from $16 per two hours) is the one closest to the

Mall. In addition to bike rental, it also provides tours. Three-hour jaunts wheel by the main sights of Capitol Hill and the National Mall. The evening rides to the monuments are particularly good.

BIKE & ROLL
CYCLING

Map p300 (☏202-842-2453; www.bikeandrolldc.com; 50 Massachusetts Ave NE; bikes per 2hr/day from $16/40; ⏰9am-7pm Jun-Aug, reduced hours Sep-May; Ⓜ Red Line to Union Station) This branch of Bike & Roll is primarily a bicycle service and repair shop, but you can also rent two-wheelers here; the price includes a lock and safety equipment. The shop is on the western side of Union Station, between the station and the National Postal Museum.

BALLPARK BOATHOUSE
KAYAKING

Map p300 (☏202-337-9642; www.boatingindc.com/boathouses/ballpark-boathouse; Potomac Ave SE; single/double kayak per hr $16/22; ⏰noon-8pm Thu & Fri, from 9am Sat & Sun mid-May–mid-Sep; Ⓜ Green Line to Navy Yard) Rent a kayak and glide along the Anacostia River. Keep your eyes open: you might spy a heron spearfishing for its lunch. Guided tours (90 minutes, per person $45) take off at sunset each evening.

ANACOSTIA RIVERWALK TRAIL
WALKING

Map p300 (www.anacostiawaterfront.org; Ⓜ Green Line to Navy Yard) The 20-mile bicycle and pedestrian path runs along both sides of the Anacostia River, rolling past Nationals Park, the Navy Yard and Kenilworth Aquatic Gardens, among other sites.

EAST POTOMAC PARK GOLF COURSE
GOLF

Map p300 (☏202-554-7660; www.golfdc.com; 972 Ohio Dr SW; 9 holes weekday/weekend from $10/13, 18 holes $30/34; ⏰sunrise-sunset; Ⓜ Orange, Silver, Blue Line to Smithsonian) It's a bit scrubby, with three courses (nine-hole red, nine-hole white and 18-hole blue). There's also a year-round driving range and a summer mini-golf course, plus the white course hosts year-round foot golf (a soccer-golf hybrid).

LANGSTON GOLF COURSE
GOLF

(☏202-397-8638; www.golfdc.com; 2600 Benning Rd NE; 18 holes weekday/weekend $25/32; ⏰sunrise-sunset, closed Mon & Tue Jan–mid-Mar; Ⓜ Red Line to Union Station then streetcar) The 18-hole course is part of the National Register of Historic Places for its role in encouraging African American golfers to take up the sport some 80 years ago. The fairways are flat, with lots of trees on the back nine. There's also a driving range. The course fringes the National Aboretum.

Downtown & Penn Quarter

Neighborhood Top Five

❶ National Archives (p130) Gawping at the Declaration of Independence, Constitution and Bill of Rights – the original founding documents of the USA, scrawled in cursive on yellowing parchment.

❷ Reynolds Center for American Art & Portraiture (p131) Browsing the world's largest collection of US art, from George Washington's official portrait to Andy Warhol's pop art.

❸ Ford's Theatre (p134) Seeing the very seat where Abraham Lincoln was assassinated, and the pistol that did the job.

❹ Newseum (p134) Reading the day's newspapers from around the globe and viewing remarkable artifacts from headline stories.

❺ National Building Museum (p134) Beholding the magnificent interior, modeled after a Renaissance-era palace, and imagining the glamorous occasions held here (ie every president's inaugural ball since 1885).

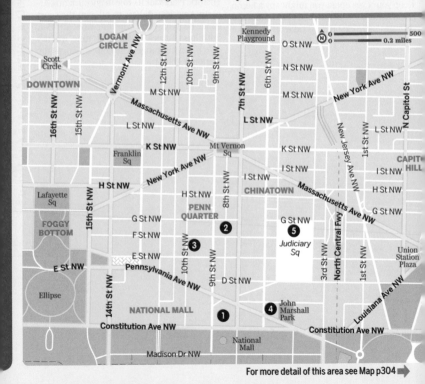

For more detail of this area see Map p304 ➤

Explore Downtown & Penn Quarter

There's a lot going on in the neighborhood, and we recommend allocating at least a full day to do it justice. Start in Penn Quarter, the area's southernmost portion named for its proximity to Pennsylvania Ave. Some of the best sights in the city are here. Take your pick for a morning visit: the National Archives (p130), where the Declaration of Independence lies enshrined for viewing; Ford's Theatre (p134), where John Wilkes Booth shot Abraham Lincoln; or the Newseum (p134), a whiz-bang, multistory collection of artifacts and current-events exhibits. In the afternoon head to the Reynolds Center for American Art & Portraiture (p131) and spend a few hours browsing famed portraits and pieces by a who's who of celebrated US artists. The elegant National Building Museum (p134) is also nearby.

Downtown stretches to the north. It's less about sightseeing and more about commerce. The Convention Center (p136) is here, along with excellent eating and drinking options in Blagden Alley and Chinatown. City-CenterDC (p142) lures shoppers.

And stay after dark. Loads of theater companies put on shows, from political shtick to Shakespeare's plays and experimental works. Something lively is usually going on at Capital One Arena (p142), home of DC's professional basketball and hockey teams. Trendy restaurants and bars keep the night humming. Michelin stars and James Beard Awards are de rigueur around the 'hood; 7th St NW and Blagden Alley are bountiful spots to get in on the action.

Local Life

➡ **Food-Truck Lunch** Join the office workers refueling at the trucks that line up around Franklin Sq, Metro Center and Gallery Place/Chinatown (on 7th and G Sts NW, beside the Reynolds Center).

➡ **Oasis** Locals seeking peace and quiet from downtown's hullabaloo head to the Reynolds Center for American Art & Portraiture (p131) and its 1st-floor interior courtyard of trees and marble benches. Many bring their food-truck lunch to munch.

➡ **Evening Movie** E Street Cinema (p142) is a quirky theater screening independent and foreign movies for neighborhood types.

Getting There & Away

➡ **Metro** All six Metro lines cross downtown, so there are several stations here. The main ones are Metro Center (where the Red, Orange, Silver and Blue Lines hub), Gallery Pl-Chinatown (where the Green, Yellow and Red Lines merge) and Mt Vernon Sq/7th St-Convention Center (on the Green, Yellow Lines).

Lonely Planet's Top Tip

Many restaurants in the neighborhood offer pretheater menus. This generally means a three-course meal for around $35, offered before 6:30pm. Rasika (p137), Brasserie Beck (p140), Jaleo (p137) and Central Michel Richard (p138) are among those that offer good pretheater deals.

 ### Best Places to Eat

➡ Dabney (p139)

➡ A Baked Joint (p138)

➡ Central Michel Richard (p138)

➡ Shouk (p138)

➡ Minibar (p138)

➡ Kinship (p140)

For reviews, see p136.

Best Places to Drink

➡ Columbia Room (p140)

➡ Dabney Cellar (p140)

➡ City Tap House (p140)

➡ La Colombe (p141)

For reviews, see p140.

Best Entertainment

➡ Woolly Mammoth Theatre Company (p141)

➡ Shakespeare Theatre Company (p141)

➡ National Theatre (p141)

➡ Capitol Steps (p141)

➡ E Street Cinema (p142)

For reviews, see p141.

DOWNTOWN & PENN QUARTER

You're in line with excitable school groups, thinking your time might be better spent elsewhere. Then you enter the dim rotunda and see them – the Declaration of Independence, Constitution and Bill of Rights – the USA's founding documents. The Archives has the real, yellowing, spidery-handwriting-scrawled parchments. And your jaw drops. There's John Hancock's signature, and Ben Franklin's and Thomas Jefferson's!

The star documents are laid out in chronological order from left to right in the rotunda. Don't expect to linger over any of them – guards make you keep moving. First up is the Declaration (1776), in which the 13 US colonies announce their sovereignty and rejection of British rule.

Next up is the Constitution (1787), which provides a framework for the new nation's government. The Bill of Rights (1789) unfurls in the next display case. This document lists 10 amendments to the Constitution that safeguard individual liberties, such as freedom of speech and religion.

The Public Vaults hold George Washington's handwritten letters and Abraham Lincoln's wartime telegrams. There's a nifty piece of paperwork from Charles 'Pa' Ingalls (of Little House on the Prairie fame) showing his grant application for 154 acres in the Dakota Territory.

A 1297 version of Magna Carta is on view in the Rubenstein Gallery. It inspired America's founding fathers with its assertion of individual rights and protections against a tyrannical ruler.

In spring and summer reserve tickets in advance on the website for $1.50 each. This lets you go through the fast-track entrance on Constitution Dr (to the right of the steps) versus the general entrance (to the left of the steps), where lines can be lengthy.

DON'T MISS

➡ Declaration of Independence

➡ Constitution

➡ Bill of Rights

➡ Magna Carta

➡ 'Pa' Ingalls' land grant, in the Public Vaults

PRACTICALITIES

➡ Map p304, D7

➡ ☎866-272-6272

➡ www.archives.gov/museum

➡ 700 Pennsylvania Ave NW, Penn Quarter

➡ admission free

➡ ⊙10am-5:30pm

➡ Ⓜ Green, Yellow Line to Archives

REYNOLDS CENTER FOR AMERICAN ART & PORTRAITURE

If you only visit one art museum in DC, make it the Reynolds Center, which combines the National Portrait Gallery and American Art Museum. There is no better collection of American art in the world than at these Smithsonian museums. It occupies three floors in the 19th-century US Patent Office building, a neoclassical beauty that hosted Lincoln's second inaugural ball.

The Experience America gallery (1st floor) hangs block-busters such as Edward Hopper's trapped woman in *Cape Cod Morning* and a slew of 1930s New Deal paintings. The nearby folk-art gallery holds a vivid collection, especially artwork by African American artists. Look for James Hampton's exquisite, foil-made throne.

The America's Presidents gallery (2nd floor) gives due to 44 past heads of state. Gilbert Stuart's rosy-cheeked *George Washington* is the most beloved. The 'cracked plate' photo of Abraham Lincoln is also here. Then seek out *Benjamin Franklin*. You'll recognize the image, as it's the same one that now graces the $100 bill. Ben's portrait enriches the American Origins gallery (1st floor). The 3rd floor has Andy Warhol's pop-art version of Michael Jackson and groovy paintings by David Hockney, Franz Kline, Wayne Thiebaud and modern blue-chip artists. The Luce Center, the museum's open storage area, spills across the 3rd and 4th floors. Wander around the trove to ogle cases of paintings and shelves stacked with sculptures, ceramics and gorgeous objets d'art.

The museum's 1st-floor inner courtyard, roofed with slanting glass and dotted with olive trees and marble benches, is a lovely spot. Bring your own picnic or order sandwiches at the cafe.

DON'T MISS

- ➡ Luce Center
- ➡ Gilbert Stuart's *George Washington*
- ➡ Joseph Siffred Duplessis' *Benjamin Franklin*
- ➡ Edward Hopper's *Cape Cod Morning*
- ➡ James Hampton's *Throne of the Third Heaven of the Nations' Millennium General Assembly*

PRACTICALITIES

- ➡ Map p304, D5
- ➡ ☏202-633-1000
- ➡ www.americanart.si.edu
- ➡ cnr 8th & F Sts NW, Penn Quarter
- ➡ admission free
- ➡ ⊙11:30am-7pm
- ➡ Ⓜ Red, Yellow, Green Line to Gallery Pl-Chinatown

National Cherry Blossom Festival

It's a rite of spring: each year in late March or early April, DC's 3700-plus cherry trees burst into a shimmering sea of pale-pink blossoms. The festival celebrates the occasion, with 1.5 million people descending on the Tidal Basin to revel in the fairy-tale sight and intoxicating scent.

Japan's Gift to DC

In 1912, the mayor of Tokyo gave 3000 cherry trees to Washington, DC, as a gift of friendship between Japan and the USA. It was actually his second gift: the first group of trees arrived two years prior, but insects and disease infested them and they had to be destroyed.

The 1912 batch fared better. First Lady Helen Herron Taft and Viscountess Chinda, wife of the Japanese ambassador, planted the first two trees in West Potomac Park on March 27. Workers placed the rest elsewhere around the Tidal Basin. Since then, the number of trees has expanded to approximately 3750. A crew of dedicated National Park Service arborists tends them.

Festival Dates & Activities

The festival kicks off on March 20 and runs for three weeks or so. Events take place all over town. The highlight is the Cherry Blossom Parade, which occurs the last Saturday of the fest and brings elaborate floats, marching bands and celebrity entertainers for a procession along Constitution Ave. Immediately afterward the Sakura Matsuri Japanese Street Festival lets loose downtown. The Kite Festival swoops and soars by the Washington Monument on a late-March

1. Looking across Tidal Basin towards the Jefferson Memorial p72 2. Cherry Blossom Parade entrant

Saturday, while Petalpalooza's fireworks at the Wharf illuminate the night sky the following weekend. Most events are kid-friendly and free. Photography workshops; boat, bike and walking tours; garden-design seminars; and theater and musical performances are also on offer.

Viewing Tips

Everyone wants to visit during the 'peak bloom' date, when 70% of the blossoms are open. The average peak bloom in recent years has been April 2. Warm weather makes it happen earlier (March 15, 1990, is the record), cold weather makes it happen later (April 18, 1958, wins the prize). The **festival website** (www.nationalcherryblossomfestival.org) tracks the predicted date via its Bloom Watch.

If you miss the Tidal Basin explosion, all is not lost. Smaller groves of cherry trees pop up at the National Arboretum and Dumbarton Oaks, and they usually peak a bit later.

TOP CHERRY BLOSSOM EXPERIENCES

➡ Snapping photos of the shimmering scene from the Jefferson Memorial or Martin Luther King Jr Memorial.

➡ Seeing the trees from the water. Try it DIY-style with a Tidal Basin Boathouse paddleboat or on a guided kayak tour with Key Bridge Boathouse.

➡ Joining the Kite Festival by the Washington Monument.

➡ Wearing pink and readying the confetti for the Cherry Blossom Parade.

◉ SIGHTS

◉ Penn Quarter

NATIONAL ARCHIVES   LANDMARK
See p130.

**REYNOLDS CENTER
FOR AMERICAN ART
& PORTRAITURE**   MUSEUM
See p131.

FORD'S THEATRE   HISTORIC SITE
Map p304 (☎202-347-4833; www.fords.org; 511 10th St NW; ⊗9am-4:30pm; Ⓜ Red, Orange, Silver, Blue Line to Metro Center) `FREE` On April 14, 1865, John Wilkes Booth assassinated Abraham Lincoln here. Timed-entry tickets provide access to the site, which has four parts: the theater itself (where you see the box seat Lincoln was sitting in when Booth shot him), the basement museum (displaying Booth's .44-caliber pistol, his muddy boot etc), Petersen House (across the street, where Lincoln died) and the aftermath exhibits. Arrive early (by 8:30am) because tickets do run out. Better yet, reserve online ($3 fee) to ensure admittance.

The play the president and Mrs Lincoln watched was *Our American Cousin*. Booth knew the farce and knew at what line the audience would laugh most. He shot Lincoln at that moment to muffle the sound. National Park Service rangers are on hand to tell the story.

The theater still holds performances, and sometimes the venue is closed to the public. It's always smart to check the schedule before heading out. Ford's posts it online, or you can call the box office to make sure the site is open. Also, not all entry tickets provide admittance to all four parts of the experience, due to occasional scheduling conflicts. Be sure to check before booking. Allow 1½ hours to see it all.

NEWSEUM   MUSEUM
Map p304 (☎202-292-6100; www.newseum.org; 555 Pennsylvania Ave NW; adult/child $25/15; ⊗9am-5pm Mon-Sat, from 10am Sun; ♿; Ⓜ Green, Yellow Line to Archives) This six-story, highly interactive news museum is worth the admission price. You can delve into the major events of recent years (the fall of the Berlin Wall, September 11, Hurricane Katrina), and spend hours watching moving film footage and perusing Pulitzer Prize–winning photographs. If nothing else, stroll up to the museum's entrance, where the front pages of newspapers from around the world – and every US state – are displayed. Tickets are usable for two consecutive days, so you can always return.

Start at the top level (Level 6), with its awesome terrace views of Pennsylvania Ave up to the Capitol, and work your way down. Level 4 has twisted wreckage from the September 11, 2001, attacks and haunting final images from Bill Biggart's camera (Biggart was the only journalist to be killed that day). Level 3 holds a memorial to journalists killed in pursuit of the truth. Level 2 has video stations where kids read news stories from a teleprompter and 'report' the news in front of a DC backdrop. The concourse level displays FBI artifacts from prominent news stories, such as the Unabomber's cabin and gangster Whitey Bulger's fishing hat.

NATIONAL BUILDING MUSEUM   MUSEUM
Map p304 (☎202-272-2448; www.nbm.org; 401 F St NW; adult/child $10/7; ⊗10am-5pm Mon-Sat, from 11am Sun; ♿; Ⓜ Red Line to Judiciary Sq) Devoted to architecture and urban design, the museum is housed in a magnificent 1887 edifice modeled after the Renaissance-era Palazzo Farnese in Rome. The space has hosted 17 inaugural balls – from Grover Cleveland's in 1885 to Donald Trump's in 2017. It's free to view the glimmering public areas; the admission fee is for the exhibits, which will please architecture buffs. Step inside to see the inventive system of windows and archways that keep the Great Hall bathed in natural light.

Four stories of ornamented balconies flank the dramatic 316ft-wide atrium, and the Corinthian columns rise 75ft high. For more information you can pick up a self-guided-tour brochure at the information desk, or join a free 45-minute docent-led tour (11:30am, 12:30pm and 1:30pm). There's also a nice cafe and a nifty bookstore inside.

The museum's Building Zone for kids is a local secret, where two- to six-year-olds stack block towers, drive toy bulldozers, and otherwise construct and destroy in the hands-on play area.

**FORD'S THEATRE CENTER FOR
EDUCATION AND LEADERSHIP**   MUSEUM
Map p304 (☎202-347-4833; www.fords.org; 514 10th St NW; ⊗9am-4:30pm; Ⓜ Red, Orange, Sil-

ver, Blue Line to Metro Center) **FREE** Across the street from the famous theater where Abraham Lincoln was shot, the center holds a gift shop on its 1st floor, as well as a 34ft tower of Lincoln books (it's actually an aluminum sculpture) – a testament to how much has been written about the 16th president. The 3rd and 4th floors have excellent exhibits covering the aftermath of his assassination. Tickets are free and include the historic theater and Petersen House. Get one at Ford's Theatre box office.

PETERSEN HOUSE   HISTORIC SITE
Map p304 (☎202-347-4833; www.fords.org; 516 10th St NW; ◷9am-4:30pm; MRed, Orange, Silver, Blue Line to Metro Center) **FREE** After being shot at Ford's Theatre, Lincoln was carried across the street to Petersen House. Its three tiny, unassuming rooms create a moving personal portrait of the president's slow and tragic end. He never regained consciousness, and died the next morning in a bed too short for his lanky frame. Entry is free but you need a ticket from the Ford's Theatre box office (across 10th St).

**FEDERAL BUREAU
OF INVESTIGATION**   NOTABLE BUILDING
Map p304 (FBI; www.fbi.gov; 935 Pennsylvania Ave NW; MGreen, Yellow Line to Archives) DC's concrete, brutalist FBI headquarters should be seen, if only to say you have laid eyes on the single ugliest building in the entire District. When it was completed in 1975, architecture critics said it was Orwellian and resembled a dreary factory.

The building is not open to the public, except via a free tour arranged by your Congressional representative one to five months in advance, if you are a US citizen.

FDR MEMORIAL STONE   MEMORIAL
Map p304 (cnr 9th St & Pennsylvania Ave NW; MGreen, Yellow Line to Archives) President Franklin Delano Roosevelt didn't want a grand monument like the one that's now on the Mall. Rather, he said if there was to be a memorial to him, he preferred it to be a plain block about the size of a desk that would be placed in front of the Archives Building. His request was honored in 1965, with this small stone slab.

**NATIONAL LAW ENFORCEMENT
OFFICERS MEMORIAL**   MONUMENT
Map p304 (www.nleomf.com; E St NW, btwn 4th & 5th Sts NW; ◷24hr; MRed Line to Judiciary Sq)

FREE This memorial in Judiciary Sq commemorates US police officers killed on duty since 1794. In the style of the Vietnam Veterans Memorial, names of the dead are carved on two marble walls curving around a plaza; new names are added during a moving candlelight vigil each year in May. Peeking over the walls, bronze lion statues protect their sleeping cubs (presumably as law enforcement officers protect us).

**NAVY MEMORIAL &
NAVAL HERITAGE CENTER**   MONUMENT
Map p304 (☎202-380-0710; www.navymemorial. org; 701 Pennsylvania Ave NW; ◷memorial 24hr, center 9:30am-5pm; MGreen, Yellow Line to Archives) **FREE** The hunched figure of the *Lone Sailor,* warding off the wind with his flipped-up pea coat, is an oft-overlooked memorial in the city. The sailor waits quietly by his duffel in a circular plaza bordered by masts sporting semaphore flags; the space evokes the vastness and the ubiquity of the sea. The Naval Heritage Center, on the same grounds, displays artifacts and a couple of ship models.

**MARTIN LUTHER
KING JR MEMORIAL LIBRARY**   LIBRARY
Map p304 (☎202-727-0321; www.dclibrary.org/ mlk; 901 G St NW; ◷9:30am-9pm Mon-Thu, to 5:30pm Fri & Sat, 1-5pm Sun; MRed, Yellow, Green Line to Gallery Pl-Chinatown) **FREE** Designed by famed modern architect Ludwig Mies van der Rohe, this low-slung, sleek central branch of the DC public-library system is an important community and cultural center. It is closed for renovations until mid-2020, when it is scheduled to reopen with new features, including creative spaces for music production and art-making, a cafe and a rooftop event space.

◉ Downtown

**NATIONAL MUSEUM
OF WOMEN IN THE ARTS**   MUSEUM
Map p304 (☎202-783-5000; www.nmwa.org; 1250 New York Ave NW; adult/child $10/free; ◷10am-5pm Mon-Sat, from noon Sun; MRed, Orange, Silver, Blue Line to Metro Center) The only US museum exclusively devoted to women's artwork fills this Renaissance Revival mansion. Its collection – some 4500 works by 1000 female artists from around the world – moves from Renaissance artists such as Lavinia Fontana to 20th-century works by

Frida Kahlo, Georgia O'Keeffe and Helen Frankenthaler. Placards give feminist interpretations of various art movements. It's free to visit on the first Sunday of each month.

The building's chandeliered interior is gorgeous. Head up the sweeping staircase to the 3rd floor, which is where most of the collection resides. The cafe on the mezzanine level provides a sumptuous refuge. Free chamber-music concerts take place on occasional Wednesdays, typically in winter and spring.

CHINATOWN   AREA
Map p304 (7th & H Sts NW; M Red, Yellow, Green Line to Gallery Pl-Chinatown) DC's dinky Chinatown is anchored on 7th and H Sts NW. It was once a major Asian American entrepôt, but today most Asian Americans in the Washington area live in the Maryland or Virginia suburbs. That said, Chinatown is still an intriguing browse. Enter through Friendship Arch, the largest single-span arch in the world.

LONG VIEW GALLERY   GALLERY
Map p304 (☑202-232-4788; www.longviewgallery dc.com; 1234 9th St NW; ⊙11am-6pm Wed-Sat, noon-5pm Sun; M Green, Yellow Line to Mt Vernon Sq/7th St-Convention Center) FREE Long View specializes in contemporary art by emerging and midcareer artists, including many from the region. The room, with its peeling paint and exposed ducting, is the perfect backdrop for edgy exhibitions of photos, paintings, multimedia and paper art. Exhibitions change monthly. Check before heading out, as the gallery is used for private events and sometimes closes to the public.

TOUCHSTONE GALLERY   GALLERY
Map p304 (☑202-347-2787; www.touchstone gallery.com; 901 New York Ave NW; ⊙11am-6pm Wed-Fri, noon-5pm Sat & Sun; M Red, Orange, Silver, Blue Line to Metro Center) FREE Touchstone Gallery exhibits contemporary pieces created by its 45 member artists. Works cover multiple media, including sculpture, painting and the occasional esoteric installation. The bright, welcoming space always has something innovative going on.

SURRATT HOUSE SITE
(WOK & ROLL)   NOTABLE BUILDING
Map p304 (604 H St NW; M Red, Yellow, Green Line to Gallery Pl-Chinatown) Today this building is the Chinese restaurant Wok & Roll, but in 1865 it was the boarding house where Abraham Lincoln's assassins met and plotted their scheme. Confederate sympathizer Mary Surratt owned and operated the business. She eventually hanged at Fort McNair for her role in Lincoln's murder – the first white woman executed by the US federal government.

WASHINGTON
CONVENTION CENTER   NOTABLE BUILDING
Map p304 (☑202-249-3000; www.dcconvention. com; 801 Mt Vernon Place NW; M Green, Yellow Line to Mt Vernon Sq/7th St-Convention Center) The hulking Convention Center hosts major trade shows, events and the occasional inaugural ball.

EATING

✖ Penn Quarter

DAIKAYA   JAPANESE $
Map p304 (☑202-589-1600; www.daikaya.com; 705 6th St NW; mains $12-14; ⊙11am-10pm Sun-Thu, to midnight Fri & Sat; M Red, Yellow, Green Line to Gallery Pl-Chinatown) Daikaya offers two options. Our favorite is downstairs, which is a casual ramen-noodle shop, where locals swarm in and slurp with friends in the slick wooden booths. Upstairs it's a sake-pouring Japanese *izakaya* (tavern), with rice-bowl lunches and small, fishy plates. Note the upstairs closes between lunch and dinner (ie between 2pm and 5pm).

RED APRON BUTCHERY   DELI $
Map p304 (☑202-524-5244; www.redapron butchery.com; 709 D St NW; mains $5-10; ⊙8:30am-8pm Mon-Fri, from 9am Sat, 9am-5pm Sun; M Green, Yellow Line to Archives) 🍽 Red Apron makes a helluva breakfast sandwich. Plop onto one of the comfy booths and wrap your lips around the ricotta, honey and pine-nut 'aristocrat' or the egg and chorizo 'buenos dias.' They're all heaped onto *tigelle* rolls, a sort of Italian flatbread. Alas, breakfast is served until 10:30am only (2:30pm on weekends). Burgers and fat sandwiches tempt thereafter.

The meat is hormone- and antibiotic-free, from animals humanely and sustainably raised by regional farmers. The surrounding foodie market sells everything from nut butters to duck fat.

TEAISM ASIAN $

Map p304 (☎202-638-6010; www.teaism.com; 400 8th St NW; mains $11-14; ☺7:30am-10pm Mon-Fri, 9:30am-9pm Sat & Sun; Ⓜ Green, Yellow Line to Archives) This small teahouse is unique in the area for its affordable lunch options – hot noodle dishes and fresh bento boxes – and its pleasantly relaxing atmosphere. It's a grand spot for a bite after a day of Mall sightseeing. The salty oat cookies are a local favorite. Wine, beer and sake are also available.

**ASTRO DOUGHNUTS
& FRIED CHICKEN** AMERICAN $

Map p304 (☎202-809-5565; www.astro doughnuts.com; 1308 G St NW; doughnuts $2.50-3.35, chicken $6-8; ☺7:30am-5:30pm Mon-Fri, 9am-5pm Sat, to 3pm Sun; Ⓜ Red, Orange, Silver, Blue Line to Metro Center) Unique doughnut flavors and fried wings – what more do you need? The chicken is the winner, cooked crisp with buttermilk or hot sriracha, though the crème brûlée doughnut also awes as you crunch the sugar crust and strike the creamy center. The chicken is available from 11:30am (11am weekends). You can even get your chicken sandwich on a doughnut 'bun.'

A couple of outdoor tables flank the door, but wee Astro is mostly for takeout.

SHAKE SHACK BURGERS $

Map p304 (☎202-800-9930; www.shakeshack. com; 800 F St NW; mains $5-10; ☺11am-11pm Sun-Thu, to midnight Fri & Sat; Ⓜ Red, Yellow, Green Line to Gallery Pl-Chinatown) The NYC chain has come to DC. The self-proclaimed 'modern roadside burger stand' is beloved for its well-griddled patties under a sweet-and-tangy Shake Sauce, crinkle-cut fries, and milkshakes made with creamy custard. Are the shakes really the nation's best? The endless crowd of happy slurpers provides the answer.

RASIKA INDIAN $$

Map p304 (☎202-637-1222; www.rasika restaurant.com; 633 D St NW; mains $14-28; ☺11:30am-2:30pm Mon-Fri, 5:30-10:30pm Mon-Thu, 5-11pm Fri & Sat; ☑; Ⓜ Green, Yellow Line to Archives) Rasika is as cutting edge as Indian food gets. The room resembles a Jaipur palace decorated by modernist art-gallery curators. Top marks go to the *murgh mussalam,* a plate of juicy tandoori chicken with cashews and quail eggs; and the deceptively simple *dal* (lentils), with just the

right kiss of sharp fenugreek. Vegetarians will feel a lot of love here.

ZAYTINYA MEDITERRANEAN $$

Map p304 (☎202-638-0800; www.zaytinya.com; 701 9th St NW; meze $8-14; ☺11am-10pm Mon & Sun, to 11pm Tue-Thu, to midnight Fri & Sat; ☑; Ⓜ Red, Yellow, Green Line to Gallery Pl-Chinatown) One of the culinary crown jewels of chef José Andrés, ever-popular Zaytinya serves superb Greek, Turkish and Lebanese meze in a long, noisy dining room with soaring ceilings and all-glass walls. It's a favorite after-work meet-up spot for wine, cocktails, and a nibble.

JALEO SPANISH $$

Map p304 (☎202-628-7949; www.jaleo.com; 480 7th St NW; tapas $9-18; ☺11am-10pm Mon, to 11pm Tue-Thu, to midnight Fri, 10am-midnight Sat, to 10pm Sun; Ⓜ Green, Yellow Line to Archives) The tapas thing has been done to death, but star chef José Andrés helped start the trend in DC, and still serves some of the best Spanish cuisine in town. The interior is an Iberian pastiche of explosive color and vintage mural-dom. Garlicky shrimps, beet salad with pistachios and housemade pork sausage with white beans are favorites in the lineup.

HILL COUNTRY BARBECUE BARBECUE $$

Map p304 (☎202-556-2050; www.hillcountry. com/dc; 410 7th St NW; mains $14-22; ☺11am-10pm Mon-Thu, to 11pm Fri, 11:30am-11pm Sat, to 9:30pm Sun; Ⓜ Green, Yellow Line to Archives) Hill Country is an anomaly for DC: a Texas-themed, cowboy-hat-filled joint, which doesn't feel corny; a barbecue spot that serves good smoked meat; and a live-music venue that hosts great honky-tonk shows. The sprawling, down-home space gets crowded on weekends, and the restaurant has been known to run out of its signature victuals by late evening.

During July and August, Hill Country operates a popular alfresco outpost on the lawn of the National Building Museum. Grab a hay-bale seat and join the fun 4pm to 9pm Thursday and Friday, and from noon on weekends.

★**CENTRAL
MICHEL RICHARD** AMERICAN $$$

Map p304 (☎202-626-0015; www.centralmichel richard.com; 1001 Pennsylvania Ave NW; mains $24-34; ☺11:30am-2:30pm Mon-Fri, 5-10pm Mon-Thu, to 10:30pm Fri & Sat, 11am-2:30pm Sun;

Ⓜ Orange, Silver, Blue Line to Federal Triangle) Michel Richard was one of Washington's first star chefs. He died in 2016, but his namesake Central blazes onward. It's a special dining experience, eating in a four-star bistro where the food is old-school, comfort-food favorites with a twist: perhaps lobster burgers, or a sinfully complex meatloaf, or fried chicken that redefines what fried chicken can be.

★ MINIBAR   AMERICAN $$$

Map p304 (☏202-393-0812; www.minibarby joseandres.com; 855 E St NW; tasting menu from $275; ⊙6pm & 8:30pm Tue-Sat; ⓂGreen, Yellow Line to Archives) Whimsical Minibar is a two-Michelin-starred foodie nirvana, where 12 lucky people get wowed by animal bits spun into cotton candy and cocktails frothed into clouds. The tasting menu, determined by chef José Andrés, is delicious and never dull. There's a sense of madcap experimentation among the 20-plus courses, as you'd expect from a molecular gastronomist. Reservations are tough to get.

Bookings become available the first Monday of the month for the following 60 days. If you don't score a reservation, or if you're looking to sample Andrés' famous food but in more casual environs, try his other local restaurants such as Jaleo (p137) and Zaytinya (p137).

FIOLA   ITALIAN $$$

Map p304 (☏202-628-2888; www.fioladc.com; 601 Pennsylvania Ave NW, enter at 678 Indiana Ave NW; mains from $50; ⊙11:30am-2:30pm & 5-10pm Mon-Thu, to 10:30pm Fri, 5-10:30pm Sat, 5-9pm Sun; ⓂGreen, Yellow Line to Archives) Dine among senators and lobbyists at this elegant, upscale trattoria off Pennsylvania Avenue, recipient of an annual Michelin star. Italian chef Fabio Trabocchi – who lords over Fiola Mare (p97) as well – adds panache to a classic Italian menu that showcases pasta and fish: think pappardelle with ragù of Scottish hare, lasagna with morels and truffles, and meatballs with a sunny-side-up egg.

✖ Downtown

★ A BAKED JOINT   CAFE $

Map p304 (☏202-408-6985; www.abakedjoint. com; 440 K St NW; mains $5-11; ⊙7am-3pm Mon-Wed, to 10pm Thu & Fri, 8am-10pm Sat, to

6pm Sun; ⓂRed, Yellow, Green Line to Gallery Pl-Chinatown) Order at the counter then take your luscious, heaped-on-housemade-bread sandwich – perhaps the fried egg and goat cheese on a fluffy biscuit, or the Nutella and banana on whole-wheat sourdough – to a bench or table in the big, open room. Natural light streams in the floor-to-ceiling windows. Not hungry? It's also a great place for a well-made latte. Beer, wine and cocktails are also available. Sweet treats come from sibling Baked & Wired (p95) in Georgetown.

★ SHOUK   ISRAELI $

Map p304 (☏202-652-1464; www.shouk.com; 655 K St NW; mains $10; ⊙11am-10pm; ☑; ⓂGreen, Yellow Line to Mt Vernon Sq/7th St-Convention Center) Fast and casual, Shouk creates big flavor in its vegan menu of Israeli street food, served with craft beer and tap wines. A crazy-good burger made of chickpeas, black beans, lentils and mushrooms gets stuffed into a toasty pita with pickled turnips, arugula and charred onions. The mushroom-and-cauliflower pita and sweet-potato fries with cashew *labneh* (creamy 'cheese') are lip smacking.

Shouk's rustic wood tables, exposed-brick walls and pantry shelves made from repurposed crates give it a funky, industrial vibe. Get ready to wrestle the crowds at lunchtime.

MATCHBOX PIZZA   PIZZA $

Map p304 (☏202-289-4441; www.matchbox restaurants.com; 713 H St NW; 10in pizzas $13-15; ⊙11am-10:30pm Mon-Thu & Sun, to 11:30pm Fri, 10am-11:30pm Sat; ⓂRed, Yellow, Green Line to Gallery Pl-Chinatown) The pizza here has a devout following of gastronomes and the restaurant's warm, exposed-brick interior is typically packed. What's so good about it? Fresh ingredients, a thin, blistered crust baked by angels, and more fresh ingredients. Oh, and the beer list rocks, with Belgian ales and hopped-up craft brews flowing from the taps. Reserve ahead to avoid a wait.

EL SOL   MEXICAN $

Map p304 (☏202-815-4789; www.elsol-dc.com; 1227 11th St NW; tacos $3-3.50, mains $10-16; ⊙10am-1am Sun-Thu, to 2am Fri & Sat; ⓂGreen, Yellow Line to Mt Vernon Sq/7th St-Convention Center) Locals love this sunny little taqueria. They fill the close-set tables at all hours to gobble tacos, tortas and other street foods made using the chef's family recipes. More than 60 types of tequila rattle behind the bar to augment the cheery scene. Alas, the food is average, but if you're hankering for a low-cost, neighborhood-vibey spot, here you go.

NANDO'S PERI-PERI
FAST FOOD $

Map p304 (☑202-898-1225; www.nandosperi peri.com; 819 7th St NW; mains $9-14; ⊙11am-10pm Mon-Wed, from noon Thu, 11am-11pm Fri & Sat, to 8pm Sun; ☎; Ⓜ Red, Yellow, Green Line to Gallery Pl-Chinatown) South African chain Nando's is about hot-spiced, flame-grilled chicken. Peri-peri, for the uninitiated, is a vinegary, chili-laden sauce in which they marinate the meat. Choose the spice level you want (from tongue-scorching to plain) and order at the counter (including beer and wine) – the meal is brought to your table. It's akin to fast food, but a winning step up.

Check out the walls: they hang original artworks by South African artists.

FULL KEE
CHINESE $

Map p304 (☑202-371-2233; www.fullkeedc.com; 509 H St NW; mains $9-15; ⊙11am-10pm Sun-Thu, to 11pm Fri & Sat; Ⓜ Red, Yellow, Green Line to Gallery Pl-Chinatown) Although you'll find more atmosphere on the moon, you won't find a better Chinese joint in the city limits. Fill yourself for next to nothing with a simple noodle dish or stir-fry, but make sure you leave room for the duck, which is divine. Try it with some mambo sauce (DC's almost citrusy version of sweet and sour).

BUSBOYS & POETS
CAFE $$

Map p304 (☑202-789-2227; www.busboysand poets.com; 1025 5th St NW; mains $12-21; ⊙7am-midnight Mon-Thu, to 1am Fri, 8am-1am Sat, 8am-midnight Sun; ☎🖉; Ⓜ Yellow, Green Line to Mt Vernon Sq/7th St-Convention Center) Busboys & Poets is a local minichain of cool cafes. Each has a multicultural, opinionated, creative vibe, along with a lengthy menu of well-priced sandwiches, Southern dishes, coffee, beer and other cafe bites, including heaps of vegetarian options. Open-mikes, literary readings, and discussions take place several nights a week.

TIGER FORK
CHINESE $$

Map p304 (☑202-733-1152; www.tigerforkdc. com; rear 922 N St NW; mains $14-22; ⊙5pm-midnight Tue-Fri, 10:30am-2:30pm & 5pm-midnight Sat & Sun; Ⓜ Green, Yellow Line to Mt Vernon Sq/7th St-Convention Center) A boisterous date-night place with a zingy interior full of lantern lights and bamboo, Tiger

Fork serves Hong Kong–style snacks and noodle dishes, such as beef *chow fun* and ginger-glazed pork ribs. A herbalist worked with the bartenders to concoct cocktails that definitely help you relax.

The restaurant is tucked back in Blagden Alley. Enter from 9th St NW or N St NW by looking for the 'Blagden' street sign and then following the brick lane in.

CAFE MOZART
GERMAN $$

Map p304 (☑202-347-5732; www.cafemozartdc. com; 1331 H St NW; mains $15-26; ⊙7am-10pm Mon-Fri, from 9am Sat, from 11am Sun; Ⓜ Red, Orange, Silver, Blue Line to Metro Center) This German grocery store/deli-bakery has a cute restaurant hiding out back that serves great sauerkraut, spaetzle and schnitzel. Best of all, it hosts accordion concerts on Tuesday, Wednesday, Thursday and Sunday, and classical-piano concerts on Friday and Saturday; they all start at 6pm. If nothing else, stop in the front to pick up some European chocolates or pastries.

★DABNEY
AMERICAN $$$

Map p304 (☑202-450-1015; www.thedabney. com; 122 Blagden Alley NW; small plates $14-23; ⊙5:30-10pm Tue-Thu, to 11pm Fri & Sat, 5-10pm Sun; Ⓜ Green, Yellow Line to Mt Vernon Sq/7th St-Convention Center) Chef Jeremiah Langhorne studied historic cookbooks, discovering recipes that used local ingredients and lesser-explored flavors in his quest to resuscitate mid-Atlantic cuisine lost to the ages. Most of the dishes are even cooked over a wood-burning hearth, as in George Washington's time. Langhorne gives it all a modern twist – enough to earn him a Michelin star.

You'll need to order two or three small plates to make a meal. The warm, wood-clad spot is tucked away in Blagden Alley. From 9th St NW look for the 'Blagden' street sign and follow the brick lane in past the mural-painted buildings and garages. Bonus: the restaurant's basement houses Dabney Cellar, an equally impressive wine bar.

★KINSHIP
AMERICAN $$$

Map p304 (☑202-737-7700; www.kinshipdc. com; 1015 7th St NW; mains $25-32; ⊙5:30-10pm; Ⓜ Yellow, Green Line to Mt Vernon Sq/7th St-Convention Center) Round up your friends and enjoy a convivial night at this Michelin-starred restaurant by James Beard Award–winning chef Eric Ziebold. Pick and choose across the menu's five categories echoing the chef's passions: ingredients (surf clams, Rohan duck), history (classics), craft (using culinary techniques), indulgence (caviar, white truffles) and 'For the Table.' The roast chicken from the last category, stuffed with a lemon-garlic-brioche mixture, is to die for.

BRASSERIE BECK

BELGIAN $$$

Map p304 (202-408-1717; www.brasseriebeck. com; 1101 K St NW; mains $26-38; 11:30am-10pm Sun-Thu, to 11:30pm Fri & Sat; Red, Orange, Silver, Blue Line to Metro Center) The chef cooks the foods of his family's Belgian homeland at boisterous Beck. It's a meaty affair, with beef braised in dark beer and duck-leg confit. Other highlights are gooey Raclette cheese, and mussels with crisp *frites* (fries). Peek in the glass-walled kitchen to see the magic happen. The beer list is hefty, and props go to the chocolate desserts.

BIBIANA

ITALIAN $$$

Map p304 (202-216-9550; www.bibianadc.com; 1100 New York Ave NW; mains $22-34; 11:30am-2:30pm Mon-Fri, 5-10pm Mon-Thu, to 11pm Fri & Sat; ; Red, Orange, Silver, Blue Line to Metro Center) Chihuly-esque glass lights dangle over a sleek dining room dotted by dark oak tables and turquoise chairs, and photo art of Vespas, the Trevi Fountain, and other Italian streetscapes. It's mostly business-people and couples on dates forking into the veal meatballs with mascarpone polenta and herbed rabbit over sunchoke puree. Reservations are wise, or wait in the mod bar-lounge. The entrance is on the corner of 12th & H Sts.

🍷 DRINKING & NIGHTLIFE

Chinatown has loads of beery drinking establishments, especially on 7th St NW around Capital One Arena. Blagden Alley (9th, 10th, M and N Sts NW) holds a clutch of smart spots for cocktails, wine or coffee.

★COLUMBIA ROOM

COCKTAIL BAR

Map p304 (202-316-9396; www.columbia roomdc.com; 124 Blagden Alley NW, Downtown; 5pm-12:30am Tue-Thu, to 1:30am Fri & Sat; Green, Yellow Line to Mt Vernon Sq/7th St-Convention Center) Serious mixology goes on at Columbia Room, the kind of place that

sources spring water from Scotland, and uses pickled cherry blossom and barley tea among its ingredients. But it's done in a re-freshingly nonsnooty environment. Choose from three areas: the festive Punch Garden on the outdoor roof deck, the comfy, leather-chair-dotted Spirits Library, or the 14-seat, prix-fixe Tasting Room.

You need tickets for the Tasting Room (the website has details), which hides be-hind a curtain out back. Book for a three- or five-course menu ($85 to $115) of cocktails with accompanying snacks. The Punch Garden and Spirits Library are walk-in seating. Columbia Room is a bit tricky to find, located in mural-splashed Blagden Alley, between 9th and 10th Sts NW.

★DABNEY CELLAR

WINE BAR

Map p304 (202-450-1015; www.thedabney. com; 1222 9th St NW, Downtown; 6pm-midnight Wed-Sat; Green, Yellow Line to Mt Vernon Sq/7th St-Convention Center) Tucked in the basement underneath the acclaimed Dabney (p139) restaurant, the Cellar pours loads of wines by the glass, including many varietals by hard-to-find, small-batch pro-ducers. The cozy, firewood-stacked room is a neighborhood favorite to drop in to for a sip along with a plate of local oysters or but-termilk bacon biscuits. Note the entrance is on 9th St (unlike the Dabney restaurant, which you enter via Blagden Alley), and it's underneath a set of stairs.

CITY TAP HOUSE

PUB

Map p304 (202-733-5333; www.penn quarter.citytap.com; 901 9th St NW, Downtown; 11:30am-midnight Mon-Wed, to 1:30am Thu, to 2:30am Fri, 11am-2:30am Sat & Sun; Red, Yel-low, Green Line to Gallery Pl-Chinatown) What's not to like about a wood-paneled, lodge-like gastropub with craft beers flowing from 40 taps? The vintage photos of folks boozing set the good-time mood. Settle in and make your own four-beer flight (4.5oz each) for around $16. The brick-oven pizzas, Korean-short-rib tacos and other upscale bar food help soak it up.

LA COLOMBE

COFFEE

Map p304 (202-289-4850; www.lacolombe. com; 924 Blagden Alley NW, Downtown; 7am-7pm Mon-Fri, from 8am Sat & Sun; ; Green, Yellow Line to Mt Vernon Sq/7th St-Convention Center) One of five DC branches of the spe-cialist coffee roaster, this La Colombe occu-pies a vintage brick garage in Blagden Alley.

The long space is drenched in natural light, and while the stools and little tables aren't the most comfy, in-the-know locals fill them while savoring great lattes and scones.

The cafe hides in Blagden Alley; enter from 9th St NW or N St NW by looking for the 'Blagden' street sign and then following the brick lane in.

COMPASS COFFEE
COFFEE

Map p304 (www.compasscoffee.com; 650 F St NW, Penn Quarter; ⊙6am-9pm; 📶; MRed, Yellow, Green Line to Gallery Pl-Chinatown) Compass is a homegrown roaster with seven locations and counting. This bright, clamorous branch sits across the street from Capital One Arena and it's always abuzz. Downtown professionals swoop in for nitro cold brews, baked goods and prepackaged sandwiches. The baristas aren't the friendliest bunch, but they do make a fine cup of joe.

ROCKET BAR
BAR

Map p304 (📞202-628-7665; www.rocketbardc. com; 714 7th St NW, Penn Quarter; ⊙4pm-2am Mon-Thu, to 3am Fri, from 3pm Sat, 12:30pm-2am Sun; MRed, Yellow, Green Line to Gallery Pl-Chinatown) Rocket Bar is an almost inexplicably popular pool hall, although there's lots more going on than shooting some stick – shuffle board, Golden Tee, all the oldies. If you're looking for a place to check out the local talent without all the pomp, circumstance and dressing up that comes with a night of clubbing, this might be your spot.

 ENTERTAINMENT

★WOOLLY MAMMOTH THEATRE COMPANY
THEATER

Map p304 (📞202-393-3939; www.woolly mammoth.net; 641 D St NW, Penn Quarter; average ticket $67; MGreen, Yellow Line to Archives) Woolly Mammoth is the edgiest of DC's experimental groups. For most shows, $20 'stampede' seats are available at the box office two hours before performances. They're limited in number, and sold first-come, first-served, so get there early.

SHAKESPEARE THEATRE COMPANY
THEATER

Map p304 (📞202-547-1122; www.shakespeare theatre.org; 450 7th St NW, Penn Quarter; average ticket $85; MGreen, Yellow Line to Archives) The nation's foremost Shakespeare company

LOCAL KNOWLEDGE

BLAGDEN ALLEY

A clutch of unique bars and restaurants hides in the maze of mural-splattered passageways between 9th, 10th, M and N Sts NW – an area known as Blagden Alley. The 19th-century buildings used to house horses and hansom cabs; now they hold venues including Tiger Fork (p139) and Columbia Room. The murals are known collectively as the DC Alley Museum; local artists change it up regularly.

presents masterful works by the Bard, as well as plays by George Bernard Shaw, Oscar Wilde, Eugene O'Neill and other greats. The season spans about a half-dozen productions annually, plus a free summer Shakespeare series on-site for two weeks in late August.

NATIONAL THEATRE
THEATER

Map p304 (📞202-628-6161; www.thenationaldc. org; 1321 Pennsylvania Ave NW, Penn Quarter; averageg ticket $65; MRed, Orange, Silver, Blue Line to Metro Center) Washington's oldest continuously operating theater shows flashy Broadway musicals and big-name productions. A lottery for $25 tickets (cash only) takes place two hours prior to every show; submit your name at the box office. Saturday mornings feature free performances for children at 9:30am and 11am; it's best to reserve tickets online in advance for these shows.

CAPITOL STEPS
COMEDY

Map p304 (📞202-397-7328; www.capsteps.com; Ronald Reagan Bldg, 1300 Pennsylvania Ave NW, Penn Quarter; tickets from $36; ⊙shows 7:30pm Fri & Sat; MOrange, Silver, Blue Line to Federal Triangle) This singing troupe claims to be the only group in America that tries to be funnier than Congress. Many of the performers are former congressional staffers, so they know their political stuff, although sometimes it can be overtly corny. The satirical, bipartisan jokes poke fun at both sides of the spectrum.

E STREET CINEMA
CINEMA

Map p304 (📞202-783-9494; www.landmark theatres.com; 555 11th St NW, Penn Quarter; tickets $12.50; MRed, Orange, Silver, Blue Line to Metro Center) The eight screens flicker

DOWNTOWN MUSEUM SHOPS

These Downtown museum shops are terrific for souvenirs and gift buying.

National Archives (p130) Whether you're looking for a Thomas Jefferson biography, a Declaration of Independence–inscribed ruler, a John Adams stuffed toy or an Elvis-meets-Nixon magnet, the Archives shop has a huge array of fun, historical goods.

National Building Museum (p134) The large shop has all kinds of gifts for architecture buffs: Frank Lloyd Wright coloring books, LEGO models of the Capitol, puzzles of the Metro system, groovy stationery and heaps of books on architecture and politics. There's also a big selection of build-it-yourself educational toys for kids.

National Museum of Women in the Arts (p135) The small room to the left of the museum entrance sells unique books, prints, posters, jewelry and handicrafts – all created by women.

with first-run independent and foreign films, documentaries and classic revivals. Crab-cake bites, empanadas, wine and craft beers stock the beyond-the-norm concession stand. This is a great neighborhood spot to see a movie.

CAPITAL ONE ARENA   STADIUM
Map p304 (☑202-628-3200; https://capital onearena.monumentalsportsnetwork.com; 601 F St NW, Penn Quarter; tickets from $40; Ⓜ Red, Yellow, Green Line to Gallery Pl-Chinatown) This ever-busy facility is DC's arena for big-name concerts and sporting events. Washington's rough-and-tumble pro-hockey team the Capitals (www.nhl.com/capitals) and pro-basketball team the Wizards (www.nba. com/wizards) both play here from October through April. The women's pro basketball team the Mystics (http://mystics.wnba. com) take over from May through August.

FORD'S THEATRE   THEATER
Map p304 (☑202-347-4833; www.fords.org; 511 10th St NW, Penn Quarter; avg ticket $45; ⊗box office 8:30am-5pm; Ⓜ Red, Orange, Silver, Blue Line to Metro Center) This historical venue – where John Wilkes Booth killed Abraham Lincoln – is still an active theater. It stages works related to Lincoln's life and times (including world premieres and musicals), as well as American classics. Shows are mostly in the evening; by day, the theater operates as a historic site (p134).

 SHOPPING

CITYCENTERDC   SHOPPING CENTER
Map p304 (☑202-289-9000; www.citycenterdc. com; H St NW, between 9th St NW & 11th St NW, Downtown; Ⓜ Red, Orange, Silver, Blue Line to Metro Center; Red, Yellow, Green Line to Gallery Pl-Chinatown) Rodeo Drive chic may not be the first way you'd think of describing Washington, but this sparkling, open-air oasis of shops and restaurants blows that notion straight out of the water. Style mavens peruse high-end boutiques, while diners indulge in haute cuisine. And the best part? The fountain-splashed courtyard tucked away from the bustle; order an espresso and relax awhile.

What used to be a run-down, best-avoided part of the city is now a glittering, 10-acre shopaholic's paradise, with swanky shops including BOSS, Bulgari, Burberry, CH Carolina Herrera, Gucci, Hermès, Kate Spade New York, Longchamp, Louis Vuitton and more.

TEAISM SHOP   FOOD & DRINKS
Map p304 (☑202-638-6010; www.teaism.com; 400 8th St NW, Penn Quarter; ⊗10am-6pm Mon-Sat, from 11am Sun; Ⓜ Green, Yellow Line to Archives) Next to the inviting cafe (p137) of the same name, Teaism sells dozens of loose-leaf teas, from smoky Lapsang souchong to organic jasmine, and rich green teas – all concealed in artful boxes behind the counter. You can also buy teapots, mugs, lovely smelling soaps and ornate display boxes (covered with handmade paper).

Dupont Circle & Kalorama

Neighborhood Top Five

1 Embassy Row (p145) Searching for Tunisia, Chile, Turkmenistan, Togo, Haiti – flags flutter above heavy doors and mark the nations inside, while dark-windowed sedans ease out of driveways ferrying diplomats to and fro.

2 Phillips Collection (p146) Standing face to face with Renoirs, Gauguins and Picassos in a restored mansion's intimate rooms.

3 Kramerbooks (p155) Browsing the stacks in the big, sunny store, then heading into the cafe to sip cocktails and stuff your face.

4 National Geographic Museum (p146) Visiting the headquarters of the famed explorers' society to see what artifacts are showing from their expeditions.

5 Woodrow Wilson House (p146) Experiencing the genteel Washingtonian lifestyle, both past and present.

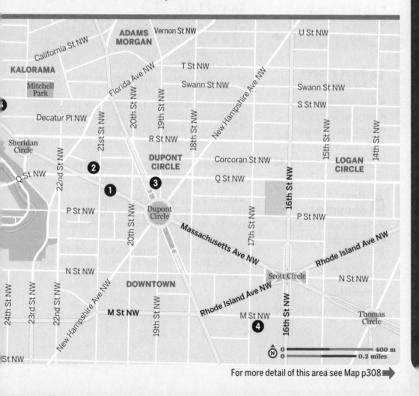

For more detail of this area see Map p308 →

Lonely Planet's Top Tip

If you really want to take advantage of the embassy scene, check out the International Club (www.internationalclubdc.com). It organizes concerts, dinners and cultural events – many held at embassies – for 'internationally minded' locals to socialize. Anyone can join and be off to dinners at the Ukrainian Embassy, concerts at the Austrian Embassy and more.

Best Places to Eat

➡ Bistrot du Coin (p149)
➡ Little Serow (p149)
➡ Bub & Pop's (p148)
➡ Blue Duck Tavern (p149)
➡ Komi (p150)
➡ Un Je Ne Sais Quoi (p148)

For reviews, see p148.➡

Best Places to Drink

➡ Board Room (p150)
➡ Bar Charley (p151)
➡ Tabard Inn Bar (p151)
➡ Larry's Lounge (p151)

For reviews, see p150.➡

Best Shopping

➡ Kramerbooks (p155)
➡ Second Story Books (p155)
➡ Dupont Circle Market (p155)
➡ Shop Made in DC (p155)

For reviews, see p155.➡

Explore Dupont Circle & Kalorama

The neighborhood is easy to explore, since almost everything radiates from the literal Dupont Circle, the traffic rotunda. Most of the sights are on the circle's west side. Spend the morning getting cultured in under-the-radar museums. Take the afternoon to wander along Massachusetts Ave NW – aka Embassy Row – and check out the captivating historic manors that hold embassies from around the globe. For an extra dose of stately mansions, mosey through Kalorama, which adjoins Dupont to the northwest. The Obamas, Ivanka Trump and Jared Kushner, and Amazon CEO Jeff Bezos all live in the neighborhood. S St NW gives a good show of the area's elegant architecture. Afterward, nifty cafes and shops beckon back toward the Dupont traffic circle, especially along Connecticut Ave NW.

Dupont is also a fab place to spend the evening. Have dinner in one of the buzzy eateries, then join the young professionals who amass here for a big night out. Romantic cocktails, crazy dance parties, retro board games and wee-hour bookstores await. What's more, Dupont is DC's center for gay nightlife, and several bars catering to the crowd are sprinkled throughout the area.

Local Life

➡ **French Treats** It seems like all of Dupont sneaks into Un Je Ne Sais Quoi (p148) at some point during the day to buy a chocolatey pastry.

➡ **Friendly Meatballs** Bub & Pop's (p148) is an endearing sandwich shop where everybody knows your name.

➡ **High Heel Race** The Tuesday before Halloween a block party erupts on 17th St, highlighted by flamboyantly dressed divas who compete in a wild sprint down the road.

Getting There & Away

➡ **Metro** Dupont Circle (Red Line) for most points. Use the Q St exit for destinations north of P St, and the 19th St exit for destinations south. Farragut North (Red Line) is closer to M St.

➡ **Bus** Catch the DC Circulator's Dupont–Georgetown–Rosslyn bus at 19th and N Sts (use the south exit from Dupont Metro Station).

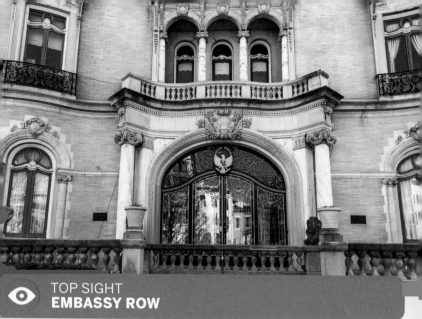

Want to take a trip around the world? Stroll northwest along Massachusetts Ave from Dupont Circle (the actual traffic circle) and you pass more than 40 embassies housed in mansions that range from elegant to imposing to discreet. Mass Ave was once Millionaire's Row, and most embassies initially were residences built by wealthy industrialists at the turn of the 20th century.

The Great Depression caused many to lose their manors, which then stood gracefully decaying until WWII's end. As nations came to Washington to set up shop, the old homes were uniquely fit to be embassies.

The **Indonesian Embassy** (pictured above; Map p308; 2020 Massachusetts Ave NW) is an impressive example. Gold-mining magnate Thomas Walsh commissioned the home in 1903, when it was the costliest house in DC (not surprising, considering the gold-flecked marble pillars). The **Luxembourg Embassy** (Map p308; 2200 Massachusetts Ave NW) is another show-stopper. Congressman Alexander Stewart built the home in 1909 in the grand court style of Louis XIV. In 1941 the Grand Duchess of Luxembourg bought it and lived here in exile during WWII. Edward Everett, inventor of the grooved bottle cap, built the structure that is now the **Turkish Ambassador's Residence** (Map p308; 1606 23rd St NW). George Oakley Totten designed the building. Totten was the official architect of Ottoman sultan Abdul Hamid II.

While Massachusetts Ave has the most embassies, New Hampshire Ave also has its share: 12 embassies, to be exact, in a four-block stretch heading northeast from Dupont Circle. Saunter along and wave to the good folks of Mozambique, Argentina, Belarus and Eritrea, among others.

For more information on the architecture of this neighborhood, see p260.

DON'T MISS

➜ Indonesian Embassy
➜ Luxembourg Embassy
➜ Turkish Ambassador's Residence

PRACTICALITIES

➜ Map p308, C4
➜ www.embassy.org
➜ Massachusetts Ave NW, btwn Observatory & Dupont Circles NW
➜ Ⓜ Red Line to Dupont Circle

⦿ SIGHTS

EMBASSY ROW   ARCHITECTURE
See p145.

★ PHILLIPS COLLECTION   MUSEUM
Map p308 (✆202-387-2151; www.phillips
collection.org; 1600 21st St NW; Tue-Fri free,
Sat & Sun $10, ticketed exhibitions per day $12;
⊙10am-5pm Tue, Wed, Fri & Sat, to 8:30pm Thu,
noon-7pm Sun; Ⓜ Red Line to Dupont Circle) The
first modern-art museum in the country
(opened in 1921) houses a small but exquisite collection of European and American
works. Renoir's *Luncheon of the Boating
Party* is a highlight, along with pieces by
Gauguin, Van Gogh, Matisse, Picasso and
many other greats. The intimate rooms, set
in a restored mansion, put you unusually
close to the artworks. The permanent collection is free on weekdays. Download the
free app or dial ✆202-595-1839 for audio
tours through the works.

The Rothko Room, which has four of the
abstract expressionist's pieces, is worth a
peek. Be aware that famous works sometimes rotate into the museum's ticketed
exhibitions (in which case admission fees
apply). The Phillips' Sunday chamber-
music series has been making sweet sounds
since 1941; concerts start at 4pm October
through May, and tickets cost $40.

**NATIONAL GEOGRAPHIC
MUSEUM**   MUSEUM
Map p308 (✆202-857-7700; www.national
geographic.org/dc; 1145 17th St NW; adult/child
$15/10; ⊙10am-6pm; Ⓜ Red Line to Farragut
North) The museum at National Geographic
Society headquarters can't compete with the
Smithsonian's more extensive offerings, but
it can be worth a stop, depending on what's
showing. Exhibits are drawn from the society's well-documented expeditions to the far
corners of the earth, and they change peri-
odically. The society also hosts films, concerts and lectures by famed researchers and
explorers; most programs have a fee.

**WOODROW
WILSON HOUSE**   MUSEUM
Map p308 (✆202-387-4062; www.woodrow
wilsonhouse.org; 2340 S St NW; adult/child $10/
free; ⊙10am-4pm Wed-Sun Mar-Dec, Fri-Sun only
Jan & Feb; Ⓜ Red Line to Dupont Circle) This
Georgian-revival mansion offers guided
hour-long tours focusing on the 28th president's life and legacy. Genteel docents discuss highlights of Wilson's career (WWI,
the League of Nations) and home, which has
been restored to the period of his residence
(1921–24). The tour features European
bronzes, a stairwell conservatory, exquisite
china and Mrs W's flapper dresses, all of
which offer a glamorous portrait of Roaring
'20s DC society.

The docents' entertaining stories spread
beyond the Wilson house: they can point
out the rich eccentrics, ambassadors and
others who live nearby.

SCOTTISH RITE TEMPLE   ARCHITECTURE
Map p308 (✆202-232-3579; www.scottishrite.org;
1733 16th St NW; ⊙10am-4:30pm Mon-Thu; Ⓜ Red
Line to Dupont Circle) **FREE** The regional headquarters of the Scottish Rite Freemasons,
also known as the House of the Temple, is
one of the most eye-catching buildings
in the District. That's because it looks like
a magic temple lifted out of a comic book,
all the more incredible for basically sitting
amid a tangle of residential row houses. It's
as if someone plopped the Parthenon in the
middle of Shady Acres suburbia.

There's a lot of heavy Masonic symbolism
and ritual associated with the temple. Thirty-
three columns surround the building, representing the 33rd Degree, an honorary dis-
tinction conferred on outstanding Masons.
Two sphinxes, Wisdom and Power, guard the
entrance, and past the gates of bronze that
front the building (really), the grand atrium
looks like a collision zone between the Egyp-
tian and Greek antiquities departments of a
major museum. Note the Pharaonic statues
and chairs modeled to resemble thrones
from the Temple of Dionysus. Guides provide
tours of all this fascinating minutiae.

DUPONT UNDERGROUND   GALLERY
Map p308 (www.dupontunderground.org; 1583
New Hampshire Ave NW; from $15; Ⓜ Red Line
to Dupont Circle) An enormous, abandoned
streetcar station lies beneath Dupont Circle,

CAPITALLY KOSHER

Two of Washington's most prominent
Judaica sights can be found amid the
brown-red bricks of Dupont Circle.

➡ Edlavitch DC Jewish Community
Center (p154)
➡ National Museum of American
Jewish Military History (p148)

and a local arts group has transformed it into a cool underground gallery of art, architecture and design. Exhibitions – maybe a sound installation or a graffiti collection – rise alongside the old tram tracks. The shows change regularly. The gallery is only open for specific events, so check the schedule online for times.

CATHEDRAL OF ST MATTHEW THE APOSTLE
CHURCH

Map p308 (☎202-347-3215; www.stmatthews cathedral.org; 1725 Rhode Island Ave NW; ⊘6:30am-6:30pm Sun-Fri, from 7:30am Sat; Ⓜ Red Line to Dupont Circle) The sturdy redbrick exterior doesn't hint at the marvelous mosaics and gilding within this 1893 Catholic cathedral, where JFK was laid in state and his funeral mass was held. Its vast central dome, altars and chapels depict biblical saints and eminent New World personages – from Simón Bolívar to Elizabeth Ann Seton – in stained glass, murals and scintillating Italianate mosaics; almost no surface is left undecorated. Pick up a self-guided-tour brochure by the entrance (beneath the guest register).

Evening is the best time to visit, when flickering candles illuminate the sanctuary, but you can attend mass on Sunday morning or slip in almost any time to look around.

STUDIO GALLERY
GALLERY

Map p308 (☎202-232-8734; www.studio gallerydc.com; 2108 R St NW; ⊘1-6pm Wed-Fri, from 11am Sat; Ⓜ Red Line to Dupont Circle) FREE Studio Gallery shows contemporary works by more than 35 emerging DC-area artists. Paintings, sculpture, mixed media and video are represented. The relatively small space spans the main floor and basement, with exhibits that always feel fresh. Openings are held on the first Friday of the month.

MANSION ON O STREET
NOTABLE BUILDING

Map p308 (☎202-496-2020; www.omansion. com; 2020 O St NW; tours from $15; ⊘11am-3pm; Ⓜ Red Line to Dupont Circle) This 100-room 1892 mansion is part inn, part gallery, part cluttered antique shop and part private event space. The decor is like a wedding at Castle Dracula: swags of velvet drapery, ornate chandeliers, candelabras, hidden doors and secret passageways. Various tours take you through. We recommend the self-guided history tour or secret door tour. Other jaunts include champagne, high tea and more. Tickets must be purchased online in advance. And bring a shopping bag: all of the oddball objects displayed are for sale.

The mansion has hosted a slew of big names over the years: Rosa Parks lived here for a decade, Chelsea Clinton had her sweet-16 party here, and every president since Teddy Roosevelt has dropped by.

SOCIETY OF THE CINCINNATI
MUSEUM

Map p308 (☎202-785-2040; www.societyof thecincinnati.org; 2118 Massachusetts Ave NW; ⊘10am-4pm Tue-Sat, from noon Sun; Ⓜ Red Line to Dupont Circle) FREE The Society of the Cincinnati is a private patriotic group that educates the public about the Revolutionary War. Who knew? What's key here is the chance to go inside the Renaissance Revival mansion (aka Anderson House) where it has its headquarters and check out the opulent interior. The gilded ballrooms, chandeliers, tapestries, sweeping staircases and marble pillars are jaw-dropping.

You can poke around a little bit on your own, but to see the majority of the rooms you'll have to go on a 45-minute, docent-guided tour (held every hour at quarter past the hour).

HEURICH HOUSE
MUSEUM

Map p308 (☎202-429-1894; www.heurichhouse. org; 1307 New Hampshire Ave NW; tours $10; ⊘tours 11:30am, 1pm & 2:30pm Thu-Sat; Ⓜ Red Line to Dupont Circle) Welcome to the castle that beer built. John Granville Myers designed the 31-room mansion for German-born brewer Christian Heurich, a man who loved beer with a passion. Entry is by guided tour only, though DIY explorations of the gardens (11am to 3pm April to October) are permitted. The hour-long jaunt takes in the home's 15 fireplaces, ornate carved-wood decor and basement beer room with its whopping stein collection.

METROPOLITAN AME CHURCH
CHURCH

Map p308 (Metropolitan African Methodist Episcopal Church; ☎202-331-1426; https://metropolitan ame.org; 1518 M St NW; ⊘10am-6pm Mon-Fri, 10am-2pm Sat, 7am-2pm Sun; Ⓜ Orange, Silver, Blue Line to McPherson Sq) Built and paid for in 1886 by former slaves, the Metropolitan AME Church occupies an imposing redbrick Gothic structure and is one of the city's most striking churches. Frederick Douglass often preached here, and his state funeral was held here in February 1895. On the day of his burial, African American schools closed, crowds packed the exterior to pay

LOCAL KNOWLEDGE

SPANISH STEPS

You're walking up 22nd St, between Decatur Pl and S St NW, and suddenly an enchanting staircase appears. The **Spanish Steps** (Map p308; 22nd St NW; M Red Line to Dupont Circle), as they're known, were modeled on those in Rome's Piazza di Spagna. Why are they here? The rise up to S St was deemed too steep, so city planners built the steps to bridge the gap. Climb up for an atmospheric view of Embassy Row.

respect and flags flew at half-mast. The funeral of civil rights activist Rosa Parks was held here in 2005.

NATIONAL MUSEUM OF AMERICAN JEWISH MILITARY HISTORY MUSEUM

Map p308 (☎202-265-6280; www.nmajmh.org; 1811 R St NW; ☺9am-5pm Mon-Fri; M Red Line to Dupont Circle) FREE The museum is a small but fascinating peek into the wartime exploits of American Jews. Displays on Jewish Medal of Honor recipients and the history of death-camp liberation – among others – are brought to life with touch screens, large-scale videos, listening stations and other multimedia experiences.

CHARLES SUMNER SCHOOL & ARCHIVES MUSEUM

Map p308 (☎202-730-0478; 1201 17th St NW; ☺9am-5pm Mon-Fri; M Red Line to Farragut North) FREE The stately, dignified Sumner building is a great example of solidly beautiful, redbrick, 19th-century, urban design, but it is an even better testament to civil rights and education. Back in 1877, this was where the first high-school class of African Americans graduated out of the public school system. Today you can find the DC Public School archives here, as well as a museum that displays local school memorabilia along with exhibits on statesman and orator Frederick Douglass.

✖ EATING

Dupont is ace for eats. Classy nouveau cuisine and upscale ethnic eateries cater to the flocks of diplomats and businesspeople, while casual cafes cater

to the more bohemian. The stretch of 17th St NW between P and Q Sts NW holds several favorites in a row. Connecticut Ave NW also has lots to offer.

★ BUB & POP'S SANDWICHES $

Map p308 (☎202-457-1111; www.bubandpops. com; 1815 M St NW; sandwiches half/whole $10/18; ☺8am-4pm Mon-Fri, 11am-4pm Sat; M Red Line to Dupont Circle) A chef tired of the fine-dining rat race opened this gourmet sandwich shop with his parents. Ingredients are made in-house from scratch – the meatballs, pickles, mayonnaise, roasted pork. Congenial mom Arlene rules the counter and can answer questions about any of it. The sandwiches are enormous, and best consumed hot off the press in the bright aqua-and-red room.

★ UN JE NE SAIS QUOI BAKERY $

Map p308 (☎202-721-0099; www.facebook. com/unjenesaisquoipastry; 1361 Connecticut Ave NW; pastries $2.50-5; ☺7:30am-7pm Mon-Thu, 7:30am-8pm Fri, 10am-8pm Sat; M Red Line to Dupont Circle) The smell of rich coffee envelops you when you enter this little bakery, where a couple of French expats bake *merveilleux*, their signature French pastry plumped with layers of meringue and ganache. It's like biting into a glorious cloud. Tarts, eclairs and other sweets are equally exquisite, served on china plates amid vintage Parisian decor.

ZORBA'S CAFE GREEK $

Map p308 (☎202-387-8555; 1612 20th St NW; mains $13-16; ☺11am-11:30pm Mon-Sat, to 10:30pm Sun; ❷; M Red Line to Dupont Circle) Generous portions of moussaka and souvlaki, as well as pitchers of Rolling Rock beer, make family-run Zorba's Cafe one of DC's best bargain haunts. On warm days the outdoor patio packs with locals. With the bouzouki music playing in the background, you can almost imagine you're in the Greek islands.

DOLCEZZA GELATO $

Map p308 (☎202-299-9116; www.dolcezza gelato.com; 1704 Connecticut Ave NW; gelato $6-8; ☺7am-10pm Mon-Thu, 7am-11pm Fri, 8am-11pm Sat, 8am-10pm Sun; ☎; M Red Line to Dupont Circle) The local mini-chain Dolcezza whips up the District's best gelati. Some flavors are unusual, such as blueberry lavender and Thai coconut milk, and change with the seasons. Traditionalists can always get their licks with chocolate, salted caramel and peppermint. Good coffee, vintage-chic decor and free wi-fi add to the pleasure.

SWEETGREEN
HEALTH FOOD $

Map p308 (📞202-387-9338; www.sweetgreen.com; 1512 Connecticut Ave NW; mains $9-12; ⏰10:30am-10pm; 🖋; Ⓜ Red Line to Dupont Circle) 🏄 Dupont Circle's branch of the healthful salad purveyor often has a line out the door. Order your huge bowl of roast chicken and kale or spicy shrimp and arugula at the counter, then take it to the communal tables to consume with the rest of the young and fit.

WELL-DRESSED BURRITO
TEX-MEX $

Map p308 (📞202-293-0515; 1220 19th St NW; mains $6-8; ⏰11:45am-2:15pm Mon-Fri; Ⓜ Red Line to Dupont Circle) The Well-Dressed Burrito deals in...well, do we need to spell it out? These burritos are big, fat and the perfect antidote to last night's alcohol overindulgence. Enter through the alley between M and N Sts.

★BISTROT DU COIN
FRENCH $$

Map p308 (📞202-234-6969; www.bistrotducoin.com; 1738 Connecticut Ave NW; mains $20-30; ⏰11:30am-midnight Mon-Wed, 11:30am-1am Thu & Fri, noon-1am Sat, noon-midnight Sun; Ⓜ Red Line to Dupont Circle) The lively and much-loved Bistrot du Coin is a neighborhood favorite for roll-up-your-sleeves, working-class French fare. The kitchen sends out consistently good onion soup, classic *steak-frites* (grilled steak and French fries), cassoulet, open-face sandwiches and nine varieties of its famous *moules* (mussels). Regional wines from around the motherland accompany the food by the glass, carafe and bottle.

The clientele is a fun mix of Dupont locals and nostalgic Europeans, and the atmosphere feels plucked out of George Orwell's *Down and Out* descriptions of Paris. Make reservations.

DUKE'S GROCERY
GASTROPUB $$

Map p308 (📞202-733-5623; www.dukesgrocery.com; 1513 17th St NW; mains $12-16; ⏰11am-10pm Mon & Tue, 11am-1am Wed & Thu, 11am-2am Fri, 10am-2am Sat, 10am-10pm Sun; 🛜; Ⓜ Red Line to Dupont Circle) 'A taste of East London in East Dupont' is Duke's tagline, and that means black pudding for brunch, curried chicken for lunch, and the famed burgers and cocktails anytime. Set over two floors in a snug row house, Duke's genial vibe invites lingering, so sometimes it's hard to score a table among the groups of chit-chatty friends and couples on low-maintenance dates.

Menu items change – and most fall into the creative, globally inspired category rather than being straight-up British – but there are usually a few vegetarian options.

AFTERWORDS CAFE
AMERICAN $$

Map p308 (📞202-387-3825; www.kramers.com; 1517 Connecticut Ave NW; mains $18-22; ⏰7:30am-1am Sun-Thu, to 3am Fri & Sat; Ⓜ Red Line to Dupont Circle) Attached to Kramerbooks (p155), this buzzing spot is not your average bookstore cafe. The packed indoor tables, wee bar and outdoor patio overflow with good cheer. The menu features tasty bistro fare and an ample beer selection, making it a prime spot for happy hour, for brunch and late night on weekends (open until 3am, baby!).

Browsing the stacks before stuffing the gut is many locals' favorite way to spend a Washington weekend.

ST ARNOLD'S MUSSEL BAR
BELGIAN $$

Map p308 (📞202-833-1321; www.starnoldsmusselbar.com; 1827 Jefferson Pl NW; mains $14-20; ⏰11am-2am Sun-Thu, to 3am Fri & Sat; Ⓜ Red Line to Farragut North) Mussels and *frites* (fries) hit the tables in innumerable varieties: in Thai curry sauce, bleu cheese and bacon sauce, and the house specialty beer sauce with caramelized shallots and duck fat, to name a few. Add the terrific Belgian beers on tap and the warm, convivial ambience, and it's easy to settle in for a while.

Another St Arnold's outpost steams up pots in Upper Northwest DC.

★LITTLE SEROW
THAI $$$

Map p308 (www.littleserow.com; 1511 17th St NW; set menu $49; ⏰5:30-10pm Tue-Thu, to 10:30pm Fri & Sat; Ⓜ Red Line to Dupont Circle) Set in a cavern-like green basement, Little Serow has no phone, no reservations and no sign on the door. It only seats groups of four or fewer (larger parties will be separated), but despite all this, people line up around the block. And what for? Superlative northern Thai cuisine. The single-option menu, which consists of six or so hot-spiced courses, changes weekly.

You might get chicken livers and long peppers, or shrimp paste, eggplant and chilies. Every dish comes with mountains of fresh herbs.

★BLUE DUCK TAVERN
AMERICAN $$$

Map p308 (📞202-419-6755; www.blueducktavern.com; 1201 24th St NW; mains $30-46; ⏰6:30am-2:30pm & 5:30-10:30pm Sun-Thu, to 11pm Fri & Sat; 🖋; Ⓜ Red Line to Dupont Circle)

A reliable rave winner, the Michelin-starred Blue Duck creates a rustic kitchen ambience in the midst of an uber-urbanized corridor of M St. The changing menu draws from farms across the country, mixing mains such as venison tartare and suckling pig sourced from Pennsylvania, crab cakes from nearby Chesapeake Bay and grits from Virginia. Weekend brunch is a big to-do.

The interior mashes up modernist clean lines and high ceilings with countrified knickknacks (baskets, barrels, vintage scales) and wooden tables and chairs. It's located inside the Park Hyatt hotel.

★KOMI   FUSION $$$
Map p308 (☎202-332-9200; www.komi restaurant.com; 1509 17th St NW; set menu $150; ⊘5:30-10pm Tue-Sat; MRed Line to Dupont Circle) There is an admirable simplicity to Komi's changing menu, which is rooted in Greece and influenced by everything – but primarily genius. Dinner comprises 12 or so dishes; say suckling pig, scallops and truffles, or roasted baby goat. Komi's cozy space doesn't take groups larger than four, and you need to reserve in advance. Call a month before your desired dining date.

Komi is one of Washington's most knockout dining experiences, with the incredible attention and measured pacing that the staff provides adding to the effect.

HANK'S OYSTER BAR   SEAFOOD $$$
Map p308 (☎202-462-4265; www.hanksoyster bar.com; 1624 Q St NW; mains $22-30; ⊘11:30am-1am Mon-Thu, 11:30am-2am Fri, 11am-2am Sat, 11am-1am Sun; MRed Line to Dupont Circle) DC has several oyster bars, but mini-chain Hank's is our favorite, mixing power-player muscle with a casual, beachy ambience. As you'd expect, the oyster menu is extensive and excellent; there are always at least four varieties on hand, along with lobster rolls, fried clams and witty cocktails. It's best to reserve ahead.

Hank's pre-theater menu (three courses for $32, offered between 5:30pm and 6:30pm) earns big praise.

SUSHI TARO   JAPANESE $$$
Map p308 (☎202-462-8999; www.sushitaro. com; 1503 17th St NW; tasting menu from $90; ⊘11:30am-2pm Mon-Fri, 5:30-10pm Mon-Sat; MRed Line to Dupont Circle) Many locals say this spare, earth-toned Japanese place serves the best sushi in town – and they were proven right when the restaurant earned a Michelin star. You can order à la carte, but the tasting menu is the way to go. The kitchen obsesses over preparing the finest, freshest fish possible, arranged with beautiful sides and garnishes.

For instance, a quivering bit of fatty tuna comes with a side of wasabi freshly grated from one long stem of Japanese horseradish into slivers of nose-tingling happiness.

TABARD INN RESTAURANT   AMERICAN $$$
Map p308 (☎202-331-8528; www.tabardinn.com; 1739 N St NW; mains $24-34; ⊘7-10am, 11:30am-2:30pm & 5:30-9:30pm Mon-Fri, 7-9am, 10am-3:30pm & 5:30-9:30pm Sat & Sun; MRed Line to Dupont Circle) Dinners are seasonal twists on classic fare – scallops with parsnip puree, veal with sugarsnap peas – but it's the deceptively normal weekend brunch menu that stands out. The poached eggs, warm, whipped-cream-topped doughnuts and oysters are sublime. Grab a table in the cozy, English manor–like interior or the splendid, ivy-walled garden courtyard. Reservations recommended.

OBELISK   ITALIAN $$$
Map p308 (☎202-872-1180; www.obeliskdc.com; 2029 P St NW; 5-course menu $78-88; ⊘6-10pm Tue-Sat; MRed Line to Dupont Circle) Obelisk's small and narrow dining room feels almost like eating at someone's kitchen table. The set-course Italian feasts are prepared with first-rate ingredients. You might sup on ricotta ravioli with green tomato sauce, or braised duck leg with pear sauce; the antipasti in particular is a revelation. The menu changes daily but doesn't give you much selection (picky eaters should call ahead). Make reservations.

🍷 DRINKING & NIGHTLIFE

DC's gay nightlife mecca, this neighborhood is packed with bars ranging from raunchy to ritzy. Regardless of your sexual orientation, there's something to keep you drinking around the circle. Chill coffeehouses, super-sleek lounges and ramshackle joints known for cheap happy hours abound.

★BOARD ROOM   BAR
Map p308 (☎202-518-7666; www.boardroomdc. com; 1737 Connecticut Ave NW; ⊘4pm-2am

Mon-Thu, 4pm-3am Fri, noon-3am Sat, noon-2am Sun; Ⓜ Red Line to Dupont Circle) Grab a table, pull up a stool and crush your opponent at Hungry Hungry Hippos. Or summon spirits with a Ouija board. Board Room lets you flash back to childhood via stacks of board games. Battleship, Risk, Operation – name it, and it's available to rent for $2. Around 20 beers flow from the taps and are available by pitcher to stoke the festivities.

★ **BAR CHARLEY** BAR

Map p308 (📞202-627-2183; 1825 18th St NW; ⏱5pm-12:30am Mon-Thu, 4pm-1:30am Fri, 10am-1:30am Sat, 10am-12:30am Sun; Ⓜ Red Line to Dupont Circle) Bar Charley draws a mixed crowd from the neighborhood – young, old, gay and straight. They come for groovy cocktails sloshing in vintage glassware and ceramic tiki mugs, served at very reasonable prices by DC standards. Try the gin and gingery Suffering Bastard. The beer list isn't huge, but it is thoughtfully chosen with some wild ales. Around 60 wines are available too.

If you're hungry, Charley serves steaks and globe-trotting small plates (poutine, curried mussels). The drinks are the prize here, though.

★ **TABARD INN BAR** BAR

Map p308 (📞202-331-8528; www.tabardinn.com; 1739 N St NW; ⏱11:30am-11pm; Ⓜ Red Line to Dupont Circle) The Tabard Inn Bar is in a hotel (p232), but plenty of locals come to swirl an old-fashioned or gin and tonic in the wood-beamed, lodge-like lounge. On warm nights, maneuver for an outdoor table on the ivy-clad patio.

★ **LARRY'S LOUNGE** GAY

Map p308 (📞202-483-1483; 1840 18th St NW; ⏱4pm-2am Mon-Thu, to 3am Fri & Sat, 2pm-2am Sun; 🏳️‍🌈; Ⓜ Red Line to Dupont Circle) An agreeably worn neighborhood joint, Larry's is known for its potently boozy drinks, dog-friendly patio and big windows perfect for people-watching. It's a gay bar, but plenty of straight patrons settle in to take advantage of its virtues. Prepare for a chat with a cast of characters.

18TH STREET LOUNGE CLUB

Map p308 (📞202-466-3922; www.eighteenthstreetlounge.com; 1212 18th St NW; ⏱5pm-2am Tue-Thu, 5pm-3am Fri, 9pm-3am Sat, 9pm-2am Sun; Ⓜ Red Line to Dupont Circle) Chandeliers, velvet sofas, antique wallpaper and a ridiculously

good-looking, dance-loving crowd adorn this multifloored mansion. The DJs – spinning funk, soul and house – are phenomenal, which is not surprising given Eric Hilton (of Thievery Corporation) is co-owner. The lack of a sign on the door proclaims the club's exclusivity. No athletic attire or sneakers. Cover charge ranges from $10 to $20.

Choose from five rooms when you get inside, each featuring different beats.

FIREFLY BAR BAR

Map p308 (📞202-861-1310; www.firefly-dc.com; 1310 New Hampshire Ave NW; ⏱4-11pm; Ⓜ Red Line to Dupont Circle) Firefly is a restaurant first – the Hotel Madera's restaurant, to be precise – but we're not listing it for those merits. We can say it's one of the coolest bars in Dupont, decked out with its surreal, magically happy 'firefly trees,' all candlelit and reminiscent of childhood summer evenings, and romantic as hell to boot. The cocktail menu is a glorious thing.

Knock back a 'vine and fig tree' (bourbon and fig cordial) and see if the world doesn't just glow a little more...wait, that's the firefly trees.

RUSSIA HOUSE LOUNGE

Map p308 (📞202-234-9433; www.russiahouselounge.com; 1800 Connecticut Ave NW; ⏱5pm-midnight Sun-Thu, to 2:30am Fri & Sat; Ⓜ Red Line to Dupont Circle) Russophiles flock to this faded but elegant Dupont gem, with its brassy chandeliers, candlelit chambers and stupefying vodka selection. It's a great spot for conversation and caviar – or heartier Continental classics like *pelemeni* (dumplings), wild-boar sausage and *shashlik* (lamb kebab).

BIER BARON TAVERN BAR

Map p308 (📞202-293-1887; http://inlovewithbier.com; 1523 22nd St NW; ⏱4pm-midnight Mon-Thu, to 2am Fri & Sat, to 11pm Sun; Ⓜ Red Line to Dupont Circle) Enter the Bier Baron's underground lair and prepare your liver for an onslaught of brews. The dark, dingy, pubby bar taps 50 different beers – emphasis on local and unusual craft suds – and offers 500 more bottled beers from around the world. Aim for a corner seat, order a sampler and settle in for an impressive taste tour.

FILTER CAFE

Map p308 (📞202-234-5837; www.filtercoffeehouse.com; 1726 20th St NW; ⏱7am-7pm Mon-Fri, 8am-7pm Sat & Sun; Ⓜ Red Line to Dupont Circle)

Local Life
A Night Out in Dupont Circle

Dupont gets busy once the sun goes down. Young professionals of all stripes and persuasions gather with friends to drink, dine and sing karaoke. They play board games, quaff sparkling wines, indulge in late-night gelati and burgers, and flirt with each other in the 3am bookshop on weekends.

❶ Wine at Bistro du Coin
Lively and much-loved Bistrot du Coin (p149) is a neighborhood favorite for roll-up-your sleeves, working-class French fare. If it's busy, try for a bar seat. Wines from around the motherland can be gulped by the glass, carafe and bottle.

❷ Board Room's Game Stash
Order a pitcher of beer and prepare to outwit your opponent at Battleship. Or unleash your tic-tac-toe skills with Connect 4. Operation, Risk, Mousetrap, Hungry Hungry Hippos – Board Room (p150) has all of your favorite childhood games to rent for $2 each.

❸ Gelato at Dolcezza
Dolcezza (p148) scoops a dozen or so creamy flavors of gelati. They're not your everyday spoonful, with varieties such as lemon ricotta cardamom and strawberry

tarragon. Don't be timid – they're divine. But they're not the only reason so many people are hanging out here. The pour-over coffee and espresso drinks provide the perfect zap for the night ahead.

❹ Late-Night Books
Open almost round the clock on weekends, Kramerbooks (p155) – along with its attached Afterwords Cafe and bar – is as much a spot for schmoozing as for shopping. Grab a meal, have a pint and flirt with comely strangers (the store is a fabled pick-up spot).

❺ Underground Art
Who knew there was a forsaken streetcar station sprawled beneath Dupont Circle? A local arts group has revamped it into Dupont Underground (p146), a cavernous gallery of art, architecture and design. Check online for exhibition times.

Bistrot du Coin p149

Set on a quiet street, Filter is a jewel-box-sized cafe with a tiny front patio, a hipster crowd, sullen baristas and, most importantly, good, locally roasted coffee. You can get a dandy flat white here.

CAFE CITRON   CLUB
Map p308 (☎202-530-8844; www.cafecitrondc.com; 1343 Connecticut Ave NW; ⊗7pm-2am Mon & Tue, 5pm-2am Wed & Thu, 5pm-3am Fri & Sat; MRed Line to Dupont Circle) Cafe Citron is one of DC's most popular Latin-music clubs (in fairness, it plays everything, but the focus is on salsa, bachata et al). Girls dance, guys watch; the hours tick on. Late night it morphs into an all-dance crowd shaking it to mega-loud music. Nights out here can be fun, if only to observe the unfolding pick-up scene.

Instructors offer free Latin dance lessons at 8pm Monday, Wednesday and Saturday, and at 9pm on Friday.

JR'S   GAY
Map p308 (☎202-328-0090; www.jrsbar-dc.com; 1519 17th St NW; ⊗4pm-2am Mon-Thu, 4pm-3am Fri, 1pm-3am Sat, 1pm-2am Sun; MRed Line to Dupont Circle) Button-down shirts are de rigueur at this gay hangout frequented by the 20- and 30-something, work-hard-and-play-hard set. Some DC residents claim that the crowd at JR's epitomizes the conservative nature of the capital's gay scene, but even if you love to hate it, as many do, JR's knows how to rock a happy hour and is teeming more often than not.

LAURIOL PLAZA   BAR
Map p308 (☎202-387-0035; www.lauriolplaza.com; 1835 18th St NW; ⊗11:30am-11pm Mon-Thu, 11:30am-midnight Fri & Sat, 11am-11pm Sun; MRed Line to Dupont Circle) Lauriol doubles as a decent Mexican restaurant by day; by night, it's extremely popular with the young and frolicsome. Most folks go for the fruit-flavored margaritas – y'know, the ones that don't taste like they've got any booze in them, and you really shouldn't have ordered another three but whatever, man, there's nothing in these...(30 minutes later)...Wooh! I love you, bro!

It's a huge, multilevel space. The outdoor patio sees the most action.

NUMBER NINE   GAY
Map p308 (☎202-986-0999; www.numberninedc.com; 1435 P St NW; ⊗5pm-2am Mon-Thu, 5pm-3am Fri, 2pm-3am Sat, 2pm-2am Sun; MRed

❻ Black Pudding at Duke's Grocery
Duke's Grocery (p149) takes its cue from East London's corner cafes and pubs. Black pudding for brunch, smoky Gouda-topped burgers for dinner – a chalkboard lists the daily-changing menu. The convivial tables spread over two floors amid mismatched armchairs and vintage photos.

❼ Karaoke at JR's
Gay hangout JR's is usually packed. While it's mostly guys aged under 40 in natty-casual attire chatting over their beers, the dark-wood and stained-glass bar is welcoming to all. Show-tunes karaoke is great fun on Monday nights.

❽ Tabard Inn Cocktails
It may be in a hotel, but lots of locals pile into the Tabard Inn Bar (p151) to linger over a brandy or an old-fashioned. The fireplace warms the lodge-like room in winter, while the ivy-swathed patio beckons in summer.

DUPONT CIRCLE & KALORAMA DRINKING & NIGHTLIFE

Line to Dupont Circle) Two-story Number Nine looks like it should be a total den of obnoxiousness, what with its super-sleek, spaceship-style furniture and Euro too-cool-for-school vibe, but then you go inside and it's a totally friendly, even laid-back gay bar. It's a good spot for gay meet-and-greet early in the evening, although things definitely get a bit more cruise-y as the night wears on.

BIG HUNT
BAR

Map p308 (☏202-785-2333; www.thebighunt.net; 1345 Connecticut Ave NW; ⊗4pm-2am Sun-Thu, 4pm-3am Fri, 5pm-3am Sat; Ⓜ Red Line to Dupont Circle) If you just said the name of this bar and smiled a little inner smile (or turned red), well, that's kind of the point. The irreverence is carried on inside via three floors of general tomfoolery, including one of the city's better rooftop patios and some arcade games. For a dive bar, Big Hunt has several surprisingly fine small-batch beers on tap.

Live comedy shows take place Wednesday through Saturday in the basement bar.

DECADES
CLUB

Map p308 (☏202-853-3498; www.decadesdc. com; 1219 Connecticut Ave NW; ⊗9pm-2am Thu, to 3am Fri & Sat; Ⓜ Red Line to Dupont Circle) Decades is a big, booming club with three levels of let-loose dance music: one each for '80s, '90s and 2000s jams. It's good fun, decorated with glowy retro decor and arcade games. No sneakers or athletic gear allowed. There's a $20 cover charge most days.

LUCKY BAR
BAR

Map p308 (☏202-331-3733; www.luckybardc. com; 1221 Connecticut Ave NW; ⊗3pm-2am Sun-Thu, to 3am Fri & Sat; Ⓜ Red Line to Dupont Circle) Lucky's interior is nothing special – your standard double-decker dark wood and cozy chairs. It's the crowd that sets it apart: an amalgamation of capital subcultures ranging from politicos, gay couples, club kids needing a break from thumpa-thumpa and the occasional tourist, everyone enjoying themselves amid a happy booze-fueled drone. Lots of sports, including international soccer, flicker on the slew of big-screen TVs.

COBALT
GAY

Map p308 (☏202-232-4416; www.facebook.com/ cobaltdc; 1639 R St NW; ⊗4pm-2am Mon-Thu, to 3am Fri & Sat, to midnight Sun; Ⓜ Red Line to Dupont Circle) Featuring lots of hair product and buff gym bodies, Cobalt tends to gather a well-dressed late-20s to 30-something crowd who come for fun (but loud!) dance parties throughout the week. The time-hallowed dance club is on the 3rd floor; the venue also has a restaurant on the 1st floor and a lounge on the 2nd.

There's no cover charge early in the week; it ranges from $3 to $12 Thursday through Saturday.

BUFFALO BILLIARDS
BAR

Map p308 (☏202-331-7665; www.buffalo billiards.com; 1330 19th St NW; ⊗4pm-2am Mon-Thu, 4pm-3am Fri, noon-3am Sat, noon-2am Sun; 🛜; Ⓜ Red Line to Dupont Circle) The 15 pool tables pull college kids and yuppies into this bright, below-street-level cave. There's usually a wait for a table, so play a little foosball, ping pong or skeeball before taking up some stick. A couple of good craft beers hide among taps.

 ## ENTERTAINMENT

If you like chamber music, don't forget about the Sunday concerts at the Phillips Collection (p146) at 4pm October through May. Tickets cost $40 and include museum admission. The soirees have been a local tradition since 1941.

DC IMPROV
COMEDY

Map p308 (☏202-296-7008; www.dcimprov. com; 1140 Connecticut Ave NW; tickets $10-22; ⊗closed Mon; Ⓜ Red Line to Farragut North) DC Improv is comedy in the traditional sense, featuring stand-up by comics from *Comedy Central*, *Saturday Night Live* and HBO in its main theater. The smaller 'lounge showroom' hosts wise-cracking, up-and-coming improv troupes, usually with cheaper ticket prices. The venue also offers workshops for those who would like to hone their laugh-getting skills.

EDLAVITCH DC JEWISH COMMUNITY CENTER
ARTS CENTER

Map p308 (☏202-777-3210; www.dcjcc.org; 1529 16th St NW; Ⓜ Red Line to Dupont Circle) The center hosts literary talks, idea symposiums, concerts and films. Its well-respected Theater J addresses the urban American Jewish experience through its plays.

The sleek, boxlike building is a treat in itself, resembling the exterior of a modern-art museum.

SHOPPING

★**KRAMERBOOKS**   BOOKS

Map p308 (☏202-387-1400; www.kramers.com; 1517 Connecticut Ave NW; ⊘7:30am-1am Sun-Thu, to 3am Fri & Sat; Ⓜ Red Line to Dupont Circle) This flagship independent – which leapt into First Amendment history when it refused to release Monica Lewinsky's book-buying list to Ken Starr's snoops – features first-rate literature, travel and politics sections.

The big, sunny bookstore attaches to fun-loving Afterwords Cafe (p149), where a frisky crowd flirts over drinks and pages into the wee hours. Author readings and other literary events take place several nights each week.

★**SECOND STORY BOOKS**   BOOKS, MUSIC

Map p308 (☏202-659-8884; www.secondstorybooks.com; 2000 P St NW; ⊘10am-10pm; Ⓜ Red Line to Dupont Circle) Packed with dusty secondhand tomes, atmospheric Second Story also sells used CDs (mostly jazz and classical), antiquarian books and old sheet music. The prices are decent and the choices are broad (particularly in the realm of history and Americana). Be sure to browse the sidewalk bins, which have books from 50¢ to $2.

DUPONT CIRCLE MARKET   MARKET

Map p308 (www.freshfarm.org; 1500 20th St NW; ⊘8:30am-1:30pm Sun; Ⓜ Red Line to Dupont Circle) The Dupont Circle Market teems with locals on Sunday morning buying fresh breads, cheeses, produce, dumplings, eggs, coffee, spirits and beers.

It's part of the Fresh Farm Market program, one of the leaders of the Chesapeake Bay region local-food movement.

SHOP MADE IN DC   ARTS & CRAFTS

Map p308 (www.shopmadeindc.com; 1330 19th Street NW; ⊘7am-8pm Mon-Fri, 11am-6pm Sat & Sun; Ⓜ Red Line to Dupont Circle) The airy space with floor-to-ceiling windows showcases – yes – locally made goods. The selection changes, but you might find nifty illustrated maps from Cherry Blossom Design or DC-themed wood block prints from art collective Ewba. Start-up restaurants offer wares in the cafe, so you can grab a coffee or Tibetan dumpling while browsing. The shop also hosts art and craft workshops (flower arranging, watercolor painting etc).

TABLETOP   HOMEWARES

Map p308 (☏202-387-7117; www.tabletopdc.com; 1608 20th St NW; ⊘noon-8pm Mon-Sat, 10am-6pm Sun; Ⓜ Red Line to Dupont Circle) Also known as the best little design store in Dupont, Tabletop is evidence that DC is a lot more stylish than some give it credit for. The whimsical candles, postmodern wine carafes and vintage table linens are sure to impress your arty and creative friends.

BEADAZZLED   JEWELRY

Map p308 (☏202-265-2323; www.beadazzled.net; 1507 Connecticut Ave NW; ⊘10am-8pm Mon-Sat, to 6pm Sun; Ⓜ Red Line to Dupont Circle) Crafty types and jewelry lovers should not miss this specialty shop, which carries all things small and stringable. The selection from around the world ranges from 5¢ clay doohickeys to expensive pearls. Helpful staff will tell you how to put them together.

BETSY FISHER   CLOTHING

Map p308 (☏202-785-1975; www.betsyfisher.com; 1224 Connecticut Ave NW; ⊘10am-7pm Mon-Fri, 10am-6pm Sat, 1-5pm Sun; Ⓜ Red Line to Dupont Circle) The sales team at this classy women's boutique makes you feel like a queen while trying on fantastic pieces by Pinko, Iris Setlakwe and other North American and European designers. The styles run the gamut from funky and fashion forward to elegant, but they're a touch on the conservative side.

PROPER TOPPER   FASHION & ACCESSORIES

Map p308 (☏202-842-3055; www.propertopper.com; 1350 Connecticut Ave NW; ⊘10am-7pm Mon-Fri, to 6pm Sat; Ⓜ Red Line to Dupont Circle) Fedoras, panama hats, short- and wide-brimmed straw hats – they're all for sale at the Proper Topper, along with children's books, wallets, jewelry, scarves and a few snazzy black dresses.

SECONDI   CLOTHING

Map p308 (☏202-667-1122; www.secondi.com; 1702 Connecticut Ave NW; ⊘11am-6pm Mon & Tue, to 7pm Wed-Fri, to 6pm Sat, 1-5pm Sun; Ⓜ Red Line to Dupont Circle) Up a narrow row of stairs, Secondi is filled with top-label, secondhand clothing for women, like Marc Jacobs jackets and slightly preloved Manolo Blahnik shoes. It's not the cheapest shop in the city (it's not a thriftshop – goods are sold on consignment), but it has a good collection of big-name designers.

Adams Morgan

Neighborhood Top Five

❶ 18th St NW (p162)
Exploring where Ethiopians, Koreans, Indians, Cubans and hard drinkers collide in a row of restaurants, music clubs, dive bars, vintage boutiques, and indie record shops like Songbyrd Record Cafe & Music House.

❷ Tail Up Goat (p161)
Pretending you're on a breezy island, sharing lemony plates of lamb ribs and sunny cocktails.

❸ Jack Rose Dining Saloon (p162) Ogling the largest whiskey collection in the western hemisphere, where more than 2600 bottles stack the infinite shelves.

❹ Dan's Cafe (p162) Indulging in a squirt bottle of booze at one of DC's premier dive bars.

❺ Madam's Organ (p163) Catching a blues band, drinking on the rooftop deck and snapping a photo of the bawdy mural outside.

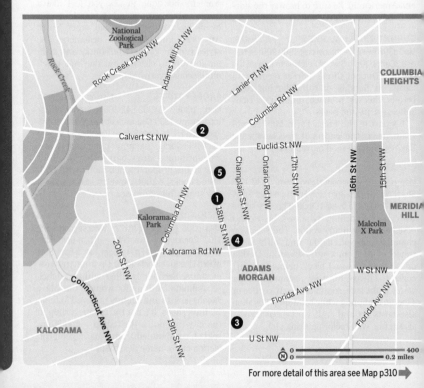

For more detail of this area see Map p310 ➡

Explore Adams Morgan

Nighttime is when Adams Morgan really lets loose and is the best time to see the neighborhood in full swing. Start at the intersection of 18th St NW and Columbia Rd NW. Several top restaurants huddle here, so choose among the smart, Michelin-starred and chef-driven spots to kick off the evening. Then head south down 18th St NW to make your way into area's wild heart. Bars and live-music clubs send out their siren call every few feet. These have long been the domain of the young and frisky, where people drink, get hammered, dance, and then stumble out in search of munchies. And it still happens – but Adams Morgan is also starting to grow up. As some of the old dive bars have fallen by the wayside, high-aiming ramen shops, taco bars and other eateries have popped up in their stead.

While AdMo (as it's called in local text message–ese) is quieter during the day, you could also spend an afternoon here taking in the area's global vibe and funky shops. Stroll 18th St NW and you'll sniff shish kebabs, Ethiopian lamb stew, jerk chicken and vegetable biryani mingling in the air from the small ethnic restaurants that line the road. Vintage boutiques, arty homewares stores, cool record shops and classic booksellers beckon from the storefronts as well, and make for good browsing.

Local Life

→ **Sip and Spin** Drink coffee with musician types during the day at Songbyrd Record Cafe & Music House (p162), then stay for DJs in the evening. The first and third Wednesday of the month are open turntable, when patrons bring their own vinyl to spin.

→ **Jazz Jam** Local musicians gather at Columbia Station (p163) for a lengthy open jam session on Sunday.

→ **Block Party** The Adams Morgan Day Festival rocks the second Sunday of September. International bands, dance and food vendors take over the streets for DC's biggest neighborhood bash.

Getting There & Away

→ **Metro** To reach most of 18th St, use the Woodley Park-Zoo/Adams Morgan station (Red Line). For points on 18th St south of Kalorama Rd, the Dupont Circle station (Red Line) is closer. Each station is about a 15-minute walk away.

→ **Bus** The DC Circulator runs from the Woodley Park-Zoo/Adams Morgan Metro to the corner of 18th and Calvert Sts (a block north of Columbia Rd), before heading east out of the neighborhood.

Lonely Planet's Top Tip

Hit the roof. Several bars and restaurants in the 'hood have rooftop decks where you can eat, drink and survey the scene playing out below. Madam's Organ (p163) and Jack Rose Dining Saloon (p162) offer swell vistas. If heights aren't your thing, settle in at ground level for alfresco drinks on the patio at Tryst (p160) or Mintwood Place (p161).

 Best Places to Eat

→ Tail Up Goat (p161)

→ Donburi (p160)

→ Mintwood Place (p161)

→ Federalist Pig (p160)

For reviews, see p160.

Best Places to Drink

→ Songbyrd Record Cafe & Music House (p162)

→ Dan's Cafe (p162)

→ Jack Rose Dining Saloon (p162)

For reviews, see p162.

Best Shopping

→ Meeps (p163)

→ Brass Knob (p163)

→ Idle Time Books (p163)

→ Tibet Shop (p164)

For reviews, see p163.

ANDREI MEDVEDEV / SHUTTERSTOCK ©

ryst p160
pular restaurant for locals.

Row houses p259
et scene showing row houses and shops
g the road.

torefront at Smash! records
4
ms Morgan is home to a range of cool
rd shops and classic booksellers.

Ethnic shops p160
neighborhood also has a global vibe,
s loaded with ethnic eateries, funky
rs, boutiques and arty homewares
es.

SUSAN ISAKSON / ALAMY STOCK PHOTO ©

SIGHTS

DISTRICT OF COLUMBIA ARTS CENTER
ARTS CENTER

Map p310 (DCAC; ☎202-462-7833; www.
dcartscenter.org; 2438 18th St NW; ⊙2-7pm
Wed-Sun; Ⓜ Red Line to Woodley Park-Zoo/
Adams Morgan) FREE The grassroots DCAC
offers emerging artists a space to showcase
their work. The 800-sq-ft gallery features
rotating visual-arts exhibits, while plays,
improv, avant-garde musicals and other
theatrical productions take place in the 50-
seat theater. The gallery is free and worth
popping into to see what's showing.

✖ EATING

**The area around 18th St NW and
Columbia Rd NW is loaded with ethnic
eateries and funky diners. Eclectic
foodie hot spots have been popping up
in their midst, bringing wood-burning
ovens, barbecued eel and Michelin stars
to the neighborhood as well.**

★ DONBURI
JAPANESE $

Map p310 (☎202-629-1047; www.donburidc.com;
2438 18th St NW; mains $11-13; ⊙11am-10pm;
Ⓜ Red Line to Woodley Park-Zoo/Adams Morgan)
Hole-in-the-wall Donburi has 15 seats at a
wooden counter where you get a front-row
view of the slicing, dicing chefs. *Donburi*
means 'bowl' in Japanese, and that's what
arrives steaming hot and filled with, say,
panko-coated shrimp atop rice and blended
with the house's sweet-and-savory sauce.
It's a simple, authentic meal. There's often
a line, but it moves quickly. No reservations.

Donburi has another venue in Dupont
Circle that's larger, but the Adams Morgan
location is the atmospheric original.

★ FEDERALIST PIG
BARBECUE $

Map p310 (☎202-827-4400; www.federalistpig.
com; 1654 Columbia Rd NW; mains $9-17; ⊙5-
10pm Wed-Fri, noon-9pm Sat & Sun; Ⓜ Green, Yellow Line to Columbia Heights) A humble, shack-
like spot with a handful of tables, Federalist Pig barbecues renowned ribs and pork
shoulder. View the menu on the tack-up
board, place your order at the counter, grab
a beer from the cooler, then wait for your
meat to arrive. It serves until the food runs
out, which happens fairly often. Updates on
Twitter (@federalistpig) when it's gone.

The sauces have a spicy kick. Top marks
to the Carolina on My Mind chopped-pork-
shoulder sandwich.

DINER
AMERICAN $

Map p310 (☎202-232-8800; www.dinerdc.com;
2453 18th St NW; mains $9-18; ⊙24hr; ☑ ♿;
Ⓜ Red Line to Woodley Park-Zoo/Adams Morgan)
The Diner serves hearty comfort food,
any time of the day or night. It's ideal for
wee-hour breakfast scarf-downs, weekend
Bloody Mary brunches (if you don't mind
crowds) or any time you want unfussy,
well-prepared American fare. Omelets, fat
pancakes, mac 'n' cheese, grilled tofu tacos
and burgers hit the tables with aplomb. It's
a good spot for kids, too.

TRYST
CAFE $

Map p310 (☎202-232-5500; www.trystdc.com;
2459 18th St NW; breakfast & sandwiches $8-12;
⊙7am-midnight Sun-Thu, to 1am Fri & Sat; ☎;
Ⓜ Red Line to Woodley Park-Zoo/Adams Morgan)
The couches, armchairs and bookshelves,
and the light flooding through streetside
windows, lure patrons so faithful they probably should pay rent at Tryst. They crowd
in for the coffee, stellar omelet and waffle
breakfasts, and creative sandwiches. Come
nightfall, baristas become bartenders,
and the cafe hosts jazzy live music several
nights a week. Tryst turns off the wi-fi on
weekends.

AMSTERDAM FALAFELSHOP
MIDDLE EASTERN $

Map p310 (☎202-234-1969; www.falafelshop.
com; 2425 18th St NW; items $6-8; ⊙11am-
midnight Sun & Mon, to 2:30am Tue-Thu, to 4am
Fri & Sat; ☑; Ⓜ Red Line to Woodley Park-Zoo/
Adams Morgan) Cheap and cheerful, fast and
delicious, the Falafelshop rocks the world
of vegetarians and those questing for late-
night munchies. Bowl up to the counter, order your falafel sandwich, then take it to the
topping bar and pile on pickles, tabbouleh,
olives and 20 other items. Take away, or
dribble away at the scattering of stools and
tables.

French fries are the only other dish on
the menu, best slathered with a mayo-and-
peanut-sauce combination from the topping bar.

PLEASANT POPS
CAFE $

Map p310 (☎202-558-5224; www.pleasantpops.
com; 1781 Florida Ave NW; mains $3-6; ⊙7:30am-
7pm Mon-Fri, from 8:30am Sat & Sun; ☎☑; Ⓜ Red

Line to Dupont Circle) Pleasant Pops cafe is definitely pleasant, with big windows that let in plenty of natural light. The 'pops' are popsicles, or Mexican *paletas* to be exact, in flavors like peach hibiscus, Mexican sweet cream and cinnamon. The good-vibe little eatery also brews zippy coffee and prepares hit-the-spot vegetarian soups and rice bowls.

CAKEROOM
BAKERY $

Map p310 (☏202-450-4462; www.cakeroombakery.com; 2006 18th St NW; baked goods $2.50-5; ⏰9am-9pm Mon-Thu, to 10pm Fri, 10am-10pm Sat, to 9pm Sun; 🛜; Ⓜ Red Line to Dupont Circle) Ogle the glass cases bursting with creamy-frosted cakes and pies. The banoffee pie (a sublime banana-toffee mix) and carrot cupcake are the sweets to beat. Fadi, the baker, is from Jordan, and he invites guests to linger on the comfy couches and armchairs upstairs in the old-timey shop.

JULIA'S EMPANADAS
LATIN AMERICAN $

Map p310 (☏202-328-6232; www.juliasempanadas.com; 2452 18th St NW; empanadas from $5; ⏰10am-midnight Mon-Thu, to 4am Fri & Sat, to 8pm Sun; Ⓜ Red Line to Woodley Park-Zoo/Adams Morgan) A frequent winner in DC's 'best late-night eats' polls, Julia's stuffs its dough bombs with chorizo, Jamaican beef curry, spinach and more. Flavors peak if you've been drinking. The little chain has a handful of takeout shops around town.

★TAIL UP GOAT
MEDITERRANEAN $$

Map p310 (☏202-986-9600; www.tailupgoat.com; 1827 Adams Mill Rd NW; mains $18-27; ⏰5:30-10pm Mon-Thu, 5-10pm Fri-Sun; Ⓜ Red Line to Woodley Park-Zoo/Adams Morgan) With its pale-blue walls, light wood decor and lantern-like lights dangling overhead, Tail Up Goat exudes a warm, island-y vibe. The lamb ribs are the specialty – crispy and lusciously fatty, with grilled lemon, figs and spices. The housemade breads and spreads star on the menu too – say, flaxseed sourdough with beets. No wonder Michelin gave it a star.

The menu is mostly sharable plates plus a handful of meat and fish mains. Lots of wines and refreshing cocktails help wash it all down.

★MINTWOOD PLACE
AMERICAN $$

Map p310 (☏202-234-6732; www.mintwoodplace.com; 1813 Columbia Rd NW; mains $18-30; ⏰5:30-10pm Tue-Thu, to 10:30pm Fri & Sat,

MIDNIGHT BITES & BRUNCH

Adams Morgan is famed for its late-night eateries. Lots of people come here postparty on weekend nights to soak up the booze. Huge slices of pizza are a traditional snack: they're sold everywhere around the neighborhood and are uniformly greasy and delicious after several libations. Other places to stuff your face in the wee hours:

➡ Diner

➡ Amsterdam Falafelshop

➡ Julia's Empanadas

Brunch is another favorite meal in the 'hood. It's usually decadent at the following places:

➡ Perry's

➡ Tryst

➡ Mintwood Place

to 9pm Sun, plus 10:30am-2:30pm Sat & Sun; Ⓜ Red Line to Woodley Park-Zoo/Adams Morgan) In a neighborhood known for jumbo pizza slices and Jell-o shots, Mintwood Place is a romantic anomaly. Take a seat in a brown-leather booth or at a reclaimed-wood table under twinkling lights. Then sniff the French-American fusion dishes that emerge from the wood-burning oven. The *flammekueche* (onion and bacon tart), chicken-liver mousse and escargot hush puppies show how it's done.

BUL
KOREAN $$

Map p310 (☏202-733-3921; www.buldc.com; 2431 18th St NW; mains $14-21; ⏰5:30-10:30pm Tue-Thu, to 2am Fri, 4:30pm-2am Sat, to 10pm Sun; Ⓜ Red Line to Woodley Park-Zoo/Adams Morgan) BUL is DC's first *pojangmacha* ('covered wagon'; Korean street-food eatery). Trendy locals love it, gobbling up grilled skewers of meat and vegetables, seafood pancakes and a fishcakey 'hangover soup.' The pork-belly fried rice comes with roasted kimchi made by the chefs' mothers.

For drinks, BUL pours seasonal flavors from a local kombucha brewery, as well as Asian spirits and beers.

PERRY'S
JAPANESE $$

Map p310 (☏202-234-6218; www.perrysam.com; 1811 Columbia Rd NW; mains $15-26; ⏰5:30-10pm Mon-Thu, to 11pm Fri & Sat, 10am-3pm &

5:30-10pm Sun; Ⓜ Red Line to Woodley Park-Zoo/Adams Morgan) You can munch sushi at Perry's, but it's the creative fusion fare that really deserves your tongue's attention. Eat in the attractive lounge or under the stars on the rooftop. Sunday brings something entirely different: drag-queen brunch. The megapopular campy show plus buffet is a scene to behold. Make reservations (up to two months in advance).

🍷 DRINKING & 🍸 NIGHTLIFE

Chic whiskey saloons and music cafes are making inroads among the rowdy dive bars. A youngish crowd predominates. Almost all of the action happens on 18th St NW.

★ **SONGBYRD RECORD CAFE & MUSIC HOUSE**   CAFE

Map p310 (☎202-450-2917; www.songbyrddc.com; 2477 18th St NW; ⊗8am-2am Sun-Thu, to 3am Fri & Sat; 🛜; Ⓜ Red Line to Woodley Park-Zoo/Adams Morgan) By day hang out in the retro cafe, drinking excellent coffee, munching sandwiches and browsing the small selection of soul and indie LPs for sale. You can even cut your own record in the vintage recording booth ($15). By night the party moves to the DJ-spinning bar, where beer and cocktails flow alongside burgers and tacos, and indie bands rock the basement club.

★ **DAN'S CAFE**   BAR

Map p310 (☎202-265-0299; 2315 18th St NW; ⊗7pm-2am Tue-Thu, to 3am Fri & Sat; Ⓜ Red Line to Woodley Park-Zoo/Adams Morgan) This is one of DC's great dive bars. The interior looks sort of like an evil Elks Club, all unironically old-school 'art,' cheap paneling and dim lights barely illuminating the unapologetic slumminess. It's famed for its whopping, mix-it-yourself drinks, where you get a ketchup-type squirt bottle of booze, a can of soda and bucket of ice for $20. Cash only.

Dan's isn't marked, as the sign fell by the wayside a while ago, so keep an eye on the surrounding street addresses.

★ **JACK ROSE DINING SALOON**   BAR

Map p310 (☎202-588-7388; www.jackrosediningsaloon.com; 2007 18th St NW; ⊗5pm-2am Sun-Thu, to 3am Fri & Sat; Ⓜ Red Line to Dupont Circle) Walk into Jack Rose and you know you've hit the whiskey jackpot. Hundreds of bottles stack the shelves – 2687 bottles, to be exact. It's the largest whiskey collection in the western hemisphere. The space contains multiple bars on three stories, each with a different feel and different cocktail menu. No wonder it's been called the center of the whiskey universe.

Here's the lineup: you've got the main Dining Saloon, where you can order from the full restaurant menu (Southern-tinged American fare) and cigar menu to go with your booze; the Open-Air Terrace, with its retractable roof and upscale snack menu; the groovy Tiki Bar, a festive seasonal space; and the basement whiskey Cellar, where entrance is by reservation only (text 202-607-1572). If you're not feeling the whiskey urge, you can also opt for unique cocktails, wines from around the world and more than 20 beers on tap.

BLACK SQUIRREL   BAR

Map p310 (☎202-232-1011; www.blacksquirreldc.com; 2427 18th St NW; ⊗5pm-1am Mon-Fri, from 11am Sat & Sun; Ⓜ Red Line to Woodley Park-Zoo/Adams Morgan) Sometimes in Adams Morgan all you want is a good friggin' beer – no suds in plastic cups, no Jaeger shots – just a stellar microbrew. The warm, exposed-brick Squirrel stocks more than 100 unusual ales, from Mexican-spiced elixirs to abbey-style triple brews. Hungry? Pair them with the gastropub grub, such as the Gruyère-smothered, house-ground burgers.

BOSSA   LOUNGE

Map p310 (☎202-650-9351; www.bossadc.com; 2463 18th St NW; ⊗5:30pm-2am Tue-Thu & Sun, to 3am Fri & Sat; Ⓜ Red Line to Woodley Park-Zoo/Adams Morgan) Dark, intimate, close and sexy – that's the scene at Bossa. The soundtrack, if you couldn't guess: jazz, flamenco and bossa nova played in the candlelit lounge. It's a relatively chilled-out spot to drink mojitos and caipirinhas early on, and then it gets its groove on, so bring your dancing feet and prepare to samba (or salsa, or bachata…).

Often there's a cover charge, but it's rarely more than $10.

BLAGUARD   IRISH PUB

Map p310 (☎202-232-9005; www.blaguarddc.com; 2003 18th St NW; ⊗5pm-2am Mon & Tue, 12:30pm-2am Wed, Thu & Sun, to 3am Fri & Sat; Ⓜ Red Line to Dupont Circle) The Blaguard is a fine bar in which to finish an Adams Morgan night. After you've had too much time dancing and screaming into someone's ear, you want a place that'll keep the party going but is a few notches lower on the crazy scale than a club. This youthful, slightly grungy neighborhood spot delivers.

HABANA VILLAGE   CLUB
Map p310 (☑202-462-6310; www.habanavillage.com; 1834 Columbia Rd NW; ⊙5:30-11pm Wed, to midnight Thu, to 2:30am Fri & Sat; ⓂRed Line to Woodley Park-Zoo/Adams Morgan) Squeezed into an old town house with a cosmopolitan bar and romantic back room, the Village is as close as DC gets to Cuba. That's not particularly close, but you do get good, stiff mojitos here, and the music – salsa, meringue, mambo and bossa nova – packs the dance floor fairly often. Instructors give salsa lessons ($10) each evening at 7:30pm.

 ENTERTAINMENT

MADAM'S ORGAN   LIVE MUSIC
Map p310 (☑202-667-5370; www.madamsorgan.com; 2461 18th St NW; cover $5-10; ⊙5pm-2am Sun-Thu, to 3am Fri & Sat; ⓂRed Line to Woodley Park-Zoo/Adams Morgan) *Playboy* magazine once named Madam's Organ one of its favorite bars in America. The ramshackle place has been around forever, and its nightly blues, rock and bluegrass shows can be downright riot-inducing. There's a raunchy bar-dancing scene and funky decor with stuffed animals and bizarre paintings on the 1st floor. The rooftop deck is more mellow. The big-boobed mural outside is a classic.

BUKOM CAFE   LIVE MUSIC
Map p310 (☑202-265-4600; 2442 18th St NW; ⊙4:30pm-2am; ⓂRed Line to Woodley Park-Zoo/Adams Morgan) Reggae and highlife bands take the stage nightly at Bukom. Be prepared for sore but happy hips as you join the mix of West African immigrants and ex–Peace Corps types who've earned their dancing chops on the continent. The music starts at 10pm (earlier weekdays); there's no cover charge. Come early and sample the chicken *yassa* and other West African fare.

COLUMBIA STATION   LIVE MUSIC
Map p310 (☑202-462-6040; www.columbiastationdc.com; 2325 18th St NW; ⊙5pm-2am Tue-Thu, to 3am Fri & Sat, 4pm-1am Sun; ⓂRed Line to Woodley Park-Zoo/Adams Morgan) Columbia Station is an intimate spot to listen to nightly jazz and blues, and if you're on a budget it's especially appealing – it doesn't have a cover charge. It's a good date spot (well, assuming your date likes jazz), with lots of low light and, natch, romantic music.

Sunday's jam session, which starts around 4:30pm, brings out a sweet group of regulars.

 SHOPPING

Funky boutiques, antique shops and stores selling ethnic knickknacks are the strong suits here.

MEEPS   VINTAGE
Map p310 (☑202-265-6546; www.meepsdc.com; 2104 18th St NW; ⊙noon-7pm Sun & Mon, to 8pm Tue-Sat; ⓂRed Line to Dupont Circle) There's this girl you know: extremely stylish and never seems to have a brand name on her body. Now, picture her wardrobe. Mod dresses, cowboy shirts, suede jackets, beaded purses, leather boots, Jackie O sunglasses and denim jumpsuits: there's Meeps mapped out for you. The store also carries a selection of clever, locally designed T-shirts.

BRASS KNOB   ANTIQUES
Map p310 (☑202-332-3370; www.thebrassknob.com; 2311 18th St NW; ⊙10:30am-6pm Mon-Sat, noon-5pm Sun; ⓂRed Line to Woodley Park-Zoo/Adams Morgan) This unique two-floor shop sells 'rescues' from old buildings: fixtures, lamps, tiles, mantelpieces and mirrors. The store's raison d'être, though, is the doorknob: brass, wooden, glass, elaborate, polished and antique. If you need to accent your crib like the interior of the best old DC row houses, look no further. Staff can help you find whatever you need.

IDLE TIME BOOKS   BOOKS
Map p310 (☑202-232-4774; www.idletimebooks.com; 2467 18th St NW; ⊙11am-10pm; ⓂRed Line to Woodley Park-Zoo/Adams Morgan) Three creaky floors are stuffed with secondhand literature and nonfiction, including one of the best secondhand political and history collections in the city. Its sci-fi, sports and humor sections are top-notch, and there's a good newsstand in its front window.

TIBET SHOP   ARTS & CRAFTS

Map p310 (☎202-287-1880; 2407 18th St NW; ⓧ10:30am-10pm Sun & Mon, to 11pm Tue, to 11:30pm Wed & Thu, to midnight Fri & Sat; Ⓜ Red Line to Woodley Park-Zoo/Adams Morgan) This long, narrow shop bursts with colorful, quality wares amid the sweet smell of incense. Singing bowls, chunky beads, prayer flags, carved masks, flowy skirts and heaps more items from the Himalayan homeland stock the shelves. The friendly Tibetan staff are happy to answer any questions about the items.

SMASH!   MUSIC

Map p310 (☎202-387-6274; www.smashrecords. com; 2314 18th St NW; ⓧnoon-9pm Mon-Thu, to 9:30pm Fri & Sat, to 7pm Sun; Ⓜ Red Line to Woodley Park-Zoo/Adams Morgan) There's a punk-rock vibe to this small shop. In addition to a solid selection of vinyl (covering mostly classic and indie rock and soul), Smash! sells used and new CDs, punky T-shirts, Doc Martens and secondhand clothing.

ADAMS MORGAN
FARMERS MARKET   MARKET

Map p310 (cnr Columbia Rd NW & 18th St NW, bank plaza; ⓧ8am-1pm Sat May-Nov; Ⓜ Red Line to Woodley Park-Zoo/Adams Morgan) On Saturday mornings the Adams Morgan Farmers Market pops up for a few brief hours. Join locals filling their reusable bags with produce, eggs, cheese, honey and cider from nearby small farms.

COMMONWEALTH   CLOTHING

Map p310 (☎202-265-1155; www.common wealth-ftgg.com; 1781 Florida Ave NW; ⓧnoon-8pm Mon-Sat, to 5pm Sun; Ⓜ Red Line to Dupont Circle) With a purely hip-hop aesthetic, Commonwealth sells one-of-a-kind sneakers, graphic T-shirts, hoodies and other street fashion. This is where rappers, DJs and NBA players get their look.

FLEET FEET   SHOES

Map p310 (☎202-387-3888; www.fleetfeetdc. com; 1841 Columbia Rd NW; ⓧ10am-8pm Mon-Fri, to 7pm Sat, noon-4pm Sun; Ⓜ Red Line to Woodley Park-Zoo/Adams Morgan) Shoes for every sporting activity are on sale at this outlet of the national chain, and the personalized service ensures your feet get what they need. The store hosts free runs at 9am Sunday; they're typically 5 miles and often swing through nearby Rock Creek Park. Women-only runs take place Wednesday at 6pm.

B&K CONVENIENCE
STORE   GIFTS & SOUVENIRS

Map p310 (2414 18th St NW; ⓧ9am-9pm; Ⓜ Red Line to Woodley Park-Zoo/Adams Morgan) B&K is primarily a pipe shop, one of the most famed among the city's stoner set. All of the glassware is, of course, to be used for tobacco smoking. Incense, energy drinks and junk-food snacks round out the heady offerings.

Logan Circle, U Street & Columbia Heights

Neighborhood Top Five

❶ **Ben's Chili Bowl** (p171) Taking a seat at this storied spot that has seen the neighborhood through good times and bad, and joining locals to eat half-smokes and gossip over sweet iced tea.

❷ **National Arboretum** (p168) Walking through wooded groves, meadows and an ethereal garden made out of Capitol pillar ruins.

❸ **Right Proper Brewing Co** (p175) Feeling the neighborhood vibe at this cheery beery brewery that was once a pool hall where Duke Ellington played.

❹ **Busboys & Poets** (p172) Discussing politics, browsing books, sipping free-trade coffee and listening to poets spout verse at this bohemian cafe.

❺ **National Museum of Health and Medicine** (p168) Gawking at Lincoln's assassination bullet and other macabre exhibits.

For more detail of this area see Map p312 ➡

Lonely Planet's Top Tip

Loosen the belt. These areas have fantastic eating and drinking options. Pick a street and meander until you find a favorite. There's 14th St in Logan Circle (trendy), 11th St in Columbia Heights (neighborly), Upshur St in Petworth (cozy) and U St in the heart of it all (budget fare and soul food).

Best Places to Eat

→ Ben's Chili Bowl (p171)
→ Himitsu (p182)
→ Chercher (p171)
→ Compass Rose (p172)
→ Busboys & Poets (p172)

For reviews, see p170.

Best Places to Drink

→ Right Proper Brewing Co (p175)
→ Primrose (p178)
→ Atlas Brew Works (p178)
→ Raven (p177)
→ U Street Music Hall (p175)

For reviews, see p175.

Best Live Music

→ Black Cat (p179)
→ 9:30 Club (p179)
→ Twins Jazz (p179)
→ DC9 (p179)

For reviews, see p179. →

Explore Logan Circle, U Street & Columbia Heights

The U St Corridor is the heart of this vast area and a fine spot to begin your explorations. A stroll here rewards with African American historic sights, soul food restaurants, mural-splashed alleys and red-hot music clubs. Spend an afternoon checking it out, or better yet, devote an evening to the nightlife scene.

U St becomes part of the larger Shaw district, which is one of DC's hottest 'hoods. But it's not annoyingly trendy. Instead, the breweries, bars and cafes that seem to pop up weekly are local places, where neighbors come to sip among neighbors. Logan Circle is next door and also booming. Walk down 14th St NW and it's stacked with dapper bars and bistros. An evening spent eating and drinking in the area is a must.

To the north, Columbia Heights is an enclave that mixes Latino immigrants and hipsters. There are no real sights, but the cheap ethnic food and unassuming punk dive bars can occupy many an evening.

Farther on, Northeast DC is a sprawl of leafy streets that hold uncommon sights. Nature lovers have a couple of groovy, free landscapes to explore, while those who like going off the beaten path can play in on-the-rise quarters such as distillery-rich Ivy City and arty, beery Brookland. You won't find many tourists out this way; it takes wheels or a lengthy public-transportation trip to reach.

Local Life

→ **Meet at the Market** On weekends, it seems like all of DC's young and hip are socializing at Union Market (p174) and noshing on foodie delights.

→ **Bang on the Drum All Day** When the weather warms, a multicultural group gathers in Meridian Hill Park (p167) for a drum circle on Sunday afternoons.

→ **Distillery Drinks** Ivy City (p178) is the go-to district for distilleries and other hot spots in revamped warehouses; locals say it's like Logan Circle's 14th St, but grittier and cheaper.

Getting There & Away

→ **Metro** The Green and Yellow Lines run in tandem to most sites. Useful stops are U St, Shaw-Howard U, Columbia Heights and Georgia Ave-Petworth. Religious sites and bars cluster near Brookland-CUA (Red Line). For Logan Circle points south of P St use McPherson Sq (Blue, Orange, Silver Lines); for points north, use the U St Metro station.

→ **Bus** D4 links the Ivy City neighborhood and Dupont Circle, but it's easier to use a rideshare service to reach the area.

👁 SIGHTS

👁 Logan Circle, U Street & Shaw

AFRICAN AMERICAN CIVIL WAR MEMORIAL
MONUMENT

Map p312 (www.afroamcivilwar.org; cnr U St & Vermont Ave NW; ⊘24hr; Ⓜ Green, Yellow Line to U St) Standing at the center of a granite plaza, this bronze memorial depicting rifle-bearing troops is DC's first major art piece by black sculptor Ed Hamilton. The statue is surrounded on three sides by the Wall of Honor, listing the names of 209,145 black troops who fought in the Union Army, as well as the 7000 white soldiers who served alongside them. To look up individual names and find their location on the memorial, check the website's 'Colored Troops Search.' To reach the plaza, depart the Metro station via the 10th St exit (follow the 'memorial' signs as you leave the train).

AFRICAN AMERICAN CIVIL WAR MUSEUM
MUSEUM

Map p312 (☎202-667-2667; www.afroamcivilwar.org; 1925 Vermont Ave NW; ⊘10am-5pm Mon, to 6:30pm Tue-Fri, to 4pm Sat & Sun; Ⓜ Green, Yellow Line to U St) FREE Set in an old schoolhouse behind the African American Civil War Memorial, the museum makes the point that for some, the Civil War was about secession versus union, but for others, it was a matter of breaking human bondage. The permanent exhibit uses photographs, videos and artifacts like slave shackles and a slave bill of sale to follow African American history from the Civil War through to the Civil Rights movement.

Knowledgeable staff answer questions and offer impromptu tours. They can also help visitors search for ancestors in databases of black troops, regiments and battles (accessible via the museum's website).

FOUNDRY GALLERY
GALLERY

Map p312 (☎202-232-0203; www.foundrygallery.org; 2118 8th St NW; ⊘1-7pm Wed-Sun; Ⓜ Green, Yellow Line to Shaw-Howard U) FREE A nonprofit member-run organization, this small gallery features a diverse range of supercontemporary art – mediums include painting, sculpture and drawings – all created by local artists. Peek in the big, street-level windows to see what's showing. Openings are held on various Saturdays.

HOWARD UNIVERSITY
UNIVERSITY

Map p312 (☎202-806-6100; www2.howard.edu; 2400 6th St NW; Ⓜ Green, Yellow Line to Shaw-Howard U) Founded in 1867, Howard remains the nation's most prestigious traditionally African American institute of higher education. Distinguished alumni include the late Supreme Court Justice Thurgood Marshall (who enrolled after he was turned away from the University of Maryland's then all-white law school), Nobel laureate Toni Morrison and former New York City mayor David Dinkins. Today Howard enrolls around 11,000 students in 13 schools. The Shaw neighborhood is as defined by Howard University as Georgetown is by its titular school.

Staff and students give free campus tours (www2.howard.edu/contact/visit). You must reserve in advance.

BETHUNE COUNCIL HOUSE
HISTORIC SITE

Map p312 (☎202-673-2402; www.nps.gov/mamc; 1318 Vermont Ave NW; ⊘9am-4pm; Ⓜ Orange, Silver, Blue Line to McPherson Sq) FREE Mary McLeod Bethune served as President Franklin Roosevelt's special advisor on minority affairs and eventually became the first African American woman to head a federal office. Her Vermont Ave home, where she lived for seven years, was the first headquarters of the National Council of Negro Women, which Bethune established in 1935. Tours cover Bethune's life, and exhibits, lectures and workshops on black history are held here as well.

In March 2018, Florida legislators voted to place a statue of Bethune in National Statuary Hall, making Bethune the first African American to be honored in this way. The site was undergoing renovation at the time of research; check for updates before heading out.

👁 Columbia Heights

MERIDIAN HILL PARK
PARK

Map p312 (www.nps.gov/mehi; btwn 15th, 16th, Euclid & W Sts NW; ⊘5am-midnight May-Oct, to 9pm Nov-Apr; Ⓜ Green, Yellow Line to Columbia Heights) This is an incredible bit of urban green space. The grounds are terraced like a hanging garden replete with waterfalls, sandstone terraces and assorted embellishments that feel almost Tuscan. The prettiest bits reside in the park's south end, including DC's only memorial to James Buchanan (the USA's 15th president). Many locals still

NATIONAL MUSEUM OF HEALTH AND MEDICINE

Macabre exhibits galore pack this Department of Defense–run **museum** (NMHM; 301-319-3300; www.medicalmuseum.mil; 2500 Linden Lane, Silver Spring, MD; ⊙10am-5:30pm; MRed Line to Forest Glen) FREE. The stomach-shaped hairball leaves a lasting impression (a 12-year-old girl ate that?), as does the megacolon (use your imagination). The showpiece is the bullet that killed Abraham Lincoln, encased alongside bits of his skull. The museum is located at Fort Detrick's Forest Glen Annex. That's officially out of the District, but just over the border in Silver Spring, MD.

Opened in 1862, the museum is one of the oldest in the DC area. The focus of the museum's eclectic collection is military medicine – the displays on Civil War combat 'nursing' are gruesome and fascinating in equal measure. It's not for the faint-hearted – visitors will see the effects of diseases, the tools used to battle them and all the messy side and after effects

Unfortunately, the Metro won't get you very close (the station is a mile from the site), so it's easiest to drive out. Parking is free. Bring photo ID.

call this Malcolm X Park from its days of hosting political rallies. The Sunday drum circle (from 3pm to 9pm) has been going on since the 1960s.

⊙ Northeast DC

★UNITED STATES
NATIONAL ARBORETUM   GARDENS

(202-245-2726; www.usna.usda.gov; R St NE; ⊙8am-5pm; MOrange, Silver, Blue Line to Stadium-Armory, then bus B2) FREE The greatest green space in Washington unfurls almost 450 acres of meadowland, sylvan theaters and a pastoral setting that feels somewhere between bucolic Americana countryside and a classical Greek ruralscape. Highlights include the Bonsai & Penjing Museum (exquisitely sculpted mini trees), the National Herb Garden (lots of hot peppers) and the otherworldly Capitol Columns Garden (studded with Corinthian pillars that were once part of the Capitol building). All are near the R St entrance.

A short distance onward, the National Grove of State Trees rises up. It sprouts everything from New York's sugar maple to California's giant sequoia. Stop at the Administration Building for a map and self-guided tour information. Prepare to do a lot of walking.

To reach the arboretum, take the Metro to bus B2. Get off on Bladensburg Rd at Rand St, which puts you a few blocks from the R St entrance. (There's another entrance on New York Ave NE, but R St is more convenient.)

KENILWORTH
AQUATIC GARDENS   GARDENS

(202-426-6905; www.nps.gov/keaq; 1550 Anacostia Ave NE; ⊙8am-4pm; MOrange Line to Deanwood) FREE DC was built on a marsh, a beautiful, brackish, low-lying ripple of saw grass and steel-blue water, wind-coaxed and tide touched by the inflow of the Potomac from Chesapeake Bay. You'd never know all that now, of course, unless you come to the USA's only national park devoted to water plants. See the natural wetlands the District sprang from; look out for beaver dams, clouds of birds and the more traditional manicured grounds, quilted in water lilies and lotus.

The gardens are a lovely refuge, and you'll likely have them to yourself. A cool boardwalk juts out into the water at the park's southwest edge. The Anacostia River Trail starts from near the visitor center. Kenilworth is about a mile walk from the Metro.

PRESIDENT
LINCOLN'S COTTAGE   HISTORIC SITE

(202-829-0436; www.lincolncottage.org; 140 Rock Creek Church Rd NW; adult/child $15/5; ⊙10am-3pm Mon-Sat, from 11am Sun; MGreen, Yellow Line to Georgia Ave-Petworth) History buffs can make the trek to President Lincoln's summer house tucked away on the grounds of the Soldiers' Retirement Home. Abe came here to beat the heat and jot notes for the Emancipation Proclamation in leafy seclusion. Guides lead one-hour tours through the abode, which is now starkly empty – audio recordings and videos to make the rooms come to life and give a feel for the man who inhabited them. Ghosts and stories float throughout. Reserve tickets in advance.

Lincoln and his family lived here for a total of 13 months between 1862 and 1864. A small museum next door holds Civil War displays and rotating Abe exhibits (about his immigration policies, his security detail at the time etc). The cottage is about a mile from the Metro station.

BASILICA OF THE NATIONAL SHRINE OF THE IMMACULATE CONCEPTION   CHURCH

(☎202-526-8300; www.nationalshrine.com; 400 Michigan Ave NE; ⊙7am-7pm Apr-Oct, to 6pm Nov-Mar; ⓂRed Line to Brookland-CUA) The largest Catholic house of worship in North America can host 6000 worshippers. It is an enormous, impressive, but somehow unimposing edifice, more Byzantine than Vatican in its aesthetic. Outlaid with some 75,000 sq ft of mosaic work and a crypt modeled after early Christian catacombs, the (literal) crowning glory is a dome that could have been lifted off the Hagia Sophia in Istanbul.

The Marian shrine sports an eclectic mix of Romanesque and Byzantine motifs, all anchored by a 329ft minaret-shaped campanile. Downstairs, the original Eastern-style crypt church has low, mosaic-covered vaulted ceilings lit by votives and chandeliers. Upstairs, the main sanctuary is lined with elaborate saints' chapels, lit by rose windows and fronted by a dazzling mosaic of a stern Christ. Hour-long guided tours cover all of it; they leave on the hour between 9am and 3pm (except at noon) from the downstairs information desk.

The church is about a half-mile from the Metro. Exit the station and head west across Catholic University's campus.

FRANCISCAN MONASTERY   MONASTERY

(☎202-526-6800; www.myfranciscan.org; 1400 Quincy St NE; ⊙9am-5pm Mon-Fri, to 6pm Sat, 8am-5pm Sun; ⓂRed Line to Brookland-CUA) ꜰꞮᴇᴇ Also known as Mt St Sepulchre, the monastery offers serene grounds with 42 acres of tulips, dogwoods, cherry trees, roses – and some peculiar re-creations of venerated places. The Order of St Francis is charged with the guardianship of the Holy Land's sacred sites, and it has interpreted that task in a unique – and broad – way here, constructing life-size, fake-granite replicas of the Tomb of Mary, Grotto at Lourdes and Stations of the Cross, among other shrines.

Inside the building the friars have reproduced the Roman Catacombs under the sanctuary floor. The dark, narrow passages wind past some fake tombs and the very real remains of Sts Innocent and Benignus; claustrophobes need not apply. You can walk around the church and grounds on your own, but the catacombs are accessible only on a guided tour (free; departs at 10am, 11am, 1pm, 2pm and 3pm Monday through Saturday, and afternoons only on Sunday). The whole place is creepy and fascinating, like a holy Disneyland. It is about a mile walk from the Metro station, through a mostly residential neighborhood.

SAINT JOHN PAUL II NATIONAL SHRINE   MUSEUM

(☎202-635-5400; www.jp2shrine.org; 3900 Harewood Rd NE; ⊙10am-5pm; ⓂRed Line to Brookland-CUA) ꜰꞮᴇᴇ An adjunct for many devotees who visit the Basilica of the National Shrine of the Immaculate Conception, this modernist-style structure is an unexpected setting for a shrine to Karol Wojtyla, the Polish lad who went on to become Pope John Paul II and eventually a saint. Exhibits feature photos, videos and papal relics (like a vial of his blood). Be sure to check out the mosaic-laden church and chapel.

The Knights of Columbus operate the site. It's about a half-mile north of the basilica on Harewood Rd NE.

GALLAUDET UNIVERSITY   UNIVERSITY

(☎202-651-5000; www.gallaudet.edu; 800 Florida Ave NE; ⓂRed Line to NoMa) The first university for deaf and hard-of-hearing students in the world occupies a lovely manicured campus of bucolic green and Gothic accents north of Capitol Hill. Notable buildings include College Hall, an antique vision in brownstone, and Chapel Hall, a gorgeous Gothic structure that screams academia. The American football huddle was invented here when the Bisons (the school team) noticed other teams were trying to interpret their sign language while they plotted their plays.

Gallaudet is a bilingual institution that provides instruction in both American Sign Language and English. The Metro station is about a half-mile west.

FORT STEVENS PARK   HISTORIC SITE

(www.nps.gov/cwdw; cnr 13th & Quackenbos Sts NW; ⊙sunrise-sunset; ⓂRed Line to Takoma) ꜰꞮᴇᴇ In a raid on July 11, 1864, Confederate General Jubal Early attacked Fort Stevens,

WORTH A DETOUR

FOOTBALL FANS

Washington's NFL team, the Redskins, plays September through to January at **FedEx Field** (☑301-276-6800; www.redskins.com; 1600 Fedex Way, Hyattsville, MD; Ⓜ Silver, Blue Lines to Morgan Blvd). The team has experienced a lot of controversy recently, and not only because of its middling play. Many groups have criticized the Redskins' name and logo as insulting to Native Americans. The US Patent and Trademark Office agreed, and revoked the team's trademark.

FedEx Field is about 10 miles east of the Capitol. The Morgan Blvd Metro station is closest; from there it's a 1-mile walk to the stadium along a sidewalk.

the northernmost of the defensive ramparts ringing DC. A small but fierce battle raged for two days – the only time the Civil War touched District soil – until Early's men withdrew across the Potomac. The fort has been partially restored, but the site is pretty neglected overall.

Abraham Lincoln himself was drawn into the shooting: the president, observing the battle from Fort Stevens' parapet, popped his head up and almost got hit by sharpshooters. It's the only time in American history that a sitting president came under direct fire from an enemy combatant.

BATTLEGROUND
NATIONAL CEMETERY
CEMETERY

(www.nps.gov/cwdw; 6625 Georgia Ave NW; ☺sunrise-sunset; Ⓜ Red Line to Takoma) The 41 Union men who died defending Fort Stevens (p169) are buried at this tiny, poignant cemetery, a half-mile north of the old fortification.

✕ EATING

✕ Logan Circle

BAAN THAI
THAI $

Map p312 (☑202-588-5889; www.baanthaidc.com; 1326 14th St NW, 2nd fl; mains $12-16; ☺11:30am-3pm & 5-10pm Mon-Thu, 11:30am-3pm & 5-11pm Fri, to 11pm Sat, 11:30am-10pm Sun; Ⓜ Orange, Silver, Blue Line to McPherson Sq) Unlike some of its 14th St neighbors, nothing particularly wild or trendy is going on at this airy restaurant. Instead you'll find solid, well-spiced northern Thai dishes, such as a yellow curry with egg noodles or deep-fried pork with sticky rice. There's sushi too, but the Thai menu reigns supreme. Save room for the coconut milk fritters.

It pays to remember that Baan Thai is on the 2nd floor – the 1st floor is occupied by a different Thai restaurant.

ESTADIO
SPANISH $$

Map p312 (☑202-319-1404; www.estadio-dc.com; 1520 14th St NW; tapas $7-17; ☺5-10pm Mon-Thu, 11:30am-2pm & 5-11pm Fri, 11am-2pm & 5-11pm Sat, 11am-2pm & 5-9pm Sun; Ⓜ Green, Yellow Line to U St) Estadio buzzes with a low-lit, date-night vibe. The tapas menu is as deep as an ocean trench. There are three variations of *ibérico* ham and a delicious foie gras, scrambled egg and truffle open-faced sandwich. Wash it down with some traditional *calimocho* (red wine and Coke). No reservations after 6pm, which usually means a wait at the bar.

ETTO
ITALIAN $$

Map p312 (☑202-232-0920; www.ettodc.com; 1541 14th St NW; mains $13-23; ☺5-10pm Mon-Thu, to 11pm Fri, noon-11pm Sat, from noon Sun; Ⓜ Green, Yellow Line to U St) The sun-splashed, tiled cafe is known for its thin-crust pizzas, salamis, anchovies and cheeses – all of which go smashingly with a nice glass of wine. The chefs are serious about quality: they grind their own flour and cure their own meats. It's worth swinging by Etto if queues at other 14th St restaurants overwhelm.

PIG
AMERICAN $$

Map p312 (☑202-290-2821; www.thepigdc.com; 1320 14th St NW; mains $17-28; ☺4-10:30pm Mon-Thu, 11:30am-11:30pm Fri, 10:30am-11:30pm Sat, from 10:30am Sun; Ⓜ Orange, Silver, Blue Line to McPherson Sq) The Pig lives up to its name, offering plenty of porcine-inspired treats, from crispy shank to a decadent cutlet-and-gruyere sandwich that will leave you lost for words. There's non-porky goodness as well, including some wonderful truffle-crusted mac and cheese and a bourbon-blasted sticky toffee pudding (that said, this isn't the best spot for herbivores). Great brunch value.

PEARL DIVE OYSTER PALACE SEAFOOD $$

Map p312 (202-319-1612; www.pearldivedc. com; 1612 14th St NW; mains $19-26; 5-10pm Mon, to 11pm Tue-Thu, 11am-11pm Fri & Sat, from 11am Sun; Green, Yellow Line to U St) Flashy Pearl Dive serves exceptional, sustainable oysters from both coasts, along with braised duck and oyster gumbo, crawfish fritters and insanely rich desserts (say, chocolate mousse cake or ricotta beignets). Fresh air from the big front windows wafts through the open industrial space, done up in a nautical, weathered-wood motif. It's wise to make reservations.

You can also wait at the upstairs bar, Black Jack, where fedora-wearing bartenders will swirl you a glamorous cocktail.

BIRCH & BARLEY AMERICAN $$

Map p312 (202-567-2576; www.birchandbarley. com; 1337 14th St NW; mains $17-29; 5:30-10pm Tue-Thu, to 11pm Fri, 11am-3pm & to 11pm Sat, 11am-3pm & 5.30-9pm Sun; Orange, Silver, Blue Line to McPherson Sq) The menu of modern comfort foods focuses on housemade pastas, flatbreads and entrees like short rib with mashed potatoes, all of which pairs with the enormous beer list. The weekend's 'boozy brunch' draws crowds by adding bottomless cups of coffee and two mind-altering cocktails to one's main dish for an extra $15.

If it's crowded, try heading to the upstairs bar Churchkey (p175), which serves pretty much the same menu.

LE DIPLOMATE FRENCH $$$

Map p312 (202-332-3333; www.lediplomatedc. com; 1601 14th St NW; mains $23-35; 5-11pm Mon-Thu, to midnight Fri, 9:30am-midnight Sat, from 9:30am Sun; Green, Yellow Line to U St) This charming French bistro is one of the hottest tables in town. DC celebrities galore cozy up in the leather banquettes and at the sidewalk tables. They come for an authentic slice of Paris, from the *coq au vin* (wine-braised chicken) and aromatic baguettes to the vintage curios and nudie photos decorating the bathrooms. Make reservations.

✗ U Street & Shaw

★ BEN'S CHILI BOWL AMERICAN $

Map p312 (202-667-0909; www.benschilibowl. com; 1213 U St NW; mains $6-10; 6am-2am Mon-Thu, to 4am Fri, 7am-4am Sat, 11am-midnight Sun; Green, Yellow Line to U St) Ben's is a DC institution. The main stock in trade is half-smokes, DC's meatier, smokier version of the hot dog, usually slathered with mustard, onions and the namesake chili. For nearly 60 years presidents, rock stars and Supreme Court justices have come to indulge in the humble diner, but despite the hype, Ben's remains a true neighborhood establishment. Cash only.

To place your order, join the locals clustered at the counter and gabbing over sweet ice tea. Ben and Virginia Ali opened the Chili Bowl in 1958. It's one of the only businesses on U St to have survived the 1968 riots and the disruption that accompanied construction of the U St Metro stop. Ben died in 2009; his sons now run the business, which includes outlets on H St NE and at Ronald Reagan Washington National Airport.

★ CHERCHER ETHIOPIAN $

Map p312 (202-299-9703; www.chercher restaurant.com; 1334 9th St NW; mains $11-17; 11am-11pm Mon-Sat, noon-10pm Sun; Green, Yellow Line to Mt Vernon Sq/7th St-Convention Center) Ethiopian expats have been known to compare Chercher's food to their grandma's home cooking. It prepares terrific *injera* (spongy bread) for dipping into hot spiced *wats* (stews). Vegetarians will find lots to devour. There's beer and honey wine from the motherland, and spices you can buy to go.

The restaurant spreads over two floors in an intimate townhouse with brightly painted walls and artwork.

FLORIDA AVENUE GRILL SOUTHERN US $

Map p312 (202-265-1586; www.floridaavenue grill.com; 1100 Florida Ave NW; mains $10-16; 8am-9pm Tue-Sat, to 4:30pm Sun; Green, Yellow Line to U St) The Grill is one of DC's quintessential diners. Be they president, Harlem Globetrotter or college student, they've all come here for more than 70 years to eat turkey legs, catfish and meatloaf served with sides of sweet tea and more character than Shakespeare's collected works.

&PIZZA PIZZA $

Map p312 (202-733-1286; www.andpizza.com; 1250 U St NW; mains $9-13; 11am-11pm Sun-Wed, to 1am Thu, to 4am Fri & Sat; Green, Yellow Line to U St) &pizza outlets are popping up all over DC, and no wonder: this is high-quality fast food. Create your own pie (enough for two meals) using housemade mozzarella, vegan mozzarella, red chickpea puree, truffle sauce and a host of other

---

LOCAL KNOWLEDGE

MURAL MANIA

Keep an eye out for the many murals splashed across the neighborhood's walls, especially around U St. Cool ones – which all happen to be by prolific local artist Aniekan Udofia – include:

➡ **The Torch**, on the west side of Ben's Chili Bowl (p171). Shows a who's who of African American trailblazers, including comedian Dave Chapelle (a DC native), the Obamas, Harriet Tubman, Prince and more.

➡ **Marvin Gaye** (Map p312; cnr S St NW & 7th St NW; MGreen, Yellow Lines to Shaw-Howard U) Depicts the soul singer – who was born and raised in DC and went to high school in Columbia Heights – crooning into a microphone.

➡ **Silent George** (Map p312; 1502 U St NW; MGreen, Yellow Lines to U St) The image of George Washington with a gag over his mouth symbolizes DC's lack of representation in Congress.

---

ingredients. Or choose a signature pizza like the Farmer's Daughter with spicy tomato, Italian sausage and an egg cracked on top.

The eatery concocts its own wild sodas (pear and fig, anise root beer) to accompany the goodness. Order at the counter and take to the scattering of communal seats. The place booms late night.

AMERICAN ICE COMPANY   BARBECUE $

Map p312 (☑202-758-3562; www.amicodc.com; 917 V St NW; mains $10-14; ☺5pm-2am Mon-Thu, to 3am Fri, 1pm-3am Sat, from 1pm Sun; MGreen, Yellow Line to U St) The usual U St–Columbia Heights crew of hipsters, policy wonks, and policy wonks who kind of look like hipsters packs the cluttered interior and much nicer outdoor patio of this casual place, which focuses on barbecue and canned beer, pretty much in that order. Try the gooey pork and cheese sandwich or the delicious swachos (aka pulled pork nachos).

SATELLITE ROOM   AMERICAN $

Map p312 (☑202-506-2496; www.satellitedc.com; 2047 9th St NW; mains $9-13; ☺5pm-2am Sun-Thu, to 3am Fri & Sat; MGreen, Yellow Line to U St) This diner-like spot is a prime place to go before or after a show at the next-door

9:30 club. Standard pizza and wings are the main course, but it's the swell tater tot selection and booze-spiked milkshakes that should be your priority.

★COMPASS ROSE   INTERNATIONAL $$

Map p312 (☑202-506-4765; www.compassrosedc.com; 1346 T St NW; small plates $8-16; ☺5pm-2am Mon-Thu, to 3am Fri & Sat, from 1am Sun; MGreen, Yellow Line to U St) Compass Rose feels like a secret garden, set in a discreet townhouse a whisker from 14th St's buzz. The exposed brick walls and sky-blue ceiling give it a casually romantic air. The menu is a mash-up of global comfort foods, so dinner might entail Korean *galbi* (short ribs), Lebanese *kefta* (ground lamb and spices) and Georgian *khachapuri* (buttery, cheese-filled bread).

They're unique flavors for DC, but Rose manages to steer clear of trendiness. No reservations, though waiting at the bar sipping offbeat wines and cocktails from around the world makes time pass quickly.

★BUSBOYS & POETS   CAFE $$

Map p312 (☑202-387-7638; www.busboysandpoets.com; 2021 14th St NW; mains $12-21; ☺7am-midnight Mon-Thu, to 2am Fri, from 8am Sat & Sun; ☏☑; MGreen, Yellow Line to U St) Busboys & Poets is one of U St's linchpins. Locals pack the place for coffee, boozy brunches, books and a progressive vibe that makes San Francisco feel conservative. The lengthy, vegetarian-friendly menu spans sandwiches, pizzas and Southern fare like shrimp and grits. Tuesday night's open-mic poetry reading ($5 admission, from 9pm to 11pm) draws big crowds.

The cafe's slate of events also includes story slams, film screenings and discussion series. The front bookstore, which stocks loads of social justice works and titles by local authors, is an inspiring browse. B&P has grown to include six locations in the DC region, but this one is the flagship.

TICO   LATIN AMERICAN $$

Map p312 (☑202-319-1400; www.ticodc.com; 1926 14th St NW; small plates $9-14; ☺11:30am-10:30pm Mon-Thu, to 11:30pm Fri, 10am-3pm & 5-11:30pm Sat, 10am-3pm & 5-10:30pm Sun; ☑; MGreen, Yellow Line to U St) Loud, fun and clattering, Tico draws a young and arty crowd for its nouveau tacos, small plates and 140 tequilas. Top honors go to the scallop ceviche, the Manchego cheese fritters and hibiscus margaritas. Vegetarians get some love from the edamame tacos, roasted cauliflower and other dishes. This bright-hued, mural-splashed eatery is popular, so make reservations.

BISTRO BOHEM   EASTERN EUROPEAN **$$**

Map p312 (☑202-735-5895; www.bistrobohem.com; 600 Florida Ave NW; mains $14-22; ☺11am-10pm Mon, to 11pm Tue-Thu, 5pm-midnight Fri, 10am-midnight Sat, from 10am Sun; 🛜; Ⓜ Green, Yellow Line to Shaw-Howard U) Cozy Bistro Bohem is a community favorite for its rib-sticking Czech schnitzels, goulash and pilsners, served with a side of local art on the walls and occasional Czech film screenings. The warm, bohemian environs make you swear you're in Prague. The action moves to the outdoor patio when the weather warms.

OOHH'S & AAHH'S   SOUTHERN US **$$**

Map p312 (☑202-667-7142; www.oohhsnaahhs.com; 1005 U St NW; mains $14-22; ☺noon-10pm Mon-Thu, to 4am Fri & Sat, to 7pm Sun; Ⓜ Green, Yellow Line to U St) Un-notch the belt: the cornbread, collard greens, meatloaf and other soul-food dishes at this bare-bones joint come in enormous portions. Not that hungry? Stop in for a piece of hummingbird (banana-pineapple) cake. Sit at the counter to be immersed in the before-U-St-became-gentrified crowd. It's a great slice of local life. A spacious dining room hides upstairs. Alas, service can be slow.

BEN'S NEXT DOOR   AMERICAN **$$**

Map p312 (☑202-667-8880; www.bensnextdoor.com; 1211 U St; mains $12-22; ☺11am-midnight Sun-Wed, to 1am Thu, to 2am Fri & Sat; Ⓜ Green, Yellow Line to U St) Ben's Next Door is, yes, next door to Ben's Chili Bowl. It offers upscale southern fare (she-crab soup, fried chicken, ribs), along with local beer and cocktails, in a warm, wood-floored room. That said, you can also get half-smokes and the rest of the Chili Bowl items over here (though we prefer to scarf them while sitting at the counter in their original environment).

✕ Columbia Heights

STICKY FINGERS   VEGAN **$**

Map p312 (☑202-299-9700; www.stickyfingersbakery.com; 1370 Park Rd NW; mains $8-11; ☺8am-8pm Tue-Thu, to 9pm Fri, 9am-9pm Sat, from 9am Sun; 🛜🖉; Ⓜ Green, Yellow Line to Columbia Heights) The tempeh bacon, gluten-free pancakes and tofu scramble are but foreplay to the (vegan) peanut butter fudge and raspberry cream cupcakes. Sticky Fingers is primarily a bakery, with a small dining area attached. Order at the counter, then enjoy your purchases at the close-quartered retro tables where fellow vegans tap away on their Macbooks.

EL CHUCHO   MEXICAN **$**

Map p312 (☑202-290-3313; www.elchuchodc.com; 3313 11th St NW; tacos $5-7, mains $12-16; ☺4pm-2am Mon-Thu, to 3am Fri, 11am-3am Sat, 11am-2am Sun; Ⓜ Green, Yellow Line to Columbia Heights) There's a Day of the Dead–inspired interior, margaritas on tap, excellent *elote* (corn) smothered in white cheese and spices, and fresh guacamole. It's home to lots of cool tattooed staff members, and the customers who love them.

PHO 14   VIETNAMESE **$**

Map p312 (☑202-986-2326; www.dcpho14.com; 1436 Park Rd NW; mains $9-16; ☺11am-9:30pm Sun-Wed, to 10pm Thu-Sat; 🖉; Ⓜ Green, Yellow Line to Columbia Heights) Smart, solid Pho 14 ladles out steaming bowls of the namesake noodle soup, as well as stir-fry dishes and *banh mi* sandwiches (baguettes filled with meat and/or spicy veggies) to brisk lunchtime and dinner crowds.

REDROCKS PIZZERIA   PIZZA **$**

Map p312 (☑202-506-1402; www.redrockscolheights.com; 1063 Park Rd NW; pizzas $11-15; ☺4-11pm Mon, from 11am Tue-Thu & Sun, 11am-midnight Fri & Sat; Ⓜ Green, Yellow Line to Columbia Heights) Red Rocks is a comfy neighborhood option where irregularly shaped, brick-fired pizzas hit the tables. You won't be shocked by any of the ingredients, but it's the quality of them that impresses: the fresh basil, flour, tomatoes and cheese are all imported from Italy.

BAD SAINT   FILIPINO **$$**

Map p312 (www.badsaintdc.com; 3226 11th St NW; mains $20-32; ☺5:30-10pm Mon, Wed & Thu, to 11pm Fri, 5-11pm Sat, from 5pm Sun; Ⓜ Green, Yellow Line to Columbia Heights) Lines form early at this wee, 24-seat restaurant. It doesn't take reservations, so expect to wait. The reward is Filipino flavors like none you've laid lips on before. The menu changes often, but you might enjoy dishes such as *kalderetang kordero* (lamb neck, sunchoke and baby carrot stew) or *ginisang tulya* (clam and coconut milk stew). It's always amazing.

NAME GAME: MALCOLM X OR MERIDIAN HILL PARK?

Officially, the park's name is Meridian Hill, because it's located on the exact longitude of DC's original milestone marker. Locals started calling it Malcolm X Park in 1970, after activist Angela Davis gave a speech there and rechristened it. Leaders then introduced a bill in Congress to change the moniker, but it was shot down because the park contains a memorial to President James Buchanan (the nation's 15th commander in chief). Thus the grounds' name cannot represent another person, according to the National Park Service, which operates the site. Locals pay the rule no mind, and many people still call it Malcolm X. Peculiar statues of Dante and Joan of Arc also dot the grounds.

With bamboo shades, low wicker chairs and antique mahjong tile decorations, the restaurant is mom-and-pop casual with a dose of funky elegance. Once you get on the wait list, head to one of the surrounding bars for drink – Room 11 next door is a fine choice. Bad Saint will text you when your table is ready.

THIP KHAO   LAOTIAN $$

Map p312 (☑202-387-5426; www.thipkhao. com; 3462 14th St NW; mains $13-24; ☺5-10pm Mon, Wed & Thu, noon-3pm & 5-11pm Fri & Sat, noon-3pm & 5-10pm Sun; ⓜGreen, Yellow Line to Columbia Heights) At this casual but trendy Laotian restaurant, chef-owner Seng Luangrath offers fabulously spicy, tart and pungent dishes from her homeland. Named for the baskets that hold sticky rice, its musttries include *naem khao,* a crispy coconut rice salad with scallions, sour pork, peanuts and cilantro; and *knap pah,* banana-leafwrapped fish grilled with herbs, dill and ginger.

If you're daring, check out the 'Jungle' part of the menu, featuring the likes of fried duck heads, pig's ears, chicken hearts, and even ant eggs.

✖ Northeast DC

UNION MARKET   MARKET $

(www.unionmarketdc.com; 1309 5th St NE; mains $6-11; ☺11am-8pm Tue-Fri, from 8am Sat & Sun; ⓜRed Line to NoMa) The cool crowd hobnobs at this food hall, where culinary entrepreneurs sell their banana-ginger chocolates, herbed goat cheeses and smoked meats. Among the stalls featuring prepared foods, everything from Burmese milkshakes to Indian dosas to Korean tacos boggle taste buds. Craft beers and coffee provide added sustenance. Tables dot the sunlit warehouse, and many locals make an afternoon of it here, nibbling and reading.

Bivalve fans should seek out the Rappahannock Oyster Bar for straight-from-Chesapeake-Bay slurping. The market also hosts lots of free events such as yoga classes and Friday night drive-in movies; check the website for the schedule. Union Market is about a half-mile walk from the NoMa Metro station, in the midst of several other food supply warehouses.

IVY CITY
SMOKEHOUSE TAVERN   SEAFOOD $$

(☑202-529-3300; www.ivycitysmokehouse.com; 1356 Okie St NE; mains $15-29; ☺5pm-midnight Mon, from 11am Tue-Thu, 11am-1am Fri & Sat, 11am-10pm Sun; ⓠD4) The sprawling Smokehouse is an exemplar of the Ivy City scene: gritty, hip and set in an old warehouse. It's part restaurant with rooftop patio, part live music venue (rock, jazz, DJs) and part seafood market (everything is smoked on site). The salmon candy and whitefish salad are standout dishes; oysters, clams and blue crabs also feature.

MASSERIA   ITALIAN $$$

(☑202-608-1330; www.masseria-dc.com; 1340 4th St NE; prix-fixe menus $92-135; ☺5:30-9:30pm Tue-Thu, to 10pm Fri, 5-10pm Sat; ⓜRed Line to NoMa) Chef Nicholas Stefanelli's Michelin-star-winning Italian oasis flourishes in the industrial neighborhood near Union Market. A festive outdoor terrace and two cozy interior rooms convey the tranquil allure of a southern Italian evening – as does the prix-fixe-only menu. Innovative dishes range from linguine with spicy sauce or beef tripe and lobster stew to venison with wild mushrooms and chestnuts.

DRINKING & NIGHTLIFE

Logan Circle, U Street & Shaw

★ RIGHT PROPER BREWING CO   BREWERY

Map p312 (202-607-2337; www.rightproper brewery.com; 624 T St NW; ⊙5pm-midnight Mon-Thu, 11:30am-1am Fri & Sat, 11:30am-11pm Sun; MGreen, Yellow Line to Shaw-Howard U) Right Proper Brewing Co makes sublime ales in a building where Duke Ellington used to play pool. It's the Shaw district's neighborhood clubhouse, a big, sunny space filled with folks gabbing at reclaimed wood tables. The tap lineup changes regularly as the brewers work their magic, but crisp farmhouse ales are an oft-flowing specialty.

Right Proper also has a larger production house (p178) and tasting room in the Brookland neighborhood, a couple of miles northeast.

★ U STREET MUSIC HALL   CLUB

Map p312 (202-588-1889; www.ustreetmusic hall.com; 1115 U St NW; Tickets $10-25; ⊙hours vary; MGreen, Yellow Line to U St) Two local DJs own and operate the basement club; it looks like a no-frills rock bar, but it has a pro sound system, a cork-cushioned dance floor and other accoutrements of a serious dance club. Alternative bands also thrash a couple of nights per week to keep it fresh. Shows start between 7pm and 10pm.

DACHA BEER GARDEN   BEER GARDEN

Map p312 (202-350-9888; www.dachadc. com; 1600 7th St NW; ⊙4-10:30pm Mon-Thu, to midnight Fri, noon-midnight Sat, from noon Sun, reduced in winter; MGreen, Yellow Line to Shaw-Howard U) Happiness reigns in Dacha's freewheeling beer garden. Kids and dogs bound around the picnic tables, while adults hoist glass boots filled with German brews. When the weather gets nippy, staff bring blankets and stoke the fire pit. And it all takes place under the sultry gaze of Elizabeth Taylor (or a mural of her, which sprawls across the back wall).

It can get packed with a bro-hugging crowd as the evening progresses, but in general everyone remains good spirited and willing to share a table. Dacha becomes an unofficial gay hangout on Sundays.

CHURCHKEY   BAR

Map p312 (202-567-2576; www.churchkeydc. com; 1337 14th St NW; ⊙4pm-1am Mon-Thu, to 2am Fri, 11:30am-2am Sat, from 11:30am Sun; MOrange, Silver, Blue Line to McPherson Sq) Coppery, mod-industrial Churchkey glows with hipness. Fifty beers flow from the taps, including five brain-walloping, cask-aged ales. If none of those please you, another 500 types of brew are available by bottle (including gluten-free suds). Churchkey is the upstairs counterpart to Birch & Barley (p171), a popular nouveau comfort-food restaurant, and you can order much of its menu at the bar.

THE COFFEE BAR   COFFEE

Map p312 (202-733-1049; www.thecoffee bardc.com; 1201 S St NW; ⊙7am-6pm Mon-Fri, 7:30am-7pm Sat & Sun; ☎; MGreen, Yellow Line to U St) Many locals point to The Coffee Bar as their favorite spot to hang out all day reading and laptop typing. Located on a quiet residential corner, with tables spilling onto the sidewalk, it feels like the lived-in neighborhood cafe you've been coming to forever. Huge windows, retro couches, hipster baristas and truly delicious coffee stoke the love.

POP-UP BAR   CAFE

Map p312 (PUB; www.popupbardc.com; 1839-1843 7th St NW; ⊙5-12:30am Mon-Thu, to 1:30am Fri, 1pm-1:30am Sat, from 1pm Sun; MGreen, Yellow Line to Shaw-Howard U) PUB opens every few months with a new, timely theme. For instance, when *Game of Thrones* started its new season, it became a GoT bar, complete with Iron Throne and Hall of Faces. Other incarnations have included a cherry-blossom-bedecked lounge and Christmas wonderland. Drink Company, the reigning champ of DC's cocktail scene, creates the booze menu.

NELLIE'S   GAY

Map p312 (202-332-6355; www.nelliessports bar.com; 900 U St NW; ⊙5pm-1am Mon-Thu, 3pm-3am Fri, 10:30am-3am Sat, from 10:30am Sun; MGreen, Yellow Line to Shaw-Howard U) The atmosphere is low-key, and Nellie's is a good place to hunker down among a friendly crowd for toothsome bar bites (including Venezuelan corn muffins), good-time events (including the weekend drag brunch) and early drink specials. Multiple plasma screens show sporting events; there's also a roof deck and board games on hand.

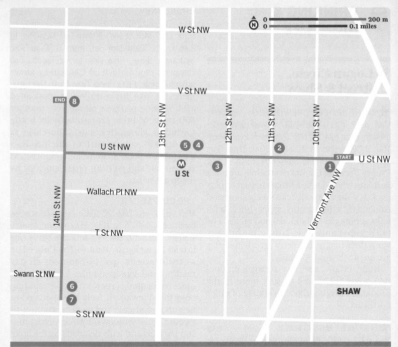

Neighborhood Walk
U Street Stroll

START AFRICAN AMERICAN CIVIL WAR MEMORIAL
END BUSBOYS & POETS
LENGTH 1 MILE; 1½ HOURS

Learn about the U St Corridor's rich African American heritage and renewal. Exit the U St Metro station at the 10th St exit and saunter around the ❶ **African American Civil War Memorial** (p167). Why is this sculpture here? Because the Metro stop, which opened in 1991, was one of the first heralds of new development in the formerly downtrodden area. The memorial reminds residents that the rebuilding of their community has been accomplished before, by ancestors who fought for their people's freedom.

Now walk west along U St – the numbered cross streets should be going up. Jazz history is everywhere, but you'll need to use your imagination to see it in its heyday. At the corner of U and 11th Sts, the former jazz club ❷ **Bohemian Caverns** (2001 11th St) hosted names like Miles Davis, John Coltrane and Duke Ellington. Speaking of the latter:

Ellington grew up in this neighborhood, and he played his first public gig in a ballroom at the landmark ❸ **True Reformer Building** (1200 U St). Cross the street and pop into ❹ **Ben's Chili Bowl** (p171), one of the city's most iconic restaurants, surviving since the 1950s. Next door, the ❺ **Lincoln Theatre** (p181) is the heart of what was once termed 'Black Broadway' – Billie Holiday, Ella Fitzgerald, Louis Armstrong and Cab Calloway all graced the stage. The '68 riots shut it down, but revitalization projects in the early '90s reopened it. Spirited shops and clubs dot 14th St. Turn left (south), and after passing T St you'll run into the ❻ **Black Cat** (p179). The Foo Fighters' Dave Grohl helped start the club. Nearby, ❼ **Home Rule** (p183) sells brightly painted homewares. Artists made the counter mosaic with smashed glass from the 1968 riots.

Head north until you reach ❽ **Busboys & Poets** (p172), a cafe and progressive bookstore that hosts readings and performances. It remains one of the artistic linchpins of the U St revival.

MARVIN
BAR

Map p312 (☎202-797-7171; www.marvindc.com; 2007 14th St NW; ☺5pm-2am Mon-Thu, to 3am Fri & Sat, from 4pm Sun; Ⓜ Green, Yellow Line to U St) Named for DC native son Marvin Gaye, this spot is a low-lit lounge and bistro downstairs, serving mostly southern fare. Upstairs, the splendid roof deck packs a mixed 14th St crowd, even in winter, when folks huddle under roaring heat lamps sipping cocktails and top-notch beers. Most nights there's live jazz or soul music, to boot.

There's a $10 cover charge after 11pm on Fridays and Saturdays.

FLASH
CLUB

Map p312 (☎202-827-8791; www.flashdc.com; 645 Florida Ave NW; tickets usually $10-15; ☺8pm-2am Wed & Thu, to 3am Fri & Sat; Ⓜ Green, Yellow Line to Shaw-Howard U) A diverse group packs into Flash. The 1st floor is a bar, while upstairs is a pocket-sized club (you pass through a photo booth into a hidden room to reach it). Deep house, techno and dubstep DJs from the East Coast and Europe spin.

BAR PILAR
BAR

Map p312 (☎202-265-1751; www.barpilar.com; 1833 14th St NW; ☺5pm-2am Mon-Thu, to 3am Fri, 11am-3am Sat, from 11am Sun; Ⓜ Green, Yellow Line to U St) This friendly neighborhood favorite serves excellent cocktails and seasonal organic tapas dishes in a snug, nicely designed space. The exposed brick walls and curious collections (hats, Hemingway regalia) give it an old-fashioned feel.

There's a 2nd-floor dining room, but it's best to stay downstairs to drink and nibble.

SALOON
BAR

Map p312 (☎202-462-2640; 1205 U St NW; ☺5pm-midnight Tue-Thu, to 2am Fri & Sat; Ⓜ Green, Yellow Line to U St) The Saloon doesn't allow patrons to pack in like sardines, with posted rules against standing between tables. That's great, because the added elbow room allows you to enjoy a brew ordered from one of the most extensive beer menus in town (Belgian ales are the tour de force).

The bar usually closes in August, when the owners go away to build schools in developing countries.

🍷 Columbia Heights

★ RAVEN
BAR

Map p312 (☎202-387-8411; 3125 Mt Pleasant St NW; ☺4pm-2am Mon & Tue, from 2pm Wed & Thu, 2pm-3am Fri & Sat, from 1pm Sun; Ⓜ Green, Yellow Line to Columbia Heights) The best jukebox in DC, a dark interior crammed with locals and lovers, that neon lighting that casts you under a glow Edward Hopper should rightly have painted, and a tough but friendly bar staff are the ingredients in this shot, which, when slammed, hits you as DC's best dive by a mile. Cash only.

WONDERLAND BALLROOM
BAR

Map p312 (☎240-542-8687; www.thewonderlandballroom.com; 1101 Kenyon St NW; ☺5pm-2am Mon-Thu, 4pm-3am Fri, 11am-3pm Sat, from 10am Sun; Ⓜ Green, Yellow Line to Columbia Heights) Wonderland embodies the edgy, eccentric Columbia Heights vibe to perfection. The interior is clapped out with so many vintage signs and found objects it could be a folk-art museum, the outdoor patio is a good spot for meeting strangers, and the upstairs dance floor is a good place to take said strangers for a bit of bump and grind.Live comedy shows take place several nights a week, mostly on Wednesday, Friday and Sunday.

RED DERBY
BAR

(☎202-291-5000; www.redderby.com; 3718 14th St NW; ☺5pm-2am Mon-Thu, to 3am Fri, 11am-3am Sat, from 11am Sun; Ⓜ Green, Yellow Line to Columbia Heights) Welcome to a hipster-punk lounge where the bartenders know patrons' names, the sweet-potato fries soak up the beer ordered from the impressively long list and cult movies play on a projector screen. The rooftop deck and board games add to the festivities. Note the brews come in cans only. The lighting is blood red and sexy; you can't help but look good under it. The bar is about a half-mile walk from the Metro north on 14th St.

QUALIA COFFEE
COFFEE

(☎202-248-6423; www.qualiacoffee.com; 3917 Georgia Ave NW; ☺7am-7pm Mon-Fri, 8am-6pm Sat & Sun; Ⓜ Green, Yellow Line to Georgia Ave-Petworth) Follow your nose a couple blocks north of the Metro to this hardcore coffee shop. Staff roast beans from around the world, and offer free tasting sessions on the

WORTH A DETOUR

IVY CITY DISTILLERIES

An industrial former rail yard, Ivy City sat forlorn for years. Then booze makers began moving in, drawn by vast warehouse spaces and cheap rent. Coffee roasters, performance venues and rooftop restaurants followed. Now the gritty neighborhood is very much an off-the-beaten-path destination. Booze hounds can take a DIY distillery crawl, hitting four makers plus a brewery in less than a mile; most offer tours and tastings. Here's the lineup, from northeast to southwest:

Jos A Magnus & Co Makes bourbon, gin and vodka and has a jazzy bar. Bonus: it occupies the same building as Atlas Brew Works (p178).

New Columbia Distillers (www.greenhatgin.com) Known for its Green Hat Gin and free tastings, but it's open on Saturday only.

Republic Restoratives Vodka, bourbon and rye whiskey are the specialties at this women-owned distillery that has an attached cocktail bar.

One Eight Distilling (www.oneeightdistilling.com) Another Saturday-only tasting room, when you can sample the housemade gin, vodka and whiskey.

second and fourth Sunday of each month at 2pm. There's not a lot of seating indoors, but tables and chairs also spill into the groovy back yard.

🍷 Northeast DC

⭐ **PRIMROSE**   WINE BAR
(☎202-248-4558; www.primrosedc.com; 3000 12th St NE; ⊙5-10pm Mon, Wed & Thu, to 11pm Fri & Sat, to 9:30pm Sun; Ⓜ Red Line to Brookland-CUA) Stepping into Primrose is like being in Paris and finding the quintessential cafe hidden down a tiny lane. The ostrich-feathered chandeliers, turquoise bar, rustic wood tables and lengthy wine list set the mood. Fifteen wines, all from France or Virginia, come by the glass. *Coq au vin* (wine-braised chicken), steak *frites* and cheeses galore are on the menu if you're hungry.

⭐ **ATLAS BREW WORKS**   BREWERY
(☎202-832-0420; www.atlasbrewworks.com; 2052 West Virginia Ave NE, Suite 102; ⊙4-10pm Mon-Thu, to 11pm Fri, 11am-11pm Sat, from 11am Sun; 🚇D4) An awesome, welcoming spot filled with local beer buffs. With its concrete floor, exposed air ducts and hodgepodge of tables, the tap room may not look like much, but when the knowledgeable bartenders fill your flight of glasses with the brewery's gose, saison and other suds, you might as well give in to being here all afternoon. Board games provide entertainment, and dogs are usually romping around. Free tours take place on Saturdays

at noon, 2pm, 4pm and 6pm; no reservations needed.

Atlas isn't easy to reach by public transportation; it's in the Ivy City neighborhood, a couple of miles northeast of Union Station. Most visitors use Uber or Lyft.

RIGHT PROPER BREWING CO BROOKLAND PRODUCTION HOUSE   BREWERY
(☎202-526-5904; www.rightproperbrewing.com; 920 Girard St NE; ⊙4-9pm Mon-Fri, from noon Sat & Sun; Ⓜ Red Line to Brookland-CUA or Rhode Island) Right Proper started out as a small brewery in Shaw (p175), but it had to expand to this Brookland facility. Now both sites make beer, with Brookland as the more copious producer. Sit down at the cherry-wood bar and order a fruit-tinged saison or sour wheat ale. Flights are a fine way to sample the 12 taps.

Be sure to check out the fantastic chalk mural of escaped zoo creatures gone wild. Free tours take place at 2pm, 4pm and 6pm Saturday and Sunday; no reservations needed. The brewery also holds yoga classes ($15, including a three-beer flight) the second Saturday of the month; sign up online in advance.

REPUBLIC RESTORATIVES   DISTILLERY
(☎202-733-3996; www.republicrestoratives.com; 1369 New York Ave NE; ⊙5-11pm Thu & Fri, from noon Sat, noon-5pm Sun; 🚇D4) Welcome to DC's largest crowd-funded distillery, and its only women-owned one at that. Vodka, bourbon, rye whiskey and apple brandy

emerge from the tanks. Drinkers of all types – young, gray haired, gay and straight – fill Republic's buzzy, mod-industrial tasting room to enjoy the creative cocktails made with the liquors. It's quite social, though the bar is smallish and gets crowded. Tours ($12 per person) take place on Saturday and Sunday, on a first come, first served basis.

JOS A MAGNUS & CO
DISTILLERY

(☑202-450-3518; www.josephmagnus.com; 2052 W Virginia Ave NE; ⊙4-10pm Wed & Thu, to midnight Fri, noon-midnight Sat, noon-7pm Sun; 🚇D4) The distillery cooks up bourbon, gin and vodka that gets stirred into cocktails in the attached cozy bar, the Murray Hill Club. It has a casually swanky, Jazz Age–meets-thrift-store vibe, which is perfect for lingering over a glass of something sweet or smoky. Tours are free and provided on demand on weekends; a five-pour tasting costs $10. Magnus shares the same building as Atlas Brew Works.

DC BRAU
BREWERY

(☑202-621-8890; www.dcbrau.com; 3178b Bladensburg Rd NE; ⊙4-9pm Mon-Wed, to 10pm Thu, 3-11pm Fri, from noon Sat & Sun; 🚇Orange, Silver, Blue Line to Stadium-Armory, then bus B2) DC Brau was the first craft brewer in town. It continues to pump out bodacious pale ales, IPAs and porters that are widely available around DC, but you can come to its small, industrial tap room to guzzle at the source. It's super laid-back, with beer poured into plastic cups; half-price Fridays and food-truck Saturdays draw lots of locals.

The brewery offers free tours on Saturdays between 1pm and 4pm. The location is pretty inconvenient to reach by public transport; it's best to rideshare here.

 ENTERTAINMENT

☆ Logan Circle, U Street & Shaw

★BLACK CAT
LIVE MUSIC

Map p312 (☑202-667-4490; www.blackcatdc.com; 1811 14th St NW; tickets $10-25; 🚇Green, Yellow Line to U St) The Black Cat is the go-to venue for music that's loud and grungy with a punk edge. The White Stripes, Arcade Fire and Foo Fighters have all thrashed here. The action divides between tiny and

intimate Backstage, downstairs, and the upstairs Mainstage, which is still small enough to see what the band is guzzling.

If you're not up for a show, head to the Red Room bar for the jukebox, billiards, pinball and strong cocktails. A vegetarian cafe is also on-site.

9:30 CLUB
LIVE MUSIC

Map p312 (☑202-265-0930; www.930.com; 815 V St NW; tickets $20-$35; 🚇Green, Yellow Line to U St) The 9:30, which can pack 1200 people into a surprisingly compact venue, is the granddaddy of the live-music scene in DC. Pretty much every big name that comes through town ends up on this stage at some point. Headliners usually begin between 10:30pm and 11:30pm.

HOWARD THEATRE
THEATER

Map p312 (☑202-803-2899; www.thehoward theatre.com; 620 T St NW; 🚇Green, Yellow Line to Shaw-Howard U) Built in 1910, Howard Theatre was the top address when U St was known as 'Black Broadway.' Duke Ellington, Ella Fitzgerald and other famed names lit the marquee. Now big-name comedians, blues, gospel and jazz acts fill the house. There's a photo op out front with the steel-and-granite statue of Ellington pounding the keys of a swirling treble clef.

The Howard was the first major theater to feature black entertainers performing for a predominantly black clientele. It closed in 1980 when the neighborhood declined, then reopened in 2012 after a $29 million renovation. The interior sparkles, from the black walnut paneling to the oak floors and huge portraits of Ellington and his jazzy friends.

TWINS JAZZ
JAZZ

Map p312 (☑202-234-0072; www.twinsjazz.com; 1344 U St NW, 2nd fl; cover charge $10-$20 most nights, plus $10 minimum for drinks; ⊙6am-midnight Sun-Thu, to 1am Fri & Sat; 🚇Green, Yellow Line to U St) Twin sisters own this long, narrow, red-walled club, and they've been staging hot jazz acts here for some 20 years. It's a jazz enthusiasts', keep-your-voice-down kind of scene, awash in cool atmosphere. Shows begin at 8pm on weekdays, and at 9pm and 11pm on weekends.

DC9
LIVE MUSIC

Map p312 (☑202-483-5000; www.dcnine.com; 1940 9th St NW; tickets usually $10-15; ⊙5pm-2am Mon-Thu, 4pm-3am Fri & Sat, from 2pm Sun; 🚇Green, Yellow Line to Shaw-Howard U) DC9 is as

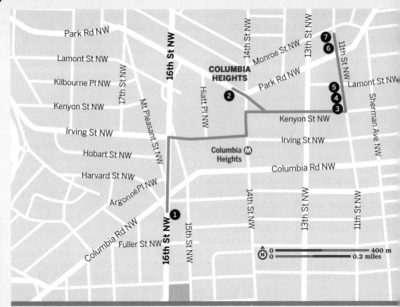

Local Life
Mixing It up in Columbia Heights

Columbia Heights (ⓂGreen, Yellow Line to Columbia Heights) booms with Latino immigrants and hipsters. A few decades ago the neighborhood was a tumbledown mess. Then the Metro station was built, followed by the slew of big-box retailers. And then – this is why you're here – it morphed into a cool-cat mix of ethnic restaurants and unassuming corner taverns chock-full of local color.

❶ Mexican Cultural Institute

The **Mexican Cultural Institute** (Map p312; ☏202-728-1628; www.instituteofmexicodc.org; 2829 16th St NW; ◷10am-6pm Mon-Fri, noon-4pm Sat) FREE looks imposing, but don't be deterred. The gilded beaux-arts mansion is open to the public and hosts excellent art and cultural exhibitions. You might see a show on Diego Rivera's art, Mayan religious artifacts or Octavio Paz's writings. Ring the doorbell for entry.

❷ Los Hermanos

When Dominican baseball players come to town to play the Nats, **Los Hermanos** (Map p312; ☏202-483-8235; www.loshermanosfordc.com; 1426-8 Park Rd NW; mains $10-14; ◷10am-9pm Mon-Sat, to 8pm Sun) is where they get their food fix. It's cafeteria-style service, so head to the counter, point to what you want behind the glass – maybe pork *mofongo* (fried green plantains) or stewed oxtail – then take it to one of the basic tables.

❸ Wonderland Ballroom

Divey Wonderland Ballroom (p177) flaunts a spacious patio with outsized wooden benches that are just right on warm evenings. The upstairs dance floor sees a mix of DJs and bands, and gets packed on weekends. The interior is clapped out in vintage signs and found objects to the point where it could be a folk-art museum.

❹ BloomBars

You never know what you'll find going on at **BloomBars** (Map p312; ☏202-567-7713; www.bloombars.com; 3222 11th St NW; by donation; ◷hours vary), a cool community arts center. By day, children's story times and music classes take place. At night, gallery shows and indie movie screenings take over.

❺ Room 11

Room 11 (Map p312; ☏202-332-3234; www.room11dc.com; 3234 11th St NW; ◷5pm-1am Mon-Thu, to 2am Fri & Sat, from 10am Sun) isn't much bigger than an ambitious living room, intimate as DC's live music venues get, and about as divey as well. Not that we're complaining; there's always a good edge on in this spot. Up-and-coming local bands, with an emphasis on indie rockers, play most nights; when the live music finishes (often around 11pm) DJs keep the place going.

On the 2nd floor, zodiac murals and diner booths set the mellow mood; downstairs you'll find a narrow shotgun bar that's often packed wall to wall. There's also a rooftop where folks gather to chill and drink.

STUDIO THEATRE
THEATER

Map p312 (☎202-332-3300; www.studiotheatre. org; 1501 14th St NW; tickets from $45; ⓜRed Line to Dupont Circle) This contemporary four-theater complex has been staging Pulitzer Prize–winning and premiere plays for more than 35 years. It cultivates a lot of local actors.

Discounted 'rush' tickets ($30) are sometimes available 30 minutes before showtime at the box office.

VELVET LOUNGE
LIVE MUSIC

Map p312 (☎202-462-3213; www.velvet loungedc.com; 915 U St NW; tickets $10; ⓜGreen, Yellow Line to Shaw-Howard U) Velvet is tiny, red and scruffy. It's a true hole in the wall, but that doesn't stop a steady stream of rock and hip-hop artists from taking the stage upstairs. Good DJs spin house, funk and R&B in the downstairs bar.

LINCOLN THEATRE
THEATER

Map p312 (☎202-888-0050; www.thelincolndc. com; 1215 U St NW; ⓜGreen, Yellow Line to U St) Duke Ellington, Louis Armstrong and Billie Holiday are among the many African American luminaries who performed in this 1922 ballroom.

The city renovated it in the 1990s to host music and theater. It's classy, but it kind of limps along with sporadic performances.

SOURCE THEATRE
THEATER

Map p312 (☎202-204-7741; www.culturaldc.org; 1835 14th St NW; ⓜGreen, Yellow Line to U St) You might see improv, Spanish-language opera or a dreamy interpretation of Strindberg at this 120-seat black-box theater, used by resident companies from an array of disciplines.

Meridian Pint

and as such it can get pretty jammed. On the plus side, everyone is friendly, the intimacy is warmly inviting on chilly winter nights and there's a spacious outdoor area for when it gets too hot inside. The low-key crowd sips excellent wines and whiz-bang cocktails.

➏ Meridian Pint
Staffed by locals, **Meridian Pint** (Map p312; ☎202-588-1075; www.meridianpint. com; 3400 11th St NW; ⏰5pm-midnight Mon-Thu, to 3am Fri, 10am-3am Sat, from 10am Sun) is the quintessential corner tavern for Columbia Heights. Strings of lights twinkle overhead, sports flicker on TV, folks play pool and shuffleboard, and impressive American craft beers flow from the 24 taps.

➐ Maple
At snug **Maple** (Map p312; ☎202-588-7442; www.dc-maple.com; 3418 11th St NW; mains $17-23; ⏰5:30-11:30pm Mon-Thu, 5pm-1am Fri, 10:30am-1am Sat, 10:30am-11pm Sun), stylish young residents eat pasta at a reclaimed-wood bar. House-made *limoncello*, Italian and craft beers, and unusual wine varietals move across the lengthy slab (the wood type, incidentally, is what gives the venue its name).

LOGAN CIRCLE, U STREET & COLUMBIA HEIGHTS ENTERTAINMENT

WORTH A DETOUR

PETWORTH

It wasn't long before Columbia Heights' gentrification spilled over to Petworth, the next stop north on the Metro. Originally a working-class community, younger, progressive types have moved in, bringing a hodgepodge of indie shops and funky bars with them. **Georgia Ave** (Map p312) is the main vein. **Upshur St** (off Map p312) is also abuzz with cute places to eat and drinking dens. Plus, President Lincoln's Cottage (p168) rises in the 'hood. Here are some favorite spots:

Himitsu (www.himitsudc.com; 828 Upshur St NW; small plates $12-18; ⊙5-10pm Tue-Thu, to 11pm Fri & Sat; ⓂGreen, Yellow Line to Georgia Ave-Petworth) This Japanese restaurant gets heaped with praise by foodie tastemakers (*Bon Appetit* magazine, James Beard Foundation) and no wonder: it's hard not to fall for the chili-spiked seafood *crudos* and candied pumpkin seed-topped eggplant, all served with exquisite care.

Ruta del Vino (☑202-248-4469; www.rutadelvinodc.com; 800 Upshur St NW; ⊙5-10pm Mon-Thu to 11pm Fri & Sat; ⓂGreen, Yellow Line to Georgia Ave-Petworth) Around 18 red and white wines are available by the glass at this homey neighborhood wine bar. Most are from Chile and Argentina, but you'll also find unusual ones from Mexico, Uruguay and other Latin American countries, along with *empanadas*, *ceviche* and other nibbles from the region. It's a relaxed place to hang out with the locals.

Hank's Cocktail Bar (☑202-290-1808; www.hankscocktailbar.com; 819 Upshur St NW; ⊙4pm-midnight Tue-Thu, to 1:30am Fri, 2pm-1:30am Sat, 2-10pm Sun; ⓂGreen, Yellow Line to Georgia Ave-Petworth) With its high-backed wooden booths, chain-wrapped lights and flickering candles, Hank's feels both modern and medieval. It's dark and slightly eerie, which is a contrast to the playful cocktails. Order a classic old-fashioned, a New Fashioned with bourbon and chai, or try a drink with mushroom-infused Scotch.

Timber Pizza (☑202-853-9746; www.timberpizza.com; 809 Upshur St NW; pizzas $12-16; ⊙5-10pm Tue-Sun; ⓂGreen, Yellow Line to Georgia Ave-Petworth) *Bon Appetit* magazine crowned Timber one of the best new restaurants in America in 2017, while the James Beard Foundation nominated the chef as a rising star. So yeah, the wood-fired pizzas are pretty damn good, especially alongside a pitcher of local beer.

Hitching Post (☑202-726-1511; www.thehpostrestaurant.com; 200 Upshur St NW; mains $16-28; ⊙4-11pm Mon-Fri, from 11am Sat, 11am-10pm Sun; ⓂGreen, Yellow Line to Georgia Avenue-Petworth) Across the street from President Lincoln's Cottage, this neighborly diner looks like a house from the outside. Inside, red-vinyl-backed booths and a bar fill the intimate room. Wait staff call customers by name and bring them plates heaped with fried chicken, the house specialty.

DC Reynolds (☑202-506-7178; 3628 Georgia Ave NW; ⊙11am-2am, to 3am Fri & Sat; ⓂGreen, Yellow Line to Georgia Ave-Petworth) This is a fine example of the dart-board-and-trivia-night corner pub genre that has colonized Petworth. The main draw is the enormous outdoor patio that's perfect for a cool beer and a pickle back (whiskey followed by pickle juice).

☆ Columbia Heights & Northeast DC

DANCE PLACE   DANCE
(☑202-269-1600; www.danceplace.org; 3225 8th St NE; ⓂRed Line to Brookland-CUA) The only truly cutting-edge dance space in the capital is tucked away in Brookland. It's run by four resident dance companies offering a year-round calendar of new work that features African dance, modern dance, step dance and other genres. It also hosts the work of top-notch national companies. The theater is a few blocks south of the Metro station.

GALA HISPANIC THEATRE   THEATER
Map p312 (☑202-234-7174; www.galatheatre.org; 3333 14th St NW; ⓂGreen, Yellow Line to Columbia Heights) Set in a converted 1920s movie palace, the Gala stages Spanish and

Latin American plays. Most performances are in Spanish with English subtitles. The theater also hosts dance, music and films from Latin countries.

 SHOPPING

Upscale boutiques, quirky design and furniture shops, galleries and vintage stores are rife along U St and 14th St as it makes its way south into Logan Circle. In Columbia Heights, Target, Giant Food and other big-box retailers throng the area around the Metro station.

★**MISS PIXIE'S** ANTIQUES
Map p312 (202-232-8171; www.misspixies.com; 1626 14th St NW; ⊙11am-7pm; MGreen, Yellow Line to U St) Bright and festive with classic pop tunes playing in the background, Miss Pixie's is a great browse. It's piled high with relics of the past, from stuffed leather armchairs to 1960s lawn ornaments. You'll find dishes, rocking chairs, farm tables, black-and-white photos, and plenty of other curiosities. New items arrive on Wednesday nights and hit the shelves by Thursday morning.

FIA'S FABULOUS FINDS CLOTHING
(202-492-8278; www.fiasfabfinds.tumblr.com; 806 Upshur St NW; ⊙noon-8pm Tue & Fri, to 7pm Wed, Thu & Sat, to 6pm Sun; MGreen, Yellow Line to Georgia Ave-Petworth) The racks are stacked tight at Fia's, which sells gently used, brand name clothes for women of all sizes. The owner lives in the neighborhood and is super welcoming. Most items cost between $20 and $30. Sales are frequent.

GOOD WOOD ANTIQUES
Map p312 (202-986-3640; www.goodwooddc.com; 1428 U St NW; ⊙noon-7pm Mon-Sat, to 5pm Sun; MGreen, Yellow Line to U St) Even if you're not in the market for a midcentury armoire, Good Wood is well worth a visit. The warm, atmospheric space holds a cool selection of antiques, including handcrafted chairs and tables, elegant lamps and wall hangings, plus modern decorative items such as candles and glassware.

HOME RULE HOMEWARES
Map p312 (202-797-5544; www.homerule.com; 1807 14th St NW; ⊙11am-7pm Mon-Sat, noon-5:30pm Sun; MGreen, Yellow Line to U St) Tired of Pottery Barn homogeneity around your house? Check out little Home Rule's amusingly original stock: frog-shaped toothbrush holders, brightly colored martini glasses, animal-shaped salt-and-pepper sets, and rugs and linens, too. The mosaic decorating the front counter symbolizes the U St district's revitalization – it's made with smashed glass from the 1968 riots.

REDEEM CLOTHING
Map p312 (202-332-7447; www.redeemus.com; 1810 14th St NW; ⊙noon-8pm Mon-Sat, to 6pm Sun; MGreen, Yellow Line to U St) 'It's never too late to change,' is the motto of this enticing little clothier on 14th St. Redeem carries indie labels and a small selection of local designers, and targets urban and hip but cashed-up customers. Look for Won Hundred denim, Colcci ankle boots, Just Female sweaters and other unique labels (for both men and women).

BIG PLANET COMICS BOOKS
Map p312 (202-342-1961; www.bigplanet comics.com; 1520 U St NW; ⊙11am-7pm Mon, Tue, Thu & Fri, to 8pm Wed, to 6pm Sat, noon-5pm Sun; MGreen, Yellow Line to U St) Not just for comic-book-loving geeks, Big Planet appeals to a surprisingly diverse audience, with an excellent collection of limited editions and graphic novels, plus posters, T-shirts, manga material and collectible stuff, all spread through a couple of musty rooms.

RED ONION RECORDS MUSIC
Map p312 (202-780-7735; www.redonion records.com; 1628 U St NW; ⊙noon-7pm Mon-Sat, to 5pm Sun; MGreen, Yellow Line to U St) Small, indie Red Onion deals in vintage vinyl. It stocks a good selection of disco, funk, jazz and classic rock. The owner will do trades if you bring in your old records. Prices are reasonable, with most items costing between $5 and $20.

🏃 **SPORTS & ACTIVITIES**

ROCK CREEK GOLF COURSE GOLF
(202-882-7332; www.golfdc.com; 6100 16th St NW; 18 holes weekday/weekend $20/25; ⊙sunrise-sunset, closed Mon & Tue Jan–mid-Mar; ⬛S2, S4) The hilly and narrow fairways have large elevation changes. Dense woods on either side replace water hazards.

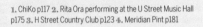

1. ChiKo p117 2. Rita Ora performing at the U Street Music Hall p175 3. H Street Country Club p123 4. Meridian Pint p181

Five Neighborhoods for a Night Out

After a day of museums and monuments, it's time to let loose. Bohemian jazz clubs? Wee-hour half-smokes? Dive bars for nighthawks? DC has several buzzy neighborhoods to make it happen. In these places, the hot spots even line up in a walkable row.

Logan Circle

North of downtown in trendy Logan Circle, 14th St NW bursts with wine bars, beer bars, tapas bars and oyster bars. Churchkey (p175) glows with the requisite hipness. DC's political glitterati cozy up nearby at Le Diplomate (p171).

U Street NW

Just north of Logan Circle, U St is DC's richest nightlife zone. DJ-savvy groovesters hit the dance floor at U Street Music Hall (p175). Late-night half-smokes await at Ben's Chili Bowl (p171).

H Street NE

Pie cafes, noodle shops and beer gardens roll out east of Union Station. Little Miss Whiskey's Golden Dollar (p122) sets the frisky standard with hallucinogenic decor and boogaloo-spinning DJs. H Street Country Club (p123) pours beer alongside a DC-themed mini-golf course.

Barracks Row

In Capitol Hill along 8th St SE, locals line up for shabby-chic Rose's Luxury (p120) and Chinese-Korean fusion at ChiKo (p117). They also sip Balkan wines at convivial Ambar (p125) and see what's on at the Fridge (p124) street-art gallery.

Columbia Heights

The main vein is 11th St NW. In good weather the patio benches at Wonderland Ballroom (p177) fill with neighborhoodies hoisting brews. It's the same scene up the road at wine-pouring Room 11 (p180) and beer-and-pool bar Meridian Pint (p181).

Upper Northwest DC

Neighborhood Top Five

1 Washington National Cathedral (p188) Admiring the esoteric assortment of sacred and profane architectural features – including an unorthodox array of gargoyles – at this massive neo-Gothic house of worship.

2 Kreeger Museum (p189) Being wowed by International Style architecture and modern art at this connoisseur's choice.

3 Hillwood Estate, Museum & Gardens (p189) Gaining an insight into the lavish lifestyle of an heiress and admiring her top-drawer decorative arts collection and manicured garden.

4 National Zoo (p189) Visiting giant pandas, Asian elephants, African lions and swinging orangutans at this Smithsonian institution.

5 Rock Creek Park (p190) Saddling up a horse, stargazing or following a hiking or cycling trail in this sprawling and wildlife-filled suburban oasis.

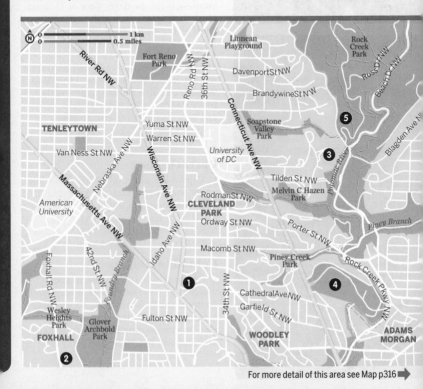

For more detail of this area see Map p316 ➡

Explore Upper Northwest DC

It's easy to fill a day or two exploring Upper Northwest. Start in residential Woodley Park, easily accessed by metro (Red Line). Join the families and school groups at the National Zoo (p189), or head to the more tranquil Hillwood Estate, Museum & Gardens (p189) in classy Forest hIlls, located near the Van Ness-UDC stop. Then grab a quick lunch (the delis and bakeries near the Van Ness-UDC metro are good choices) and spend your after-noon· hiking or horse-riding in Rock Creek Park (p190), an urban oasis managed by the National Park Service. On your second day, visit the architecturally resplend-ent Kreeger Museum (p189) and Washington National Cathedral (p188), have lunch at Open City (p192) in the cathedral grounds and then take a pleasant walk or bus trip to Georgetown or to Connecticut Ave, Upper North-west's main dining and nightlife strip.

Local Life

➡ **Literary Salon** Author readings and talks, moderated conversations and book launches are held almost every night and weekend afternoon at the intellectually curious Politics and Prose Bookstore (p194).

➡ **Poetry Stars** On Sunday afternoons in summer, the Joaquin Miller Poetry Series takes place in Rock Creek Park's planetarium (p190).

➡ **Indie Cinema** The much-loved art-deco Avalon Theatre (p193) hosts family-themed weekend events and shows a wide range of films. You can also watch a film with a wine or beer in hand.

Getting There & Away

➡ **Metro** The Red Line is your best option. Stations include Woodley Park (for restaurants), Cleveland Park (the National Zoo and restaurants), Van Ness-UDC (Hillwood Estate, Museum & Gardens, restaurants) and Friendship Heights (Rock Creek Park's Nature Center & Planetarium).

➡ **Bus** L1 and L2 buses travel along Connecticut Ave NW and pick up from the Woodley Park, Cleveland Park and Van Ness-UDC Metro stations; 30-series buses run along Wisconsin Ave NW and pick up from the Tenleytown-AU Metro station. The N2, N3, N4 and N6 bus lines head up Massachusetts Ave from Dupont Circle to Washington National Cathedral, and bus D6 travels from the Farragut North Metro station to a stop near Kreeger Museum.

Lonely Planet's Top Tip

Remember your geography. Upper Northwest may seem far from the action, but it's right next door to George-town (to the southwest), Dupont (to the southeast), and Adams-Morgan (to the west). You can easily walk to any of these neighborhoods and their rich stock of res-taurants and nightlife.

 **Best Parks & Gardens**

➡ Rock Creek Park (p190)

➡ Hillwood Estate, Museum & Gardens (p189)

➡ Glover Archbold Park (p190)

➡ Battery Kemble Park (p190)

For reviews, see p189. ➡

 Best Places to Eat

➡ Comet Ping Pong (p191)

➡ 2 Amys (p191)

➡ Buck's Fishing & Camping (p192)

➡ Bread Furst (p191)

➡ Indique (p193)

➡ Macon (p193)

For reviews, see p191. ➡

 Best Places to Drink

➡ St Arnold's Mussel Bar (p193)

➡ Nanny O'Brien's Irish Pub (p193)

For reviews, see p193. ➡

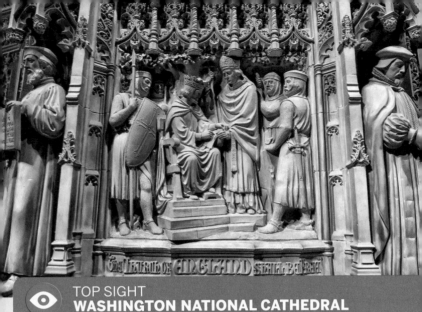

The grand Gothic cathedrals of Western Europe provided the design inspiration for this landmark building, which features flying buttresses, carved stone gargoyles, a vaulted ceiling and oodles of stained-glass. The sixth-largest cathedral in the world, it has played a pivotal role in the city's religious life since its cornerstone was laid in 1907.

What's fascinating here are the distinctive American accents. A lunar rock is embedded in the 'Scientists and Technicians' stained-glass window, and Darth Vader's head is represented among the 112 gargoyles. Carvings depict figures including Mother Teresa, Rosa Parks, Eleanor Roosevelt, Helen Keller and John Walker, the first black bishop of Washington. Stained-glass features include a magnificent rose window made from 10,000 pieces of richly colored glass, and the controversial Jackson-Lee window honoring the two Confederate generals. Elements in the latter window representing Confederate flags were removed in 2016 and the Cathedral's governing body is currently considering replacing it entirely.

In the main sanctuary, look for the Canterbury Pulpit, where Martin Luther King Jr gave his last Sunday sermon; the High Altar (made from limestone taken from an ancient quarry outside Jerusalem); and the Holy Spirit Chapel, which houses painted oak panels by noted American artist NC Wyeth.

If visiting in the afternoon, try to stay to hear the choristers at Evensong (5:30pm Mondays to Fridays and 4pm on Sundays during the school year). You can also join a guided highlights tour (Monday to Saturday), which is included in the ticket price.

DON'T MISS

➜ Gargoyles
➜ High Altar
➜ Rose window
➜ Canterbury Pulpit
➜ 'Scientists and Technicians' window
➜ Holy Spirit Chapel

PRACTICALITIES

➜ Map p316, B4
➜ ☎202-537-6200
➜ www.cathedral.org
➜ 3101 Wisconsin Ave NW, Cathedral Heights
➜ adult/child 5-17yr $12/8, Sun free
➜ ⊙10am-5pm Mon-Fri, 10am-4pm Sat, 12:45-4pm Sun
➜ 🚍N2, N3, N4, N6 from Dupont Circle

⊙ SIGHTS

**WASHINGTON NATIONAL
CATHEDRAL**   CHURCH
See p188.

⭐ **KREEGER MUSEUM**   MUSEUM
(📞202-337-3050; www.kreegermuseum.org;
2401 Foxhall Rd NW, Foxhall Crescent; adult/
student $10/8; ☺10am-4pm Tue-Sat, closed Aug;
Ⓜ Red Line to Farragut North or Dupont Circle, then
bus D6) One of DC's top attractions for architecture buffs and those with an interest in 20th-century art, this museum is housed in a stunning 1963 International Style building designed by American architect Philip Johnson. Clad in travertine, it features a distinctive roofline, light-saturated interior salons and an expansive sculpture terrace that is home to works by artists including Jean Arp and Henry Moore. Inside, artworks from the top-drawer personal collection of David and Carem Kreeger are displayed.

Exhibits are constantly rotated, so you're just as likely to see Monet's dappled impressionism as Edvard Munch's dark expressionism. There are plenty of masterpieces, including works by Picasso, van Gogh and Cézanne. Guided tours are offered at 10:30am and 1:30pm from Tuesday to Friday, and at 10:30am, noon and 2pm on Saturday. If heading here by bus, alight at Hoban Rd NW and walk north up Foxhall Rd.

⭐ **HILLWOOD ESTATE,
MUSEUM & GARDENS**   MUSEUM, GARDENS
Map p316 (📞202-686-5807; www.hillwood
museum.org; 4155 Linnean Ave NW, Forest Hills;
adult/student/child 6-18yr $18/10/5; ☺10am-
5pm Tue-Sat; Ⓜ Red Line to Van Ness-UDC) The former estate of Marjorie Merriweather Post of Post cereal fame, this lavishly decorated 1920s mansion showcases her extraordinary collections of Russian imperial art (icons, paintings, jewelry, Fabergé eggs) and French 18th-century decorative artwork (Sèvres porcelain, Louis XVI furniture). Wandering through the mansion is fascinating – the state-of-the-art 1950s kitchen, modern staff quarters and opulent, objet-laden entertaining and living areas give a wonderful insight into her privileged life and role as a notable society hostess.

As a bonus, the 25-acre estate incorporates some lovely gardens, which include Post's dog cemetery, a greenhouse and a museum shop. The on-site cafe serves light fare, such as sandwiches, salads and soups. It's worth joining a free one-hour guided tour of the mansion – held at 11:30am and 1:30pm Tuesday through Thursday with an extra 3:30pm tour Friday through Sunday – to hear stories about Post's lifestyle. Alternatively, take advantage of the downloadable audio guide. The estate is a mile walk from the Van Ness-UDC Metro station.

NATIONAL ZOO   ZOO
Map p316 (📞202-633-4888; www.nationalzoo.
si.edu; 3001 Connecticut Ave NW, Woodley Park;
☺9am-6pm mid-Mar–Sep, to 4pm Oct–mid-Mar,
grounds 8am-7pm mid-Mar–Sep, to 5pm Oct–mid-
Mar; Ⓜ Red Line to Cleveland Park or Woodley Park)
FREE Home to more than 1800 animals and more than 300 species in natural habitats, the National Zoo is famed for its giant pandas Mei Xiang, Tian Tian and Bei Bei. Other highlights include the African lion pride, Asian elephants, and orangutans swinging 50ft overhead from steel cables and interconnected towers (aka the 'O Line').

This Smithsonian Institution zoo was founded in 1889 and planned by Frederick Law Olmsted, designer of New York's Central Park. The zoo's grounds follow the natural contours of a woodland canyon, and the exhibits are noted for their natural-habitat settings. The zoo is intensively involved in worldwide ecological study and species-preservation work. High points in the past decade include giant panda and lowland gorilla births – a happy change from the early 2000s, when the zoo faced controversy over mismanagement and the deaths of several animals.

Even non-zoo fans will find the National Zoo entertaining. The panda house offers fun facts on the creatures' sex lives (they only go at it three days per year – indeed Mei Xiang's pregnancy was the result of artificial insemination) and bowel production (behold the hefty replica poo). Big-cat fans will enjoy visiting the Cheetah Conservation Station and most visitors seem to find the Electric Fishes Demonstration Lab in the Amazonia exhibit quite fascinating.

ⓘ EASIEST WAY TO THE ZOO

The National Zoo is pretty much equidistant between the Cleveland Park and Woodley Park Metro stops, but the walk is flat if you get off at Cleveland Park (it's uphill from Woodley Park).

The grounds are well-marked, but there is a map on the zoo's website and printed versions can be purchased at the main entrance. Check the sign there for each day's event program, including animal feedings. Note that the Bird House is undergoing a major renovation and is closed until 2021. If coming by Metro, the walk from Woodley Park is uphill and the walk from Cleveland Park is flat. If driving, parking costs $25.

ROCK
CREEK PARK   PARK
Map p316 (www.nps.gov/rocr; ☉sunrise-sunset; ⓂRed Line to Friendship Heights; Red, Green, Yellow Line to Fort Totten; then bus E4 from both) At 1700-plus acres, Rock Creek is twice the size of New York's Central Park and feels wilder. Terrific trails for hiking, biking and horseback riding extend the entire length, and the boundaries enclose Civil War forts, dense forest and wildflower-strewn fields.

Beach Drive is undergoing extensive renovation and various sections will be closed to vehicles over the course of several years. Visit www.nps.gov/rocr to learn more.

Rock Creek Park begins at the Potomac's east bank near Georgetown and extends to and beyond the northern city boundaries. Narrow in its southern stretches, where it hews to the winding course of the waterway it's named for, it broadens into wide, peaceful parklands in Upper Northwest DC.

You can pick up maps, source hiking information and sign up for ranger-led programs at the Nature Center & Planetarium in the northern part of the park. Cell phone 'tours' are stationed around the park. When you see a dial-and-discover sign, just call the listed number and enter the stop number – you can then listen to a ranger give a two-minute narration about that part of the park. Southwest of the Nature Center, the Soapstone Valley Park extension, off Connecticut Ave at Albemarle St NW, preserves quarries where the area's original Algonquin residents dug soapstone for shaping their cookware.

SOAPSTONE
VALLEY TRAIL   PARK
Map p316 (Forest Hills; ⓂRed Line to Van Ness-UDC) This rugged 1-mile trail follows along Soapstone Creek and makes a nice add-on to a hike in Rock Creek Park. Access the trailhead on Ablemarle St NW, about one block east of Connecticut Ave.

NATURE CENTER
& PLANETARIUM   NATURE CENTER
(☎202-895-6000; www.nps.gov/rocr; 5200 Glover Rd NW, Rock Creek Park, off Military Rd; ☉9am-5pm Wed-Sun; ⓂRed Line to Friendship Heights or Red, Green, Yellow Line to Fort Totten; then bus E4 from both) FREE The Nature Center & Planetarium is the main visitor center for Rock Creek Park. Besides exhibits on park flora, fauna and history, it can provide hiking information, maps and field guides. A 'touch table' is set up for kids, and rangers lead child-oriented nature walks. Free ranger-led astronomy programs happen inside the planetarium at 1pm and 4pm on Saturday and Sunday; there's also a kids program at 4pm on Wednesday.

If you're coming via public transportation, take the E4 bus to the intersection of Military and Glover roads. Look to your left and follow the trail up to the Nature Center.

A bit further north of here, on the west side of Beach Dr, is Joaquin Miller Cabin, a log house that once sheltered the famed nature poet.

GLOVER
ARCHBOLD PARK   PARK
Map p316 (Westchester; ⓂRed Line to Dupont Circle) Glover is a sinuous, winding park, extending from Van Ness St NW in Tenleytown down to the western border of Georgetown University. Its 180 tree-covered acres follow the course of little Foundry Branch Creek, along which runs a pretty nature trail. You can take either bus D2 or D6 from Dupont Circle to get to this park

This park is a good bird-watching destination. It's also a favorite for trail runners. To make a 6-mile loop, start at the C&O Canal and run north through the park, turn west on the greenway along Edmunds St to Palisades Park, then continue south back to the canal and then east to your starting point.

BATTERY KEMBLE PARK   PARK
(Foxhall Crescent; ⓂRed Line to Dupont Circle) Skinny Battery Kemble Park, about a mile long but less than a quarter-mile wide, separates the wealthy Foxhall and Palisades neighborhoods of far northwestern DC. Managed by the National Park Service, the park preserves the site of a little two-gun battery that helped defend western DC against Confederate troops during the Civil War. Take bus D6 from the Dupont Circle station to get to this park.

PEIRCE MILL
HISTORIC BUILDING

Map p316 (www.nps.gov/pimi; 2401 Tilden St NW, Rock Creek Park; ⊙10am-4pm Sat & Sun Apr-Oct; MRed Line to Van Ness-UDC) **FREE** Alongside Rock Creek, the 1829 Peirce Mill is a beautiful fieldstone building that houses a recently restored gristmill – the last of the mills that once flourished along the creek. Milling demonstrations are given between 11am and 2pm on the 2nd and 4th Saturdays from April to October.

KAHLIL GIBRAN
MEMORIAL GARDEN
GARDENS

Map p316 (3100 Massachusetts Ave NW, Woodley Park; MRed Line to Dupont Circle, then bus N2, N4 or N6) Located within a wooded ravine known as Woodland-Normanstone Park, this garden memorializes the arch-deity of soupy spiritual poetry. Its centerpieces are a bust of the Lebanese mystic and a star-shaped fountain surrounded by flowers, hedges and limestone benches engraved with various Gibranisms such as 'We live only to discover beauty. All else is a form of waiting.' From a path just north of the garden, you can hop onto trails that link to Rock Creek and Glover Archbold parks.

ISLAMIC CENTER
MOSQUE

Map p316 (2551 Massachusetts Ave NW, Embassy Row; ⊙10am-5pm; MRed LIne to Dupont Circle) Topped with a 160ft minaret, this pale limestone structure on Embassy Row is the national mosque for American Muslims and dates from 1957. Inside, the mosque glows with bright floral tiling, thick Persian rugs and gilt-trimmed ceilings detailed with more Quranic verse. Visitors may enter but must remove their shoes before doing so and women must cover their hair with a scarf.

✕ EATING

Restaurants, cafes and delis are dotted along the length of Connecticut Ave, particularly around the Cleveland Park and Woodley Park metro stops. There are also plenty of choices on Wisconsin Ave NW near Washington National Cathedral.

★COMET PING PONG
PIZZA $

Map p316 (☏202-364-0404; www.cometping pong.com; 5037 Connecticut Ave NW, Chevy Chase; pizzas $9-19; ⊙5-9:30pm Mon-Thu, 11:30am-10:45pm Fri & Sat, 11:30am-9:30pm Sun; ⌖; MRed Line to Van Ness-UDC) Proving that DC is more than a city of suits and corporate offices, Comet Ping Pong offers a fun and festive counterpoint to most of the city's eateries. On offer are ping-pong tables, an industrial-chic interior and delicious pizzas cooked in a wood-burning oven. Reservations are not required.

Play a round on the tables while you wait for a seat, then feast on creative pizzas such as Smoky, which is topped with smoked bacon, Gouda and mushrooms. Wash it down with a draft from Atlas Brew Works. It's popular with families in the early evening, but as the night progresses older kids – the 25- to 65-year-old crowd – take over. Bands take the stage from time to time.

★BREAD FURST
BAKERY $

Map p316 (☏202-765-1200; www.breadfurst.com; 4434 Connecticut Ave NW, Van Ness/Forest Hills; sandwiches $8-10, cakes $6; ⊙7am-7pm Mon-Fri, 8am-5pm Sat & Sun; ⌖; MRed Line to Van Ness-UDC) 🌿 Watch the bakers hand-shape artisan breads and traditional pastries at this bustling bakery. Owner Mark Furstenberg was dubbed 'Outstanding Baker of the US' by the James Beard Foundation in 2017 and the accolade is well deserved – sample a delicious sandwich or baguette, brownie, cake, pastry or muffin to see why. Challah is available on Fridays.

★2 AMYS
PIZZA $

Map p316 (☏202-885-5700; www.2amysdc.com; 3715 Macomb St NW, Cleveland Park; pizzas $9-15; ⊙5-10pm Mon, 11am-10pm Tue-Thu, 11am-11pm Fri & Sat, noon-10pm Sun; ⌖⌖; MRed Line to Tenleytown-AU, then southbound bus 31, 32, 36, 37) A stone's throw from Washington National Cathedral, 2 Amys serves Neapolitan-style pizza and calzones to a crowd of regulars. It's particularly popular with local families. Toppings are traditional – marinara, margherita, calabrese – and the pizzas are cooked in a wood-fired oven that is the centrepiece of the open kitchen. Dessert treats include house-made gelato and cannoli.

The rear wine bar is a *molto simpatico* spot to enjoy a glass or two of local or European beer, a cocktail or your choice of Italian wines offered by the bottle and glass. You can snack on excellent antipasti – frittata, crostini, *salumi* platters – here, too.

OPEN CITY
AMERICAN $

Map p316 (☏202-332-2331; www.opencitydc.com; 2331 Calvert St NW, Woodley Park; breakfast dishes $7-16, mains $12-18; ⊙7am-late; ⌖; MRed

CIVIL WAR FORTS

The remains of Civil War forts that dot Rock Creek Park are among its most fascinating sites. During the war, Washington was, essentially, a massive urban armory and supply house for the Union Army. Its position near the Confederate lines made it vulnerable to attack, so forts were hastily erected on the city's high points. By spring 1865, 68 forts and 93 batteries bristled on the hilltops around DC. See Civil War Defenses of Washington (www.nps.gov/cwdw) for more on the subject.

Line to Woodley Park) Open City is a bedrock breakfast and brunch spot in Woodley Park, drawing a mix of diners including young families and old-time regulars. You'll find the usual assortment of egg- and pancake-centric dishes, along with brick-oven pizzas, pot roast, sandwiches and other comfort fare. Bartenders whip up an excellent Bloody Mary. Breakfast is served all day.

Though fairly quiet during the week, you'll need to arrive early for weekend brunch to beat the huge crowds that begin forming by 11am.

OPEN CITY AT THE
NATIONAL CATHEDRAL   CAFE $

Map p316 (☑202-965-7670; www.opencity cathedraldc.com; 3101 Wisconsin Ave NW, Cathedral Heights; brunch dishes $4-11, sandwiches $8-10; ☺7am-6pm; ☏; ⓜTenleytown-AU, then bus 31, 32, 36, 37) Located in the grounds of Washington National Cathedral, this atmospheric cafe with indoor and outdoor seating serves sweet and savory waffles, grilled sandwiches, salads, soups, pastries and well-brewed coffees. It occupies an octagonal building that formerly served as the baptistry. Despite its proximity to a busy tourist site, this cafe is a much-loved local haunt.

BINDAAS   INDIAN $

Map p316 (☑202-244-6550; www.bindaasdc.com; 3309 Connecticut Ave NW, Cleveland Park; brunch dishes $6-12, dinner mains $8-15; ☺5-11pm Mon-Fri, 11am-11pm Sat, 11am-9pm Sun; ⓜRed Line to Cleveland Park) Serving modern riffs on traditional Indian street food, this stylish eatery is a popular choice for weekend brunch, when its puris, *pakoras*, bhajis, masala omelettes and coconut jaggery pancakes provide a wonderfully spicy start to the day. At dinner, wraps, shashliks and *uttapams* are the offerings, accompanied by a decent selection of wines and beers.

SOAPSTONE MARKET   DELI $

Map p316 (☑202-750-4100; www.soapstone market.com; 4465 Connecticut Ave NW, Van

Ness/Forest Hills; mains $8-15, sandwiches $8-12; ☺8am-9pm Sun-Thu, to 10pm Fri & Sat; Ⓟ☏☑; ⓜRed Line to Van Ness-UDC) The aisles of this designer grocery store showcase plenty of specialty products, many of which feature in the excellent dishes produced in its huge deli section. Choose from salads, an abundance of vegetable dishes, hearty soups at $3 per cup and delicious sandwiches. Order at the counter and then grab a seat – there are indoor and outdoor options.

Patrons receive 90 minutes of free parking at the nearby Park Van Ness garage.

VACE DELI   ITALIAN $

Map p316 (☑202-363-1999; www.vaceitaliandeli. com; 3315 Connecticut Ave NW, Cleveland Park; whole pizza $9-11; ☺9am-9pm Mon-Fri, to 8pm Sat, 10am-5pm Sun; ⓜRed Line to Cleveland Park) If you're going on a picnic in Rock Creek Park, you can source *salumi*, cheese, bread, olives and wine from Vace, perhaps the best-loved Italian deli in DC. Treat yourself to some of its pizzas, too; they're *delizioso*.

ROCKLANDS BARBECUE   SOUTHERN US $

Map p316 (☑202-333-2558; www.rocklands.com; 2418 Wisconsin Ave NW, Glover Park; mains $6-20; ☺11am-9pm Sun-Wed, to 10pm Thu-Sat; ⓜRed Line to Tenleytown-AU, then bus 30, 32, 34 or 36) We say Southern, but really, it's just about the barbecue here: slow smoked, red oak and hickory, no electricity, no gas, Texas-style and pretty good for the East Coast. The ribs, as you might guess, are the way to go. Eat in or order at the take-out counter.

★BUCK'S FISHING
& CAMPING   AMERICAN $$

Map p316 (☑202-364-0777; www.bucksfishing andcamping.com; 5031 Connecticut Ave NW, Chevy Chase; mains $15-39; ☺5-9:30pm Sun-Thu, to 10pm Fri & Sat; ⓜRed Line to Van Ness-UDC) Buck's is popular for its vibe: haute lakeside fishing camp complete with modern banquettes, red-and-white checked tablecloths and canoes on the walls. The menu showcases high-end comfort food at its best, with the kitchen cranking out seasonally in-spired mains and year-round wood-grilled burgers. Make reservations on weekend eve-nings to avoid painfully long waits.

★ INDIQUE INDIAN $$

Map p316 (☎202-244-6600; www.indique.com; 1312-14 Connecticut Ave NW, Cleveland Park; mains $13-24; ☺5-10pm Mon-Thu, noon-3pm & 5-10:30pm Fri, 11am-3pm & 5:30-10pm Sat & Sun; ☻☑; Ⓜ Red Line to Cleveland Park) The jew-eled colors and ornate architecture of tra-ditional Rajasthani mansions provide the decorative inspiration for this modern In-dian restaurant, but the menu is influenced by multiple Indian regions. The dishes from Kerala are particularly delicious. Try the starters, which pay homage to street-food culture, and the creative cocktails, such as Mumbai Mule and Shantarum.

★ MACON FUSION $$

(☎202-248-7807; www.maconbistro.com; 5520 Connecticut Ave NW, Chevy Chase; brunch mains $12-20, dinner mains $21-27; ☺5-10pm Mon-Thu, 5-11pm Fri, 10am-2pm & 5-11pm Sat, 10am-2pm & 5-10pm Sun; Ⓜ Red Line to Friendship Heights, then bus L1 & L2) Macon, Georgia, meets Mâcon, France, in this wild mash-up of delectable Southern cooking with classic French cuisine. Regulars head here to feast on Southern favorites including short-ribs and lobster and grits, or on French favorites such as steak *frites* and duck confit. Deviled eggs and biscuits with honey butter and pepper jelly are staples at the popular week-end brunch. Thanks to a stylish refit, the interior of this landmark 1925 building now features an open kitchen and a bold flash-bulb-lit sign above the 20-seat bar – which is, incidentally, a great spot for solo diners. The 3-course prix fixe menu ($35) offered from 5pm to 6.30pm offers great value.

ST ARNOLD'S MUSSEL BAR BELGIAN $$

Map p316 (☎202-621-6719; www.starnolds musselbar.com; 3433 Connecticut Ave NW, Cleve-land Park; mains $12-20; ☺4pm-2am Mon-Thu, 11am-3am Fri & 11am-4pm Sun; Ⓜ Red Line to Cleveland Park) This lively open-air spot in Cleveland Park makes a fine destination when you want to combine a bit of eating and drinking. Mussel lovers will appreciate the huge selection of dishes, and the Belgian-heavy beer selection is outstanding. There's also a cozy all-wood tavern downstairs. Come between 4pm and 7pm on weekdays to enjoy $11 mussel pots and $5 beers.

LEBANESE TAVERNA MIDDLE EASTERN $$

Map p316 (☎202-265-8681; www.lebaneset averna.com; 2641 Connecticut Ave NW, Woodley Park; mains $18-29; ☺11:30am-10pm Sun-Thu, to 11pm Fri & Sat; ☻; Ⓜ Red Line to Woodley Park) Family-run, this Lebanese restaurant has been serving mezes, kibbe, shawarma and other traditional dishes for more than three decades. It's vegetarian-friendly. Eat in the high-ceilinged room or outside under the umbrellas.

🍷 DRINKING & NIGHTLIFE

Most places tend to be of the quiet neighborhood pub variety. The exception is a small cluster of rowdy Irish bars around Connecticut Ave in Cleveland Park, near Uptown Theater. This is probably Upper Northwest's most concentrated nightlife strip; the crowd here is young, international and determined to party.

NANNY O'BRIENS IRISH PUB IRISH PUB

Map p316 (☎202-686-9189; www.nannyobriens. com; 3319 Connecticut Ave NW, Cleveland Park; ☺noon-2am Sun-Thu, to 3am Fri & Sat; Ⓜ Red Line to Cleveland Park) Washington's most authen-tic Irish pub has been a favorite with real and wannabe Irish people for decades. You won't find any cheesy shamrock schlock or shameless promotions here; this bar would rather concentrate on serving stiff drinks along with a good soundtrack. There's live music from 10pm on Saturdays and a happy hour daily from 4pm to 8pm.

☆ ENTERTAINMENT

AVALON THEATRE CINEMA

(☎202-966-6000; www.theavalon.org; 5612 Con-necticut Ave NW, Chevy Chase; adult/child 12yr & under $12.50/9.50; ☻; Ⓜ Red Line to Friendship Heights, then bus L1 or L2) Dating from the 1920s, this handsomely restored art-deco movie house shows a mix of independent, foreign and first-run films. It's operated by the local community, who rallied to save the building when it was threatened with demolition in the early 2000s. If you're traveling with kids, don't miss the week-end family matinees. There's a popular cafe and snack bar (with wine, beer and freshly baked snacks) inside.

LA MAISON FRANÇAISE
MUSIC, THEATER

Map p316 (📞202-944-6192; www.frenchculture. org/events; 4101 Reservoir Rd NW; Ⓜ Red Line to Farragut North) La Maison is otherwise known as the French embassy. The beating heart of Gallic DC occupies eight elegantly landscaped acres, anchored by the marble, modernesque embassy itself. Countless cultural activities are held here every week; check the website for listings. Reservations are required for all events. To get here, take bus D6 from the metro station.

AMC LOEWS UPTOWN 1
CINEMA

Map p316 (www.amctheatres.com; 3426 Connecticut Ave NW, Cleveland Park; Ⓜ Red Line to Cleveland Park) Housed in a historic building, this one-screen theater near the Cleveland Park Metro station shows first-run films. Sadly, nothing remains of the original 1936 interior.

🛍 SHOPPING

Don't forget the well-stocked gift shops at Hillwood Estate, Museum & Gardens (p189) or Washington National Cathedral (p188).

POLITICS AND PROSE
BOOKSTORE
BOOKS

Map p316 (📞202-364-1919; www.politics-prose. com; 5015 Connecticut Ave NW, Chevy Chase; ⏰8am-10pm Mon-Sat, to 8pm Sun; 📶; Ⓜ Van Ness-UDC, then bus L1 or L2) A much-loved DC literary hub, this independent bookstore carries an excellent selection of fiction and nonfiction, has knowledgeable staff and is fiercely supportive of local authors. It's known for hosting readings and book clubs. The basement coffeehouse and wine bar (sandwiches $9 to $10) hosts cultural and music events, and offers happy hour from 4pm to 7pm Monday to Friday.

BARSTONS CHILD'S PLAY
TOYS

(📞202-244-3602; www.barstonschildsplay. com; 5536 Connecticut Ave NW, Chevy Chase; ⏰9:30am-7pm Mon-Fri, to 6pm Sat, 11:30am-5pm Sun; 📶; Ⓜ Friendship Heights) This much-loved toy shop may look small on the outside, but it has a fantastic selection with all the latest kid pleasers. A daily storytime session is held at 10:30am. Either of these buses (L1 or L2) from the Friendship Heights Metro station will take you here.

KRÖN CHOCOLATIER
FOOD & DRINKS

(📞202-966-4946; www.krondc.com; 5300 Wisconsin Ave NW, Mazza Gallerie, Chevy Chase; ⏰10am-8pm Mon-Fri, 10am-6pm Sat, noon-6pm Sun; Ⓜ Red Line to Friendship Heights) This shop is known for hand-dipped truffles and amusing novelties, such as edible golf balls, laptops and iPhones.

MAZZA GALLERIE
MALL

(📞202-966-6114; www.mazzagallerie.com; 5300 Wisconsin Ave NW, Chevy Chase; ⏰10am-8pm Mon-Fri, to 7pm Sat, noon-6pm Sun; Ⓜ Red Line to Friendship Heights) If you need an upscale mall, this one has the requisite Neiman-Marcus, Saks etc. Downstairs is a seven-screen AMC movie theater. It's right beside the metro and a stone's throw from the Maryland border.

🏃 SPORTS & ACTIVITIES

FLETCHER'S BOATHOUSE
WATER SPORTS

(📞202-244-0461; www.boatingindc.com/boathouses/fletchers-boathouse; 4940 Canal Rd NW, Foxhall Crescent; watercraft per hr/day from $16/30; ⏰7am-6pm late-Mar–Oct, to 7pm Memorial Day–Labor Day; Ⓜ Red Line to Farragut North, then bus D6) This boathouse is a few miles upriver from Georgetown and is accessible by bike from the C&O Canal & Towpath or by car from Canal Rd. Canoes, kayaks, rowboats, stand-up paddleboards and bicycles can be hired, fishing licenses and tackle are available, and canoe and stand-up paddleboard tours are offered.

Take Reservoir Rd west, which merges with Canal Rd.

ROCK CREEK PARK
HORSE CENTER
HORSEBACK RIDING

Map p316 (📞202-362-0117; www.rockcreekhorsecenter.com; 5100 Glover Rd NW, Rock Creek Park; guided trail rides $42; Ⓜ Red Line to Friendship Heights, then bus E2 or E3) Thirteen miles of wide dirt trails crisscross the northern part of Rock Creek Park, with an equitation field nearby. This center offers guided trail rides, lessons and pony rides. Reservations are required. Weekday rides are only available during summer, while weekend rides run from April to October. One to three rides are scheduled daily so check the website for times.

Northern Virginia

Neighborhood Top Five

1 **Arlington National Cemetery** (p197) Paying your respects at the Tomb of the Unknown Soldier, John F Kennedy Memorial, Challenger Memorial and other places of commemoration and contemplation.

2 **Steven F Udvar-Hazy Center** (p202) Marvelling at an extraordinary collection

of planes, jets and even a space shuttle.

3 **Mount Vernon Trail** (p206) Cycling to Theodore Roosevelt Island, Old Town Alexandria and George Washington's estate.

4 **Freedom House Museum** (p200) Coming face to face with the horrors of slavery.

5 **Pentagon** (p198) Checking out the world's largest office building and its memorial to those killed on site in the September 11, 2001, terrorist attack.

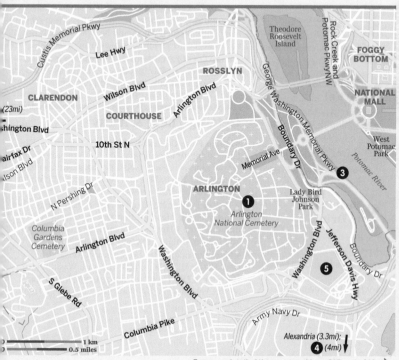

For more detail of this area see Map p315 and p318 ➡

Lonely Planet's Top Tip

Take a day and cycle to Mount Vernon along the eponymous 18-mile trail (p206), which starts at the Theodore Roosevelt Island parking lot. If you start in Alexandria, it's about 12 miles onward. The path hugs the river much of the way and you'll pedal past a lighthouse, bird-filled marsh and 19th-century fort before heading uphill to George Washington's manor.

Best Museums

➡ Steven F Udvar-Hazy Center (p202)

➡ Freedom House Museum (p200)

➡ National Inventors Hall of Fame & Museum (p200)

➡ Stabler-Leadbeater Apothecary Museum (p200)

For reviews, see p199.➡

Best Places to Eat

➡ Brabo Tasting Room (p203)

➡ Del Ray Cafe (p203)

➡ Stomping Ground (p203)

For reviews, see p202.➡

Best Places to Drink

➡ Captain Gregory's (p205)

➡ Bar PX (p205)

➡ Ireland's Four Courts (p204)

➡ Whitlow's on Wilson (p204)

For reviews, see p204.➡

Explore Northern Virginia

We concentrate on the towns of Arlington and Alexandria, which combine crucial capital sites with historic sites, cozy pubs and a buzzing food scene.

Start with Arlington. It's quite close, just a Metro stop from DC, and it holds the two main reasons to cross the border: Arlington National Cemetery (p197) and the Pentagon (p198). Plan on a half-day for these two sights alone. Beyond Arlington you'll find the jaw-dropping Steven F Udvar-Hazy Center (p202), aka the annex of the National Air and Space Museum, which holds three times as many jets and rockets as the Mall building.

The charming town of Alexandria is 5 miles and 250 years away from Washington. Once a salty port, Alexandria – known as 'Old Town' to locals – is today a posh collection of redbrick homes, cobblestone streets, gas lamps and a waterfront promenade. Boutiques, outdoor cafes and bars pack the main thoroughfare, making the town a fine afternoon or evening jaunt. It's also a jumping-off spot for excursions to Mount Vernon (p209).

Local Life

➡ **Stay Cool** When temperatures rise, those in the know head to Theodore Roosevelt Island (p199). It's quiet too, since no bikes or cars are permitted.

➡ **Hangout** Whitlow's on Wilson (p204) is everything a neighborhood hangout should be: boisterous, brunch-awesome, beer-rich and band-savvy on weekends.

➡ **Shop Local** Farmers markets in Alexandria's Old Town (p206), Del Ray (p206) and Arlington (p206) are popular destinations on weekend mornings.

Getting There & Away

➡ **Metro** From DC, use the Arlington Cemetery (Blue Line) to get to the cemetery and the Pentagon (Blue and Yellow Lines) stations to visit Pentagon sites. Ride the King St-Old Town (Blue and Yellow Lines) station for most of Alexandria's sights.

➡ **Trolley** In Alexandria, a free trolley runs along King St between the Metro station and waterfront every 15 minutes from 10am to 10:15pm Sunday to Wednesday, and until midnight Thursday to Saturday.

➡ **Boat** Seasonal water taxis connect Alexandria with National Harbour, MD, and with Washington Harbour in DC. There are also seasonal boat trips to Mount Vernon from SW Waterfront in DC and from Alexandria.

ARLINGTON NATIONAL CEMETERY

At America's national military cemetery, simple white headstones mark the sacrifice of more than 400,000 service members and their dependents. The 624-acre grounds contain the dead of every war the US has fought since the Revolution. Still in active use, it's not uncommon to see families gathered around flag-draped caskets or hear a lone bugle's heartrending lament.

The **Tomb of the Unknown Soldier** (Map p318; off Wilson Dr) contains the remains of unidentified US service members from both world wars and the Korean War. A special military unit of white-gloved, rifle-toting sentinels maintains a round-the-clock vigil. The elaborate changing of the guard (every hour on the hour October through March, every half hour April through September) is one of Arlington's most moving sights.

An eternal flame marks the grave of **John F Kennedy** (Map p318; off Sheridan Dr), next to those of Jacqueline Kennedy Onassis and their two children who died in infancy.

The **Space Shuttle Challenger Memorial** (Map p318; off Memorial Dr) is near the Tomb of the Unknown Soldier. Other points of interest include the tomb of DC city planner **Pierre L'Enfant** (Map p318; off Sherman Dr), near the Kennedy graves, and the **Women in Military Service for America Memorial** (Map p318; www.womensmemorial.org; Schley Dr), near the cemetery entrance. The **Iwo Jima Memorial** (Map p318; Ord & Weitzel Dr), displaying the famous raising of the flag over Mt Suribachi, is on the cemetery's northern fringes.

Pick up a free cemetery map at the cemetery's **Welcome Center** (Map p318; ⊙8am-7pm Apr-Sep, to 5pm Oct-Mar). Hop-on, hop-off bus tours (adult/child $13.50/6.75) are an easy way to hit the highlights. They depart continuously from the visitors center.

DON'T MISS

➡ Kennedy graves and eternal flame
➡ Tomb of the Unknown Soldier
➡ Iwo Jima Memorial
➡ Challenger Memorial
➡ Women in Military Service for America Memorial

PRACTICALITIES

➡ Map p318, E3
➡ ☏877-907-8585
➡ www.arlington cemetery.mil
➡ Memorial Ave
➡ admission free
➡ ⊙8am-7pm Apr-Sep, to 5pm Oct-Mar
➡ Ⓜ Blue Line to Arlington Cemetery

TOP SIGHT
PENTAGON

More than 23,000 people work in this massive polygon, the largest office building in the world. As the headquarters of the US Department of Defense, the Army, Navy and Air Force top brass are all here, as are the Joint Chiefs of Staff. With serious preplanning, you can tour inside. The outdoor Pentagon Memorial is open to anyone, any time.

The Building

Just how big is the Pentagon? The entire Capitol could fit into any one of its five wedge-shaped sections. It has three times the floor space of New York's Empire State Building. The parking lots hold 8770 cars. The building's 17.5 miles of corridors hold 284 bathrooms (side note here: architects designed the building with twice the number of bathrooms needed per number of employees, because segregated Virginia required separate facilities for 'white' and 'colored' persons). The Pentagon's post office handles 1.2 million pieces of mail monthly. Unlike other monumental federal buildings around DC, the Pentagon was built without using marble. That's because, when construction was going on during WWII, Italy – the source of marble – was an enemy country.

Pentagon Memorial

While the formidable edifice appears impenetrable, 184 people were killed here on September 11, 2001, when American Airlines Flight 77 crashed into the west side of the building. Just outside of the Pentagon is a tranquil memorial to these victims, including passengers of flight 77. The grounds consist of 184 benches, each engraved with a victim's name, reaching over a small pool of water. The benches are arranged according to the victims' ages and where they were during the crash (Pentagon versus the airplane). The youngest victim was three-year-old Dana Falkenberg (who was on board flight 77); the oldest was John Yamnicky, 71, a Navy veteran also on the flight.

To reach the memorial, follow the signs from the Pentagon Metro station and go all the way through the parking lot to the end; it's about a 10-minute walk. It is OK to take photos at the memorial, but nowhere else on Pentagon grounds.

Building Tours

The Pentagon offers free, hour-long tours. During the 1.5-mile jaunt, informative guides discuss the military divisions (Army, Air Force, Navy, Marine Corps) housed here; show you the Hall of Heroes and a Medal of Honor; and take you through the Pentagon Memorial. You'll also get an eyeful of artwork and historic memorabilia in the long corridors. Tours depart from the Metro station. No electronics allowed inside.

Top Tips

➡ To tour the building, you need to make a reservation 14 to 90 days in advance. Book online (https://pentagontours.osd.mil/tours) as early as possible.

➡ A free audio tour of the memorial can be downloaded before visiting, or accessed on-site by calling ☎202-741-1004.

DON'T MISS

➡ Memorial audio tour
➡ Flight 77 point of impact
➡ Memorial age lines
➡ Building tours (via preregistration)
➡ Medal of Honor (on the building tour)

PRACTICALITIES

➡ Map p318, F6
➡ https://pentagontours.osd.mil/tours
➡ Arlington
➡ ⊙memorial 24hr, tours by appointment 10am-4pm Mon-Thu, noon-4pm Fri
➡ Ⓜ Blue, Yellow Line to Pentagon

⊙ SIGHTS

⊙ Arlington

**ARLINGTON
NATIONAL CEMETERY** CEMETERY
See p197.

PENTAGON NOTABLE BUILDING
See p198.

ARLINGTON HOUSE HISTORIC SITE
Map p318 (✆703-235-1530; www.nps.gov/
arho; Sherman Dr, Arlington National Cemetery;
⊙9:30am-4:30pm; MBlue Line to Arlington
Cemetery) FREE Set on a hill overlooking
the cemetery, this 1802 Greek Revival–style
mansion is the former home of Confederate
General Robert E Lee and his wife Mary
Anna Custis Lee (aka Martha Washington's
great-granddaughter). Union troops seized
the property once Lee left to command
Virginia's army in the Civil War, and used
the grounds to bury Union war casualties.
The house interior can be visited, but is unfurnished and in sore need of restoration.
Arlington National Cemetery Tours buses
stop outside.

After the war, the Lee family sued the
federal government for reimbursement: the
government paid them off, and Arlington
Cemetery was born. Ranger-guided tours
of the house are held on weekends on the
hour from 10am to 3pm.

AIR FORCE MEMORIAL MEMORIAL
Map p318 (✆703-462-4093; www.airforce
memorial.org; 1 Air Force Memorial Dr; ⊙9am-
9pm Apr-Sep, 8am-8pm Oct-Mar; MBlue, Yellow
Line to Pentagon) FREE Overlooking the Pentagon and adjacent to Arlington National
Cemetery, three graceful stainless-steel
arcs soar 270ft into the air. This shimmering memorial – meant to evoke the con-
trails of jets – pays tribute to the millions of
men and women who served in the air force
and its predecessor organizations.

**THEODORE ROOSEVELT
ISLAND** PARK
Map p318 (www.nps.gov/this; off George Washington Memorial Pkwy; ⊙6am-10pm; ♿; MBlue,
Orange, Silver Line to Rosslyn) This 91-acre
wooded island in the Potomac is a wilderness preserve honoring the conservation-
minded 26th US president. A large memorial plaza and statue of Teddy dominate the

island's center, and 2½ miles of trails and
boardwalks snake around the shorelines.
The island's swampy fringes shelter birds,
raccoons and other small animals. There
are great views of the Kennedy Center and
Georgetown University across the river.
Note that bikes aren't permitted on the island itself; lock them up in the parking lot.

Originally a Native American fishing
village, the island has been owned by a
Caribbean sea captain, home to the Mason
family, and safeguarded by Union troops
during the Civil War. In 1932 the Theodore
Roosevelt Memorial Association purchased
the land with the aim of creating a memorial. Famed landscape architect Frederick
Law Olmsted is credited with renaturaliz-
ing the setting. It was finally dedicated in
1967. The island is accessible only from the
northbound lanes of the George Washington Memorial Pkwy. If you're walking from
Rosslyn, the closest Metro station, find the
pedestrian bridge that takes you across the
parkway (at the corner of North Lynn St
and Lee Hwy).

**GEORGE WASHINGTON
MEMORIAL PARKWAY** PARKWAY
Map p318 (✆703-289-2500; www.nps.gov/
gwmp) The 25-mile Virginia portion of the
highway honors its namesake with recreation areas and memorials all the way south
to his old estate at Mount Vernon. It's lined
with remnants of George Washington's
life and works, such as his old Patowmack
Company canal (in Great Falls National
Park) and parks that were once part of his
farmlands (Riverside Park, Fort Hunt Park).
The 18.5-mile-long Mount Vernon Trail
(p206) parallels the parkway.

The road is a pleasant alternative to the
traffic-choked highway arteries further
away from the river, but you need to pull off
to really appreciate the sites.

DEA MUSEUM MUSEUM
Map p318 (United States Drug Enforcement
Agency Museum; ✆202-307-3463; www.dea
museum.org; 700 Army Navy Dr; ⊙10am-4pm
Tue-Fri; MBlue, Yellow Line to Pentagon City)
FREE The propaganda is served up with
nary a chuckle at this heavy-handed museum brought to you by the Drug Enforcement Agency (DEA). Exhibits cover the last
150 years of drug use, from the opium par-
lors of the 19th century to 1920s cocaine-
dispensing apothecaries, on to the trippy
days of the 1960s, the crack epidemic of

NORTHERN VIRGINIA SIGHTS

the 1980s, and more recent days of crystal-meth labs and the powder drugs favored by the 24-hour party people of today. The entrance is on S Hayes St.

⊙ Alexandria

FREEDOM HOUSE MUSEUM   MUSEUM
Map p315 (☎708-836-2858; www.visitalexandria va.com; 1315 Duke St; ☺10am-3pm Mon-Fri, guided tours & weekends by appointment only; Ⓜ Blue, Yellow Line to King St-Old Town) FREE This demure Federal-style row house holds a tragic story. At a time when Alexandria was the nation's second-largest slave center (after New Orleans), a flourishing slave-trading business occupied this building and adjoining space. A well-presented basement museum, developed by the Northern Virginia Urban League, powerfully tells the stories of the thousands of enslaved people who passed through. Personal video narratives and artifacts are on view in a heartbreaking setting.

Up to 150 slaves were kept in the holding pen outside (since torn down). Among those likely held here was Solomon Northup, a free black man who in 1841 was kidnapped from Washington and sold into bondage in the south. His story was portrayed in the film *Twelve Years a Slave*. There's no admission, but donations are encouraged. The museum isn't signed; look for the Franklin and Armfield Slave Office information panel.

NATIONAL INVENTORS
HALL OF FAME & MUSEUM   MUSEUM
(☎571-272-0095; www.invent.org/honor/hall-of-fame-museum; 600 Dulany St, Madison Bldg; ☺10am-5pm Mon-Fri, 11am-3pm Sat; Ⓜ Blue, Yellow Line to King St-Old Town) FREE Housed in the atrium of the US Patent and Trademark Office, this museum tells the history of the US patent. Step inside to see where the story started in 1917 in Memphis, Tennessee, when a wholesale grocer named Clarence Saunders invented and patented what he called 'self-servicing' stores, now commonly known as supermarkets.

Incidentally, Saunders went from rags to riches and almost back to rags again, but you'll have to visit the museum to get the rest of the story, along with displays depicting other famous and influential patents. It is about a third of a mile from the King St Metro station; take Diagonal Rd south to Dulany St.

STABLER-LEADBEATER
APOTHECARY MUSEUM   MUSEUM
Map p315 (☎703-746-3852; www.alexandriava gov/Apothecary; 105-107 S Fairfax St; adult/child 5-12yr $5/3; ☺10am-5pm Tue-Sat, 1-5pm Sun & Mon Apr-Oct, 11am-4pm Wed-Sat, 1-4pm Sun Nov-Mar; Ⓜ Blue, Yellow Line to King St-Old Town) In 1792 Edward Stabler opened up his apothecary (pharmacy) – a family business that would operate until 1933, when the Depression forced its doors to close. Unused and untouched since that time, it's now a museum. Shelves on two floors are lined with 900 beautiful hand-blown apothecary bottles storing remedies and potions. Harry Potter fans will adore the atmospheric upstairs preparation room, which resembles Professor Snape's potions room at Hogwarts – it even has jars of 'dragon's blood' hemlock and mandrake root

GEORGE WASHINGTON
MASONIC NATIONAL
MEMORIAL   MONUMENT
(☎703-683-2007; www.gwmemorial.org; 101 Callahan Dr at King St; adult/child under 13yr $15/free; ☺9am-5pm; Ⓜ Blue, Yellow Line to King St-Old Town) Alexandria's most prominent landmark features a fine view from the observation deck of its 333ft tower. Modeled after Egypt's Lighthouse of Alexandria, it honors the first president (who was initiated into the Masons in Fredericksburg in 1752 and later became Worshipful Master of Alexandria Lodge No 22). After paying admission, you can explore exhibits on the 1st and 2nd floors, but to visit the tower and see Washington-family artifacts, you must take a 60-minute guided tour.

Tours depart at 9:30am, 11am, 1pm 2:30pm and 4pm. If you ask one too many questions about masonic symbolism and the *National Treasure* movies a trapdoor will open and drop you into the parking lot. We jest, it's all quite welcoming and fascinating

Tickets to the observation deck are free and general admission is discounted to $10 for holders of the Alexandria Museum Pass

CARLYLE HOUSE   HISTORIC BUILDING
Map p315 (☎703-549-2997; www.novaparks com; 121 N Fairfax St; adult/child 5-12yr $5/3 ☺10am-4pm Tue-Sat, noon-4pm Sun; Ⓜ Blue, Yellow Line to King St-Old Town) If you have time for just one historic house tour in Alexandria, make it this one. The house dates from 1753 when merchant and city founder, John Carlyle, built the most lavish mansion in

own (which in those days was little more than log cabins and muddy lanes). The Georgian Palladian–style house is decorated with paintings, historic relics and period furnishings that help bring the past to life. Visits are by one-hour guided tour.

Free tours are given on the hour and half hour. Take the trolley from King St station.

ALEXANDRIA BLACK HISTORY MUSEUM
MUSEUM

Map p315 (☑703-746-4356; www.alexblackhistory.org; 902 Wythe St; suggested donation $2; ⊗10am-4pm Tue-Sat; MBlue, Yellow Line to Braddock Rd) Paintings, photographs, books and other memorabilia documenting the African American experience in Alexandria, one of the nation's major slave ports, are on display at this small resource center (enter from Wythe St). Pick up a brochure for self-guided walking tours of important African American history sites in Alexandria. In the next-door annex, the Watson Reading Room has a wealth of books and documents on African American topics.

Operated by the museum, the African American Heritage Park is worth a stop to see headstones from a 19th-century African American cemetery. The park is about a half mile southeast of the King St Metro. From the station, take Reinekers Lane south, go left on Duke St, then right on Holland Lane.

FORT WARD MUSEUM & HISTORIC SITE
FORTRESS

(☑703-746-4848; www.alexandriava.gov/fortward; 4301 W Braddock Rd; ⊗park 9am-dusk daily, museum 10am-5pm Tue-Sat, noon-5pm Sun) FREE Washington, DC's best-preserved Civil War fort is surprisingly hidden away in a residential Alexandria neighborhood. But there it is, a vivid foray into the life and times of occupied Alexandria and what it took to protect the federal capital from Confederate attack. The reconstructed headquarters houses a small museum with period uniforms, medical equipment and a model of the original fort. A road winds through 45 tree-shaded acres, with signs and maps interpreting the fort's landscape.

Fort Ward is considered a model of 19th-century engineering. Designed for 36 guns mounted in five bastions, it boasts nearly 95 percent of its original earthen walls, an authentically reconstructed bastion, the ceremonial entrance gate and underground bomb shelters to house 500 men. Check for frequent reenactments that interpret

ⓘ ALEXANDRIA MUSEUM PASS

The **Alexandria Museum Pass** ($15; www.visitalexandriava.com) gives entry to eight historic sites in Alexandria and a 40% discount to Mount Vernon. It represents a possible saving of $34. Valid for one year, it can be purchased at the town's **visitor center** (Map p315; ☑703-838-6494; www.visitalexandriava.com; 221 King St; ⊗10am-6pm Sun-Wed, to 8pm Thu-Sat Apr-Sep, to 5pm Oct-Mar; MBlue, Yellow Line to King St-Old Town).

Civil War soldier and civilian life, including infantry drills, artillery demonstrations, camp life, torchlight tours and more. The easiest access to the fort is by car.

ALEXANDRIA ARCHAEOLOGY MUSEUM
MUSEUM

Map p315 (☑703-746-4399; www.alexandriava.gov/archaeology; 3rd fl, 105 N Union St, Torpedo Art Center; ⊗10am-3pm Tue-Fri, to 5pm Sat, 1-5pm Sun; MBlue, Yellow Line to King St-Old Town) FREE Alexandria is known for its landmark archaeological protection code – one of the first in the US – which encourages local archaeologists and developers to work together to preserve the past. This small museum on the 3rd floor of the Torpedo Factory houses a laboratory where archaeologists clean up and catalog the artifacts they have unearthed at local digs. First-hand observation of the work, excavation exhibits and hands-on discovery kits allow visitors to witness and participate in the reconstruction of history.

CONTRABANDS & FREEDMEN CEMETERY
CEMETERY

(www.alexandriava.gov/FreedmenMemorial; 1001 S Washington St; MBlue, Yellow Line to King St-Old Town) During the Civil War, the Union-controlled southern city of Alexandria, VA, became a safe haven for formerly enslaved African Americans. Though they had been freed from bondage, their lives were difficult, with disease and death rampant in their shantytown homes. Some 1800 contrabands (as freed slaves were called) and freedmen were buried at this cemetery on Alexandria's southern edge. A memorial park was developed on the site, including

WORTH A DETOUR

STEVEN F UDVAR-HAZY CENTER

The National Air and Space Museum in the Mall is so awesome they made an attic for it: the **Steven F Udvar-Hazy Center** (📞703-572-4118; www.airandspace.si.edu; 14390 Air & Space Museum Pkwy; ⊙10am-5:30pm; 🚻; Ⓜ Silver Line to Wiehle-Reston East for bus 983) FREE in Chantilly, VA. It's three times the size of the DC museum and sprawls through massive hangars near Washington Dulles International Airport. Highlights include the SR-71 Blackbird (the fastest jet in the world), space shuttle *Discovery* (fresh from the clouds after its 2011 retirement) and the Enola Gay (the B-29 that dropped the atomic bomb on Hiroshima).

Visitors can hang out in the observation tower and watch the planes take off and land at Dulles, go on a simulator (piloting a jet, taking a space walk), or catch shows at the on-site Airbus IMAX Theater. Free 90-minute tours through the collection are offered at 10:30am and 1pm daily.

If you're driving, take I-66 West to VA 267 West, then VA 28 South, then follow the signs. Parking is $15 (free after 4pm).

the sculpture, *The Path of Thorns and Roses*, symbolizing the freedom struggle.

The cemetery is about 1.5 miles southeast of the King St Metro station. From the station, take Reinekers Lane south, go left on Duke St, then right on S Washington St.

GADSBY'S TAVERN MUSEUM   MUSEUM

Map p315 (📞703-746-4242; www.gadsbys tavern.org; 134 N Royal St; adult/child 5-12yr $5/3; ⊙10am-5pm Tue-Sat, 1-5pm Sun & Mon Apr-Oct, to 4pm Nov-Mar; Ⓜ Blue, Yellow Line to King St-Old Town) Once a real tavern (operated by John Gadsby from 1796 to 1808), this building now houses a museum demonstrating the prominent role of the tavern in Alexandria during the 18th century. As the center of local political, business and social life, it was frequented by anybody who was anybody, including George Washington, Thomas Jefferson and the Marquis de Lafayette. Take a self-guided tour or join a guided tour at quarter to and quarter past the hour.

The rooms are restored to their 18th-century appearance, but are sparsely furnished.

FRIENDSHIP FIREHOUSE MUSEUM   MUSEUM

Map p315 (📞703-746-3891; www.alexandriava. gov/friendshipfirehouse; 107 S Alfred St; $2; ⊙1-4pm Sat & Sun; 🚻; Ⓜ Blue, Yellow Line to King St-Old Town) This 1855 Italianate firehouse displays historic firefighting gear – a great draw for kids. Local legend has it that George Washington helped found this volunteer fire company, served as its captain and even paid for a new fire engine.

LEE-FENDALL HOUSE   HISTORIC BUILDING

Map p315 (📞703-548-1789; www.leefendall house.org; 614 Oronoco St; adult/child 5-17yr $5/3; ⊙10am-4pm Wed-Sat, 1-4pm Sun; Ⓜ Blue, Yellow Line to Braddock Rd or King Street-Old Town) Between 1785 and 1903, generations of the famous Lee family lived in this architecturally impressive house. Guided tours (on the hour) show the restored house as it probably was in the 1850s and 1860s, showcasing Lee-family heirlooms and personal effects, and period furniture.

CHRIST CHURCH   CHURCH

Map p315 (📞703-549-1450; www.historicchrist church.org; 118 N Washington St, cnr Columbus & Cameron Sts; $5; ⊙9am-4pm Mon-Sat, 2-4:30pm Sun; Ⓜ Blue, Yellow Line to King St-Old Town) Built in 1773, this brown-brick Georgian-style church has welcomed worshipers from George Washington to Robert E Lee. The cemetery contains the mass grave of Confederate soldiers.

✕ EATING

There are plenty of compelling choices in Alexandria, but the districts close to the Arlington National Cemetery and Pentagon are culinary wastelands.

✕ Arlington

EL POLLO RICO   LATIN AMERICAN $

Map p318 (📞703-522-3220; www.elpollorico restaurant.com; 932 N Kenmore St; chicken with

ides $8-17; ⊗11am-10pm; MSilver, Orange Line
ᵒ Clarendon/Virginia Sq-GMU) *Polla a la brasa*
rotisserie chicken) fiends queue outside
he door of this no-frills Peruvian chicken
ᵒoint every night, keen to feast on its ten-
der, juicy, flavor-packed birds served with
succulent (highly addictive) dipping sauces,
crunchy fries and sloppy 'slaw.

BUZZ BAKESHOP
BAKERY $

☑703-650-9676; www.buzbakeshop.com; 818
N Quincy St, Ballston; ⊗7am-9pm Tue-
10pm Fri, 8am-10pm Sat, 8am-9pm Sun; MSilver,
Orange Line to Ballston-MU) Need a break from
sightseeing? Step inside this contemporary
but inviting bakery on the corner of Wilson
and N Quincy to relax and check your mes-
sages over a coffee and cupcake or cookie.
Close to a bike-share station.

✕ Alexandria

★STOMPING GROUND
BREAKFAST $

☑703-567-6616; www.stompdelray.com; 309
Mt Vernon Ave; mains $7-12; ⊗7am-3pm Tue-
Sat, 9am-3pm Sun; MBlue, Yellow Line to Braddock Rd/King St-Old Town) Did somebody say
biscuit? Oh yes they did. And make that a
scratch-made buttermilk biscuit piled with
fillings of your choice (Benton's bacon, eggs,
veggie frittata, avocado and many more)
and with gouda grits on the side. Or just
stop by this stylish Del Ray spot for coffee
and to work on your laptop. Order and collect at the counter.

EAMONN'S DUBLIN CHIPPER
PUB FOOD $

Map p315 (☑703-299-8384; www.eamonns
dublinchipper.com; 728 King St; mains $9-15;
⊗11:30am-10pm Mon-Wed, to 11pm Thu, to midnight Fri, noon-midnight Sat, noon-9pm Sun;
MBlue, Yellow Line to King St-Old Town) You'll
find no better execution of the fish-and-
chips genre than at this classic Irish-style
chipper. How authentic is it? Well, it im-
ports Batchelor's baked beans from Ireland,
but it also serves deep-fried Mars Bars,
Milky Way and Snickers. Like many resto-
pubs in this part of Old Town, Eamonn's is
a good place for a drink on weekend nights.

CAPHE BANH MI
VIETNAMESE $

Map p315 (☑703-549-0800; www.caphebahnmi.
com; 407 Cameron St; dishes $5-12; ⊗11am-3pm
& 5-9pm Mon-Fri, to 9pm Sat, to 8pm Sun; MBlue,
Yellow Line to King St-Old Town) Stop in this
neighborhood favorite for delicious banh

mi sandwiches, big bowls of pho, pork-belly
steamed buns and other simple but well-
executed Vietnamese dishes. The small but
cozy space always draws a crowd, so go early to beat the dinner rush. Drinks include
beer and bubble tea.

★DEL RAY CAFE
MODERN AMERICAN $$

(☑703-717-9151; www.delraycafe.com; 205 E
Howell St; mains brunch & lunch $10-16, dinner
$21-29; ⊗8am-2:30pm daily, 5-9pm Mon-Thu, to
10pm Fri & Sat; 🛜🚻; MBlue, Yellow Line to Brad-
dock Rd) In a beautifully restored two-story
1925 house, this family-friendly cafe serves
up excellent French and American cooking.
The owner, who hails from Alsace, sources
from local farms to create a tempting menu
of old- and new-world comfort fare. It's a
long walk from King St; take bus 10 from
Braddock Rd or King St-Old Town Metro
stations.

★BRABO
TASTING ROOM
INTERNATIONAL $$

Map p315 (☑703-894-5252; www.brabo
restaurant.com; 1600 King St; sandwiches $14-
16, mains $13-22; ⊗7-10:30am & 11:30am-10pm
Mon-Thu, to 11pm Fri, 8-11am & 11:30am-11pm Sat,
to 10pm Sun; MBlue, Yellow Line to King St-Old
Town) The inviting and sunlit Brabo Tasting
Room serves its signature mussels, tasty
wood-fired tarts and gourmet sandwiches
with a good beer and wine selection. In the
morning, stop by for brioche French toast
and Bloody Marys. Brabo restaurant, next
door, is the high-end counterpart serving
seasonal fare (mains $22 to $45).

HANK'S OYSTER BAR
SEAFOOD $$

Map p315 (☑703-739-4265; www.hanksoyster
bar.com; 1024 King St; mains $18-31; ⊗11:30am-
midnight Mon-Fri, from 11am Sat & Sun; MBlue, Yel-
low Line to King St-Old Town) Get your oyster fix
during happy hour (3pm to 7pm and 10pm to
midnight Monday to Friday) when the briny
critters are only $1.25 apiece at this outpost
of the popular Dupont Circle business. If
you're not sure which oysters to pick from
the long list, opt for a sampler. There are also
seafood and meat dishes on offer.

SONOMA CELLARS
CALIFORNIAN $$

Map p315 (☑703-566-9867; www.mysonoma
cellar.com; 703 King St; mains $14-24; ⊗4-10pm
Mon, to 11pm Tue-Fri, 10am-11pm Sat, to 10pm Sun;
MBlue, Yellow Line to King St-Old Town) Drinking California wines (particularly those
from Napa and Sonoma) is de rigueur at

FARMERS MARKETS

Virginia's farmland bounty is on display weekend mornings at:

➡ Arlington Farmers Market (p206)
➡ Old Town Farmers Market (p206)
➡ Del Ray Farmers Market (p206)

this West Coast outpost. Duck in for a glass of chardonnay and a cheese and charcuterie plate ($18 to $22), or settle in for the evening to graze on tacos, quesadillas, burgers and salads piled with sun-drenched produce. In warmer weather, most action occurs in the rear courtyard.

MOMO SUSHI
& CAFE
JAPANESE $$

Map p315 (☎703-299-9092; www.mymomo sushi.com; 212 Queen St; sushi/sashimi combos $11-25, dinner boxes $15-25; ⊗11:30am-2:30pm & 4-10pm Mon-Fri, noon-10pm Sat, 4-9:30pm Sun; Ⓜ Blue, Yellow Line to King St-Old Town) Momo is tiny and has just 13 seats, but it serves excellent sushi. A well-priced bento box ($11) is available at lunch.

FISH MARKET
SEAFOOD $$

Map p315 (☎703-836-5676; www.fishmarketva. com; 105 King St; mains $24-35; ⊗11:30am-10pm Sun-Thu, to 11:30pm Fri & Sat; Ⓜ Blue, Yellow Line to King St-Old Town) This rambling, 400-seat Old Town landmark restaurant has been serving up Chesapeake-style seafood since 1976. Occupying a 19th-century warehouse at the corner of King and Union Sts, it's known for its crab cakes, jambalaya, raw oysters, and 32-ounce 'schooners' of beer. Seating is on a first-come, first-served basis.

Drop in for happy hour at the Anchor Bar. Best seat: the balcony, from which you can watch King St's bustle. The bar is open until midnight Sunday to Thursday and 1am Friday and Saturday.

GADSBY'S TAVERN
RESTAURANT
AMERICAN $$

Map p315 (☎703-548-1288; www.gadsbys tavernrestaurant.com; 138 N Royal St; mains lunch $11-15, dinner $22-30; ⊗11:30am-3pm & 5:30-10pm Mon-Sat, 11am-3pm & 5:30-10pm Sun; Ⓜ Blue, Yellow Line to King St-Old Town) The food isn't all that memorable, but Gadsby's scores high on novelty. Named after

the Englishman who operated the tavern from 1796 to 1808 (when it was the center of Alexandria's social life), it works hard to emulate an 18th-century hostelry; waitstaff even wear period costumes. Kitsch but fun

DRINKING & NIGHTLIFE

In Alexandria you can stroll to a number of bars in Old Town, while there are quite a few inviting patios in Del Ray. Arlington's drinking is mainly done in pubs and clubs.

📍 Arlington

★ IRELAND'S FOUR COURTS
IRISH PUB

Map p318 (☎703-525-3600; www.irelandsfour courts.com; 2051 Wilson Blvd; ⊗11am-2am Mon-Fri, 8am-2am Sat & Sun; Ⓜ Silver, Orange Line to Court House) Buckets of Guinness lubricate the O'Connors and McDonoughs at Arlington's favorite Irish pub. Fish and chips ($11) and other pub grub is on offer, as is live music (from 9pm Wednesday to Saturday).

★ WHITLOW'S ON WILSON
BAR

Map p318 (☎703-276-9693; www.whitlows.com; 2854 Wilson Blvd; ⊗11am-2am Mon-Fri, 9am-2am Sat & Sun; Ⓜ Silver, Orange Line to Clarendon) Occupying almost an entire block just east of Clarendon Metro, Whitlow's on Wilson has something for everyone: burgers, brunch and comfort food on the menu; happening happy hours and positive pickup potential; plus 12 brews on tap, a pool table, jukebox, live music and an easygoing atmosphere. Head to the rooftop tiki bar in warmer months.

CONTINENTAL
LOUNGE

Map p318 (☎703-465-7675; www.continental poollounge.com; 1911 N Fort Myer Dr; ⊗11:30am-2am Mon-Fri, 6pm-2am Sat & Sun; Ⓜ Blue, Orange, Silver Line to Rosslyn) This buzzing pool lounge evokes a trippy, tropical vibe with its murals of palm trees, oversized tiki heads and color-saturated bar stools. All of which sets the stage for an alternative night of shooting pool on one of the six tables, playing Ping-Pong or trying your hand at shuffleboard.

🍷 Alexandria

⭐ CAPTAIN GREGORY'S COCKTAIL BAR
Map p315 (www.captaingregorys.com; 804 N Henry St; ⏰5:30-11:30pm Wed & Thu, to 1am Fri & Sat, to 10:30pm Sun; Ⓜ Blue, Yellow Line to Braddock Rd) This nautical-themed speakeasy is hidden inside a Sugar Shack doughnut shop, which explains the decadent gourmet doughnuts on the menu. As for drinks, from Anais Needs a Vacay to Moaning Myrtles Morning Tea, the names are as diverse as the ingredients. Think flavored liqueurs, infused spirits and a range of fruit and spices. The cocktail menu changes frequently. Reservation recommended.

⭐ BAR PX BAR
Map p315 (www.barpx.com; 728 King St; ⏰6pm-midnight Wed & Thu, to 1:30am Fri & Sat; Ⓜ Blue, Yellow Line to King St-Old Town) This elegant, low-lit drinking den is a magical spot to linger over a cocktail or two. Bartenders shake up beautifully hued elixirs for a well-dressed crowd, in keeping with the speakeasy theme. True to form, there's no sign, just a blue light and a red door to mark the entrance (on S Columbus St). It's best to reserve ahead.

KILLER ESP CAFE
Map p315 (1012 King St; ⏰7am-9pm Sun-Thu, to 11pm Fri & Sat; 🛜; Ⓜ Blue, Yellow Line to King St-Old Town) Killer by name and execution, this hipster haven serves Alexandria's best coffee. Enjoy an espresso, drip, cold brew or pour-over example with a gluten-free cookie ($2), French pastry ($2) or empanada ($5). Tables out front, comfy couches out back.

UNION STREET PUBLIC HOUSE PUB
Map p315 (📞703-548-1785; www.unionstreet publichouse.com; 121 S Union St; ⏰3-10pm Mon-Thu, 11:30am-11pm Fri, 11am-11pm Sat & Sun; Ⓜ Blue, Yellow Line to King St-Old Town) Gas lamps out front welcome tourists and locals into this spacious taproom for frosty brews, raw-bar delights and nightly dinner specials.

PIZZERIA BIRRERIA PARADISO BAR
Map p315 (📞703-837-1245; www.eatyourpizza. com; 124 King St; pizzas $13-21; ⏰11:30am-10pm Mon-Thu, to 11pm Fri & Sat, noon-10pm Sun; Ⓜ Blue, Yellow Line to King St-Old Town) Sure, the focus is pizza, but the beer list here is outstanding. With 14 brews on draft, 190 or so bottle varieties and one rotating cask selection, you won't lack for options. It's a comfy spot for hopheads to sit back and indulge in small-batch suds chased with piping-hot pizza from a wood-fired stone oven.

☆ ENTERTAINMENT

ARLINGTON CINEMA & DRAFTHOUSE CINEMA
Map p318 (📞703-486-2345; www.arlington drafthouse.com; 2903 Columbia Pike; matinee/ evening screening $8/10; Ⓜ Blue, Yellow Line to Pentagon City, then bus 16) Ice-cold beer and arthouse and first-run films at bargain prices? Count us in. You'll find comfy chairs for flick-viewing, a menu of sandwiches, pizzas and popcorn, as well as brews, wine and cocktails (this is one of the few places in DC where you can drink and catch a movie at the same time). Admission is discounted by $2 on Mondays evenings.

Some nights the theater skips the movies and hosts stand-up comedy instead. There are also family-oriented programs some weekends. It's about a mile from the Metro; grab a cab or the route 16 bus from the station. You need to be at least 21 years to enter (or with a parent, but only for sessions before 9pm).

CLARENDON BALLROOM LIVE MUSIC
Map p318 (📞703-469-2244; www.clarendonball room.com; 3185 Wilson Blvd; ⏰Tue-Sat; Ⓜ Silver, Orange Line to Clarendon) A ballroom done up to look like a big-band-era dance hall, the Clarendon is a NoVa cornerstone that attracts throngs of 20- and 30-somethings to bump and grind on weekend nights. The upstairs deck is perfect for lingering over a sunset cocktail. There is an $8 cover some nights. It's regularly closed for private events; check the website for an update before heading here.

BIRCHMERE LIVE MUSIC
(📞703-549-7500; www.birchmere.com; 3701 Mt Vernon Ave; tickets $30-100; ⏰box office 5-9pm, shows 7:30pm; Ⓜ Blue, Yellow Line to Pentagon City) This 50-year-old place, hailing itself as 'America's Legendary Music Hall,' hosts a wide range of fare, from old-time folk musicians to country, blues and R&B stars. The lineup also features the odd burlesque show, indie rock bands and the occasional one-person comedy act.

The talent that graces the stage is reason enough to come, but the venue is pretty great too: it sort of looks like a warehouse that collided with an army of LSD-affected muralists. Located north of Old Town Alexandria, off Glebe Rd. Take bus 10A from Pentagon City station.

BASIN STREET LOUNGE
JAZZ

Map p315 (☎703-549-1141; www.219restaurant.com; 219 King St; admission Fri & Sat $5; ⊙shows 9pm Tue-Sat; ⓜBlue, Yellow Line to King St-Old Town) Tortoiseshell glasses and black turtlenecks ought to be the uniform of choice at this low-key jazz venue and cigar bar, located above the 219 Restaurant. The extensive whiskey selection, amber lighting and long wooden bar make a fine backdrop to bluesy jazz performances.

 SHOPPING

★TORPEDO
FACTORY ART CENTER
ARTS & CRAFTS

Map p315 (☎703-746-4570; www.torpedofactory.org; 105 N Union St; ⊙10am-6pm Fri-Wed, to 9pm Thu; ⓜBlue, Yellow Line to King St-Old Town) The former munitions factory today houses studios in which 165 artists and craftspeople sell their creations directly to the customer. There are also seven galleries. It is a distinctive setup, and there's a good chance you'll head home with a reasonably priced, one-of-a-kind painting, textile or piece of jewelry.

FASHION CENTRE AT PENTAGON CITY
MALL

Map p318 (☎703-415-2401; www.simon.com; 1100 S Hayes St; ⊙10am-9:30pm Mon-Sat, 11am-6pm Sun; ⓜBlue, Yellow Line to Pentagon City) It houses 170 shops and restaurants, including Apple, Macy's and Nordstrom, as well as a food court beneath skylights. It's your average, convenient mall – with the fun bonus of being where Monica Lewinsky got busted by Ken Starr's troopers back in '98.

ARLINGTON FARMERS MARKET
MARKET

Map p318 (www.community-foodworks.org/arlington-courthouse-market; cnr N Courthouse Rd & N 14th St; ⊙8am-noon Sat Jun-Oct; ⓜSilver, Orange Line to Court House) A local favorite in Arlington.

OLD TOWN FARMERS MARKET
MARKET

Map p315 (www.alexandriava.gov/farmersmarket; 301 King St, Market Sq; ⊙7am-noon Sat; ⓜBlue, Yellow Line to King St-Old Town) This popular fruit-and-veg market is open year-round. There's free parking in the Market Sq car park during market hours.

DEL RAY FARMERS MARKET
MARKET

(www.alexandriava.gov/farmersmarket; 2311 Mt Vernon Ave; ⊙8am-noon Sat; ⓜBlue, Yellow Line to Braddock Rd, then bus 10A or 10B) This local favorite in Del Ray sells everything from Amish cheese to fresh pasta.

 SPORTS & ACTIVITIES

★MOUNT
VERNON TRAIL
CYCLING

Map p318 (www.nps.gov; ⊙6am-10pm; ⓜArlington Cemetery, Ronald Reagan Washington National Airport & Rosslyn) The 18-mile-long Mount Vernon Trail is a paved riverside path that is a favorite with local cyclists. From the Francis Scott Key Bridge, it follows the Potomac River south past Roosevelt Island, Arlington National Cemetery and Ronald Reagan Washington National Airport, through Old Town Alexandria, all the way to Mount Vernon.

Sights along the way include **Lady Bird Johnson Park** (Map p318; www.nps.gov; ⊙6am-10pm; ⓜArlington Cemetery), which commemorates the First Lady who tried to beautify the capital via greenery-planting campaigns; swathes of tulips and daffodils bloom here in spring. Gravelly Point, just north of the airport, provides a vantage point for watching the planes take off and land. Roaches Run Waterfowl Sanctuary lets you check out naturally airborne creatures including ospreys and green herons.

The trail is mostly flat, except the long climb up the hill to George Washington's house at the end. The scenery is magnificent – DC skylines and all – and the historical component is certainly unique.

WASHINGTON & OLD DOMINION TRAIL
CYCLING

(W&OD; www.nvrpa.org; ⊙Shirlington-Herndon 5am-9pm, elsewhere to dusk; ⓜEast Falls

CYCLING THE MOUNT VERNON TRAIL

The 18-mile paved multi-use Mount Vernon Trail stretches along the banks of the Potomac River from the Francis Scott Key Bridge near Theodore Roosevelt Island (p199) to George Washington's Mount Vernon (p209) estate. The trail connects with other regional routes including the Potomac Heritage, Custis, Rock Creek, Four Mile Run, and Woodrow Wilson Bridge Trails.

Walkers and runners use the trail, but it is most popular with cyclists, who appreciate its predominantly flat terrain and wonderful views of the Potomac and DC monuments. Cultural stops along the way include Mount Vernon, Old Town Alexandria and Arlington National Cemetery (p197).

The trail can be tricky to follow as it passes through Alexandria because there are two route choices, both of which are on-street. The more popular route is along the waterfront, via Union St. The last mile heading toward Mount Vernon involves a reasonably significant climb. There are restrooms (May to September only) and water fountains along the route.

Capital Bikeshare (p270) has bike stations at the Kennedy Center; on the corner of Virginia Ave and 25th St NW; in the Georgetown Waterfront Park; and near the Iwo Jima Memorial (p197) at the Arlington National Cemetery. All of these are close to Theodore Roosevelt Island. Remember that no bikes are allowed on the island's trails; you'll need to ride across the Theodore Roosevelt Bridge from The Mall or across the Francis Scott Key Bridge from Georgetown.

Church) The Washington & Old Dominion Trail starts in southern Arlington and follows the old railway bed through historic Leesburg and on to Purcellville, in the Allegheny foothills. Its 45 miles are paved and spacious, winding their way through the Virginia suburbs. The easiest place to pick up the trail is outside the East Falls Church Metro station: exit right and turn right again onto Tuckahoe St, then follow the signs. For the truly ambitious, it's a short jump from here to the 2000 miles of Appalachian Trail going south to Georgia and north to Maine.

BIKE & ROLL   CYCLING

Map p315 (☎202-842-2453; www.bikethesites.com; 1 Wales Alley; per 2hr/day from $16/40; ☺10am-6pm Wed-Sun mid-Mar–Oct; Ⓜ Blue, Yellow Line to King St-Old Town) Rent a bike and hop on the Mount Vernon Trail one block south. You'll have to call ahead, though, since bikes are available only by advance reservation (no walk-ins). Ask about package deals (including picnic provisions, admission fees and one-way boat trips) to George Washington's estate. The shop is located off Strand St. Kids' bikes are also available (per hour/day $10/25).

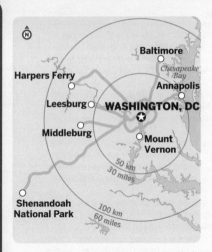

Day Trips from Washington, DC

Mount Vernon p209

The beautiful estate of George Washington is a great place to explore the legacy of one of America's great visionaries.

Baltimore p210

The city has a vibrant waterfront, top-notch art and history museums, and a totally underrated eating and drinking scene.

Annapolis p214

Maryland's small, historic capital has 18th-century architecture, excellent seafood restaurants and a scenic harbor.

Harpers Ferry p216

Peaceful Harpers Ferry is packed with historic sites and charming cafes. Great hikes and bike rides begin just outside of town.

Leesburg & Middleburg p218

Leesburg and nearby Middleburg have grand estates and delightful restaurants. Virginia's thriving wine region beckons nearby.

Shenandoah National Park p221

This vast wilderness has hundreds of miles of hiking trails, plus plenty of scenic overlooks to take in the rolling verdure of the Blue Ridge Mountains.

A visit to George Washington's much-loved home near the banks of the Potomac is an easy escape from the city — one that the president himself enjoyed. It's also a journey through history: the country estate of this quintessential gentleman has been meticulously restored and affords a glimpse of rural gentility and the lives of the slaves who supported it.

Mount Vernon's 21-room mansion displays George and Martha's colonial tastes. At over 11,000 sq ft in size, the 2½-story home (with full cellar) was over 10 times the size of the average Virginia home when it was built. Highlights include the architecturally rich and art-filled New Room, used to receive visitors; the little parlor, where the family hosted social gatherings of music and dancing; the study where Washington wrote and read; and a river-facing two-story piazza, which functioned as the family living room in warm weather. George and Martha are both buried on the grounds.

Also on-site, the Reynolds Museum and Education Center gives insight into Washington's life through exhibits, information panels, interactive displays and the immersive 4-D 'Revolutionary War Experience' spectacular. Artifacts include period furnishings, clothing and jewelry (Martha was quite taken with finery), and George's unusual dentures (made of human, cow and horse teeth as well as ivory).

Three miles south of Mount Vernon, you can learn about Washington's prowess at farming and making whiskey, with actors in period costume demonstrating how it all worked.

Mount Vernon is 16 miles south of DC, off the Mount Vernon Memorial Hwy. Potomac Riverboat Co (p270) runs ferries from Alexandria, and the Spirit of Mount Vernon (p272) departs from the SW Waterfront in DC.

DON'T MISS

➡ The mansion
➡ Outbuildings
➡ Museum and Education Center
➡ Pioneer farm
➡ Distillery

PRACTICALITIES

➡ ☎ 703-780-2000
➡ www.mountvernon.org
➡ 3200 Mount Vernon Memorial Hwy
➡ adult/child 6-11yr $20/12
➡ ⏱ 9am-5pm Apr-Oct, to 4pm Nov-Mar
➡ Ⓜ Yellow Line to Huntington, then Fairfax Connector bus 101

Baltimore

Explore

Once among the most important port towns in America, Baltimore – or 'Bawlmer' to locals – is a city of contradictions. It remains a defiant, working-class city tied to its nautical past, but in recent years has earned acclaim for impressive, up-to-the-minute entrepreneurial ventures, from new boutique hotels and edgy exhibits at world-class museums to forgotten neighborhoods now bustling with trendy food courts and farm-to-table restaurants.

For travelers, a visit to B'more (another nickname) should include one trip to the waterfront, whether it's the Disney-fied Inner Harbor, the cobblestoned streets of portside Fells Point or the shores of Fort McHenry, birthplace of America's national anthem, 'The Star-Spangled Banner.' As you'll discover, there's an intense, sincere friendliness here, which is why Baltimore lives up to its final, most accurate nickname: 'Charm City.'

The Best...

→ **Sight** American Visionary Art Museum (p212)
→ **Place to Eat** Woodberry Kitchen (p213)
→ **Place to Drink** Brewer's Art (p213)

Top Tip

The free green-and-purple **Charm City Circulator** (☑410-350-0456; www.charmcitycirculator.com) FREE shuttles are handy. The Purple Route connects the Inner Harbor, Mt Vernon and Federal Hill. The Green Route runs through Fells Point. The Banner Route runs from the Inner Harbor to Fort McHenry.

Getting There & Away

Train Maryland Rail Commuter (MARC) operates weekday commuter trains between **Penn Station** (https://mta.maryland.gov/marc-train; 1500 N Charles St, Charles North) and **Union Station** (www.unionstationdc.com; 50 Massachusetts Ave NE)in Washington, DC ($8, about one hour), on the Penn Line.

Car Take I-295 (Baltimore–Washington Pkwy) north to Russell St, which terminates west of the Inner Harbor. Or take I-95 north to I-395, which spills out downtown as Howard St. Beware of this drive during rush hour; outside of peak times it should take 45 to 60 minutes.

Need to Know

→ **Area Code** ☑410, 443, 667
→ **Location** 45 miles northeast of Washington, DC.
→ **Visitor Center** (☑877-225-8466; www.baltimore.org; 401 Light St, Inner Harbor; ⊙10am-5pm, closed Mon Jan & Feb; ☎)

◉ SIGHTS

⊙ Harborplace & Inner Harbor

NATIONAL AQUARIUM AQUARIUM
(☑410-576-3800; www.aqua.org; 501 E Pratt St, Piers 3 & 4; adult/child $40/25; ⊙9am-5pm Sun-Thu, to 8pm Fri, to 6pm Sat, varies seasonally; ☀) Standing seven stories high and capped by a glass pyramid, this is widely considered to be America's best aquarium, with almost 20,000 creatures from more than 700 species, a rooftop rainforest, a multistory shark tank and a vast re-creation of an Indo-Pacific reef that is home to blacktip reef sharks, a green sea turtle and stingrays. There's also a reconstruction of the Umbrawarra Gorge in Australia's Northern Territory, complete with 35ft waterfall, rocky cliffs and free-roaming birds and lizards.

HISTORIC SHIPS IN BALTIMORE MUSEUM
(☑410-539-1797; www.historicships.org; 301 E Pratt St, Piers 1, 3 & 5; adult/student/child from $15/13/7; ⊙10am-5pm, hours vary seasonally; ☀) Ship lovers can tour four historic ships: a coast guard cutter that saw action in Pearl Harbor, a 1930 lightship, a submarine active in WWII and the USS Constellation – one of the last sail-powered warships built (in 1797) by the US Navy. You can opt for a two- or four-vessel admission ticket. If you only see two, include the four-deck USS *Constellation*, which spotlights the stories of past crew members. Admission to the 1856 Seven Foot Knoll Lighthouse, on Pier 5, is free.

⊙ Downtown & Little Italy

NATIONAL GREAT BLACKS IN WAX MUSEUM
MUSEUM

(☑410-563-3404; www.greatblacksinwax.org; 1601 E North Ave; adult/student/child $15/14/12; ⊙9am-5pm Tue-Sat, from noon Sun) This simple but thought-provoking African American history museum has exhibits spotlighting Frederick Douglass, Jackie Robinson, Dr Martin Luther King Jr and Barack Obama, as well as lesser-known figures such as explorer Matthew Henson. It also covers slavery, the Jim Crow era and African leaders – all told in surreal but informative fashion through Madame Tussaud–style wax figures.

Unflinching exhibits about the horrors of slave ships and lynchings are graphic and may not be well suited to younger children.

EDGAR ALLAN POE HOUSE & MUSEUM
MUSEUM

(☑410-462-1763; www.poeinbaltimore.org; 203 N Amity St; adult/student/child $5/4/free; ⊙11am-4pm Thu-Sun) Home to Baltimore's most famous adopted son from 1832 to 1835, it was here that the macabre poet and writer first found fame after winning a $50 short-story contest. After moving around, Poe returned in 1849 to Baltimore, where he died under mysterious circumstances.

His **grave** (☑410-706-2072; www.westminsterhall.org; 519 W Fayette St, cnr N Greene St, Westminster Hall; ⊙grounds 8am-dusk) can be found in nearby Westminster Cemetery. The home is unfurnished and there are few artifacts, but the small house feels fittingly eerie.

STAR-SPANGLED BANNER FLAG HOUSE & 1812 MUSEUM
MUSEUM

(☑410-837-1793; www.flaghouse.org; 844 E Pratt St; adult/child $9/7; ⊙10am-4pm Tue-Sat; 🖼) This historic home, built in 1793, is where Mary Pickersgill sewed the gigantic flag that inspired America's national anthem. Costumed interpreters and 19th-century artifacts transport visitors back in time to dark days during the War of 1812; there's also a hands-on discovery gallery for kids.

⊙ Mt Vernon

★ WALTERS ART MUSEUM
MUSEUM

(☑410-547-9000; www.thewalters.org; 600 N Charles St; ⊙10am-5pm Wed & Fri-Sun, to 9pm Thu) **FREE** The magnificent Chamber of Wonders re-creates the library of an imagined 17th-century scholar, one with a taste for the exotic. The abutting Hall of Arms and Armor displays the most impressive collection of medieval weaponry you'll see this side of *Game of Thrones*. In sum, don't pass up this excellent, eclectic museum. It spans more than 55 centuries, from ancient to contemporary, with top-notch displays of Asian treasures, rare and ornate manuscripts and books, and a comprehensive French paintings collection.

MARYLAND HISTORICAL SOCIETY
MUSEUM

(☑410-685-3650; www.mdhs.org; 201 W Monument St; adult/child $9/6; ⊙10am-5pm Wed-Sat, from noon Sun) With more than 350,000 objects and seven million books and documents, this is among the world's largest collections of Americana. Highlights include one of two surviving Revolutionary War officer's uniforms, photographs from the Civil Rights movement in Baltimore, and Francis Scott Key's original manuscript of 'The Star-Spangled Banner' (displayed at the top of the hour). The 10ft-tall replica mastodon – the original was preserved by artist and Maryland native Charles Wilson Peale – is impressive. A few original bones are displayed.

WASHINGTON MONUMENT
MONUMENT

(☑410-962-5070; www.mvpconservancy.org; 699 Washington Pl; adult/child $6/4; ⊙10am-5pm Wed-Sun) For the best views of Baltimore, climb the 227 marble steps of the 178ft-tall Doric column dedicated to America's founding father, George Washington. The monument was designed by Robert Mills, who also created DC's Washington Monument, and is looking better than ever following a $6-million restoration project. The ground floor contains a museum about Washington's life. To climb the monument, buy a ticket on-site or reserve online. Spaces are limited. The 1st-floor gallery is free.

⊙ Federal Hill & Around

★AMERICAN VISIONARY ART MUSEUM
MUSEUM

(AVAM; ☑410-244-1900; www.avam.org; 800 Key Hwy; adult/child $16/10; ⊗10am-6pm Tue-Sun) Housing a jaw-dropping collection of self-taught (or 'outsider' art), AVAM is a celebration of unbridled creativity utterly free of arts-scene pretension. Across two buildings and two sculpture parks, you'll find broken-mirror collages, homemade robots and flying apparatuses, elaborate sculptural works made of needlepoint, and gigantic model ships painstakingly created from matchsticks. The whimsical automatons in the Cabaret Mechanical Theater are worth a closer look.

And don't miss the famous Flatulence Post and its, er, 'fart art' in the Basement Gallery.

FORT McHENRY NATIONAL MONUMENT & HISTORIC SHRINE
HISTORIC SITE

(☑410-962-4290; www.nps.gov/fomc; 2400 E Fort Ave; adult/child $10/free; ⊗9am-5pm; P) On September 13 and 14, 1814, this star-shaped fort successfully repelled a British navy attack during the Battle of Baltimore. After a long night of bombs bursting in the air, shipbound prisoner Francis Scott Key saw, 'by dawn's early light,' the tattered flag still waving. Inspired, he penned 'The Star-Spangled Banner,' which was set to the tune of a popular drinking song.

⊙ Fell's Point & Canton

Once the center of Baltimore's shipbuilding industry, the historic cobblestoned neighborhood of Fell's Point is now a gentrified mix of 18th-century homes and restaurants, bars and shops. The neighborhood has been the setting for several films and TV series, most notably *Homicide: Life on the Street*.

Further east, the slightly more sophisticated streets of Canton fan out, with its grassy square surrounded by great restaurants and bars.

⊙ North Baltimore

★EVERGREEN MUSEUM
MUSEUM

(☑410-516-0341; http://museums.jhu.edu; 4545 N Charles St; adult/child $8/5; ⊗11am-4pm Tue-Fri, from noon Sat & Sun; P) Well worth the 7-mile drive north from the Inner Harbor, this grand 19th-century mansion provides a fascinating glimpse into upper-class Baltimore life of the 1800s. The house is packed with fine art and masterpieces of the decorative arts – including paintings by Modigliani, glass by Louis Comfort Tiffany and exquisite Asian porcelain – not to mention the astounding rare book collection, numbering some 32,000 volumes. Visits are by guided tour offered on the hour until 3pm.

✗ EATING

HANDLEBAR CAFE
AMERICAN; MEXICAN $

(☑443-438-7065; www.handlebarcafe.com; 511 S Caroline St, Fells Point; mains breakfast $7-13, lunch & dinner $8-15; ⊗7am-2am Tue-Sun, to 3pm Mon) Owned by X-Games champ Marla Streb, this friendly bike shop and bistro – adorned with mountain bikes and gear-themed decor – serves burritos and wood-fired pizzas behind its big garage door. Craft beer, live music and an indoor sprint series too. The vibe is so darn cool even the clumsiest goof in town will be considering a career in trick dirt biking.

★THAMES ST OYSTER HOUSE
SEAFOOD $$

(☑443-449-7726; www.thamesstreetoyster house.com; 1728 Thames St, Fells Point; mains $12-29; ⊗5-9:30pm Sun-Thu, to 10:30pm Fri & Sat, plus 11:30am-2:30pm Wed-Sun) A Fells Point icon, this vintage dining and drinking hall serves some of Baltimore's best seafood. Dine in the polished upstairs dining room with waterfront views, take a seat in the backyard, or plunk down at the bar in front (which stays open till midnight) and watch the drink-makers and oyster-shuckers in action. The lobster rolls are recommended too.

★HELMAND
AFGHANI $$

(☑410-752-0311; www.helmand.com; 806 N Charles St, Mt Vernon; mains $14-25; ⊗5-10pm Sun-Thu, to 11pm Fri & Sat) The Helmand is a longtime favorite for its *kaddo borawni* (pumpkin in yogurt-garlic sauce), vegetable platters and flavorful beef-and-lamb meatballs, followed by cardamom ice cream. If you've never tried Afghan cuisine, this is a great place to do so.

FAIDLEY'S   SEAFOOD $$

(☑410-727-4898; www.faidleyscrabcakes.com; 203 N Paca St, Lexington Market; lump crab cakes $15; ☺10am-5pm Mon-Wed, to 5:30pm Thu-Sat) Here's a fine example of a place that the press and the tourists 'discovered' long ago, yet whose brilliance hasn't been dimmed by the publicity. Faidley's is best known for its crab cakes, in-claw meat, backfin (body meat) or all lump (the biggest chunks of body meat). Tuck in at a stand-up counter with a cold beer and know happiness.

★WOODBERRY KITCHEN   AMERICAN $$$

(☑410-464-8000; www.woodberrykitchen.com; 2010 Clipper Park Rd, Woodberry; mains brunch $13-23, dinner $21-45; ☺5-10pm Mon-Thu, to 11pm Fri & Sat, to 9pm Sun, plus brunch 10am-2pm Sat & Sun) The Woodberry takes everything the Chesapeake region has to offer, plops it into a former flour mill and creates culinary magic. The menu is a playful romp through the best of regional produce, seafood and meats, from Maryland rockfish with Carolina Gold grits to Shenandoah Valley lamb with collard greens, and hearty vegetable dishes plucked from nearby farms. Reserve ahead.

DRINKING

BREWER'S ART   PUB

(☑410-547-6925; www.thebrewersart.com; 1106 N Charles St, Mt Vernon; ☺4pm-1:45am Mon-Fri, from noon Sat & Sun) In a vintage early-20th-century mansion, Brewer's Art serves well-crafted Belgian-style microbrews to a laid-back Mt Vernon crowd. There's tasty pub fare (mac 'n' cheese, cheeseburgers) in the bar, and upscale American cuisine in the elegant back dining room. Head to the subterranean drinking den for a more raucous crowd. During happy hour (4pm to 7pm) house drafts are just $4.

ONE-EYED MIKE'S   BAR

(☑410-327-0445; www.oneeyedmikes.com; 708 S Bond St, Fells Point; ☺noon-2am Mon-Thu, from 11am Fri-Sun) Santa Claus sent us a shot of Grand Marnier during a December jaunt to this cozy gastropub where bottles of the orange-flavored liqueur line the shelves. You too can buy a lifetime membership ($175) to the bar's Grand Marnier Club, more than 2900 strong, and your bottle will be forever reserved. Good cheer and top-notch pub grub are draws too.

☆ ENTERTAINMENT

★ORIOLE PARK AT
CAMDEN YARDS   STADIUM

(☑888-848-2473; www.orioles.com; 333 W Camden St, Downtown) The Baltimore Orioles play here, arguably the best ballpark in America, from April through September. Daily tours of the stadium are offered April through November; tours cost $9 for adults, $6 for children under 15 years of age.

🛏 SLEEPING

HI BALTIMORE HOSTEL   HOSTEL $

(☑410-576-8880; www.hiusa.org/baltimore; 17 W Mulberry St, Mt Vernon; dm $30-31; P❋@🛜) Located in a beautifully restored 1857 mansion, the HI Baltimore has dorms with four, eight and 12 beds. Helpful management, a nice location between Mt Vernon and downtown, and a filigreed classical-chic look make this one of the region's best hostels. Twenty-four-hour front desk. Breakfast is included. Parking is $8 per night.

HOTEL BREXTON   HOTEL $$

(☑443-478-2100; www.hotelbrexton.com; 868 Park Ave, Mt Vernon; r $159-219; P❋🛜🐾) This redbrick 19th-century landmark has recently been reborn as an appealing, if not overly lavish, hotel. Rooms offer a mix of wood floors or carpeting, comfy mattresses, mirrored armoires and framed art prints on the walls. Curious historical footnote: Wallis Simpson, the woman for whom Britain's King Edward VIII abdicated the throne, lived in this building as a young girl.

It's in a good location, just a short walk to the heart of Mt Vernon. There are six free spots for parking, first-come, first-served, plus four guaranteed spots for an extra $25 per night. Otherwise, check the website for details about using Parking Panda. Continental breakfast included. Pets are $50 per night per pet.

★ SAGAMORE PENDRY   BOUTIQUE HOTEL $$$
(☑443-552-1400; www.pendryhotels.com; 1715 Thames St, Fells Point; r/ste from $399/759; P🛋❋❋) Hunkered commandingly on the historic Recreation (Rec) Pier, this new luxury property is a game changer, bringing a big dose of charm and panache to Baltimore's favorite party neighborhood. With local art on the walls, nautical and equestrian touches in the common areas, and an 18th-century cannon on display (unearthed during construction), the hotel embraces Charm City's culture and history.

Annapolis

Explore

Annapolis is as charming as state capitals get. The Colonial architecture, cobblestones, flickering lamps and brick row houses are worthy of Victorian author Charles Dickens, but the effect isn't artificial: this city has preserved, rather than created, its heritage.

Perched on Chesapeake Bay, Annapolis revolves around the city's rich maritime traditions. It's home to the US Naval Academy, whose 'middies' (midshipmen students) stroll through town in their starched white uniforms. Sailing is not just a hobby here but a way of life, and the city docks are crammed with vessels of all shapes and sizes. With its historic sights, water adventures and great dining and shopping, Annapolis is worthy getaway.

The Best...

➡ **Sight** US Naval Academy

➡ **Activity** Cruises on the Bay

➡ **Place to Eat** Vin 909

Top Tip

With the Chesapeake Bay at its doorstep, Annapolis has superb seafood. The recent openings of several farm-to-table-minded restaurants have added depth to the dining scene along Main St and near the dock.

Getting There & Away

Bus Greyhound (☑800-231-2222; www.greyhound.com; 275 Harry S Truman Pkwy)
runs daily buses ($8 to $10) to Washington, DC, from a pickup and drop-off stop 5 miles west of the historic downtown.

Car Hwy 50 east goes from DC into downtown Annapolis.

Need to Know

➡ **Area Code** ☑410, 443, 667

➡ **Location** 30 miles east of Washington, DC.

➡ **Tourist Office** (☑410-280-0445; www.visitannapolis.org; 26 West St; ⊙9am-5pm)

◉ SIGHTS

US NAVAL ACADEMY   UNIVERSITY
(☑visitor center 410-293-8687; www.usnabsd.com/for-visitors; Randall St, btwn Prince George & King George Sts; ⊙visitor center 9am-5pm Mar-Dec, to 4pm Mon-Fri Jan & Feb) The undergraduate college of the US Navy is one of the most selective universities in America. The **Armel-Leftwich Visitor Center** (☑410-293-8687; www.usnabsd.com/for-visitors; 52 King George St, Gate 1, City Dock entrance; tours adult/child $11.50/9.50; ⊙9am-5pm Mar-Dec, to 4pm Jan & Feb) is the place to book tours (adult/child $11.50/9.50; 75 minutes) and immerse in all things Academy-related. Come for the formation weekdays at 12:05pm sharp, when the 4000 students conduct a 20-minute military marching display in the yard. Photo ID is required for entry. If you've got a thing for American naval history, revel in the well-done **Naval Academy Museum** (☑410-293-2108; www.usna.edu/Museum/index.php; 118 Maryland Ave; ⊙9am-5pm Mon-Sat, from 11am Sun) FREE.

HAMMOND
HARWOOD HOUSE   MUSEUM
(☑410-263-4683; www.hammondharwoodhouse.org; 19 Maryland Ave; adult/child $10/5; ⊙noon-5pm Tue-Sun Apr-Dec) Of the many historical homes in town, the Hammond Harwood House, dating from 1774, is the one to visit. It has a superb collection of decorative arts, including 18th-century furniture, paintings and ephemera, and is one of the finest existing British Colonial homes in America. Knowledgeable guides help bring the past to life on 50-minute house tours (held at the top of the hour).

MARYLAND STATE HOUSE
HISTORIC BUILDING

(☎410-260-6445; http://msa.maryland.gov/msa/mdstatehouse/html/home.html; 99 State Circle; ☺9am-5pm) FREE The country's oldest state capitol in continuous legislative use, the grand 1772 State House also served as national capital from 1783 to 1784. Notably, General George Washington returned his commission here as Commander-in-Chief of the Continental Army in 1783 after the Revolutionary War, ensuring that governmental power would be shared with Congress. The exhibits and portraits here are impressive and include Washington's copy of his speech resigning his commission. Pick up a self-guided tour map on the 1st floor.

WILLIAM PACA HOUSE & GARDEN
HISTORIC BUILDING

(☎410-990-4543; www.annapolis.org; 186 Prince George St; garden tours $5, house & garden tours from $8; ☺10am-5pm Mon-Sat, from noon Sun late Mar-Dec) Take a tour (offered hourly on the half hour) through this Georgian mansion for insight into 18th-century life for the upper class in Maryland. Don't miss the blooming garden in spring. The home and gardens are closed from January through late March.

EATING

CHICK & RUTH'S DELLY
DINER $

(☎410-269-6737; www.chickandruths.com; 165 Main St; mains breakfast & lunch $8-15, dinner $5-23; ☺6:30am-11:30pm Sun-Thu, to 12:30am Fri & Sat; 👪) A cornerstone of Annapolis, the-squeeze-'em-in-tight Delly bursts with affable quirkiness and a big menu, heavy on sandwiches and breakfast fare. Patriots can relive grade-school days reciting the Pledge of Allegiance weekdays at 8:30am and Saturdays and Sundays at 9:30am. Breakfast served all day.

★VIN 909
AMERICAN $$

(☎410-990-1846; www.vin909.com; 909 Bay Ridge Ave; small plates $12-20; ☺5:30-10pm Wed & Thu, to 11pm Fri, 5-11pm Sat, 5-9pm Sun, plus noon-3pm Wed-Sat, closes at 9pm Tue & Sun in winter) Perched on a little wooded hill and boasting intimate but enjoyably casual ambience, Vin is the best thing happening in Annapolis for food. Farm-sourced goodness features in the form of duck confit, dry-aged Angus-beef sliders and homemade pizzas with toppings such as wild-boar meatballs or honey-braised squash with applewood bacon.

★JIMMY CANTLER'S RIVERSIDE INN
SEAFOOD $$

(☎410-757-1311; www.cantlers.com; 458 Forest Beach Rd; mains $10-32; ☺11am-10pm Sun-Thu, to 11pm Fri & Sat) One of the best crab shacks in the state, where eating a steamed crab has been elevated to an art form: a hands-on, messy endeavor, normally accompanied by corn on the cob and ice-cold beer. Cantler's is a little ways outside of Annapolis, but can be approached by road or boat (a waterfront location is a crab-house industry standard).

IRON ROOSTER
BREAKFAST $$

(☎410-990-1600; www.ironroosterallday.com; 12 Market Space; mains breakfast & lunch $9-20, dinner $10-25; ☺7am-10pm Mon-Sat, to 8pm Sun) From the crab-cake Benedict layered with lump crab, poached eggs and hollandaise to the buttermilk fried chicken and waffles with black-pepper pan gravy, everything sounds good at this rustic-chic enclave near Dock St that brings in appreciative breakfast crowds. Other highlights include gourmet pop tarts and the bacon Bloody Mary.

BOATYARD BAR & GRILL
SEAFOOD $$

(☎410-216-6206; www.boatyardbarandgrill.com; 400 4th St, Eastport; mains $10-27; ☺7:30am-midnight Mon-Fri, from 8am Sat & Sun; 👪) This bright, nautically themed restaurant with a big central bar is a festive and welcoming spot for crab cakes, fish and chips, oysters, fish tacos and other seafood. Happy hour (3pm to 7pm Monday to Friday) draws in the crowds with $3 drafts. Patty's Fatty's oysters are $1 on Sundays.

 SPORTS & ACTIVITIES

CRUISES ON THE BAY
CRUISE

(☎410-268-7601; www.cruisesonthebay.com; City Dock; 40min cruise adult/child $17/6; ☺late Mar–mid-Nov) The best way to explore the city's maritime heritage is on the water. Watermark, which also operates the Four Centuries Walking Tour (p216), offers a variety of cruise options, with frequent departures.

FOUR CENTURIES WALKING TOUR
WALKING

([📞]410-268-7601; www.annapolistours.com; 26 West St; 2¼hr tour adult/child $20/10) A costumed docent leads this great introduction to all things Annapolis. The 10:30am tour leaves from the visitor center; the 1:30pm tour from the information booth at City Dock. There's a slight variation in sights visited by each, but both cover the country's largest concentration of 18th-century buildings, influential African Americans and colonial spirits who don't want to leave.

The associated one-hour **Pirates of the Chesapeake Cruise** ([📞]410-263-0002; www.chesapeakepirates.com; 311 3rd St; $22; ☉daily mid-Apr–Aug, Sat & Sun only Sep & Oct; [👶]) is good 'yar'-worthy fun, especially for the kids.

WOODWIND
CRUISE

([📞]410-263-7837; www.schoonerwoodwind.com; 80 Compromise St; adult/child 2hr sail $43/29, sunset cruise $46/29; ☉Tue-Sun mid-Apr–Oct) This beautiful 74ft schooner offers two-hour day and sunset cruises. Or splurge for the Woodwind 'boat & breakfast' package (rooms $319, including breakfast), one of the more unique lodging options in town.

🛏 SLEEPING

SCOTLAUR INN
GUESTHOUSE **$**

([📞]410-268-5665; www.scotlaurinn.com; 165 Main St; r $119-149; [P][❄][🛜]) The folks from Chick & Ruth's Delly (p215) offer 10 rooms above the restaurant, each with wrought-iron beds, floral wallpaper and private bath. The quarters are small but have a cozy and familial atmosphere (the guesthouse is named after the owners' children Scott and Lauren, whose photos adorn the hallways). Breakfast included. Two-night minimum stay on weekends.

HISTORIC INNS OF ANNAPOLIS
HOTEL **$$**

([📞]410-263-2641; www.historicinnsofannapolis.com; 58 State Circle; r from $209; [P][❄][🛜]) The Historic Inns comprise three different boutique guesthouses, each set in a heritage building in the heart of old Annapolis: the Maryland Inn, the Governor Calvert House and the Robert Johnson House. Common areas are packed with period details, and the best rooms boast antiques, fireplaces and attractive views (the cheapest can be small). Check in at Governor Calvert House.

Harpers Ferry

Explore

History lives on in this attractive town, set with steep cobblestoned streets, and framed by the Shenandoah Mountains and the confluence of the Potomac and Shenandoah Rivers. The lower town functions as an open-air museum, with more than a dozen buildings that you can explore to get a taste of 19th-century, small-town life. Exhibits narrate the town's role at the forefront of westward expansion, American industry and, most famously, the slavery debate – in 1859 old John Brown tried to spark a slave uprising here and was hanged for his efforts; the incident rubbed friction between North and South into the fires of Civil War.

Harpers Ferry sits beside the Appalachian Trail across the Potomac from the C&O Canal bike path, so there are lots of outdoorsy types here.

The Best...

➡ **Sight** Harpers Ferry National Historic Park

➡ **Activity** Hiking the town loop (p218)

➡ **Place to Eat** Anvil

Top Tip

Parking is limited in Harpers Ferry proper. Instead head to the visitor center of the Harpers Ferry National Historic Park (p217) off Hwy 340. You can park and take a free shuttle into town from there.

Getting There & Away

Train Amtrak (www.amtrak.com) trains run from the Harpers Ferry Station to DC's Union Station (daily, 90 minutes) on the Capitol Limited route. MARC trains (http://mta.maryland.gov) run to DC's Union Station several times per day (Monday to Friday) on the Brunswick Line.

Car From Washington take I-495 north to I-270, which turns into I-70. Merge onto Hwy 340 west and follow the signs for downtown Harpers Ferry. Travel time is 90 minutes.

Need to Know

➤ **Area Code** ☑304, 681

➤ **Location** In West Virginia, 66 miles northwest of DC.

➤ **Tourist Office** (☑304-535-2627; www.discoveritallwv.com; 37 Washington St; ⊙9am-5pm)

◉ SIGHTS

HARPERS FERRY NATIONAL HISTORIC PARK
PARK

(☑304-535-6029; www.nps.gov/hafe; 171 Shoreline Dr; per person on foot or bicycle $5, vehicle $10; ⊙trails sunrise-sunset, visitor center 9am-5pm; ℗♿) Historic buildings and museums are accessible to those with passes, which can be found, along with parking and shuttles, north of town at the Harpers Ferry National Historic Park Visitor Center off Hwy 340. Parking is incredibly limited in Harpers Ferry proper so plan to park at the visitor center and catch the frequent shuttle. It's a short and scenic ride.

JOHN BROWN MUSEUM
MUSEUM

(www.nps.gov/hafe; Shenandoah St; ⊙9am-5pm) **FREE** Across from Arsenal Sq and one of the park's museums, this three-room gallery gives a fine overview (through videos and period relics) of the events surrounding John Brown's famous raid.

THE POINT
NATURAL FEATURE

(www.npd.gov/hafe; Potomac St) At the southern end of Potomac St, just a few steps from the lower town, take in a view of three states – Maryland, Virginia, West Virginia – from the confluence of the Potomac and Shenandoah Rivers.

MASTER ARMORER'S HOUSE
HISTORIC SITE

(☑304-535-6029; www.nps.gov/hafe; Shenandoah St; ⊙9am-5pm) **FREE** Among the free sites in the historic district, this 1858 house explains how rifle technology developed here went on to revolutionize the firearms industry. Has a small information center and helpful exhibits about the town and its history.

EATING & DRINKING

CANNONBALL DELI
SANDWICHES $

(☑304-535-1762; 148 High St; sandwiches $4-11; ⊙10am-6pm) From the High St entrance near the national park, head underground for tasty subs, gyros and sandwiches. On a pretty day, walk through the tiny kitchen to the back deck, which has a view of Potomac St and the railroad. Convenient to the C&O cycling path just across the Potomoc Bridge.

ANVIL
AMERICAN $$

(☑304-535-2582; www.anvilrestaurant.com; 1290 W Washington St, Bolivar; lunch mains $9-14, dinner mains $11-28; ⊙11am-9pm Wed-Sun) Local trout melting in honey-pecan butter and an elegant Federal dining room equal excellence at Anvil, in next-door Bolivar. Stop by for solid bar food – cheeseburger, crab-cake sandwich, Reuben – in the pub at lunch.

GUIDE SHACK CAFE
COFFEE

(☑304-995-6022; www.guideshackcafe.com; 1102 Washington St; ⊙6:30am-6:30pm Mon-Fri, 7am-7pm Sat & Sun; 🛜) Well of course there's a mini-climbing wall in the back of this coffee shop: the place is a short walk from both the Appalachian Trail and the C&O Canal cycling path. Stop here for a bit of conversation and the sweet and creamy iced coffee, which is refreshing on a hot day.

🏃 SPORTS & ACTIVITIES

C&O CANAL NATIONAL HISTORIC PARK
CYCLING, HIKING

(www.nps.gov/choh) The 184.5-mile towpath passes along the Potomac River on the Maryland side. From the historic downtown you can reach it via the Appalachian Trail across the Potomac Bridge. Check www.nps.gov/hafe for additional access points to the towpath and a list of bike-rental companies.

RIVER RIDERS
ADVENTURE SPORTS; CYCLING

(☑304-535-2663; www.riverriders.com; 408 Alstadts Hill Rd; guided kayaking trip per person $74; ⊙8am-6pm Jun-Aug, hours vary rest of year) The go-to place for rafting, canoeing, tubing, kayaking and multiday cycling trips, plus cycle rental (two hours is $34 per person). There's even a 1200ft zipline.

HIKING THE HARPERS FERRY TOWN LOOP

This 1.5-mile walk serves up an enticing mix of history, scenery and trail camaraderie on a steep loop that links river views with lower-town Harpers Ferry.

The camaraderie starts at the **Appalachian Trail Conservancy** (ATC; ☑304-535-6331; www.appalachiantrail.org; 799 Washington St, cnr Washington & Jackson Sts; ☉9am-5pm), the headquarters of the 2160-mile **Appalachian Trail** (AT), which stretches through 14 states from Maine to Georgia. Questions are encouraged, and the folks here have maps galore, including one that covers the parameters of the town loop. From here, the loop crosses the grounds of now-closed **Storer College** (www.nps.gov/hafe; Fillmore St) atop Camp Hill. Storer began as a one-room schoolhouse for freed slaves. Today, part of the grounds serves as a training facility for the National Park Service.

Follow the blue blazes to the AT, which rolls through West Virginia for a mere 4 miles, the shortest distance in any of the AT states. The woodsy path opens up to a fine river vista at **Jefferson Rock** (off Church St, Appalachian Trail), named for President Thomas Jefferson. Jefferson stopped here in 1783 and had this to say about the view: 'The passage of the Patowmac through the Blue Ridge is perhaps one of the most stupendous scenes in Nature.' Alrighty then.

From here you can check out Harpers Cemetery, which dates to the 1780s, then continue down to lower town, passing St Peter Catholic Church, built in 1833, along the way. Before heading up High St to the ATC, follow the AT to The Point (p217), which sits prettily at the convergence of the Potomac and Shenandoah Rivers.

🛏 SLEEPING

TOWN'S INN
INN **$**

(☑304-932-0677; www.thetownsinn.com; 179 High St; dm $35, r $120-150; ❋☎) Spread between two neighboring pre–Civil War residences, the Town's Inn has rooms ranging from small and minimalist to charming heritage-style quarters. Also offers a six-bed hostel dorm room. It's set in the middle of the historic district and has a simple indoor-outdoor cafe (open 10am to 6pm) as well.

TEAHORSE HOSTEL
HOSTEL **$**

(☑304-535-6848; www.teahorsehostel.com; 1312 Washington St; dm $35, ste $140-350; ☉Mar-Oct; ℗❋@☎) Popular with cyclists on the C&O Canal towpath and hikers on the Appalachian Trail, Teahorse is a welcoming place with comfy rooms and common areas (including an outdoor patio). It's located 1 mile (uphill) from the historic lower town of Harpers Ferry.

JACKSON ROSE
B&B **$$**

(☑304-535-1528; www.thejacksonrose.com; 1167 W Washington St; r weekday/weekend $140/160, closed Jan & Feb; ℗❋☎) This marvelous 18th-century brick residence with stately gardens has three attractive guestrooms, including a room where Stonewall Jackson lodged briefly during the Civil War. Antique furnishings and vintage curios are sprinkled about the house, and the cooked breakfast is excellent. It's a 600m walk downhill to the historic district. No children under 12.

Leesburg & Middleburg

Explore

Leesburg is one of northern Virginia's oldest towns, and King St in its colonial-era center is lined with handsome buildings housing restaurants, offices and shops. The town sits along the Washington & Old Dominion Trail, and makes an excellent destination for cyclists.

Lying 19 miles southwest of Leesburg, Middleburg is a quaint town with colonial buildings that host some enticing restaurants and boutiques. It is located in a particularly affluent pocket of Virginia that holds its traditions dear – the Middleburg Fox Hunt still meets regularly, and meticulously maintained horse farms dot the surrounding green countryside. Either town makes a terrific base for visiting the Loudoun Wine Trail.

The Best...

➡ **Sight** Oatlands Historic House & Gardens

➡ **Place to Eat** Red Fox Tavern

➡ **Place to Drink** Breaux Vineyards (p220)

Top Tip

On the first Friday of every month, you can join in **Leesburg's First Friday** (www.leesburgfirstfriday.com; ⊘6-9pm Feb-Dec), when shops and galleries in the historic downtown area stay open till 9pm.

Getting There & Away

Bicycle Pick up the Washington & Old Dominion Trail (p206) outside the East Falls Church Metro station in Arlington and head west to Leesburg.

Car Take I-66 to the Dulles Toll Rd exit (Hwy 267). When it turns into the Dulles Greenway, continue 13 miles to the end. Exit left and take the first right exit to Leesburg Business. Follow King St to Loudoun St, the center of historic Leesburg. Middleburg is 19 miles southwest. Take Hwy 15 south and turn right on Hwy 50. Travel time is 40 minutes by car.

Need to Know

➡ **Area Code** ☑703

➡ **Location** Leesburg is 40 miles northwest of DC; Middleburg is 42 miles west of DC.

➡ **Tourist Office** (☑703-771-2170; www.visitloudoun.org; 112g South St, Market Station; ⊘9am-5pm)

⊙ SIGHTS

OATLANDS HISTORIC HOUSE & GARDENS HISTORIC SITE

(☑703-777-3174; www.oatlands.org; 20850 Oatlands Plantation Lane, Leesburg; adult/child 6-16yr $15/10, grounds only $10; ⊘10am-5pm Mon-Sat, 1-5pm Sun Apr-Dec, closed Jan-Mar) Established in 1803 by a great-grandson of Robert 'King' Carter, a wealthy pre-Revolutionary planter, this plantation has as its focal point a lovingly restored Greek Revival mansion surrounded by 4 acres of formal gardens. Tours of the mansion are by anecdote-filled guided tour. The property is located on US 15, about 6 miles south of Leesburg.

NATIONAL SPORTING MUSEUM MUSEUM

(☑540-687-6542; www.nationalsporting.org; 102 The Plains Rd, Middleburg; museum adult/child 13-18yr $10/8, Wed free; ⊘10am-5pm Wed-Sun) Middleburg is foxhunting territory (Middleburg's Hunt meets regularly), so it's not surprising that its main museum takes as its focus equine sports. Housed in the handsome Vine Hill mansion, the attractively presented collection includes plenty of paintings of horses, hounds and bewhiskered men in top hats and red coats; most are 19th-century British works. There are also exhibits on horse- racing (the Seabiscuit display is particularly interesting), angling and field sports. A library and research center is in a building nearby.

EATING & DRINKING

SHOE'S CUP & CORK CAFE $$

(☑703-771-7463; www.shoescupandcork.com; 17 N King St, Leesburg; mains $10-20; ⊘7am-5pm Mon & Tue, to 9pm Wed & Thu, to 10pm Fri, 9am-10pm Sat, 9am-5pm Sun) Across from the courthouse, this quirky cafe in an old shoe store serves up excellent fare for breakfast, lunch and dinner. Think warm brie sandwiches, kale and quinoa salads and wild-mushroom ravioli. Good drinks (coffee made with house-roasted beans, microbrews, malbecs) add to the appeal – as does the outdoor patio with bocce court.

WINE KITCHEN WINE BAR $$

(☑703-777-9463; www.thewinekitchen.com; 7 S King St, Leesburg; lunch mains $10-16, dinner mains $16-27; ⊘11:30am-9pm Tue-Thu, to 10:30pm Fri & Sat, 11am-3pm & 4-9pm Sun; 🖉) After a day of exploring, kick back at this welcoming and upbeat wine bar in the historic district. The menu has seasonal offerings from the field (great for vegetarians), land (including locally produced meat and poultry) and sea. Over 40 wines are available by the glass, and there are also plenty of craft beers.

★RED FOX TAVERN AMERICAN $$$

(☑540-687-6301; www.redfox.com/tavern; 2 E Washington St, Middleburg; mains $28-46; ⊘8-10am & 5-9pm Mon-Fri, 11:30am-2:30pm & 5-9pm Sat, 11:30am-2:30pm & 5-8pm Sun) Hallmarks here are the elegant surrounds and delicious dishes created using top-quality local produce. Take a seat by the fireplace of this

LOUDOUN WINE TRAIL

There are more than 40 wineries and vineyards in Loudoun County, which is also known as DC's Wine Country. The soil and climate are well suited to white varietals – viognier and chardonnay thrive – but decent reds are also produced here. There are six regional clusters: Snicker's Gap, Mosby, Harmony, Waterford, Loudoun Heights and Potomac. Loudoun Heights and Snicker's Gap are particularly impressive. Many of the wineries have restaurants, and most sell cheese and charcuterie plates or picnic provisions. Go to loudounfarms.org/craft-beverages/wine-trail/ for an interactive map. There's plenty more information at www.visitloudoun.org/things-to-do/wine-country/. Top choices for a visit:

Breaux Vineyards (📞540-668-6299; www.breauxvineyards.com; 36888 Breaux Vineyards Lane, Hillsboro; tastings $15; ⏱11am-6pm mid-Mar–Oct, to 5pm Nov-early Mar; 🐾) The best-known vineyard in the Loudoun Heights cluster, Breaux produces a wide range of wines, the best of which are the the Madeleine chardonnay and the Meritage blend of five Bordeaux varietals. Views from the tasting-room terrace are lovely. Tastings cover six wines.

Bluemont Vineyard (📞540-554-8439; www.bluemontvineyard.com; 18755 Foggy Bottom Rd, Bluemont; tastings $15; ⏱11am-6pm Sat-Thu, to 8pm Fri, reduced hours winter; 🐾) Producing an award-winning Petit Manseng, this winery between Winchester and Leesburg is a wonderful lunch stop due to its spectacular location at the crest of a 950ft hill commanding sweeping views over the countryside.

Sunset Hills Vineyard (📞540-882-4560; www.sunsethillsvineyard.com; 38295 Fremont Overlook Lane, Purcellville; tastings $10; ⏱noon-5pm Mon-Thu, to 6pm Fri, 11am-6pm Sat & Sun; 🅿) 🍃 A relative newcomer to the Loudon district, this solar-powered 20-acre winery in the Waterford Cluster incorporates meticulously restored and rebuilt Amish farm buildings dating from the 1870s. The winemakers have received plenty of plaudits for their viognier and mosaic (Bordeaux-style) wines.

Tarara Vineyard (📞703-771-7100; www.tarara.com; 13648 Tarara Lane; tastings $10-20; ⏱11am-5pm Mon-Thu, to 6pm Fri-Sun, closed Tue & Wed Nov-Mar; 🐾) On a bluff overlooking the Potomac, this 475-acre estate is one of the most attractive vineyards in Virginia. The winery has a 6000-sq-ft cave/cellar, and visitors can enjoy tastings of wines including its well-regarded Navaeh red and white blends followed by a picnic on the lakeside lawn.

Otium Cellars (📞540-338-2027; www.otiumcellars.com; 18050 Tranquility Rd, Purcellville; tastings $10; ⏱11am-5pm Mon & Thu, to 10pm Fri, to 9pm Sat, to 5pm Sun) Produces some unusual Austrian- and German-style wines, including a Grüner Veltliner, Blaufränkisch and Dornfelder. Often stages live music and hosts food trucks.

antique-festooned 1728 inn and feast on perfectly cooked steaks, hickory-bourbon-glazed salmon or famous fried chicken with mac 'n' cheese. The cosy Night Fox Pub in the building opens every weekday evening and from noon on weekends.

KING ST OYSTER BAR　BAR
(📞540-883-3156; 1 E Washington St, Middleburg; 12 oysters $24-36; ⏱11am-10pm Sun-Thu, to 11pm Fri & Sat) Housed in a grandiose neoclassical building, this joint jumps every afternoon during its happy hour (3pm to 6:30pm), when locals slurp on freshly shucked oys-

ters and sip on $5 craft beer and cocktails. At lunch and dinner, seafood dishes dominate the menu (mains $15 to $59).

🛏 SLEEPING

LEESBURG
COLONIAL INN　GUESTHOUSE $$
(📞703-777-5000; www.theleesburgcolonialinn.com; 19 S King St, Leesburg; r $129-179; 🐾) In the center of Leesburg, this simple 10-room guesthouse has a great location and unbeatable prices. On the downside, street and

downstairs restaurant noise can be an issue for light sleepers, and some rooms could use a heavier hand in the housekeeping department. Rooms 8, 9 and 10 are the nicest rooms.

★RED FOX INN   BOUTIQUE HOTEL $$$
(☎540-687-6301;   www.redfox.com/inn;   2 East Washington St, Middleburg; r $245-505; Ⓟ♿❄🖥) The antique four-poster beds here are so high that step ladders are sometimes provided to enable guests to hit the pillows. They're one of the many unusual features of this charming boutique hotel. Individually decorated rooms are offered on the upstairs floors of the 1728 tavern and in two annexe buildings. A generous breakfast is enjoyed in the tavern.

Shenandoah National Park

Explore

Shenandoah National Park is mighty easy on the eyes, set against a backdrop of the dreamy Blue Ridge Mountains, ancient granite and metamorphic formations that are more than one billion years old. The park itself was founded in 1935 as a retreat for East Coast urban populations. It is an accessible day-trip destination from DC, but you should aim to stay longer if you can. The 500 miles of hiking trails, 75 scenic overlooks, 30 fishing streams, seven picnic areas and four campgrounds are sure to keep you entertained.

Skyline Dr is the breathtaking road that follows the main ridge of the Blue Ridge Mountains and winds 105 miles through the center of the park. It begins in Front Royal at the western end of I-66, and ends in the southern part of the range at Rockfish Gap near I-64. It's a glorious drive, though bendy and slow going.

The Best...

➡ **Sight** Luray Caverns

➡ **Hiking** Old Rag Mountain (p222)

➡ **Place to Eat** Spottswood Dining Room (p222)

Top Tip

To beat the crowds, avoid going on weekends – especially in the summer – when there is a lot of traffic in the park.

Getting There & Away

Bus The **Virginia Breeze** (☎877-462-6342; www.catchthevabreeze.com; tickets $15-50) bus service to/from Washington, DC, stops at Front Royal and Staunton near the main park entrances/exits.

Car From Washington, DC, take I-66 west for around 65 miles. Take exit 13 for Hwy 55/79/Front Royal. The park's entrance at Front Royal is some 7 miles onward. The overall trip takes 90 minutes.

Need to Know

➡ **Area Code** ☎540

➡ **Location** 75 miles west of Washington, DC.

➡ **Visitor Center** (www.nps.gov/shen; Mile 4.6, Skyline Dr; ⏱9am-5pm Mon-Fri, to 6pm Sat & Sun, closed late Nov-early Apr)

◉ SIGHTS

★SHENANDOAH
NATIONAL PARK   NATIONAL PARK
(☎540-999-3500;   www.nps.gov/shen;   Skyline Dr; 1-week pass per car $25; ⏱year-round) One of the most spectacular national parks in the country, Shenandoah is a showcase of natural color and beauty: in spring and summer the wildflowers explode, in fall the leaves burn bright red and orange, and in winter a cold, starkly beautiful hibernation period sets in. White-tailed deer are a common sight and, if you're lucky, you might spot a black bear, bobcat or wild turkey. The park lies just 75 miles west of Washington, DC.

★LURAY CAVERNS   CAVE
(☎540-743-6551;   www.luraycaverns.com;   970 US Hwy 211 W, Luray; adult/child 6-12yr $27/14; ⏱9am-7pm daily mid-Jun-Aug, to 6pm Sep-Nov & Apr–mid-Jun, to 4pm Mon-Fri, to 5pm Sat & Sun Dec-Mar) If you can only fit one cavern into your Shenandoah itinerary, head 25 miles south from Front Royal to the world-class Luray Caverns and hear the 'Stalacpipe Organ' – hyped as the largest musical instrument on earth. Tours can feel like a

HIKING OLD RAG MOUNTAIN

One of the most popular day hikes in the Shenandoah National Park, the 9.2-mile circuit to the summit of **Old Rag Mountain** (www.nps.gov/shen; Rte 600) is also one of the most challenging, with lots of scrambling and climbing – this isn't for novices or the unfit, and families with young children should probably give it a miss. The hike will take seven or eight hours; try to hike on weekdays, as the trail can be unpleasantly crowded on weekends.

Park in the lot off Rte 602 on the park's eastern boundary. Then walk along Rte 600. Pass the Nicholson Hollow Trailhead on the right and then should take the blue-blazed Ridge Trail to the left (it's well marked). The first 2 miles of the trail pass through wooded landscape where deer and other wildlife can often be spotted; there's also a profusion of wildflowers during the spring, summer, and fall. You'll then come to the challenging part of the hike – crossing the rock scramble – before reaching the summit and admiring a simply extraordinary view over the national park.

Returning, you should descend on the Saddle Trail (also blue-blazed and well marked), which becomes a fire road after you pass Old Rag Shelter. At the T-intersection, go right and immediately right again at the fork onto Weakley Hollow Fire Road (yellow-blazed) to return to your starting point.

For more information go to www.nps.gov/shen/planyourvisit/old-rag-hike-prep.htm.

cattle call on busy weekends, but the stunning underground formations make up for all the elbow-bumping. To save time at the entrance, buy your ticket online ahead of time, then join the entry line.

HAWKSBILL MOUNTAIN　　　　MOUNTAIN
(Mile 45.6, Skyline Dr) The highest peak in the park (4050ft) is also a well-known nesting area for peregrine falcons. Stand on the rustic stone observation platform at the end of the trail for long-lasting impressions of the park's wondrous beauty.

EATING

**SPOTTSWOOD
DINING ROOM**　　　　AMERICAN **$$**
(www.visitshenandoah.com; Mile 51.3, Skyline Dr, Big Meadows Lodge; lunch mains $8-17, dinner mains $12-28; ⊘7:30-10am, noon-2pm & 5:30-9pm early May-early Nov;) The wide-ranging menu at the dining room in Big Meadows Lodge makes the most of locally sourced ingredients. Complement your food with Virginian wines and local microbrews, all enjoyed in an old-fashioned rustic-lodge ambience. There's also a taproom (2pm to 11pm) with a limited menu and live entertainment.

POLLOCK DINING ROOM　　　　AMERICAN **$$**
(www.visitshenandoah.com; Mile 41.7, Skyline Dr, Skyland Resort; mains lunch $9-20, dinner $12-28;

⊘7:30-10:30am, noon-2:30pm & 5-9pm late Mar-late Nov) The food is solid, if not life altering, in Skyland's dining room. But the view of the leafy park though the big windows? Now that's a different story. Lunch means sandwiches and burgers, while dinner aims a little fancier – stick to classics like Rapidan Camp Trout and Roosevelt Chicken. The adjacent taproom (2pm to 10pm) serves cocktails, local beers and a limited menu of sandwiches and a few specialties.

SPORTS & ACTIVITIES

Shenandoah has more than 500 miles of hiking trails, including 101 miles of the famous Appalachian Trail (AT). You can easily access the AT from Skyline Dr, which roughly parallels the trail.

HAWKSBILL SUMMIT　　　　HIKING
(Mile 45.6, Skyline Dr) This tremendous climb to the park's highest peak offers an unforgettable picture of the mountain landscape. There are two options for this climb: either a 2.9-mile loop or 1.7-mile up-and-back.

BEARFENCE MOUNTAIN　　　　HIKING
(Skyline Dr) A short trail leads to a spectacular 360-degree viewpoint. The circuit hike is only 1.2 miles, but one section involves an adventurous scramble over rocks.

BIG MEADOWS   HIKING

(Skyline Dr) A very popular area with four easy-to-medium-difficulty hikes. The Lewis Falls and Rose River trails run by the park's most spectacular waterfalls; the former accesses the Appalachian Trail.

DARK HOLLOW FALLS   HIKING

This small waterfall is only 0.7 miles away from the Skyline Dr parking area, but the rocky terrain makes for a tough hike in certain sections, and the return trip is all uphill. It's not unusual for hikers to suffer accidents here, so take extra caution when stepping over slippery rocks and make use of those handrails – they're there for a darn good reason!

🛏 SLEEPING

LEWIS MOUNTAIN CABINS   CABIN $

(☑855-470-6005; www.goshenandoah.com; Mile 57.6, Skyline Dr; 1- & 2-bed cabins $133-138, d bunk cabins $37-42; ☉early Mar-late Nov; 🅿 🌸) The most rustic accommodation option in the area short of camping, this place has several pleasantly furnished one- and two-bedroom cabins complete with private bathrooms for a hot shower after a day's hiking. There are also small cabins with bunk beds, but no linen or bathroom. Bear in mind many cabins are attached, although we've never heard our neighbors here.

SKYLAND RESORT   RESORT $$

(☑855-470-6005; www.goshenandoah.com; Mile 41.7, Skyline Dr; r $141-265, cabins $130-281; ☉late Mar–mid-Nov; 🅿🌸🛜🛏) Founded in 1888, this spectacularly located resort commands views over the countryside. You'll find a variety of room types, including recently renovated premium rooms; rustic but comfy cabins; a taproom with a live entertainment program; and a full-service dining room. You can also arrange horseback rides from here. Opens a month or so before Big Meadows in the spring.

BIG MEADOWS LODGE   LODGE $$

(☑855-470-6005; www.goshenandoah.com; Mile 51.2, Skyline Dr; r $122-206, cabins $140-145; ☉early May-early Nov; 🅿🌸🛜) The historic Big Meadows Lodge has 29 cozy woodpaneled rooms and five rustic cabins. The on-site Spottswood Dining Room serves three hearty meals a day; reserve well in advance. Free, family-friendly entertainment is presented nightly in the bar.

🛏 Sleeping

Many DC lodgings are imbued with history that few other American cities can match: when rooms here are called the 'Roosevelt suite,' it's because Teddy actually slept in them. The best digs are monuments of Victorian and jazz-era opulence. Groovy design-driven hotels, straightforward chain hotels, B&Bs and apartments blanket the cityscape, too. But nothing comes cheap...

Seasons & Prices

The high-season apex is late March through June (cherry blossom season and school-group visiting time). September and October are also busy. Book well in advance if traveling during these months. Prices are lowest in August, January (assuming it's not an inauguration year) and February. Rates on weekends (Friday and Saturday) are typically less than on weekdays.

Hotels

More and more hotels are joining the pack, rising up at a particularly rapid pace around downtown, the White House area, Capitol Hill and southwest DC. All big-box chains have outposts (usually several) here. Hip, design-savvy hotels abound, as do uber-luxury hotels catering to presidents, prime ministers and other heads of state.

B&Bs

DC has quite a few B&Bs. Set in elegant old row houses and Victorian mansions, they cluster around Dupont Circle and Adams Morgan. Many are redolent of Old Washington (in a sip-sherry-at-noon way) and are atmospheric as hell. They're generally cheaper than big hotels.

Hostels

Several hostels are sprinkled around, typically in locations that are a bit far-flung. The District has one Hostelling International (www.hiusa.org) property and several independent hostels that do not require membership. Browse listings at www.hostels.com and www.hostelworld.com.

Apartments

Given all the interns, politicos and business folk who come to town for extended stays, apartment rentals are popular. They're usually great value compared to hotels. Airbnb (www.airbnb.com) does a booming business in the District.

Amenities

In-room wi-fi, air-conditioning and a private bathroom are standard, unless noted otherwise. Breakfast is rarely included at top-end hotels, while midrange and budget properties often include a continental breakfast.

Tipping

➡ **Hotel porters** $2 per bag

➡ **Housekeeping staff** $2 to $5 daily (high end of range for suites or particularly messy rooms)

➡ **Parking valets** $2 to $5 when you're handed back the keys

➡ **Room service** 15% to 20%

➡ **Concierges** Up to $20 (for securing last-minute restaurant reservations, sold-out show tickets etc)

Lonely Planet's Top Choices

Sofitel Lafayette Square (p227) Bright, airy rooms in a revamped historic building tinged with Parisian chic.

Kimpton George Hotel (p230) Mod lodging near the Capitol with pop-art accents.

Chester Arthur House (p235) Logan Circle manor stuffed with chandeliers, oriental rugs and character.

Hotel Hive (p227) What it lacks in space it makes up for in stylish cool.

Henley Park Hotel (p230) Historic building with character, charm, paisley, plaid and afternoon tea.

Best By Budget

$

Hostelling International – Washington DC (p230) Big, amenity-laden hostel that draws an international crowd.

Adam's Inn (p234) Twenty-seven rooms in which to make yourself at home, in a couple of Adams Morgan town houses.

HighRoad Hostel (p234) Modern dorms and upscale amenities near nightlife.

$$

Kimpton Carlyle (p232) Oft-overlooked, art-deco beauty sitting amid Dupont Circle's embassies.

Pod DC Hotel (p230) Small rooms but big hipster perks like an on-site diner, rooftop bar and reasonable rates.

Phoenix Park Hotel (p229) Irish hospitality and homey rooms by Union Station.

$$$

Hay-Adams Hotel (p228) Old-school luxury a stone's throw from the White House.

Watergate Hotel (p228) Designer property where you hobnob with the jetset crowd.

Jefferson (p234) Luxurious, romantic, Parisian and often considered DC's top address.

Best Contemporary Cool

Line Hotel DC (p234) Repurposed church with airy rooms and a radio station broadcasting from the lobby.

Kimpton Mason & Rook Hotel (p235) Rooms like a chic apartment, plus free bicycles and a rooftop bar.

Graham Georgetown (p228) Stately and stylish digs, right in the heart of Georgetown.

Best For Political Intrigue

Willard InterContinental Hotel (p228) The center of Washington, where the term lobbyist was coined and MLK wrote his 'Dream' speech.

Mayflower Renaissance Hotel (p227) JKF, J Edgar Hoover and Eliot Spitzer enjoyed the hotel's pleasures.

Washington Hilton (p235) Where President Reagan was shot; now a popular business hotel.

Best For Romantics

Akwaaba (p232) Literary-minded B&B with some very sexy rooms.

Embassy Circle Guest House (p232) French country-style home near Embassy Row that'll feed you silly.

Kimpton Hotel Madera (p233) Intimate hotel near Dupont's fancy restaurants and with a cozy bar onsite.

NEED TO KNOW

Price Ranges
The following price ranges refer to a double room with bathroom (excluding tax and breakfast, unless otherwise stated).

$	less than $200
$$	$200–$350
$$$	more than $350

Tax
Washington, DC's room tax is 14.8%. Northern Virginia's tax is around 13.25% (amount varies by county). Taxes typically are not included in quoted rates. Some hotels also tack on a 'facilities fee' of around $25 per night. (The Kimpton brand is known for this.) Always check to avoid surprises.

Parking Costs
Figure on $35 to $57 per day for in-and-out privileges.

Checking In & Out
Normally 3pm/noon. Many places will allow early check-in if the room is available (or will store your luggage if not).

SLEEPING

Where to Stay

NEIGHBORHOOD	FOR	AGAINST
White House Area & Foggy Bottom	Central location dripping with monumental buildings and luxury lodgings where DC's powerbrokers concentrate.	Expensive, not much of a neighborhood feeling.
Georgetown	Lovely, leafy, moneyed neighborhood with accommodations to match	There's no Metro service, so it's not as convenient as other areas for getting around.
Capitol Hill & South DC	Still amid the political intrigue, but more laid-back than the White House Area; wide range of hotels, suites and hostels.	Much of the area is quiet come nighttime.
Downtown & Penn Quarter	Bustles with trendy bars, restaurants and theaters; near the Mall for tourists and Convention Center for business travelers.	Pricey, and the scene can be a bit raucous.
Dupont Circle & Kalorama	It is DC's most lodging-laden 'hood. Great B&Bs and boutique hotels mix among town homes and embassies; cool shops, bistros, bars and sights at your doorstep.	Main areas can be congested and rowdy at night.
Adams Morgan	Young, quirky, B&B-filled area with a cache of ethnic eateries and musical nightlife.	Isolated from the Metro; most properties are a 15-minute walk from the nearest station.
Logan Circle, U Street & Columbia Heights	Gentrifying region with fresh hotels joining scattered B&Bs and guesthouses; good for urban explorer types.	Most lodgings are at least a half-mile from the Metro, and you're a haul from the Mall.
Upper Northwest DC	Quiet, family-oriented residential enclave; accommodations cluster around Woodley Park, convenient to the Metro and restaurants.	Far from the top-draw sights.
Northern Virginia	Cheaper than the District, especially if you have a car (many places offer free parking).	Lodgings tend to be big-box chains without much character.

🛏 White House Area & Foggy Bottom

HOTEL RL
HOTEL $

Map p296 (📞202-223-4320; www.redlion.com/washington-dc; 1823 L St NW; r from $89; Ⓟ☺✳@🛜🐾; Ⓜ Red, Orange, Silver, Blue Line to Farragut North, Farragut West) Hotel RL styles itself as a boutique choice, but it's too worn for that category. Still, it has a bouncy vibe and quirky edge, with free bike hire and gym passes, a games room and a space in the lobby where performances and lectures are staged. Rooms are large, and have a kitchenette; free coffee is available downstairs each morning.

Note that multinight minimum stays sometimes apply.

⭐ SOFITEL LAFAYETTE SQUARE
HOTEL $$

Map p296 (📞202-730-8800; www.sofitel washingtondc.com; 806 15th St NW; r $199-730, ste $260-1500; Ⓟ☺✳@🛜🐾; Ⓜ Orange, Silver, Blue Line to McPherson Sq) We rarely give establishments a 10 out of 10 score, but that's what this splendid hotel deserves. Not as large as its five-star DC competitors, it has a classy and calm ambience and offers exemplary levels of service. Decor is decidedly Parisian and everything about the rooms (beds, bathrooms, amenities, facilities) is top-notch, especially in the luxury rooms and suites.

⭐ HOTEL HIVE
DESIGN HOTEL $$

Map p296 (📞202-849-8499; www.hotelhive.com; 2224 F St NW; r $99-299, loft r $149-329; ✳🛜🐾; Ⓜ Orange, Silver, Blue Line to Foggy Bottom-GWU) There's plenty of buzz around DC's first micro-hotel. The 83 rooms are small (twin and bunk-bed rooms are tiny, and don't have closets – opt for a king loft if possible). Clever design features include under-bed luggage storage and a small work desk. A hip bar and branch of the trendy **&pizza** eatery are downstairs, and there's a rooftop bar, too.

For on-the-go types who don't mind the lack of space and hostel vibe, it's good value for the location (right by the George Washington University campus, and a short walk to the Mall). Bargain hunters can save even more money by choosing rooms that are below the lobby and viewless, or above the bar and noisier.

MAYFLOWER RENAISSANCE HOTEL
HISTORIC HOTEL $$

Map p296 (📞202-347-3000; www.themayflower hotel.com; 1127 Connecticut Ave NW; r $210-400; Ⓟ☺✳@🛜🐾; Ⓜ Red, Orange, Silver, Blue Line to Farragut North) Although not the exclusive establishment it once was (the restaurant is named after J Edgar Hoover, who lunched here daily; John F Kennedy reportedly trysted in its rooms), this huge four-star choice retains its regal 1925 foyer and sense of history. The contemporary guest rooms are businesslike, though they do sport sleek bathrooms and good-quality bedding.

MELROSE HOTEL
HOTEL $$

Map p296 (📞202-955-6400; www.melrose hoteldc.com; 2430 Pennsylvania Ave NW; r $99-350; Ⓟ☺✳@🛜; Ⓜ Orange, Silver, Blue Line to Foggy Bottom-GWU) A decent three-star choice, the Melrose is popular with business travelers, who appreciate its good-sized rooms with recently updated – if slightly cramped – bathrooms. The location is close to Rock Creek Park, so Georgetown's eating and drinking options are a short walk away, as are the upmarket eateries around Washington Circle.

RIVER INN
HOTEL $$

Map p296 (📞202-337-7600; www.the riverinn.com; 924 25th St NW; ste $89-429; Ⓟ☺✳@🛜🐾; Ⓜ Orange, Silver, Blue Line to Foggy Bottom-GWU) Despite the name, this hotel is not actually on the river, but on a quiet residential street near the Kennedy Center. The location provides easy access to both Georgetown and the White House. The well-sized suites sport corporate-apartment-like decor and equipped kitchenettes; some have river views. There's a restaurant, gym and coin-operated laundry on site.

HOTEL LOMBARDY
BOUTIQUE HOTEL $$

Map p296 (📞202-828-2600; www.hotel lombardy.com; 2019 Pennsylvania Ave NW; r $109-299; Ⓟ☺✳🛜; Ⓜ Orange, Silver, Blue Line to Foggy Bottom-GWU) The Lombardy first welcomed guests in the 1970s, when its intimate Venetian-style decor (shuttered doors, warm gold walls) was an instant hit with visiting Europeans. The well-maintained rooms have worn well, but are in need of a refresh – furnishings are worn and bathrooms dated. Opt for an upper-floor room on the east side of the building. The restaurant is disappointing.

CLUB QUARTERS
HOTEL $$

Map p296 (📞202-463-6400; www.clubquarters.com/washington-dc; 839 17th St NW; r $110-450; 🅿️🅗❋@🛜; Ⓜ️Orange, Silver, Blue Line to Farragut West) Club Quarters is a favorite with business travelers on the go. Rooms are small and without views, lacking any semblance of charm or quirk, but the bed is comfortable, the desk workable, the wi-fi fast enough and the coffee maker well stocked. Oh, and the prices are reasonable in an area where they're usually sky-high.

★HAY-ADAMS HOTEL
HERITAGE HOTEL $$$

Map p296 (📞202-638-6600; www.hayadams.com; 800 16th St NW; r from $400; 🅿️❋@🛜; Ⓜ️Orange, Silver, Blue Line to McPherson Sq) One of the city's great heritage hotels, the Hay is a beautiful old building where 'nothing is overlooked but the White House.' The property has the best rooms of the old-school luxury genre in the city, sporting elegant decor, top-quality fittings, hugely comfortable beds and luxe bathrooms. Facilities include a gym, restaurant and popular basement bar (p88).

The hotel is named for two 1884 mansions that once stood on the site (owned by secretary of state John Hay and historian Henry Adams) that were the nexus of Washington's political and intellectual elite. It's also a site of scandal: in the 1980s the Hay-Adams was where Oliver North wooed contributors to his illegal Contra-funding scheme.

★WATERGATE HOTEL
DESIGN HOTEL $$$

Map p296 (📞202-827-1600; www.thewatergatehotel.com; 2650 Virginia Ave NW; r from $399, ste from $669; 🅿️❋@🛜🏊❋; Ⓜ️Orange, Silver, Blue Line to Foggy Bottom-GWU) The 2016 unveiling of this iconic hotel's redesign had DC's smart set all aflutter, and the general consensus seems to be that Ron Arad's sleek interior treats Luigi Moretti's 1965 design with the respect it deserves. Public areas have plenty of pizzazz (the Next Whisky Bar in the lobby is a knockout) and the spacious rooms successfully meld comfort and style.

Additional services and features include a spa with gym and indoor saltwater swimming pool, plus a rooftop bar and lounge offering glorious river views and a small ice-rink in winter.

WILLARD INTER-CONTINENTAL HOTEL
HISTORIC HOTEL $$$

Map p296 (📞202-628-9100; www.washington.intercontinental.com; 1401 Pennsylvania Ave NW; r from $300, ste from $600; 🅿️❋❋@🛜❋; Ⓜ️Red, Orange, Silver, Blue Line to Metro Center) The Willard is where MLK wrote his 'I Have a Dream' speech; where the term 'lobbyist' was coined (by President Grant to describe political wranglers trolling the lobby); and where many presidents have lain their heads. The 335 spacious rooms are slowly being renovated: Premium options overlook the Washington Monument. Families appreciate the kids concierge and program. Breakfast costs $34.

The chandelier-hung hallways are still thick with lobbyists and corporate aristocrats buffing their loafers on the dense carpets. Upon entering the marble lobby, you'll be forgiven for expecting Jay Gatsby to stumble down the stairs clutching a bourbon. Speaking of which: the superb Round Robin (p88) bar on-site claims to be the mint julep's birthplace.

ST REGIS WASHINGTON
HOTEL $$$

Map p296 (📞202-638-2626; www.stregiswashingtondc.com; 923 16th St NW; r from $350, ste from $550; 🅿️❋@🛜❋; Ⓜ️Orange, Silver, Blue Line to McPherson Sq) The neo-renaissance St Regis is one of the grandest hotels in the city. What else can you say about a building designed to resemble nothing less than an Italian palace? Rooms are as gilded as you'd expect, with hand-carved armoires, double-basin marble sinks and luxe Italian bedlinen.

🛏 Georgetown

GRAHAM GEORGETOWN
BOUTIQUE HOTEL $$

Map p302 (📞202-337-0900; www.thegrahamgeorgetown.com; 1075 Thomas Jefferson St NW; r $275-375; 🅿️❋@🛜; 🚌Circulator) Set smack in the heart of Georgetown, the Graham occupies the intersection between stately tradition and modernist hip. Good-sized rooms have tasteful silver, cream and chocolate decor with pops of ruby and geometric accents. Even the most basic rooms have linens by Liddell Ireland and L'Occitane bath amenities, which means you'll be as fresh, clean and beautiful as the surrounding Georgetown glitterati. The rooftop lounge lets you ogle monument views while sweet beats thump in the background. The basement speakeasy is good for a quieter cocktail.

GEORGETOWN INN
HOTEL **$$**

Map p302 (☑202-333-8900; www.georgetown inn.com; 1310 Wisconsin Ave NW; r $250-350; P⊖❋@🛜; 🚌Circulator) Georgetown University alumni and parents on college weekends favor this property parked in the center of the neighborhood's action. The inn has a Revolutionary War–period look (think old Europe meets American colonial) and spreads through a collection of restored 18th-century townhouses. The stately decor (sturdy wood headboards, furniture with feet) is aging, but slowly getting spruced up.

GEORGETOWN SUITES
HOTEL **$$**

Map p302 (☑202-298-7800; www.george townsuites.com; 1111 30th St NW; ste $275-385; P⊖❋@🛜; 🚌Circulator) If you don't mind trading style for ho-hum practicality (and 1980s decor), the Georgetown Suites provide good value for the neighborhood. The most common units are 500-sq-ft studios and 800-sq-ft one-bedroom suites. It's more space than you'll get in a typical hotel room, plus all units have kitchens for self-catering. Free continental breakfast and wi-fi are included.

The property splits into a second building at 1000 29th St (a block away), which tends to be noisier. M St's shopping and dining bonanza, the waterfront and C&O Canal are within spitting distance.

🛏 Capitol Hill & South DC

WILLIAM PENN HOUSE
HOSTEL **$**

Map p300 (☑202-543-5560; www.william pennhouse.org; 515 E Capitol St; dm $45-55; ⊖❋@; 🚇Orange, Silver, Blue Line to Capitol South or Eastern Market) This friendly Quaker-run guesthouse with garden offers clean, well-maintained dorms, though it could use more bathrooms. There are 30 beds in total, including two 10-bed dorms, two four-bed dorms and one two-bed room. The facility doesn't require religious observance, but there is a religious theme throughout, and it prefers guests who are active in progressive causes. Rates include continental breakfast.

The curious and spiritually minded can rise for the 7:30am worship service.

CITY HOUSE HOSTEL WASHINGTON DC
HOSTEL **$**

Map p300 (☑202-370-6390; www.cityhouse hostels.com; 506 H St NE; dm $25-40; ⊖❋@🛜; 🚇Red Line to Union Station) This small, jolly hostel puts you a few blocks from H St's rollicking nightlife. The rooms, in shades of sky blue, tomato red and other bright paints, have bunk beds for four to 12 people. One quibble: if the hostel is near full, waits for the bathrooms can be an issue. The free-beer happy hour rocks each evening.

There's a game room and big TV hooked up to cable, Netflix and Hulu for communal movie nights. Note the hostel has a no-shoe policy inside.

PHOENIX PARK HOTEL
HOTEL **$$**

Map p300 (☑202-638-6900; www.phoenix parkhotel.com; 520 N Capitol St NW; r $170-300; P⊖❋@🛜; 🚇Red Line to Union Station) Though it may look bland from the outside, the Phoenix is all Irish warmth, polished wood and Waterford crystal chandeliers inside. The hotel has long been home away from home for visiting Irish politicians. The rooms – upstairs from the Dubliner pub – are tidy and trim, done up in shades of crisp white and royal blue. They're not big, but they feel like home.

CAPITOL HILL HOTEL
HOTEL **$$**

Map p300 (☑202-543-6000; www.capitol hillhotel-dc.com; 200 C St SE; r $180-320; P⊖❋🛜🏊; 🚇Orange, Silver, Blue Line to Capitol South) This friendly, 153-room hotel occupies a sober-looking building near the Capitol. Dark walnut furnishings and white cushiony beds dot the spacious, clean-lined chambers. Smaller rooms have kitchenettes, while larger rooms have a full kitchen. Lots of political workers stay here, as it is the only hotel that is actually on the Hill. Continental breakfast and a wine happy hour are included.

Self-service laundry, free bicycle use (sign up early, as supply is limited) and a cute lobby with fireplace are part of the package. Highchairs, games and more are available for families.

LIAISON
HOTEL **$$**

Map p300 (☑202-638-1616; www.jdvhotels.com/ liaisondc; 415 New Jersey Ave NW; r $199-369; P❋@🛜🏊🏊; 🚇Red Line to Union Station) The jazzy, 343-room Liaison draws a mix of business types and tourists. Modernist rooms come in a stately, slate-to-earth tone color palette; they feel the right mix of corporate and playful. That said, the seasonal rooftop is all the latter: there's trippy house music and a pool that seems perpetually occupied by attractive folks. And it's all within spitting distance of the Capitol.

WASHINGTON COURT HOTEL   HOTEL **$$**

Map p300 (202-628-2100; www.washington courthotel.com; 525 New Jersey Ave NW; r $199-329; P❄✳@🐾🛜; M Red Line to Union Station) The Washington Court won't wow you with design pizzazz, but the large rooms with spruce, earth-toned decor and a convenient perch next to Union Station make up for it. If you luck out, you might get a room with a view of the Capitol. Then again, you might get one with a view of a government office building.

⭐**KIMPTON GEORGE HOTEL**   HOTEL **$$$**

Map p300 (202-347-4200; www.hotelgeorge. com; 15 E St NW; r $269-429; P❄✳@🐾🛜; M Red Line to Union Station) Nods to namesake George Washington are pervasive at this hotel, which is the hippest lodging on the Hill. Rooms exude a cool, creamy-white Zen and feature large bathrooms, Colonial-inspired work desks, fun presidential pop art and wallpaper adorned with Washington's cursive-written inaugural address. The handy location puts you between Union Station and the Capitol.

Service is top notch. The on-site French bistro provides refreshment, as does the free-wine happy hour each evening. Children and pets receive beyond-the-norm treatment via the Kimpton brand's special programs. A limited number of free bicycles are also available for guests.

🛏 Downtown & Penn Quarter

⭐**HOSTELLING INTERNATIONAL – WASHINGTON DC**   HOSTEL **$**

Map p304 (202-737-2333; www.hiwashington dc.org; 1009 11th St NW, Downtown; dm $33-55, d $110-150; ❄✳@🛜; M Red, Orange, Silver, Blue Line to Metro Center) Top of the budget picks, this large, friendly hostel attracts a laid-back international crowd and has loads of amenities: lounge rooms, a pool table, a 60in TV for movie nights, free tours of vari-

ous neighborhoods and historic sites, free continental breakfast, and free wi-fi.

The dorm rooms are clean and well kept, in configurations ranging from four to 10 beds; there are a few private, en-suite rooms, too. Tours include night explorations of the monuments, Dupont Circle pub crawls and the like. Reservations are recommended March to October.

HOTEL HARRINGTON   HOTEL **$**

Map p304 (202-628-8140; www.hotel-harrington.com; 436 11th St NW, Penn Quarter; d $130-200; P❄✳@🛜; M Orange, Silver, Blue Line to Federal Triangle) One of the most affordable options near the Mall, the aging family-run Harrington has small, basic rooms that are clean but in definite need of an update. Helpful service and a prime location make it great value for travelers who don't mind the dowdy rooms. It's a popular crash pad for school groups, budget-minded families, and international guests.

CAPITAL VIEW HOSTEL   HOSTEL **$**

Map p304 (202-450-3450; www.capital hostels.com; 301 I St NW, Downtown; dm $35; ❄✳@🛜; M Red, Yellow, Green Line to Gallery Pl-Chinatown) Set in a redbrick house at Downtown's far edge, the Capital View is a decent backpacker option. The groovy, hammock-hanging roof deck is the showpiece. The dorms – some mixed gender, others single sex, each with two to six beds in metal frame bunks – are tidy. Alas, the bathrooms are pretty grungy, and the area can be a bit forlorn at night.

⭐**HENLEY PARK HOTEL**   BOUTIQUE HOTEL **$**

Map p304 (202-638-5200; www.henleypark. com; 926 Massachusetts Ave NW, Downtown; r $150-270; P❄✳@🛜; M Green, Yellow Line to Mt Vernon Sq/7th St-Convention Center) This beautiful Tudor-style structure used to be an apartment building for Senators and Congressmen. The rooms – decked in tasteful plaids, paisleys, and dark wood furniture – are as elegant as the edifice. The property has tons of character, with a charming bar and restaurant serving afternoon tea. Some noise seeps in from the street outside, but overall it's excellent value.

⭐**POD DC HOTEL**   DESIGN HOTEL **$**

Map p304 (202-847-4444; www.thepodhotel. com; 627 H St NW, Downtown; d $140-240; ✳🛜; M Red, Yellow, Green Line to Gallery Pl-Chinatown) The Pod is a micro-hotel with teeny rooms

But that's not necessarily bad, especially if you crave hipness at a reasonable price. Under-bed luggage storage and a work desk are among the clever design features. There's a comfort food diner and whiskey bar, a rooftop bar with free happy hour snacks, and a savvy young staff presiding over it all.

The vibe is a bit like a hostel. It's a stone's throw from the Metro station and China-town Gate, and while there are plenty of people around, this stretch of street feels a tad sketchy at night.

MORRISON-CLARK INN   HISTORIC HOTEL $$

Map p304 (☑202-898-1200; www.morrison clark.com; 1011 L St NW, Downtown; d $180-330; ⓟ☺✳@☎☂; Ⓜ Green, Yellow Line to Mt Vernon Sq/7th St-Convention Center) Listed on the Register of Historic Places and helmed by a doting staff, the 114-room Morrison-Clark comprises two 1864 Victorian residences filled with fine antiques, tear-drop chande-liers and gilded mirrors, and a newer wing with Asian-influenced decor set in the re-purposed Chinese church next door. It may sound odd, but the overall effect is lovely and dignified.

All of the rooms have modern furnish-ings (flat-screen TV, wired-up work desk, free wi-fi), and a tasteful cream-and-taupe color scheme, though some are on the small side. Located near the Convention Center, the inn attracts lots of business people who prefer a bit of grace and style to the sur-rounding corporate hotels.

ELDON SUITES   APARTMENT $$

Map p304 (☑202-540-5000; www.eldonsuites. com; 933 L St NW, Downtown; apt $220-320; ⓟ☺✳☎; Ⓜ Green, Yellow Line to Mt Vernon Sq/7th St-Convention Center) Given its loca-tion spitting distance from the Convention Center, Eldon Suites puts up plenty of busi-ness folk. Families dig it, too. You get much more space than in similarly priced hotels. Even the smallest unit has 600 sq ft, along with a fully equipped kitchen and separate living area. The neutral decor is nothing fancy, but ah, so much room!

There's lots of construction going on in this part of the city, so noise and blocked sidewalks can be an issue.

KIMPTON HOTEL
MONACO DC   HOTEL $$$

Map p304 (☑202-628-7177; www.monaco-dc. com; 700 F St NW, Penn Quarter; d $280-450; ⓟ☺✳@☎☂; Ⓜ Red, Yellow, Green Line to Gallery Pl-Chinatown) A bold-green, art-deco-inspired interior helps polish the cool-cat vibe at this temple to glamour. Set in the 1839 Tariff Building, a neoclassical land-mark, the Monaco wows in its public areas. Some rooms are on the small side, but they feel fresh thanks to a champagne-and-blue palette, high ceiling, and a lion's head archi-tectural medallion gazing out from the wall.

The location works well for families: it's near lots of quick-bite restaurants, and it's four blocks from the Mall. Kids get special toys and treats, adults sip free happy-hour wine, and active types can ride the compli-mentary bicycles, as per all Kimpton-brand properties.

TRUMP INTERNATIONAL
HOTEL WASHINGTON DC   HOTEL $$$

Map p304 (☑202-695-1100; www.trumphotels. com/washington-dc; 1100 Pennsylvania Ave NW, Penn Quarter; d $360-1000; ⓟ☺✳@☎☂; Ⓜ Red, Orange, Blue, Silver Line to Metro Center) Trump's company took the historic Old Post Office and gave it a $200 million makeover, transforming the Richardsonian Roman-esque structure into a 263-room (and 35 suite) hotel palace that opened in 2016, complete with crystal chandeliers, exqui-site millwork and a nine-story, light-filled atrium. To the surprise of no one, the venue has become a hub for Trump supporters.

🛏 Dupont Circle & Kalorama

EMBASSY INN   HOTEL $

Map p308 (☑202-234-7800; www.embassy-inn-hotel-dc.com; 1627 16th St NW; r $120-170; ☺✳@☎; Ⓜ Red Line to Dupont Circle) The Em-bassy Inn shows up on hostel booking sites, which gives you an indication of its no-frills ambience. Rooms are small and dark with thin walls, but there's a veneer of quaint-ness here. And the location rocks, flanked by the food-and-drink paradises of Dupont and Logan Circle. Wi-fi can be hit or miss.

Basically, the Embassy works in a pinch, when you turn up in town during a busy time and prices elsewhere are skewing sky high.

WINDSOR INN   HOTEL $

Map p308 (☑202-667-0300; www.windsor-inn-hotel-dc.com; 1842 16th St NW; r $120-170; ☺✳☎; Ⓜ Green, Yellow Line to U St) The

TOP PET-FRIENDLY HOTELS

A fair number of DC hotels allow pets, but the best of the bunch also provide food and water bowls, pickup bags, maps of neighborhood dog-walk areas, and Milk-Bone treats. The best also do not charge for pets or have size or weight restrictions. These properties are top of the heap for Fido:

➡ Kimpton Hotel Palomar DC

➡ Kimpton Mason & Rook Hotel (p235)

➡ Kimpton George Hotel (p230)

➡ Kimpton Carlyle Hotel

Windsor offers spare, fusty rooms. Non-fastidious travelers just looking for a place to crash at night will be fine, and grateful for the affable service and happenin' Dupont Circle/U St Corridor location. Wi-fi is free, but temperamental.

★ **KIMPTON CARLYLE HOTEL**   HOTEL **$$**

Map p308 (☏202-234-3200; www.carlylehotel dc.com; 1731 New Hampshire Ave NW; r $179-349; P🐾❄@🛜🏊🐕; ⓂRed Line to Dupont Circle) In-the-know business travelers, families and couples make their way to the overlooked Carlyle, set amid embassies. The art-deco gem offers quiet, handsomely furnished rooms with crisp white linens, luxury mattresses, 37in flat-screen TVs and kitchenettes (in some). As part of the snazzy Kimpton brand, guests have access to freebies such as bicycles to use, an evening wine happy hour and yoga mats in rooms.

Families can get cribs and roll-away beds for children. Pet owners can get beds and treats for Fido.

★ **AKWAABA**   B&B **$$**

Map p308 (☏202-328-3510; www.dcakwaaba. com; 1708 16th St NW; r $175-285; P🐾❄🐕; ⓂRed Line to Dupont Circle) Part of a small chain of B&Bs that emphasizes African American heritage in its properties, DC's Akwaaba outpost fills a handsome, late-19th-century mansion. Rooms are themed from literary abstractions ('Inspiration,' which has fine, airy ceilings and a slanting skylight) to authors ('Zora,' an all-red room that's as romantic as can be). The cooked breakfast gets rave reviews, and the Dupont vibe is at your doorstep.

EMBASSY CIRCLE GUEST HOUSE   B&B **$$**

Map p308 (☏202-232-7744; www.dcinns.com; 2224 R St NW; r $200-350; 🐾❄🛜; ⓂRed Line to Dupont Circle) Embassies surround this 1902 French country–style home, which sits a few blocks from Dupont's nightlife hubbub. The 11 big-windowed rooms are decked out with Persian carpets and original art on the walls; they don't have TVs, though they do each have wi-fi. Staff feed you well throughout the day, with a hot organic breakfast, afternoon cookies, and an evening wine-and-beer soirée.

Embassy Circle's sister property – the Woodley Park Guest House (p236) in farther-flung northwest DC – is also a hot spot.

KIMPTON HOTEL PALOMAR DC   HOTEL **$$**

Map p308 (☏202-448-1800; www.hotel palomar-dc.com; 2121 P St NW; r $240-380; P🐾❄@🛜🏊🐕; ⓂRed Line to Dupont Circle) The Palomar attracts a stylish business clientele, plus a whole lot of pooches. Room decor is midcentury modernish, with geometric lamps, a muted color palette, comfy bed, nicely powered-up work desk and 55in TV. Palomar's free evening wine hour is a packed scene. The seasonal pool and deck go beyond the norm. Then there's the pet-friendly vibe, which the hotel does up big time.

Not only does your dog get pampered each night with gourmet treats at turndown, he can also get a massage or other concierge-arranged services. The closest dog-walking park is a few blocks away.

TABARD INN   BOUTIQUE HOTEL **$$**

Map p308 (☏202-785-1277; www.tabardinn.com; 1739 N St NW; r $200-270, without bath $125-170; 🐾❄@🛜; ⓂRed Line to Dupont Circle) Named for the inn in *The Canterbury Tales,* the Tabard spreads through a trio of Victorian-era row houses. The 40 rooms are hard to generalize: all come with vintage quirks such as iron bed frames and old armoires, though little accents distinguish them – a Matisse-like painted headboard here, Amish-looking quilts there. There are no TVs, and wi-fi can be dodgy, but the of-yore atmospherics prevail.

Downstairs in the parlor, the beautiful restaurant (p150) and bar (p151) have low ceilings and old furniture, highly conducive to curling up with a vintage port and the Sunday *Post.* Guests receive a $15 voucher for food and beverages.

KIMPTON HOTEL MADERA
HOTEL **$$**

Map p308 (☎202-296-7600; www.hotelmadera.com; 1310 New Hampshire Ave NW; r $200-370; P☺❄@🏠🐕; Ⓜ Red Line to Dupont Circle) Cozy yet cosmopolitan, the Madera is one of DC's 10 Kimpton-brand properties, the focus here being more of a small, intimate boutique than large funk-da-house hipster haunt. The 82 earth-tone rooms sport bright batik pillows, cushy beds, 42in flat-screen TVs and decent-sized work desks, though bathrooms are small. Some rooms have balconies overlooking New Hampshire Ave. Firefly, the on-site bar, stirs romance.

A free-wine happy hour, in-room yoga gear and first-come access to the hotel's loaner bicycles are also part of the package. Heaps of eating and drinking options are within a few blocks.

SWANN HOUSE
B&B **$$**

Map p308 (☎202-265-4414; www.swannhouse.com; 1808 New Hampshire Ave NW; r $279-379; ☺❄@🏠🐕; Ⓜ Red Line to Dupont Circle) A dozen rooms sprinkled throughout an exquisite 1883 Romanesque mansion, all set off enough from Dupont Circle to be quiet, but close enough to be an easy walk from the action. The rooms are highly individualized: some are flowery and frilly while others are more subdued and contemporary. The backyard pool is unique for a B&B.

Staff serves the bountiful breakfast at tables in the chandeliered dining room or outside on the covered front porch. Afternoon sweets and evening sherry are also part of the package.

KIMPTON ROUGE HOTEL
HOTEL **$$**

Map p308 (☎202-232-8000; www.rougehotel.com; 1315 16th St NW; r $198-378; P☺❄@🏠🐕; Ⓜ Red Line to Dupont Circle) Rouge's decor is definitely red – deep crimson, to be precise – with bold designs, funky furniture and hip photo art decorating the good-sized rooms, though the style feels a bit like a burlesque club. Specialty rooms have bunk beds and Xbox 360 games, while others come with kitchenettes. Rouge often shows up on hotel deal apps, where rates can be quite reasonable.

Free wine each evening, in-room yoga mats and loaner bikes (if you can snag one) are nice perks. The hotel sits amid embassies and is a short walk from the restaurant scenes of both Dupont Circle and Logan Circle.

KIMPTON TOPAZ HOTEL
HOTEL **$$**

Map p308 (☎202-393-3000; www.topazhotel.com; 1733 N St NW; r $185-365; P☺❄@🏠🐕; Ⓜ Red Line to Dupont Circle) Abracadabra: the door swings open at the Topaz to reveal an Arabian Nights–style decor. Jewel-tone colors dominate the rooms – purple love seats, sapphire-blue drapes and pale-green striped walls, all set off by satiny white beds and pillows. While it's a bit faded and could use a refresh, it's still flush with the genial service and free-flowing wine you expect at Kimpton-brand hotels.

The location puts you near plenty of hip bars and restaurants. Healthy perks include in-room yoga gear and free access to a nearby fitness club.

MADISON
HOTEL **$$**

Map p308 (☎202-862-1600; www3.hilton.com; 1177 15th St NW; r $260-370; P☺❄@🏠🐕; Ⓜ Red Line to Farragut North) The Madison has hosted every US president since JFK. The attractive rooms are midsized, with silver-gray walls, fluffy white beds, a sturdy work desk and wingback chair to relax in. Alas, the rooms aren't very soundproof. As a side note, the Madison is supposedly the first hotel in the world to have introduced the minibar – thanks, guys.

The hotel has bounced around between corporate owners in recent years. It became a Hilton property in late 2017.

HILTON GARDEN INN/
GEORGETOWN AREA
HOTEL **$$**

Map p308 (☎202-974-6010; www.hiltongardeninn.com; 2201 M St NW; r $240-400; P☺❄@🏠🐕; Ⓜ Orange, Silver, Blue Line to Foggy Bottom-GWU) 🌿 Like most trusty Hilton Garden Inns, this one caters to lots of business travelers and families. Unlike most, this one is in a glittering Silver LEED-certified building. The spacious rooms have easeful beds, a powered-up work desk, Keurig coffeemaker and fridge. The rooftop frolics with an outdoor pool and garden terrace.

The location is a trifecta of easy walking goodness between Dupont Circle, Foggy Bottom and Georgetown.

ST GREGORY
HOTEL **$$**

Map p308 (☎202-530-3600; www.stgregoryhotelwdc.com; 2033 M St NW; r $219-389; P☺❄🏠; Ⓜ Red Line to Dupont Circle or Farragut North) Step into the St Gregory's lobby and you're greeted by a cool, midcentury modern–infused space with a fireplace, bookshelves, wingback chairs and groovy bar. At the time of research, the good-sized rooms were being revamped to match, with wood floors, white walls and clean-lined, modern-meets-heritage decor. The location is ace, a short stroll away from Dupont's bars and bistros.

EMBASSY SUITES WASHINGTON DC
HOTEL **$$**

Map p308 (☑202-857-3388; www.washingtondc. embassysuites.com; ste $270-370; P ❋ @ ⟦⟧ ⟦⟧; MRed Line to Dupont Circle) This Embassy displays the chain's typical hallmarks: all the units are two-room suites (living room with sofa bed in front, bedroom in back), there's a cooked-to-order bacon, egg and pancake breakfast each morning (often quite crowded), there's free wine each evening, and there's an indoor, kiddie-mobbed pool. The property does those basics well. Wi-fi costs $10 to $14 per day.

The location between Georgetown and Dupont Circle is handy. Families will appreciate being two blocks from Rock Creek Park, where the little ones can let off steam. Rooms on the 8th and 9th floors have views over Georgetown.

★ THE JEFFERSON
HOTEL **$$$**

Map p308 (☑202-448-2300; www.jefferson dc.com; 1200 16th St NW; r from $450; P ❋ ❋ @ ⟦⟧ ⟦⟧; MRed Line to Farragut North) The elegant, two-winged 1923 mansion has an ornate porte-cochère, beaux-arts architecture and a luxurious interior full of crystal and velvet, all meant to evoke namesake Thomas Jefferson's digs when he lived in Paris. Favored by diplomatic visitors, the hotel's antique-furnished rooms waft cushy beds, marble bathrooms, tobacco and earth tones, and Gilded Age class.

The 99-room property regularly places near the top of Washington's best-hotel lists. The on-site cocktail bar is superb for a nightcap while listening to the gentleman piano player.

🛏 Adams Morgan

ADAM'S INN
B&B **$**

Map p310 (☑202-745-3600; www.adamsinn. com; 1746 Lanier Pl NW; r $119-199, without bath $99-160; P ❋ ❋ @ ⟦⟧; MRed Line to Woodley Park-Zoo/Adams Morgan) Tucked on a shady

residential street, this 27-room inn is known for its personalized service, fluffy linens and handy location just a few blocks from 18th St's global smorgasbord. Inviting, homey rooms sprawl through two adjacent townhouses and a carriage house. The common areas have a nice garden patio, and there's a general sense of sherry-scented chintz.

Breakfast is DIY continental style. It is 0.75 miles from the Metro.

HIGHROAD HOSTEL
HOSTEL **$**

Map p310 (☑202-735-3622; www.highroad hostels.com; 1804 Belmont Rd NW; dm $42-60; ❋ ⟦⟧; MRed Line to Woodley Park-Zoo/Adams Morgan) HighRoad's Victorian row-house exterior belies its modern interior. The dorms come in various configurations, from four to 14 beds – some co-ed, others gender-specific. All have stark white walls, gray metal bunks and black lockers. There's a fancy (though small) community kitchen and common room with a fireplace, chandelier and a jumbo, Netflix-wired TV. Nighthawks will groove on nearby 18th St's bounty.

Free movie nights, pasta dinners, outings to local bars and other group activities take place several times a week.

THE LINE HOTEL DC
DESIGN HOTEL **$$**

Map p310 (☑202-588-0525; www.theline hotel.com/dc; 1770 Euclid St NW; r $229-399; P ❋ @ ⟦⟧; MRed Line to Woodley Park-Zoo/Adams Morgan) Opened in early 2018, the Line breathes fresh energy into an old church. It's as on-trend as you can get, with three restaurants and two bars by local celebrity chefs, 24-hour room service and an internet radio station that broadcasts from the lobby. The 220 rooms are airy, white-walled visions of low-key cool, sporting vintage radios, sculptural dangling lights and hardwood floors.

Adams Morgan's nightlife is steps away. Columbia Heights' scene is nearby, as well.

AMERICAN GUEST HOUSE
B&B **$$**

Map p310 (☑202-588-1180; www.american guesthouse.com; 2005 Columbia Rd NW; r $160-260; ❋ ❋ @ ⟦⟧; MRed Line to Dupont Circle) The 12-room American Guest House earns high marks for its intimate sense of service, bountiful omelet-y breakfasts and elegant, individualized rooms. Decor runs the gamut from Victorian vibe (Room 203) to New England cottage (Room 304) to colonial love nest (Room 303). Some quarters are rather small.

WASHINGTON HILTON
BUSINESS HOTEL **$$**

Map p310 (📞202-483-3000; www.hilton.com; 1919 Connecticut Ave NW; r $230-335; 🅿️✳️@🛜🏊🐕; MRed Line to Dupont Circle) The 1960s-style semicircular structure has all the amenities you expect at a big business hotel. The rooms are corporate blah, but considering the service you get and the nifty location near food and drink hot spots, it's not a bad deal. Wi-fi costs $13 per day.

The Hilton is famed as the site of John Hinckley's attempt to assassinate President Ronald Reagan, on March 30, 1981. Hoping to impress the actor Jodie Foster, the disturbed young man shot Reagan, his press secretary and an FBI agent near the T St NW entrance.

🛏️ Logan Circle, U Street & Columbia Heights

ASANTE SANA INN
GUESTHOUSE **$**

Map p312 (📞202-570-1281; www.asantesana.us; 1207 Kenyon St NW; r $140-165; ✳️🛜🐕; MGreen, Yellow Line to Columbia Heights) This is a basic guesthouse with six modest rooms (all with private bath, though in some cases not en suite) and a communal kitchen for self-catering (there's a grocery store nearby). It's nothing fancy. The selling point for adventurous types is that it's in a cool, off-the-beaten-path neighborhood, near ethnic eats, hipster dive bars and the Metro.

HILLTOP HOSTEL
HOSTEL **$**

(📞202-291-9591; www.hilltophosteldc.com; 300 Carroll St; dm $28, r $70; @🛜; MRed Line to Takoma) The rough-and-ready Hilltop is in the bohemian, politically leftist neighborhood of Takoma, in far northeast DC. Set in a century-old Victorian mansion, it is pretty darn beat-up, but that doesn't stop international backpackers looking for cheap digs from staying here. The backyard barbecue and hammock inspire frequent impromptu parties.

Don't be put off by the hostel's distance from downtown: it's across the street from the Metro, which gets you to Capitol Hill in about 15 minutes. Besides, Takoma has its own strip of antique shops and vegetarian restaurants to explore.

⭐CHESTER ARTHUR HOUSE
B&B **$$**

Map p312 (📞877-893-3233; www.chesterarthurhouse.com; 23 Logan Circle NW; r $185-225; 🚍✳️🛜; MGreen, Yellow Line to U St) Snooze in one of four rooms in this beautiful Logan Circle row house, located a stumble from the restaurant boom along P and 14th Sts. The 1883 abode is stuffed with crystal chandeliers, antique oil paintings, oriental rugs and a mahogany paneled staircase, plus ephemera from the hosts' global expeditions.

Alas, President Arthur never lived here. It's a gimmick, though the house was built by a Treasury undersecretary in Arthur's administration.

KIMPTON MASON & ROOK HOTEL
HOTEL **$$**

Map p312 (📞202-742-3100; www.masonandrookhotel.com; 1430 Rhode Island Ave NW; r $189-399; 🅿️🚍✳️@🛜🏊🐕; MOrange, Silver, Blue Line to McPherson Sq) 🌱 Snuggled into a tree-lined neighborhood near trendy 14th St, Mason & Rook feels like your urbane friend's chic apartment. The lobby resembles a handsome living room, with comfy seating, bookshelves and eclectic art. The large guest rooms invite lingering with plush fabrics, rich dark wood and leather decor, and marble bathrooms with walk-in rain showers.

The free bicycles are handy for cruising around town. Be sure to check out the seasonal rooftop bar, where chaise lounges cluster around a small swimming pool. Drinks and light bites are available as you take in an expansive view of the city's iconic skyline.

But it's not just for hipsters: the hotel welcomes kids and pets, too. Child-safety kits, cribs and toys are available for families, while plush bed loaners, treats and water bowls make furry family members feel at home.

CAMBRIA WASHINGTON DC CONVENTION CENTER
HOTEL **$$**

Map p312 (📞202-552-5427; www.cambriadc.com; 899 O St NW; r $219-349; 🅿️🚍✳️@🛜🏊; MGreen, Yellow Line to Mt Vernon Sq/7th St-Convention Center) 🌱 The Cambria racks up bonus points for its vast rooms. The shiny dove-gray and white chambers come equipped with a sofa sleeper, powered-up work desk and two flat-screen TVs in addition to a big, comfy bed or two. The 10th-floor rooftop terrace and small indoor pool are also deft touches, though other public areas feel a bit cold and sterile.

Lots of business travelers stay here thanks to the Convention Center proximity. The space is great for families, too, though be aware you're a haul from the Mall and other sights. The next-door grocery store stocks good bottles of wine and snacks.

⌂ Upper Northwest DC

KIMPTON GLOVER
PARK HOTEL
HOTEL $

Map p316 (☏202-337-9700; www.gloverpark hotel.com; 2505 Wisconsin Ave NW, Glover Park; $120-375; P☻❋@☎☏; ⓂRed Line to Woodley Park) This 154-room hotel in residential Glover Park, near Georgetown, has a decidedly boutique feel. It also offers excellent value. The surroundings are stylish, there's a well-regarded Italian restaurant on-site and fitness devotees will appreciate the gym and in-room yoga mats. You'll find comfortable beds and quality amenities in all the rooms, and kitchenettes in 21 of them.

The hotel's accessiblity credentials are strong. A Metro stop is 1.3 miles away and a free hotel shuttle is provided. Wi-fi is not free.

WOODLEY PARK
GUEST HOUSE
B&B $

Map p316 (☏202-667-0218; www.dcinns.com; 2647 Woodley Rd NW, Woodley Park; r $180-250, without bath $130-165; P❋@☎; ⓂRed Line to Woodley Park) This elegant, 1920s-era home, close to the Metro stop, offers excellent value. Upper-floor rooms are nice and sunny; those in the basement have low ceilings and windows overlooking the carpark. Note that rooms don't have TVs, and that those with shared bathrooms have an occupancy of one person only. Breakfast is a bountiful, organic, communal affair.

Woodley Park's sister property – Embassy Circle Guest House (p232) near Dupont Circle – is also a winner.

KALORAMA GUEST HOUSE
B&B $$

Map p316 (☏202-588-8188; www.kalorama guesthouse.com; 2700 Cathedral Ave NW, Woodley Park; r $175-290, without bath $79-135, ste $600; P❋@☎; ⓂRed Line to Woodley Park) Set in two cozy Victorian row houses, Kalorama offers 11 flowery, antique-furnished rooms. Nine of them have private baths and the other two rooms share a bathroom.

Some rooms are in the basement, so let them know when booking if you prefer a brighter upstairs unit. Breakfast is a self-serve affair consumed at a communal table in the main house.

OMNI SHOREHAM HOTEL
HOTEL $$

Map p316 (☏202-234-0700; www.omnishoreham hotel.com; 2500 Calvert St NW, Woodley Park; r $160-430; P☻❋@☎; ⓂRed Line to Woodley Park) The 836-room Omni is a favorite with conventioneers, but it's good for families too. It is a stroller's roll to the National Zoo and Rock Creek Park, and just a couple of blocks to the metro that can whisk you to DC's main sights in four stops. Rooms are worn; wi-fi is not free.

Child guests receive backpacks with toys and games, as well as a milk-and-cookie service on their first night. And you'll have a hell of a time extracting them from the lovely heated outdoor pool.

⌂ Northern Virginia

Chain and business hotels are found around the Rosslyn and Pentagon City Metro stations, a short trip from DC proper. Old Town Alexandria's lodgings are further away (though still on the Metro) and prices are higher, but the neighborhood is much more alluring.

OLD COLONY INN
MOTEL $

(☏703-739-2222; www.oldcolonyinnalexandria. com; 1101 N Washington St; r from $67; P☎☎; ⓂBlue, Yellow Line to Braddock Rd) Offers good-value rooms, proximity to Old Town, a fitness center and complimentary breakfasts. There's also a free shuttle service to Reagan airport, the Old Town (just under a mile away) and to the Metro station.

LORIEN HOTEL & SPA
HOTEL $$

Map p315 (☏703-894-3434; www.lorien hotelandspa.com; 1600 King St; r $199-399; P☻❋☎☎; ⓂBlue, Yellow Line to King St-Old Town) Hidden behind King St shopfronts, this is Alexandria's best accommodation option. Recently renovated rooms are comfortable and well sized, but it's the added extras here that matter: a communal wine hour in the early evening, complimentary morning coffee in the foyer, spa treatments (massages $115 to $250), a gym and a steam room. Meals can be enjoyed in the attached Brabo Tasting Room (p203).

Understand Washington, DC

Washington, DC Today

The District supports a bill introduced in Congress that would make it the nation's 51st state. It's part of Washington's ongoing battle for autonomy from the federal government and to keep Congress from interfering with its laws, such as assisted suicide. The city's economy is proceeding apace, though its largest employer is shedding jobs. Meanwhile, development continues big time around downtown and the Southwest Waterfront.

Best on Film

All the President's Men (1976) Dramatic portrayal of two journalists who uncover the USA's biggest political scandal: Watergate.

Mr Smith Goes to Washington (1939) Frank Capra classic of an idealist do-gooder (played by Jimmy Stewart) taking on the established power brokers of Washington.

The Post (2017) True story of *Washington Post* publisher Katharine Graham (played by Meryl Streep) and what happens when she decides to expose a government cover-up.

Best in Print

Lost in the City (Edward P Jones; 1992) Critically acclaimed collection of short stories set in African American DC during the tumultuous 1960s and '70s.

Hard Revolution (George Pelecanos; 2004) Two brothers, one a rookie police officer and the other a Vietnam veteran, get caught up in DC's 1968 race riots.

The Lost Symbol (Dan Brown; 2009) Harvard 'symbologist' Robert Langdon is in a deadly race to decode the city's Masonic secrets and hidden history in a formulaic but fun page-turner.

The 51st State?

Since she was elected in late 2014, Mayor Muriel Bowser has been leading the charge to make Washington, DC, the 51st state. For years, DC residents have paid billions in taxes but have had no voting representation in either house of Congress – despite having a population larger than two states (Vermont and Wyoming). It's no wonder that residents are proud of their license plates, which brandish the slogan 'Taxation Without Representation.'

In November 2016, nearly 80% of District voters approved a referendum for statehood. A few months later, a bill called the Washington, DC Admission Act was introduced on Capitol Hill. It had a record-setting 116 cosponsors in the House (cosponsors are Congressional members who back the bill before it's officially proposed). Despite this, the chance of passage is slim, given Congress' current conservative makeup. But Bowser and her colleagues continue to push and keep the issue at the forefront of local politics.

At the time of research, Bowser was poised to be elected for a second term. Besides statehood, issues on her plate include the Metro, the USA's second-busiest subway system, which everyone loves to hate for its service snafus. To win back riders, it started a program in early 2018 to provide refunds for passengers delayed more than 15 minutes during rush hour. The lack of affordable housing is another persistent problem in the city.

Autonomy Issues

Here's why DC statehood is a big deal: without it, the Feds can swoop in and interfere with civic affairs. Take the District's Death with Dignity Act, which gives physicians the right to prescribe lethal medication to terminally ill patients who have less than six months to live. The law went into effect in February 2017. Congress, however, attempted to crush the measure via a spending bill. US representatives claim it is within their rights to do so, since under the Home Rule Charter of 1973, Congress must review and approve any law passed by the local government – and lawmakers can foil laws they don't like through the budgeting process. This has happened with other recent laws, including the legalization of marijuana and the Reproductive Health Non-Discrimination Act. Needless to say, DC officials and democracy activists seek more autonomy for the city to prevent such intrusions.

Capital Economics

After Washington's GRP (the regional equivalent for GDP) shrank by 0.8% in 2013, it has been working its way back in a slow and steady fashion. It is projected to reach 2.8% in 2018, putting it slightly ahead of the national average.

However, there are a couple of issues that complicate the long-term picture. One is that the federal workforce has lost jobs. The federal government is, of course, the city's largest employer. When the Trump administration took office, it implemented a hiring freeze at many agencies, and its subsequent budgets have called for staff cuts in several departments. DC also is experiencing a decline in population growth. In 2016 more millennials left DC than moved there, citing things like high housing costs and lengthy commutes to work as factors. Immigrants in neighborhoods such as Columbia Heights are also leaving the city as rent costs spike, heading into the suburbs of neighboring Maryland.

Nonstop Building

Given all the construction and high-flying cranes hovering around town, you'd think Washington's economic growth was booming rather than proceeding at an average pace. Heaps of mixed residential and commercial developments are rising around the Convention Center downtown (an area also known as Mt Vernon Triangle). Capital Hill and South DC are seeing similar action at the Navy Yard and NoMa (north of Mass Ave), while the Wharf is the neighborhood's star – a $2.5-billion waterfront complex of freshly built restaurants, entertainment venues and public piers, with more to come over the next several years. The city's new $300 million soccer stadium, Audi Field, shines nearby, as does the glossy new home of the International Spy Museum, which adds some architectural heft to L'Enfant Plaza.

population per sq mile

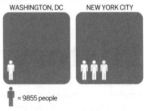

WASHINGTON, DC   NEW YORK CITY

≈ 9855 people

birthplace
(% of population)

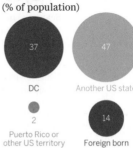

37 — DC

47 — Another US state

2 — Puerto Rico or other US territory

14 — Foreign born

if Washington, DC, were 100 people

48 would be African American
36 would be white
11 would be Latino
4 would be Asian
1 would be other

History

A compromise in a fragile new nation, Washington, DC, was built from scratch on a strategically chosen site between north and south. Following the Civil War, tiny Washington grew quickly, and became a vital job creator during the Great Depression and WWII. The 20th century brought turmoil: civil-rights struggles, political scandals and urban blight. By the 21st century, however, Washington's stricken neighborhoods saw revitalization, even as DC remains the focal point for America's increasingly divided political views.

Early Settlement

Before the first European colonists sailed up from Chesapeake Bay, Native Americans, primarily the Piscataway tribe of the Algonquin language group, made their home near the confluence of the Potomac and Anacostia Rivers. The first recorded white contact with the Piscataway was in 1608 by the English Captain John Smith, who set out from Jamestown colony to explore the upper Potomac.

Relations with the peaceful Piscataway were amicable at first, but soon turned ruinous for the Native Americans, who suffered from European diseases. By 1700 the few remaining Piscataway migrated out of the region to Iroquois territory in Pennsylvania and New York.

Empire of Mud (2014), by JD Dickey, provides an eye-opening account of Washington's early days as a city of tenements, malaria, open slave-trading and political corruption.

The first European settlers in the region were traders and fur trappers, who plied the woodlands beyond the Allegheny Mountains, often working with local Algonquin communities. English and Scots-Irish settlers followed, turning the forests into farmland.

By the late 1600s, expansive agricultural estates lined both sides of the Potomac. These tidewater planters became a colonial aristocracy, dominating regional affairs. Their most lucrative crop was the precious sotweed – tobacco – which was tended by African indentured servants and slaves. The river ports of Alexandria and Georgetown became famous for their prosperous commercial centers.

TIMELINE	1608	1791–92	1800
	Piscataway people, who live around the Potomac and Anacostia Rivers, encounter John Smith on his journey up the Potomac – a word that may mean 'trading place' in Algonquin.	As a compromise to the growing antagonism between north and south, the site for the new federal capital is chosen. Virginia and Maryland both cede land for the 100-sq-mile territory.	Congress convenes in Washington for the first time. Despite the grandeur of L'Enfant's plan, the new capital remains a sparsely populated, muddy frontier town.

Fight for Independence

In the 1770s, growing hostilities with Britain led the colonies (now calling themselves states) to draft the Declaration of Independence, severing ties with Britain. Perhaps the most empowering section of the declaration stated that Americans were 'resolved to die free men rather than live as slaves.'

At the outset of the war, the colonies faced tremendous obstacles. The colonial leaders' belief in their ultimate success was both visionary and utterly improbable. They had neither a professional army nor a navy – only a ragtag group of poorly trained militiamen fighting against the most powerful army and navy on the planet. The king expected a quick suppression of the revolt.

Instead, the British faced off against George Washington, a highly skilled and charismatic military tactician whose courage under fire (in the French and Indian War) was well known. Washington was appointed commander in chief of the 20,000-odd men – a number that would swell to more than 200,000 by the war's end.

Incredibly, the war would rage on for eight years, with more soldiers dying from disease and exposure during the long bitter winters than from battle wounds. The war also brought other European powers into the fray, with France providing arms and munitions, and eventually troops and naval power.

Despite numerous losses, Washington's army prevailed. The British surrendered at Yorktown in 1783 and later ceded all formerly British-held territories to the American colonies.

A Visionary New City

Following the Revolutionary War, the fledgling US Congress set up a temporary capital in Philadelphia while searching for a more permanent home. The Constitution, ratified in 1788, specified that a federal territory, no greater than 10 sq miles, should be established for the nation's capital. Northerners and southerners both wanted the capital in their territory, and archrivals Thomas Jefferson (a Virginian) and Alexander Hamilton (a New Yorker) struck a compromise, agreeing to construct a new city on the border between north and south. The precise location was left up to the newly inaugurated and wildly popular President George Washington.

Washington chose a site some 20 miles from his own Mount Vernon estate – a place he loved and knew well. The site on the Potomac proved a strategic location for commerce and river traffic, and was politically

Despite popular belief (asserted even by some congressmen), Washington, DC, was not built on a swamp. When surveying the capital, L'Enfant found fields, forests and bluffs. Some marshy areas near the river were prone to tidal fluctuations and periodic floods, but most of the new federal city was not marshy.

1814	1835	1846	1860
As the War of 1812 rages, British troops attack the capital, destroying many public buildings (including the White House and Capitol). President Madison flees to Virginia.	Issue of slavery is dividing the nation. The Snow Riots erupt in Washington, with white mobs attacking blacks. In response, Congress passes laws restricting blacks' economic rights.	Allying more with slaveholders and Southern interests, Alexandria County residents successfully petition to return the area to Virginia. It's an indication of the north-south divide.	Abraham Lincoln is elected president. The South secedes from the Union and war is declared the following April. Washingtonians live in fear of attack from rebels, across the river in Virginia.

pleasing to both northern and southern concerns. Maryland and Virginia agreed to cede land to the new capital.

Over drinks at Suter's tavern in Georgetown, Washington persuaded local landowners to sell their holdings to the government for $66 an acre. In March 1791 the African American mathematician Benjamin Banneker and surveyor Andrew Ellicott mapped out a diamond-shaped territory that spanned the Potomac and Anacostia Rivers. Its four corners were at the cardinal points of the compass, and it embraced the river ports of Georgetown and Alexandria (the latter eventually returned to Virginia). Pierre Charles L'Enfant, a French officer in the Revolutionary War, sketched plans for a grand European-style capital of monumental buildings and majestic boulevards. It was named the Territory of Columbia (to honor Christopher Columbus), while the federal city within would be called 'the city of Washington.'

L'Enfant, despite his great vision for the city, would be dismissed within a year. He refused to answer to anyone aside from Washington, and when he challenged the commissioning authority above him, he was eventually fired. Nevertheless, his plan for the city would play a major role in its eventual design – and no one, aside from Washington, had a greater influence upon its development. After Washington fired his planner, land speculators grabbed prized properties and buildings sprang up haphazardly along mucky lanes. In 1793 construction began on the President's House and the Capitol, the geographic center points of the city. In 1800 John Adams became the first president to occupy the still uncompleted mansion. His wife Abigail hung the family's laundry in the East Room. The city remained a half-built, sparsely populated work in progress.

City residents for their part still associated themselves with the states from which they'd come. This began to change in 1801 when DC residents lost the right to vote in Virginia and Maryland elections. According to the Constitution, Congress alone would control the federal district, which intentionally or not, disenfranchised District residents. In 1820 DC held its first mayoral and city council elections, which voters took part in – though this would not always be the case.

Want to read the Constitution, Emancipation Proclamation, Federalist Papers and much, much more? Peruse the National Archives at www.archives. gov or '100 Milestone Documents' at www.ourdocuments.gov.

War of 1812: Washington Burns

In the early 19th century, the young nation had yet to become a formidable force in world affairs. US merchants and seamen were regularly bullied on the high seas by the British Navy. Responding to congressional hawks, President James Madison declared war in 1812. In retaliation for the razing of York (Toronto) by US troops, the British assaulted Wash-

1862	1863	1864	1865
Slavery is abolished throughout DC. Washington becomes an army camp as the Civil War continues. Supply depots, warehouses and factories bring workers into the city.	President Lincoln issues the Emancipation Proclamation, freeing all slaves. By the end of the Civil War, some four million African Americans will be freed.	The war comes to Washington when the Confederate army attacks Fort Stevens – the only battle fought on capital soil. After a two-day skirmish, the Union army prevails.	After Sherman's crippling, scorched-earth drive across the South, Confederate General Robert E Lee surrenders to Ulysses S Grant at Appomattox Court House in Virginia.

ington. Work was barely complete on the Capitol in August 1814 when redcoats marched into Washington and sacked and burned the city's most important buildings (but left private houses largely unharmed). President Madison fled to the Virginia suburbs. Upon returning, the president took up temporary residence in the Octagon (now the Octagon Museum), the home of Colonel John Taylor, where he ratified the Treaty of Ghent, which ended the war. He remained there until the refurbishing of the White House was complete.

Although the British were expelled and the city rebuilt, Washington was slow to recover. A congressional initiative to abandon the dispirited capital was lost by just nine votes.

Slavery in the Federal City

When Congress first convened in Washington in 1800, the city had about 14,000 residents. It was even then a town heavily populated by African Americans: slaves, and free blacks composed 29% of the population. Free blacks lived in the port of Georgetown, where a vibrant African American community emerged. They worked alongside and socialized with the city's slaves.

Since its introduction in Jamestown colony in 1619, slave labor had become an essential part of the regional tobacco economy. In 1800 more than half of the nation's 700,000 slaves lived in Maryland and Virginia. The capital of America's slave trade at that time, Washington, DC, contained slave markets and holding pens.

The city's slave population steadily declined throughout the 19th century, while the number of free blacks increased. They migrated to the city, establishing churches and schools.

Washington, DC, became a front line in the intensifying conflict between the north and south over slavery. The city was a strategic stop on the clandestine Underground Railroad, shuttling fugitive slaves to freedom in the northern states. The abolitionist movement fueled further racial tensions. In 1835 the Snow Riots erupted as white mobs attacked black Washingtonians. When the rampage subsided, legislation restricting the economic rights of the city's free blacks was passed. At last, Congress outlawed the slave trade in Washington in 1850; the District Emancipation Act abolished slavery outright in 1862.

The Civil War & Its Aftermath

The 1860 election of Abraham Lincoln meant that the office of president would no longer protect southern interests in the increasingly

HISTORY SLAVERY IN THE FEDERAL CITY

1865	1865	1865-67	1870-80
Five days after the Confederate surrender, Lincoln is shot in the head by the well-known actor John Wilkes Booth in Washington's Ford's Theatre. He dies hours later.	Andrew Johnson takes office and does little to help newly freed blacks. For violating the Tenure of Office Act, he is impeached and narrowly avoids being removed from office in 1868.	After the war Congress establishes the Freedman's Bureau to help former slaves transition to free society. In 1867 Howard University is founded.	The city doubles in size during the postwar boom. Board of Public Works head Alexander 'Boss' Shepherd helps modernize the city with paved streets, sewers and parks.

Civil War on Film

....

Civil War (1990)

....

Glory (1989)

....

Gods & Generals (2003)

....

Gettysburg (1993)

....

Gone with the Wind (1939)

irreconcilable rift over slavery. Rather than abide by the electoral outcome, southern secessionists opted to exit the Union, igniting a horrific four-year war that would leave over half a million dead. Washington was a prized target and the front lines of fighting often came quite near the capital. Indeed when the war began, city residents (including Lincoln) remained fearful of a siege from the Confederates, whose campfires were visible just across the Potomac in Virginia. Had Maryland joined the Confederate side – and it very nearly did – the capital would have been completely isolated from the North, with disastrous results for the city and country. A ring of earthwork forts was hastily erected, but Washington saw only one battle on its soil: Confederate General Jubal Early's unsuccessful attack on Fort Stevens in northern DC, in July 1864. Nevertheless, Washingtonians lived in constant anxiety, as bloody battles raged nearby at Antietam, Gettysburg and Manassas.

As the war raged on, soldiers, volunteers, civil servants and ex-slaves flooded into the capital. Within three months of the first shots fired at Fort Sumter, over 50,000 enlistees descended on the capital to join the Union Army. Throughout the war, Washington would serve as an important rearguard position for troop encampments and supply operations. Among those who spent time here was local resident Matthew Brady, whose compelling photographs provide a vivid document of the war. Poet Walt Whitman was also a Washington resident then, volunteering at a makeshift hospital in the converted Patent Office – today the National Portrait Gallery; his poem 'The Wound Dresser' is based on his experiences tending the injured and dying. This building, incidentally, also hosted President Lincoln's inauguration ball, after his re-election in 1865.

Lincoln's second term would be short-lived. One month later – and five days after Confederate General Robert E Lee surrendered to Union General Ulysses S Grant at Appomattox – Lincoln was assassinated by John Wilkes Booth in downtown Washington at Ford's Theatre.

The Civil War had a lasting impact on the city. The war strengthened the power of the federal government, marking the first efforts to conscript young men into military service and to collect income tax from private households. Warfare brought new bureaucracies, workers and buildings to the capital. Between the war's start and end, the city's population nearly doubled to more than 130,000. One of the largest influxes of newcomers was freed blacks.

Vice-president Andrew Johnson, a southerner from Tennessee, assumed the presidency following Lincoln's death, but did little to help the freed African Americans; he even vetoed the first Civil Rights bill.

1901	1907	1913	1916–19
The McMillan Commission revives L'Enfant's original design for the rapidly growing capital, beautifying the Mall and solidifying the grandeur of Washington.	The grand beaux arts–style Union Station opens and serves as a key terminus between North and South (with 200,000 passengers a day). Today it receives over 32 million visitors annually.	President Woodrow Wilson starts a policy of segregation in federal offices (including lunchrooms and bathrooms) for the first time since 1863. It continues until the 1950s.	WWI draws thousands of people to Washington for the administration of the war. By war's end, the city's population is over half a million.

TRAGEDY AT FORD'S THEATRE

In 1865, just days after the Confederate Army surrendered, President Abraham Lincoln was gunned down in cold blood. John Wilkes Booth – Marylander, famous actor and diehard believer in the Confederate cause – had long harbored ambitions to bring the US leadership to its knees. On April 14, when he stopped by Ford's Theatre to retrieve his mail, he learned the president would be attending a play that evening. Booth decided it was time to strike. He met with his co-conspirators and hatched a plan: Lewis Powell would kill Secretary of State William Seward at his home, while George Atzerodt killed Vice President Andrew Johnson at his residence and Booth struck Lincoln – all would happen simultaneously around 10pm. As it turns out, only Booth would succeed in his mission.

That night, as Booth strolled up to Lincoln's box, no one questioned him, as he was a well-known actor at Ford's. He crept inside and barricaded the outer door behind him (Lincoln's bodyguard had headed to a nearby pub at intermission and never returned). Booth knew the play well, and waited to act until he heard the funniest line of the play – '... you sockdologizing old man-trap!' As the audience predictably erupted in laughter, Booth crept behind Lincoln and shot him in the head. The president's lifeless body slumped forward. Mary Lincoln screamed and Major Henry Rathbone, also in Lincoln's box, tried to seize the assassin. Booth stabbed him then leaped onto the stage. His foot, however, became entangled in the flag decorating the box, and he landed badly, fracturing his leg. He stumbled to his feet and held the bloody dagger aloft, saying 'Sic semper tyrannis!' ('Thus to all tyrants!'). Booth fled the theater, mounted his waiting horse and galloped off to meet his co-conspirators.

Lincoln never regained consciousness. He was carried across the street to the Petersen House, where he died early the next morning. In a massive manhunt, Booth was hunted down and shot to death less than two weeks later. His alleged co-conspirators were also discovered, brought to trial and executed on July 7.

Congress, however, did attempt to help blacks make the transition to free society, and in 1867 Howard University, the nation's first African American institute of higher learning, was founded. By this time, blacks composed nearly a quarter of the population.

Washington's economy was bolstered by a postwar boom. Although in some ways a Southern city, Washington was already part of the commercial networks of the north. The B&O Railroad connected the city via Baltimore to the industry of the northeast, while the Chesapeake and Ohio Canal opened a waterway to the agriculture of the Midwest. In 1871 President Ulysses S Grant appointed a Board of Public Works to upgrade the urban infrastructure and improve living conditions.

1919	1920	1920s–1960s	1922
Following the armistice, decommissioned soldiers and civilians look for work, and racial tensions lead to race riots in Washington and dozens of other cities.	The 19th Amendment to the Constitution grants women the right to vote. Early activists such as Susan B Anthony (1820–1906) are instrumental in its success.	The '20s see the start of an African American cultural boom; U St, which became home to more than 300 black businesses, becomes known as 'Black Broadway.'	The city experiences its worst natural disaster: heavy snowfall – 18in – causes the collapse of the roof of the Knickerbocker Theatre, killing nearly 100 people inside.

The board was led by Alexander Shepherd, who energetically took on the assignment. He paved streets, put in sewers, installed gaslights, planted trees, filled in swamps and carved out parklands. But he also ran over budget by some $20 million and was sacked by Congress, who reclaimed responsibility for city affairs. 'Boss' Shepherd was the closest thing that DC would have to self-government for 100 years.

Turn of the American Century

In 1900 Senator James McMillan of Michigan formed an all-star city-planning commission to makeover the capital, whose population now surpassed a quarter-million. The McMillan plan effectively revived L'Enfant's vision of a resplendent capital on par with Europe's best cities. The plan proposed grand public buildings in the beaux-arts style, which reconnected the city to its neoclassical republican roots, but with an eclectic flair. It was impressive, orderly and upper class. The plan entailed an extensive beautification project. It removed the scrubby trees and coal-fired locomotives that belched black smoke from the National Mall, and created the expansive lawn and reflecting pools that exist today.

The Mall became a showcase of the symbols of American ambition and power: monumental tributes to the founding fathers; the enshrinement of the Declaration of Independence and Constitution in a Greek-style temple; and the majestic Memorial Bridge leading to Arlington National Cemetery. Washington had become the nation's civic center, infused with the spirit of history, heroes and myths. The imagery was embraced by the country's budding political class.

The cornerstone of the Jefferson Memorial (p72) hides a copy of the Declaration of Independence and Constitution. The White House also stashed a time capsule, this one buried in the garden by George W Bush for the building's 200th anniversary. It holds a cellphone and a computer chip, among other objects.

The plan improved living conditions for middle-class public servants and professionals. New 'suburbs,' such as Woodley Park and Mt Pleasant, offered better-off residents a respite from the hot inner city, and electric trolleys crisscrossed the streets. However, the daily life of many Washingtonians was less promising. Slums like Murder Bay and Swamppoodle stood near government buildings, and about 20,000 impoverished blacks still dwelled in dirty alleyways.

A World & Washington at War

Two world wars and one Great Depression changed forever the place of Washington in American society. These events hastened a concentration of power in the federal government in general and the executive branch in particular. National security and social welfare became

1931	1932–35	1941–44	1954
The Great Depression devastates the country. In 1931 Hunger Marchers protest in DC followed by encampments of 20,000 jobless WWI vets known as the Bonus Army.	Roosevelt is elected president. His New Deal programs put people to work, and Washington sees a host of construction projects, including the National Archives and the Supreme Court.	The expanding federal government and its wartime bureaucracy lead to another population boom. More big projects are bankrolled, including construction of the Pentagon.	The Supreme Court rules that segregation in public schools is 'inherently unequal' and orders desegregation. The fight to integrate schools spurs the Civil Rights movement

the high-growth sectors of public administration. City life transformed from southern quaintness into cosmopolitan clamor.

WWI witnessed a surge of immigration. The administration of war had an unquenchable thirst for clerks, soldiers, nurses and other military support staff. By war's end, the city's population was over half a million.

The 1920s brought prosperity to Washington and other parts of the country, but the free-spending days wouldn't last. The stock market crash of 1929 heralded the dawn of the Great Depression, the severe economic downturn that had catastrophic implications for many

FROM SLAVE TO STATESMAN: FREDERICK DOUGLASS

Born Frederick Augustus Washington Bailey in 1818 on a slave plantation along Maryland's Eastern Shore, Frederick Douglass is remembered as one of the country's most influential and outstanding black leaders of the 19th-century.

In 1838, at 20 years old, he escaped wretched treatment at the hands of Maryland planters and established himself as a freeman in New Bedford, Massachusetts, eventually working for abolitionist William Lloyd Garrison's antislavery paper, the *Liberator*. After his escape, he took his new last name from a character in the Sir Walter Scott book *The Lady of the Lake*. Largely self-educated, Douglass had a natural gift for eloquence. In 1841 he won the admiration of New England abolitionists with an impromptu speech at an antislavery convention, introducing himself as 'a recent graduate from the institution of slavery,' with his 'diploma' (ie whip marks on his back).

Douglass' effectiveness so angered proslavery forces that his supporters urged him to flee to England to escape seizure and punishment under the Fugitive Slave Law. He followed their advice and kept lecturing in England until admirers contributed enough money ($710.96) to enable him to purchase his freedom and return home in 1847.

Douglass then became the self-proclaimed station master and conductor of the Underground Railroad in Rochester, NY, working with other famed abolitionists such as Harriet Tubman and John Brown. In 1860 Douglass campaigned for Abraham Lincoln, and when the Civil War broke out, helped raise two regiments of black soldiers – the Massachusetts 54th and 55th – to fight for the Union.

After the war, Douglass went to Washington to lend his support to the 13th, 14th and 15th Constitutional Amendments, which abolished slavery, granted citizenship to former slaves and guaranteed citizens the right to vote.

In 1895 Douglass died at his Anacostia home, Cedar Hill, now the Frederick Douglass National Historic Site.

1961	1963	1968	1969–71
The states ratify an amendment to the Constitution that allows DC residents to participate (with three Electoral College votes) in presidential elections.	Martin Luther King Jr leads the Civil Rights march on the National Mall. He delivers his 'I Have a Dream' speech at Lincoln Memorial before a crowd of 200,000.	King is assassinated in Memphis; Washington and other cities erupt in violence. Twelve people are killed in the ensuing riots, with small businesses torched.	As the war in Vietnam claims thousands of American lives, many citizens come to Washington to protest. Over 500,000 march in 1969, followed by many more in 1970 and 1971.

Most Haunted Buildings

....

Capitol

....

Decatur House

....

Hay-Adams Hotel

....

St John's Church

Americans. As more and more lost their jobs and went hungry, people turned to Washington for help. Thousands gathered in Hunger Marches on Washington in 1931 and 1932; they were followed by some 40,000 protesters who set up makeshift camps throughout the city, waiting for Congress to award them cash payment for service certificates issued in bonds – they became known as the Bonus Army. President Hoover ordered the US Army to evacuate them, and the troops attacked their encampments, killing several and wounding hundreds of others.

Franklin Roosevelt's New Deal extended the reach of the federal government. Federal regulators acquired greater power to intervene in business and financial affairs. Dozens of relief agencies were created to administer the social guarantees of the nascent welfare state. In Washington, New Deal work projects included tree planting on the Mall, the construction and refurbishment of public buildings and park infrastructure and repairs to institutions like the Lincoln Memorial and the Supreme Court.

The Great Depression didn't really end until the arrival of WWII, when Washington again experienced enormous growth. A burgeoning organizational infrastructure supported the new national security state. The US Army's city-based civilian employee roll grew from 7000 to 41,000 in the first year of the war. The world's largest office building, the Pentagon, was built across the river as the command headquarters. National Airport (today called Ronald Reagan Washington National Airport) opened in 1941.

Cold War

The Cold War defined much of US foreign – and to some degree, domestic – policy in the decades following WWII. The USA's battle with the USSR was not fought face to face, but through countries such as Korea, Vietnam, Cambodia, Mozambique and Afghanistan – all pawns in a geopolitical, economic and ideological battle. Red fever swept the US, as Washington organized witch hunts, like those investigated by the House Committee on Un-American Activities (HUAC), which aimed to blacklist communist subversives.

The Cuban Missile Crisis, which took place over 12 days in October 1962, brought the US and the Soviet Union perilously close to nuclear war, and some historians believe that without the effective diplomacy of John F Kennedy and Secretary of State Robert McNamara, the nation would have gone into battle.

During the Cold War, many covert battles were waged on foreign soil. Perhaps the most famous was the Iran-Contra affair in the 1980s, dur-

1974	1975	1976	1970s–'80s
Five burglars working for President Nixon are arrested breaking into Democratic campaign headquarters at the Watergate Hotel. The ensuing investigation leads to Nixon's resignation.	Following the Home Rule Act, passed in 1973, disenfranchised Washingtonians are finally given the right to effectively govern themselves. Voters elect Walter Washington.	Metrorail opens to serve the growing suburban community. Despite intense lobbying by the automobile industry, several freeway projects through the city are never realized.	Washington, like other American cities, enters a period of urban blight. Its population is falling as increased crime rates and social decay drive many residents out into the suburbs.

ing Ronald Reagan's tenure as president. Staff in his administration, along with the CIA, secretly and illegally sold arms to Iran and then used the proceeds to finance the Contras, an anti-communist guerilla army in Nicaragua.

The Cold War furthered the concentration of political power in Washington-based bureaucracies, a trend that continued in the 1980s.

Segregation & the Civil Rights Movement

In the early 20th century, Washington adopted racial segregation policies, like those of the South. Its business establishments and public spaces became, in practice if not in law, 'whites only.' The 'progressive' Woodrow Wilson administration reinforced discrimination by refusing to hire African American federal employees and insisting on segregated government offices.

Following WWI, decommissioned soldiers returned en masse from the front, bringing to a head festering racial tensions in society. In the steamy summer of 1919, the tinderbox ignited when a white mob marched through the streets attacking random African American residents with bricks, pipes and, later, guns. In the following two days, whites and African Americans alike mobilized and the violence escalated. President Wilson called in 2000 troops to put an end to the chaos, but by then nine people had been killed (dozens more would die from their wounds) and hundreds injured. It was but a foreshadowing of more chronic race riots in the future.

In response, organized hate groups tried, without much success, to organize in the capital. In 1925 the Ku Klux Klan marched on the Mall. Nonetheless, Washington was an African American cultural capital in the early 20th century. Shaw and LeDroit Park, near Howard University, sheltered a lively African American–owned business district, and African American theater and music flourished along U St NW, which became known as 'Black Broadway' – Washington's own version of the Harlem Renaissance. African Americans from the South continued to move to the city in search of better economic opportunities. Citywide segregation eased somewhat with the New Deal (which brought new African American federal workers to the capital) and WWII (which brought lots more).

In 1939 the DC-based Daughters of the American Revolution barred the African American contralto Marian Anderson from singing at Constitution Hall. At Eleanor Roosevelt's insistence, Anderson instead sang at the Lincoln Memorial before an audience of 200,000. That was the

Few films are devoted to first ladies, as they're usually side players in their husband's story, but *Jackie* (2016) breaks the mold. Natalie Portman stars as Jacqueline Kennedy in the days immediately following JFK's assassination.

1981	1990	1992–94	1998
Reagan survives an assassination attempt outside the Washington Hilton. The attack disables press secretary James Brady, who becomes a leading advocate for gun control.	In 1990 Mayor Marion Barry is arrested after being videotaped smoking crack. His arrest angers supporters, who decry the FBI 'entrapment.' Barry serves six months in prison.	Despite serving a prison term, Marion Barry quickly rejoins Washington political life; he is elected to the city council in 1992, then re-elected as mayor (his fourth term) in 1994.	The Monica Lewinsky scandal breaks, with evidence of nine sexual encounters with President Bill Clinton, the first president since Andrew Johnson (in 1868) to be impeached.

beginning of the growing movement toward equality – though the process would be long with demonstrations, sit-ins, boycotts and lawsuits.

Parks and recreational facilities were legally desegregated in 1954; schools followed soon thereafter. President John F Kennedy appointed the city's first African American federal commissioner in 1961. The Home Rule Act was approved in 1973, giving the city some autonomy from its federal overseers. The 1974 popular election of Walter Washington brought the first African American mayor to office. The capital became one of the most prominent African American–governed cities in the country.

Washington hosted key events in the national Civil Rights movement. In 1963 Reverend Martin Luther King Jr led the March on Washington to lobby for passage of the Civil Rights Act. His stirring 'I Have a Dream' speech, delivered before 200,000 people on the steps of the Lincoln Memorial, was a defining moment of the campaign. The assassination of King in Memphis in 1968 sent the nation reeling. Race riots erupted in DC – as they did in more than 100 other American cities. The city exploded in two nights of riots and arson (centered on 14th and U Sts NW in the Shaw district). Twelve people died, more than 1000 were injured, and hundreds of mostly African American–owned businesses were torched. White residents fled the city en masse, and downtown Washington north of the Mall (especially the Shaw district) faded into decades of economic slump.

The legacy of segregation proved difficult to overcome. For the next quarter-century, white and African American Washington grew further apart. By 1970 the city center's population declined to 750,000, while the wealthier suburbs boomed to nearly three million. When the sleek, federally funded Metrorail system opened in 1976, it bypassed the poorer African American neighborhoods in favor of linking downtown with the largely white suburbs.

Decay & Decline

President Lyndon Johnson, until then lauded for his ambitious civil rights and social programs, sank his reputation on the disastrous war in Vietnam, which the US had entered in the 1950s. Toward the end of the 1960s hundreds of thousands of Americans had participated in protests against the continuing conflict.

The political upheaval that began in the 1960s continued unchecked into the next decade. The year 1970 marked the first time DC was granted a nonvoting delegate to the House of Representatives. Three years later the Home Rule Act paved the way for the District's first mayoral election in more than a century.

Civil Rights on Film

King (1970)

Mississippi Burning (1988)

The Long Walk Home (1991)

Selma (2014)

Loving (2016)

1999	1999–2007	2000	2001
Barry's fourth term ends following a budgetary crisis inherited from his predecessor. A new Republican-controlled Congress overrules many of the mayor's fiscal decisions.	Washingtonians elect the sober, less-controversial Anthony Williams as the city's fourth mayor. During his two terms he helps restore the city's finances.	Washington's real-estate boom is underway, with gentrification transforming formerly African American neighborhoods. George W Bush is elected president.	Hijacked planes destroy the World Trade Center in New York and crash into the Pentagon. Another presumed intended for the Capitol or White House, crashes in Pennsylvania

These were two rare positives in an otherwise gloomy decade. The city's most famous scandal splashed across the world's newspapers when operatives of President Richard Nixon were arrested breaking into the Democratic National Committee campaign headquarters at the Watergate Hotel. The ensuing cover-up and Nixon's disgraceful exit was not a shining moment in presidential history.

Meanwhile, life on the streets was no more glorious, as neighborhoods continued to decay; crack-cocaine hit District streets with a vengeance and housing projects turned into zones of violence. By the late 1980s, DC had earned the tagline 'Murder Capital of America.' In truth, urban blight was hitting most American cities.

Jimmy Carter became president in 1977. Gas prices, unemployment and inflation climbed to all-time highs. The taking of American hostages in Iran in 1979, and his perceived bungling of their release, effectively ended his political career. In November 1980, Ronald Reagan, a former actor and California governor, was elected president.

Reagan, who was ideologically opposed to big government, nevertheless presided over the enormous growth of the Washington bureaucracy, particularly in the military-industrial complex.

Local politics entered an unusual period when Marion Barry, a veteran of the Civil Rights movement, was elected mayor in 1978. Combative and charismatic, he became a racially polarizing figure in the city. On January 18, 1990, Barry and his companion, ex-model Hazel 'Rasheeda' Moore, were apprehended in a narcotics sting at the Vista Hotel. The FBI and DC police arrested the mayor for crack-cocaine possession.

When Barry emerged from jail, his supporters, believing he'd been framed, re-elected him to a fourth and lackluster term. As city revenues fell under his watch, Congress lost patience and seized control of the city, ending yet another episode of Home Rule.

> In *The Souls of Black Folk* (1903), WEB Du Bois, who helped found the National Association for the Advancement of Colored People (NAACP), eloquently describes the racial dilemmas of politics and culture facing early-20th-century America.

21st Century

The 2000 presidential election went off with a history-making glitch. On election night, November 7, the media prematurely declared the winner twice, based on exit-poll speculation, before finally concluding that the Florida race outcome was too close to call. It would eventually take a month before the election was officially certified. Numerous court challenges and recounts proceeded, and the Supreme Court eventually intervened, declaring George W Bush the winner.

Bush's presidency unfolded during the nation's worst terrorist attacks. On September 11, 2001, 30 minutes after the attack on New York's World Trade Center, a plane departing Washington Dulles International

> **Oscar-Nominated Presidential Movies**
>
> *JFK (1991)*
>
> *Lincoln (2012)*
>
> *Frost/Nixon (2008)*

2001	2002–03	2005	2008–09
The Bush administration invades Afghanistan and later Iraq. The resulting war lasts over a decade, claiming the lives of over 180,000 Iraqis and 6800 Americans.	In the run-up to the Iraq invasion, mass protests against the planned war are held in Washington and other cities. An estimated 30 million protesters take part.	As Montréal weeps, Washington receives a new professional baseball team, the Washington Nationals (and former Expos). They eventually move into a custom-built stadium in 2008.	Barack Obama becomes the first African American president. An estimated 1.8 million people attend his inauguration.

Airport was hijacked and crashed into the Pentagon's west side, penetrating the building's third ring. Sixty-six passengers and crew, as well as 125 Pentagon personnel, were killed in the suicide attack.

Meanwhile President Bush's tenure in office was marred by controversy on many fronts. The war in Iraq – launched in 2003 to seize Iraq's (nonexistent) stockpiles of weapons of mass destruction – continued until the end of his second term, and sent the government deeply into debt. Bush was also criticized for the bungling of federal relief efforts to victims of Hurricane Katrina, which devastated New Orleans in 2005.

ESPIONAGE: A CAPITAL GAME

Near the hallowed halls of power, Washington, DC, has long played a role in the subterfuge-filled world of intelligence operations. A few of the darker moments in cloak-and-dagger diplomacy:

On September 21, 1976, the Chilean diplomat Orlando Letelier and his American colleague Ronni Karpen Moffitt were killed by a car bombing in Sheridan Circle. Letelier served as the US ambassador appointed by President Salvador Allende before he was overthrown by General Augusto Pinochet. Several men were convicted for playing a role in the assassination, including the American Michael Townley, a former CIA operative, and Manuel Contreras, Chilean Secret Police Chief – both of whom implicated Pinochet in the killing. Pinochet, who died in 2006, was never brought to justice for the assassination.

In the 1980s, the FBI and NSA constructed a tunnel under the Russian embassy – right under their decoding room – on Wisconsin Ave. US operatives were never able to successfully eavesdrop, however, owing to a betrayal to the Soviets by FBI agent Robert Hanssen. The embassy, incidentally, is where Vitaly Yurchenko, a former high-ranking KGB operative-turned-CIA informant, re-defected after giving his CIA handlers the slip in a Georgetown restaurant. The KGB allegedly interrogated Yurchenko after his return, while he was under the influence of a truth serum, to ensure his return was not a CIA ploy.

Some historians suggest that Yurchenko's re-defection was really just a cover to protect one of the USSR's most important CIA informants. Aldrich Ames, a counter-intelligence analyst in DC, began supplying secrets to the Soviets in 1985, and continued on a grand scale for some nine years. His betrayal led to the execution of at least 10 Soviet agents spying for the US and compromised scores of operations. In return the Soviets paid him over $4 million. The CIA slowly realized there was a mole in their organization, but it took years before Ames was discovered – in part because he fooled several polygraph tests (although the $540,000 Arlington home purchased in cash was a slight tip-off). Ames, who narrowly avoided the death penalty, is serving a life sentence in a Pennsylvania penitentiary.

2008–09	2010	2011	2011
The stock market crashes due to catastrophic mismanagement by major American financial institutions. The crisis spreads worldwide.	Despite Congressional attempts to block it, same-sex marriage becomes legal in Washington, DC. The capital joins five other states in legalizing gay marriage (legal today nationwide).	The Martin Luther King Jr Memorial opens on the Tidal Basin. It's the first memorial in the Mall area dedicated to a non-president and to an African American.	A magnitude 5.8 earthquake strikes the East Coast. No one was killed, though the quake causes millions of dollars of damage to the Washington Monument and National Cathedral.

The 2008 election featured one of the most hotly debated presidential contests in American history. In the end, Barack Obama became the nation's first African American president. Obama had run on a platform of hope and change in an era of increasingly divisive American politics. Following the financial meltdown in 2008, the Obama administration pumped money into the flailing economy. He also took on the growing crisis in Afghanistan and the complicated issue of health-care reform.

Obama's second term saw the country emerge from the Great Recession, as the president presided over a growing economy, rock-bottom gas prices and low unemployment. However, Congress put the screws on the federal budget, cutting spending and slashing jobs in Washington, DC. It also continued to meddle in the city's affairs, such as marijuana legalization.

The situation certainly didn't improve in 2016. That's when the federal government shifted to the right after a hugely divisive election. Donald Trump took over in the White House, while Republicans took over both houses of Congress. Top of the new legislative agenda: cracking down on illegal immigrants, dismantling Obama's health-care reform and 'draining the swamp,' – that is, ridding the government of its old, business-as-usual practices. All of this has had a major impact on Washington and its residents.

Chocolate City: A History of Race and Democracy in the Nation's Capital (2017), by Chris Myers Asch and George Derek Musgrove, covers four centuries of politics, promises and realities in America's first black-majority city.

HISTORY 21ST CENTURY

2014	2016	2017	2018
Voters in DC vote to legalize marijuana use. Despite approval by 70% of the voters, Congress swoops in and blocks the law (which is why you still can't buy or sell pot in the city).	The National Museum of African American History and Culture opens on the Mall. It quickly becomes one of the Smithsonian's most popular attractions.	Donald Trump becomes the 45th president, riding a populist wave into the White House with a vow to 'drain the swamp' (ie fix the government's problems).	The federal government shuts down twice during the first six weeks of the year (once for a few days, once for a few hours) because Congress can't agree on a budget.

Arts & Media

Washington has made no small contribution to the American arts, courtesy of home-town musical legends like Duke Ellington and Marvin Gaye, and literary luminaries such as Frederick Douglass and Henry Adams. DC's journalists and news organizations continue to break new ground in one of the great media capitals of the world. And for something lighter, DC features prominently as a backdrop in disaster films, political sagas and spy thrillers.

Famous DC Musicians

Duke Ellington (jazz)

Marvin Gaye (soul)

Chuck Brown (go-go)

Henry Rollins (hard-core punk)

Bad Brains (hard-core punk)

Thievery Corporation (electronic)

Salad Days: A Decade Of Punk In Washington, DC (1980-90) is a 2014 documentary that takes a look at the city's famed scene. Interviewees include thrashers from the area such as Dave Grohl and Henry Rollins.

Music

In the early 20th century, segregation of entertainment venues meant that black Washington had to create its own arts scene. Jazz, big band and swing flourished at clubs and theaters around DC, particularly in the Shaw district. Greats such as Duke Ellington, Pearl Bailey, Shirley Horn, Johnny Hodges and Ben Webster all got their start in the clubs of U St NW. Today, this district has been reborn, with new clubs and theaters open in its historic buildings. Other venues in the area – such as the Black Cat and the 9:30 Club – have become mainstays of DC rock, blues and hip-hop.

The scene at these clubs is varied, but not unique to DC. The exception is where it builds on its local roots in go-go and punk. Go-go (p258), which stomped into the city in the 1970s, is an infectiously rhythmic dance music combining elements of funk, rap, soul and Latin percussion. These days, go-go soul blends with hip-hop and reggae's rhythm.

DC's hard-core take on punk, embodied by such bands as Fugazi and Dag Nasty, combined superfast guitar with a socially conscious mind-set and flourished at venues in the 1990s. Arlington-based Dischord Records grew out of the punk scene and remains a fierce promoter of local bands. While punk is no longer the musical force it once was, its influence on grunge and other modern genres is undeniable.

Showing off its southern roots, DC has spawned some folk and country stars of its own too, including Emmylou Harris, Mary Chapin Carpenter and John Fahey (who named his seminal folk-record label, Takoma, for Takoma Park, his boyhood home).

The immensely talented Marvin Gaye was born in Washington and delved into music early on, singing in a church choir and performing with local groups before his discovery in a DC nightclub by Bo Diddley when he was 19. He later signed on with Motown Records and created some of the unsurpassed hits of the 1960s and '70s, including 'What's Going On?,' 'Let's Get It On' and 'Sexual Healing.' His tumultuous life led him into troubles with drugs and the Internal Revenue Service (he lived in Belgium for a time), and in and out of marriages. During an argument following his return home, he was shot and killed by his father one day before his 45th birthday on April 1, 1984.

Popular African American R&B and soul artist Roberta Flack was raised in Arlington, VA. Before establishing her music career, she was the first black student teacher in an all-white school in posh Chevy

THE DUKE

DC's most famous musical son, jazz immortal Edward Kennedy 'Duke' Ellington (1899–1974), was born in the West End neighborhood and spent his youth in Shaw. In the segregated DC of the early 20th century, Shaw hosted one of the country's finest black arts scenes – drawing famed actors, musicians and singers to perform at venues such as the Howard Theatre – so the Duke took root in rich soil. Plus both of his parents played a mean piano.

As a tot, Ellington purportedly first tackled the keyboard under the tutelage of a teacher by the name of Mrs Clinkscales. He honed his chops by listening to local ragtime pianists such as Doc Perry, Louis Thomas and Louis Brown at Frank Holliday's T St poolroom. His first composition, written at 16, was the 'Soda Fountain Rag'; next came 'What You Gonna Do When the Bed Breaks Down?' The handsome, suave young Duke played clubs and cabarets all over black Washington before decamping to New York in 1923.

There, Ellington started out as a Harlem stride pianist, performing at Barron's and the Hollywood Club, but he soon moved to the famed Cotton Club, where he matured into an innovative bandleader, composer and arranger. He collaborated with innumerable artists, including Louis Armstrong and Ella Fitzgerald, but his most celebrated collaboration was with composer-arranger Billy Strayhorn, who gave the Ellington Orchestra its theme, 'Take the "A" Train,' in 1941.

Ellington's big-band compositions, with their infectious melodies, harmonic sophistication and ever-present swing, made him one of the 20th century's most revered American composers. His huge volume of work – more than 1500 pieces – is preserved in its entirety at the Smithsonian Institution in his old hometown.

For more on the Duke, check out his witty memoir *Music Is My Mistress*, which details his DC childhood and later accomplishments.

Chase, MD. She was discovered at the Capitol Hill jazz club, Mr Henry's, where the owners eventually constructed an elaborate stage for her.

Currently, the rapper Wale is perhaps DC's best-known music export.

Cinema

Hollywood directors can't resist the black limousines, white marble, counterintelligence subterfuges and political scandal that official Washington embodies.

One of Hollywood's favorite Washington themes involves the political naïf who stumbles into combat with corrupt capital veterans. Such is the story of the Frank Capra film *Mr Smith Goes to Washington,* in which Jimmy Stewart and his troop of 'Boy Rangers' defeat big, bad government and preserve democracy for the rest of the country. This theme reappears in the 1950 hit *Born Yesterday,* as well as in *Dave, Legally Blonde 2* and *Being There*.

Another popular theme for DC-based cinema is the total destruction of the nation's capital by aliens. Along these lines *X-Men: Days of Future Past, 2012, Independence Day,* the spoof *Mars Attacks!* and the Cold War–era *Earth Vs the Flying Saucers* all feature DC on the edge of destruction.

Not surprisingly, DC is a popular setting for political thrillers: *In the Line of Fire* (Clint Eastwood as a savvy Secret Service agent protecting the president), *Patriot Games* (Harrison Ford as a tough CIA agent battling Irish terrorists) and *No Way Out* (Kevin Costner as a Navy officer outracing Russian spies) are entertaining stories set amid DC landmarks.

The finest satire of the Cold War is probably Stanley Kubrick's 1964 *Dr Strangelove*. Set inside the Pentagon, the plot revolves around a power-mad general who brings the world to the brink of annihilation because he fears a communist takeover of his 'precious bodily fluids.'

Hollywood made a movie about the famed National Archives photo of Elvis and Nixon shaking hands in the Oval Office. *Elvis & Nixon* (2016) tells how Elvis showed up at the White House wearing a jumpsuit, toting a pistol and requesting to be made a federal agent.

Real-life intrigue has been the subject of a handful of DC films, including the 1976 *All the President's Men*, which is based on Carl Bernstein's and Bob Woodward's firsthand account of exposing the Watergate scandal (Robert Redford and Dustin Hoffman play the reporters). 2017's *The Post* tells a similar true story, this one about *Washington Post* publisher Katharine Graham (played by Meryl Streep) and what happens when she and her staff decide to print the Pentagon Papers, which detail a government cover-up during the Vietnam War.

Curiously, films featuring a character in the form of a US president typically depict him with absurd idealism: *Air Force One, The American President* and *Thirteen Days* are all rather fanciful portraits of a good, if not downright heroic, chief executive. Variations on the theme include the parody *Wag the Dog,* a story of a presidential adviser (Robert De Niro) who hires a Hollywood producer (Dustin Hoffman) to 'produce' a war in order to distract voters from an unfolding sex scandal. Bizarrely, the film was released just a month before the Clinton-Lewinsky affair became headline news.

Only a select few films set in Washington, DC, are not about politics, espionage or cataclysmic destruction. The horrific highlight is the *Exorcist,* the cult horror flick set in Georgetown. The creepy long staircase in the movie – descending from Prospect St to M St in reality – has become known as the Exorcist Stairs (p94). Another classic Georgetown movie is the 1980s brat-pack flick *St Elmo's Fire*. Demi Moore and Judd Nelson's characters are supposed to be Georgetown graduates, but the college campus is actually the University of Maryland in College Park.

DC also serves as the backdrop to numerous TV series. Top picks include *Veep* (2012–), a satire about a fictional vice president and her awesomely dysfunctional staff; *Homeland* (2011–), a thriller about a bipolar female CIA agent and her covert work; *House of Cards* (2013–2018), about a ruthless politician and his wife; and *The Americans* (2013–18), a period drama about two Soviet spies posing as a married American couple.

Literature

Washington's literary legacy is, not surprisingly, deeply entwined with US political history. The city's best-known early literature consists of writings and books that hammered out the machinery of US democracy. From Thomas Jefferson's *Notes on the State of Virginia* to James Madison's *The Federalist Papers* and Abraham Lincoln's historic speeches and proclamations, this literature fascinates modern readers – not only because it is the cornerstone of the US political system, but because of the grace and beauty of its prose.

In the 19th century, Washington outsiders – who came here by circumstance, professional obligation or wanderlust – made notable contributions to the city's oeuvre. Walt Whitman's *The Wound Dresser* and *Specimen Days* and Louisa May Alcott's *Hospital Sketches* were based on the authors' harrowing experiences as Civil War nurses at Washington's hospitals. Mark Twain had an ill-starred (and short) career as a senator's speechwriter, memorialized in *Washington in 1868*.

Frederick Douglass (1818–95), the abolitionist, editor, memoirist and former slave, is one of Washington's most respected writers. His seminal antislavery works *The Life & Times of Frederick Douglass* and *My Bondage & My Freedom* were written in DC, where Douglass lived on Capitol Hill and in Anacostia.

In DC, the Harlem Renaissance is sometimes called the New Negro Movement, named after the famous volume by Howard University professor Alain Locke. *The New Negro* (1925) – the bible of the Renaissance – is a collection of essays, poems and stories written by Locke and his

Best Films Showing DC Locations

The Exorcist (1973)

Wag the Dog (1997)

The Day the Earth Stood Still (1951)

The American President (1995)

'The truth, no matter how bad, is never as dangerous as a lie in the long run.'

Washington Post newspaper

colleagues. The writing is energetic and subversive; as a snapshot of the Renaissance and the African American experience it is invaluable.

Throughout the 20th century, Washington literature remained a deeply political beast, defined by works such as Carl Bernstein and Bob Woodward's *All the President's Men* (1974).

Gore Vidal grew up in DC and often aimed his satirical pieces at the city. His six-volume series of historical novels about the American past includes *Washington, DC* (1967), an insightful examination of the period from the New Deal to the McCarthy era from the perspective of the capital.

Many more purely literary writers have appeared on the scene, too. Edward P Jones does a superb job of capturing the streets, sounds and sights of DC. His collection of stories *Lost in the City* (1992) is set in inner-city DC in the 1960s and '70s, and portrays a raw and very real city, with characters grappling with the complexities of American life.

George Saunders' best-selling *Lincoln in the Bardo* (2017) takes place in Oak Hill Cemetery, where President Lincoln's son Willie was initially interred after he died of typhoid. The novel paints a haunting picture of the grief-stricken president and the cemetery's other residents, who rise up to tell their own stories of life during DC's early days. The poignant book has spawned a mini tourist boom in the Georgetown graveyard.

On a less elevated note, DC has also inspired hundreds of potboilers. Dan Brown's *The Lost Symbol* (2009) brings his Harvard 'symbologist' to the nation's capital on a suspenseful – if formulaic – journey into the secrets of DC's coded (Freemason-filled) history. Crime novelist and DC native George Pelecanos has written 20 books, with most set in the District, such as *Hard Revolution* (2004). Even Bill Clinton is getting in on the action. He and prolific author James Patterson teamed up to write

Best of DC on TV

Homeland (2011–)

Veep (2012–)

House of Cards (2013–18)

The Americans (2013–18)

GO-GO

Go-go is DC's homegrown sound. It's percussion-heavy and funky, a little bit soul, salsa and rap. The average band has 10 or so people playing drums, keyboards, cowbells and timbales. You'll want to dance.

It started in the mid-1970s with local bandleader Chuck Brown. He came up with the idea of danceable music that never stopped as a way to compete with DJs. It became go-go, aka music that just goes and goes.

Brown died in 2012, but several bands keep the sound alive:

Rare Essence (www.rareessence.com) Together since 1976, they began playing in a basement in southeast DC.

Backyard Band (backyardbanddc.com) Brings a hard-core rap-influenced sound to go-go that attracts younger audiences.

Team Familiar (www.teamfamiliar.com) Newer band known for playing R&B over go-go riffs.

Junkyard Band (www.junkyardband.us) Formed in 1980, when they were DC kids in a housing project jamming on makeshift instruments.

Check the websites for upcoming gigs around Washington.

The President Is Missing (2018), a thriller that tries to figure out how the most prominent person in the world has vanished without a trace.

Media

Widely read and widely respected, the daily *Washington Post* (www.washingtonpost.com) is considered one of the nation's top newspapers. Its competitor, the *Washington Times* (www.washingtontimes.com) is owned by the Unification Church and provides a more conservative perspective. The national newspaper *USA Today* (www.usatoday.com) is based across the Potomac in McLean, VA. Several TV programs are also based in DC, including the PBS *NewsHour* with longtime host Jim Lehrer and all of the major networks' Sunday-morning news programs.

Also based in DC is National Public Radio (NPR; www.npr.org), the most renowned noncommercial radio broadcaster in the nation. Popular shows include *Morning Edition* and *All Things Considered.* NPR's offices are in the heart of the hip, redeveloped NoMa neighborhood. Another key Washington media organization is Politico (www.politico.com), which keeps its audience informed of breaking political stories via its free newspaper, podcasts and website.

Washington has some excellent sources of independent media. The *Washington City Paper* (www.washingtoncitypaper.com) keeps an alternative but informed eye on local politics and trends. Smaller rags filled with juicy Capitol gossip include *The Hill* (www.thehill.com) and *Roll Call* (www.rollcall.com).

For amusing and decidedly left-wing political-cartoon humor, check out www.markfiore.com. The Pulitzer Prize–winning artist, whose work has appeared in newspapers across the country, pens weekly animated skits that take aim at the Washington ruling elite.

The city has several Instagram-worthy murals brightening its walls. The Department of Public Works commissions them; its website Murals DC (http://muralsdcproject.com) provides the lowdown on the works and their locations. Hot spots include the U Street Corridor, NoMa neighborhood and Blagden Alley.

Architecture

Washington's architecture and city design are the products of its founding fathers and city planners, who intended to construct a capital city befitting a powerful nation. The early architecture of Washington, DC, was shaped by two influences: Pierre Charles L'Enfant's 1791 city plan, and the infant nation's desire to prove to European powers that its capital possessed political and artistic sophistication rivaling the ancient, majestic cities of the Continent.

L'Enfant Plan & Federal Period

The L'Enfant plan imposed a street grid marked by diagonal avenues, roundabouts and grand vistas. L'Enfant had in mind the magisterial boulevards of Europe. To highlight the primacy of the city's political buildings, he intended that no building would rise higher than the Capitol. This rule rescued DC from the dark, skyscraper-filled fate of most modern American cities.

In an effort to rival European cities, Washington's early architects – many of them self-taught 'gentlemen architects' – depended heavily upon the Classic Revival and Romantic Revival styles, with their ionic columns and marble facades. Federal-style row houses dominated contemporary domestic architecture and still line the streets of Capitol Hill and Georgetown.

Other fine examples from the Federal period are the Sewall-Belmont House (now the Belmont-Paul Women's Equality National Monument) and the uniquely shaped Octagon Museum. The colonnaded Treasury Building, built by Robert Mills in the mid-19th century, represented the first major divergence from the L'Enfant plan, as it blocked the visual line between the White House and the Capitol. Mills also designed the stark, simple Washington Monument, another architectural anomaly and not only because it is 555ft high (taller than the Capitol). Later, other styles would soften the lines of the cityscape, with creations such as the French-inspired Renwick Gallery, designed by James Renwick.

McMillan Plan

At the turn of the 20th century, the McMillan plan (1901–02) revived many elements of the L'Enfant plan. It restored public spaces downtown, lent formal lines to the Mall and Capitol grounds, and added more classically inspired buildings. During this period, John Russell Pope built the Scottish Rite Masonic Temple, which was modeled after the mausoleum at Halicarnassus, as well as the National Archives. Here are some of the best examples of this eclectic French-inspired design that has become so emblematic of Washingtonian architecture:

- **Historical Society of Washington, DC** (www.dchistory.org) Built with funds donated by Andrew Carnegie, the former main public library of DC occupies a majestic position at the center of Mount Vernon Sq.

Conspiracy theories abound about the secret symbols planted in the nation's capital by its masonic architects. The evidence: draw lines along the avenues between major DC points and you get key Masonic symbols – the pentagram, square and compass. To delve deeper, read *The Secrets of Masonic Washington* by James Wasserman.

AMBASSADORIAL ARCHITECTURE

Some of Washington's most interesting buildings, by dint of design or history, are its embassies (p145), mainly concentrated in the Dupont Circle area and Upper Northwest DC. Note that you'll generally have to appreciate these buildings from the outside.

Indonesian Embassy (2020 Massachusetts Ave NW) The extravagant 61-room former mansion of 19th-century gold-mining baron Thomas Walsh was built in a curving neo-baroque style, and originally contained a slab of gold ore embedded in the front porch. Not one for subtlety, Walsh once threw a New Year's Eve party where 325 guests knocked back 480 quarts of champagne, 288 fifths of Scotch, 48 quarts of cocktails, 40 gallons of beer and 35 bottles of miscellaneous liqueurs (according to a piece in the New York Times).

Embassy of Italy Chancery (3000 Whitehaven St NW) This odd, starkly geometric structure was actually fashioned to resemble the original 10-sq-mile plan of the District itself – its layout a giant diamond cut by a glass atrium, meant to represent the curving Potomac.

Danish Embassy (3200 Whitehaven St NW) Stark and simple, this 1960 modernist building, designed by Vilhelm Lauritzen, provides a dramatic counterpoint to a city of sometimes overwrought beaux-arts design.

Finnish Embassy (3301 Massachusetts Ave NW) This sleek and modern building embodies the design principles of famed Finnish architect Alvar Aalto. Designed by Mikko Heikkinen and Markku Komonen, the constructivist, ivy-clad design features a glass wall that juts over Rock Creek Park.

Embassy of Bangladesh Chancery (3510 International Dr NW) Because water is such an important feature of the Bangladeshi landscape, the inverted roof gable atop this innovative structure is meant to resemble a water lily, while the interior, composed of different grades of slate and other materials, evokes a riverbed.

Embassy of Brunei Darussalam (3520 International Ct NW) With its post-and-beam construction and pitched roof, this deceptively modern-looking embassy is inspired by the rustic designs of traditional houses in Brunei Darussalam (a sultanate in Southeast Asia) – simple stilt structures built over water.

House of Sweden (2900 K St NW) Architects Gert Wingårdh and Tomas Hansen designed this contemporary, clean-lined building made of glass, light wood and stone. The 2006 stunner exemplifies Scandinavian simplicity and practicality, and is especially dramatic given its location on the waterfront in Georgetown. It houses the embassies of Sweden and Iceland.

➡ **Corcoran School of the Arts & Design** (p89) The Corcoran was once described by Frank Lloyd Wright as the best designed building in the city. Fittingly, the grand structure now houses an art and design school.

➡ **Meridian International Center** (1630 Crescent Pl NW) A limestone chateau by John Russell Pope.

➡ **Willard InterContinental Hotel** (p228) Grand beaux-arts hotel that has hosted high-society guests for over a century.

➡ **Union Station** (p269) The archetypal example of the neoclassical beauty and grandeur of beaux arts during the age of railroads.

WWII to the Present

Classicism came to a screaming halt during and after WWII, whe war workers flooded the city. Temporary offices were thrown onto th

Mall and new materials that were developed during wartime enabled the construction of huge office blocks. Slum clearance after the war – particularly in southwest DC – meant the wholesale loss of old neighborhoods in favor of brutalist concrete boxes, such as the monolithic government agencies that currently dominate the ironically named L'Enfant Plaza.

Today, Washington architecture is of uncertain identity. Many new buildings, particularly those downtown, pay homage to their classical neighbors while striving toward a sleeker, postmodern monumentalism.

A handful of world-renowned architects have left examples of their work in the city. The National Gallery of Art is a perfect example. Franklin Delano Roosevelt opened the original building, designed by John Russell Pope, in March 1941. Now called the West Building, Pope's symmetrical, neoclassical gallery overwhelms the eye at first glimpse. Two wings lacking external windows stretch for 400ft on either side of the main floor's massive central rotunda, which has a sky-high dome supported by 24 black ionic columns. From the center vaulted corridors lead to each wing, ending with an internal skylight and fountain and a plant-speckled garden court.

The East Building of the gallery is perhaps even more spectacular. Designed in 1978 by IM Pei, the ethereal structure is all straight lines that create a triangular shape. The building design was initially difficult to conceive, as Pei was given a strange-shaped block of land between 3rd and 4th Sts. He solved the problem by making only the marble walls permanent. The rest of the internal structure can be shaped at will, according to the size of various temporary exhibitions. The design is striking, resembling the Louvre in Paris, with pyramidal skylights rising out of the ground (look up from the ground floor of the museum and you'll see a glassed-in waterfall).

Other famous buildings include Ludwig Mies van der Rohe's Martin Luther King Jr Memorial Library and Eero Saarinen's Washington Dulles International Airport.

The architecture of DC tells much about American political ideals and their occasionally awkward application to reality. The National Mall of today is a perfect example. The western half contains a mix of sleek modern creations and neoclassical marble temples disguised as memorials. The eastern side is an entirely different story, a mishmash of sometimes awesome and sometimes appalling architecture.

One of the most successful 21st-century designs to grace the Mall is the National Museum of the American Indian, which opened in 2004. Designed by Canadian architect and Native North American Douglas Cardinal, it is a curving, almost undulating building with a rough-hewn Kasota limestone facade that references the natural wind- and rain-sculpted rock formations of the southwest. The museum's garden has more than 150 different species of plants and wildflowers that are native to the Atlantic coastal plain and the Appalachian Mountains, which add to the element of naturalism in the building and its landscape.

Other key designs include the National Museum of African American History and Culture, a striking 374,000-sq-ft space modeled on the Yoruban aesthetic of a three-tiered crown. Geometrical and bronze-clad panels give the building a dynamic quality, as do other thoughtful elements like an internal waterfall and the uplifting sculptural tilt of the roof. Celebrated architect David Adjaye designed the eye-popper, which opened in late 2016.

Ugliest Structures in DC?

Federal Bureau of Investigation (935 Pennsylvania Ave NW)

Department of Labor Building (200 Constitution Ave NW)

HUD Federal Building (451 7th St SW)

Lauinger Library (Georgetown University)

Department of Energy Building (1000 Independence Ave SW)

Design hounds shouldn't miss Architecture Month, when you can get behind-the-scenes tours of captivating buildings. It's held throughout April. Visit www.aiadc.com/featured-events for more info.

Politics

It's hard to escape from politics in Washington, DC. While LA attracts wannabe film-makers and actors, and New York draws creative and financial types, DC draws folks wanting to be close to the corridors of power. So banter at cafes, restaurants and bars – at least downtown – tends to revolve around the latest gossip about Capitol Hill or the White House.

The Political Vortex

Even those who have no professed interest in politics can't help but follow the decisions – which often have national or even global implications – being made just up the road. You won't find many other cities where such a large number of cab drivers listen to National Public Radio (NPR.)

Power, it must be said, has enormous appeal, which is perhaps why DC emits such a palpable buzz. It draws the best and brightest, from congressional staffers and foreign diplomats to policy analysts at think tanks, NGOs and the World Bank, to name but a few of many important offices headquartered here – every one contributing to the political pageantry in all its glory and shame.

Hand in hand with power comes corruption, and Washingtonians love a good scandal (particularly if it's happening to those who belong to the other party). And there's rarely a dull news day in this town. Congressional brawls, egregious abuses of power and, of course, sexual scandals are all par for the course in the ever-changing news cycle of US politics.

Not surprisingly, the denigration of federal politicians is a widely practiced pursuit – being called a Washington insider, after all, can ruin a career. Amid the current climate of antigovernment sentiment – and the scandals that help fuel the resentment – sometimes it's easy to forget the momentous events precipitated by legislators, judges and presidents. Ending slavery, creating jobs during the darkest days of the Great Depression, sending astronauts to the moon, putting an end to institutionalized racial discrimination: all the work of so-called Washington insiders. US government at work is a messy business, but at times it has brought dramatic changes for the better to the lives of its citizens.

Understanding US Politics: Separation of Powers

Everyone knows Americans do things their own way – spelling, measuring, sports – and the democratic process is no exception.

It begins with citizens being watchful and suspicious of their government. The entire country was founded by anti-authoritarian colonists, while the Civil War was fought over how much power Washington, DC, could exert over the states (among other things). Obsessed with keep-

WASHINGTON'S SITES OF SCANDAL

Washington media loves a good takedown. Here are a few ill-fated sites where some of the big stories began:

Watergate: Towering over the Potomac, this chichi apartment-hotel complex has lent its name to decades of political crime. It all started when Committee to Re-Elect the President operatives were found here, trying to bug Democratic National Committee headquarters; it ended with President Nixon's resignation.

Tidal Basin: In 1974 Wilbur Mills, 65-year-old Arkansas representative and chairman of the House Ways & Means Committee, was stopped for speeding, whereupon his companion – 38-year-old stripper Fanne Foxe, known as the 'Argentine Firecracker' – leapt into the Basin to escape. Unfortunately for Mills' political career, a TV cameraman was there to film it.

The Westin City Center (formerly the Vista Hotel): Former DC mayor Marion Barry was in Room 727 when the FBI caught him taking a puff of crack cocaine in the company of ex-model (and police informant) Hazel 'Rasheeda' Moore. The widely broadcast FBI video of his toke horrified a city lacerated by crack violence, but didn't stop it from reelecting Barry in 1994.

Pentagon City food court: It was by the sushi bar that Monica Lewinsky awaited Linda Tripp, her lunch date (and betrayer), who led Ken Starr's agents down the mall escalators to snag her up for questioning in the nearby Ritz-Carlton Hotel in 1998.

Capitol steps: John Jenrette was a little-known South Carolina representative until he embroiled himself in a bribery scandal. Jenrette's troubles were compounded when his ex-wife Rita revealed in a 1981 issue of *Playboy* (in which she also posed nude) that she and her erstwhile husband used to slip out during dull late-night congressional sessions for an alfresco quickie on the Capitol's hallowed marble steps. The comedy group Capitol Steps takes its name from this famous frolic.

ing government in check, the founding fathers devised a system that disperses power through three branches that keep each other in check.

You can visit those branches starting on Capitol Hill, where the legislative branch, better known as Congress, convenes. Put simply, Congress writes laws. There are two bodies assigned to this task: the House of Representatives and the Senate. In the House, there are 435 voting representatives, who are allotted proportionally by state population – Wyoming, the least populous state, has one, and California, with the largest population, has 53. There are 100 senators: two for each state, a way of giving smaller states equal footing with more populous ones. Congress not only writes laws, it can also impeach the president, determine the jurisdictional limits of courts and vote out its own members.

Behind the Capitol dome is the Supreme Court, whose nine justices are appointed by the president to life terms. The court's job is to determine how true to the Constitution laws are. Arguably the weakest branch, it nonetheless has a crucial role in the democratic process. While the public face of many causes in the USA are crowds of protesters, actual change is often practically affected through the courts, from the Supreme Court on down. This was the case with the Scopes Trial, which allowed evolution to be taught in public schools, the African American Civil Rights movement and the bid for gay marriage.

A little way down Pennsylvania Ave sits the White House, where the president heads the executive branch. Unlike a prime minister, the president is both head of state and head of government, and possesses the power to veto (override) Congress' bills, pardon criminals, and appoint a cabinet, judges and ambassadors.

Suspicious of political factoids? So are we – particularly during political elections. Turn to bipartisan www.factcheck.org to help discern truth from 'fake news.'

While the powers are separated, they are not isolated from each other. The founding fathers figured that each branch's ability to check its partners would generate a healthy tension. This uneasy equality makes compromise a necessity for movement on issues, and it is the true bedrock of US politics.

The Media & Washington

It's hard to imagine an area that packs so many journalists into such a small space. Politics is a game of public perception, and the gatekeepers of that opinion are the media. Politicians – even the ones who publicly lambaste journalists – must maintain a working relationship with the press corps. On the other hand, reporters must ostensibly be merciless, brutally honest and somehow removed from the politicians they cover. In reality, to gain access to the sources they require for their stories, the profiler often forges a relationships with the profiled.

That said, social media – and Twitter, in particular – has shaken up the scene. Politicians can use the online service to reach their constituents and thus bypass the traditional press. Social media also has been the facilitator of 'fake news' – ie misinformation that's spread rapidly and in a targeted fashion using sites like Twitter and Facebook.

Lobbyists

'Lobbyist' is one of the dirtiest words in the American political lexicon, yet its meaning is fairly innocuous. Essentially, a lobbyist is someone who makes a living advocating special interests. This isn't Europe, where causes form their own party and seek power through a parliamentary coalition (though there are lobbyists there, too, of course). Here the agenda-pushers directly thrust their message onto elected officials.

Lobbying is traditionally dated to the late 19th century, but it took off as a vital component of US politics during the money-minded 1980s. Most politicos see lobbyists as a necessary evil, and while it's the rare politician who admits to being influenced by them, everyone understands their importance: lobbyists are the go-betweens in a city built on client-patron relationships. For better or worse, they have become a vital rung on DC's power ladder.

Labor unions and tree huggers, gun nuts and industrialists, every group gets its say here through the work of well-paid and connected advocates. Lobbying ranks, largely based on K St (to the point that the two terms are synonymous), are swelled by those who know how to navigate the complex social webs of the capital; some watchdogs estimate as many as 40% of former congresspeople rejoin the private sector as lobbyists. In a city where getting anything done is often based on personal relationships, a lobbyist can be worth far more than, say, an embassy with rotating staff. Indeed, many countries keep embassies for ritual value and leave the real legwork of diplomacy to DC lobbying firms.

Wining, dining, vacation packages and the art of giving all of the above without violating campaign-contribution laws is a delicate dance. Every year legislation is introduced to keep lobbyists off the floor of Congress (figuratively and sometimes literally), but lobbyists are probably too ingrained in the political landscape to ever be completely removed from it.

Democracy in Action

One of the great paradoxes of US politics is how simultaneously accessible and impenetrable the system is. Visitors can walk into congressional hearings dressed in jeans and a T-shirt and address their elected

Americans vote most of their leaders into office, but not the president. Instead, they vote indirectly through the Electoral College. It is the College and its electors who actually pick the president every four years. This is meant to ensure geographically fair elections: even small states can command electoral attention.

representatives, in public, with relative ease. Mass protests have rocked the foundations of government and seared themselves on the national psyche forever. Yet most of the decisions that influence US government are made between small groups of well-connected policy wonks, lobbyists and special interests who are mainly concerned with perpetuating their own organizations.

Many Americans believe changing the system requires going to DC and coming face to face with their elected officials (there's even a cinematic subgenre devoted to the idea, from *Mr Smith Goes to Washington* to *Legally Blonde 2*). On a grand scale, this equation is partly true. Large protests, often held on the National Mall, can shift public perception a few points toward a particular cause. But smaller delegations usually require lots of money and clout to effect change.

It's maddening, but the surface of the process is surprisingly open to travelers. Check www.house.gov and www.senate.gov to get the schedules for congressional committee hearings.

MALL OF JUSTICE

The Mall has long provided a forum for people seeking to make their grievances heard by the government. Suffragists, veterans, peaceniks, civil rights activists and more have all staged rallies here over the years. Among the key events:

Bonus Army (1932) WWI veterans, left unemployed by the Great Depression, petitioned the government for an early payment of promised bonuses for their wartime service. As many as 10,000 veterans settled in for an extended protest, pitching tents on the Mall and the Capitol lawn. President Hoover dispatched Douglas MacArthur to evict the 'Bonus Army;' the violence of the eviction helped cement Hoover's reputation as an uncaring president.

'I Have a Dream' (1963) At the zenith of the Civil Rights movement's struggle for racial equality, Reverend Martin Luther King delivered a stirring speech from the steps of the Lincoln Memorial to 200,000 supporters.

Antiwar Protests (1971) In April 1971 an estimated 500,000 Vietnam veterans and students gathered on the Mall to oppose continued hostilities. Several thousand arrests were made.

AIDS Memorial Quilt (1996) Gay and lesbian activists drew more than 300,000 supporters in a show of solidarity for equal rights under the law and to display the ever-growing AIDS quilt, which covered the entire eastern flank of the Mall from the Capitol to the Washington Monument.

Million-Mom March (2000) A half-million people convened on the Mall on Mother's Day to draw attention to handgun violence and to demand that Congress pass stricter gun-ownership laws.

Bring Them Home Now Tour (2005) Led by families who lost loved ones in the war, this gathering of over 100,000 protesters demanded the withdrawal of American soldiers from Iraq.

Rally to Restore Sanity and/or Fear (2010) Comedians Jon Stewart and Stephen Colbert gathered some 200,000 to oppose the trend of radicalization in politics. This was a counterpoint to Glenn Beck's conservative Rally to Restore Honor held a few months earlier.

Women's March (2017) The day after President Donald Trump's inauguration, some 500,000 people gathered on the Mall to advocate for women's rights and other issues. Concurrent marches were held in cities around the globe.

Current Issues

The documentary film *Get Me Roger Stone* (2017) follows the titular character, a longtime Republican strategist and lobbyist, and his dark tactics to upend traditional politics. Creating controversy and manipulating media, his methods reach their peak when anti-establishment candidate Donald Trump – whom he advises – wins the 2016 election.

US politics remains ever divided, with Republicans and Democrats rarely seeing eye to eye. The role of government is at the center of the ideological divide: those on the right believe fewer taxes, lower deficits and a smaller government will help spur economic growth, while those on the left believe government should take an active role in spending and in maintaining a social safety net.

One thing they do agree on, however, is the enormous challenges the US still faces. While the economy seems to be doing well – unemployment down to 4.1%, GDP growing at a respectable 2.6% and consumer confidence up at the time of writing – there's a nagging feeling that many people aren't sharing in this good fortune. How to address income inequality and the widening chasm between the ultrawealthy and everyone else remains one of the hot-button topics of today.

Other issues include immigration, same-sex marriage and environmental regulations. Republicans and Democrats are widely split on how to address these matters. And the rift is getting worse: a 2017 study by the Pew Research Center showed the partisan split in America is the highest it has been in two decades, with a 36-point gap between the parties on key issues. The widest breaks were in views about race (that discrimination exists and hinders people of color) and government aid to the poor.

It's not helping that Republicans and Democrats don't view each other kindly. According to the Pew study, 16% of Democrats said they held a very unfavorable opinion of Republicans during the survey in 1994. By 2017, the number had jumped to 44%. The percentages were almost identical when flipped and Republicans were asked about Democrats.

Other major debates in the US revolve around health-care access, gun control and US foreign policy (ie play a role in foreign affairs, or not? Ensure peace through good diplomacy, or through military strength?).

Last but not least, allegations of Russian interference in the 2016 election have been much argued around town. A special counsel has been investigating whether Russia hacked into election systems and used social media to influence US voters to bolster the Trump campaign and undermine Hillary Clinton. The probe also has been looking into whether there was any collusion between the Trump campaign and Russia. Democrats tend toward the meddling and conspiring theory, while Republicans say the evidence isn't there.

Survival Guide

Transportation

ARRIVING IN WASHINGTON, DC

Most visitors arrive by air. The city has two airports: Dulles International Airport is larger and handles most of the international flights, as well as domestic flights. Ronald Reagan Washington National Airport handles domestic services plus some flights to Canada. Reagan is more convenient, as it's closer to the city and has a Metro stop. Baltimore's airport is a third, often-cheaper option. It's connected to DC by commuter rail, though it's not handy if you're arriving at night.

Buses are a popular means of getting to DC from nearby cities such New York, Philadelphia and Richmond, VA. Tickets are cheap, the routes are direct to the city center, and the buses usually have free wi-fi and power outlets.

It's also easy to reach DC by train from major east-coast cities. The fast, commuter-oriented Acela train links Boston, New York and Philly to DC's Union Station.

Flights, cars and tours can be booked online at lonely-planet.com/bookings.

Ronald Reagan Washington National Airport

Ronald Reagan Washington National Airport (DCA; www.flyreagan.com) 4.5 miles south of downtown in Arlington, VA. It has free wi-fi, several eateries and a currency exchange (National Hall, Concourse Level).

Metro

The airport has its own Metro (www.wmata.com) station on the Blue and Yellow Lines. Trains (around $2.65) depart every 10 minutes or so between 5am (from 7am weekends) and 11:30pm (to 1am Friday and Saturday); they reach the city center in 20 minutes. It connects to the concourse level of terminals B and C.

Bus

The Supershuttle (www.supershuttle.com) door-to-door shared-van service goes downtown for $16. It takes 10 to 30 minutes and runs from 5:30am to 12:30am.

Taxi

Rides to the city center take 10 to 30 minutes (depending on traffic) and cost $19 to $26. Taxis queue outside the baggage-claim area at each terminal.

Dulles International Airport

Dulles International Airport (IAD; ☎703-572-2700; www.flydulles.com) In the Virginia suburbs 26 miles west of DC. It has free wi-fi, several currency exchanges and restaurants throughout the terminals. Famed architect Eero Saarinen designed the swooping main building. The Metro Silver Line is slated to reach Dulles in 2020, providing a transfer-free ride at long last.

Bus & Metro

The Silver Line Express bus run by Washington Flyer (www.washfly.com) operates every 15 to 20 minutes from Dulles (main terminal, arrivals level door 4) to the Wiehle-Reston East Metro station between 6am and 10:40pm (from 7:45am weekends). Total time to DC's center is 60 to 75 minutes; total bus-Metro cost around $11.

Metrobus 5A (www.wmata.com) runs every 30 to 40 minutes from Dulles to Rosslyn Metro (Blue, Orange and Silver Lines) and on to central DC (L'Enfant Plaza) between 5:50am (6:30am weekends) and 11:35pm. Total time to the center is around 60 minutes; total fare is $7.50.

The Supershuttle (www.supershuttle.com) door-to-door shared-van service goes downtown for $30. It takes 30 to 60 minutes and runs from 5:30am to 12:30am.

Taxi

Taxi rides to the city center take 30 to 60 minutes (depending on traffic) and cost $62 to $73. Follow the 'Ground Transportation' or 'Taxi' signs to where they queue.

Baltimore/ Washington International Thurgood Marshall Airport

Baltimore/Washington International Thurgood Marshall Airport (BWI; ☏410-859-7111; www.bwiairport.com; 7035 Elm Rd; ☎) 30 miles northeast of DC in Maryland.

Bus & Metro

Metrobus B30 (www.wmata. com) runs from BWI to the Greenbelt Metro station (last stop on the Green Line); it departs every 60 minutes from bus stops on the lower level of the international concourse and concourse A/B. The total bus-Metro fare is about $12. Total trip time is around 75 minutes.

The Supershuttle (www. supershuttle.com) door-to-door shared-van service goes to downtown DC for $37. The ride takes 45 min-

utes to an hour and runs from 5:30am to 12:30am.

Train

Both Maryland Rail Commuter (MARC; www.mta.mary land.gov) and Amtrak (www. amtrak.com) trains travel to DC's Union Station.

They depart from a terminal 1 mile from BWI; a free bus shuttles passengers there. Trains leave once or twice per hour, but there's no service after 9:30pm (and limited service on weekends). It takes 30 to 40 minutes; fares start at $7. MARC typically is cheaper than Amtrak.

Taxi

A taxi to DC takes 45 minutes or so and costs $90. Taxis queue outside the baggage-claim area of the Marshall terminal.

Union Station

Magnificent, beaux-arts **Union Station** (Map p300; ☏202-289-1908; www.unionsta tiondc.com; 50 Massachusetts Ave NE; ☺24hr; Ⓜ Red Line to Union Station) is the city's rail hub. There's a handy Metro station (Red Line) here for transport onward in the city.

Amtrak (www.amtrak. com) arrives at least once per hour from major East Coast cities. Its Northeast Regional trains are cheaper but slower (about 3½ hours between NYC and DC).

Amtrak's Acela Express trains are more expensive but faster (2¾ hours between NYC and DC; 6½ hours between Boston and DC). The express trains also have bigger seats and other business-class amenities.

MARC (www.mta. maryland.gov) trains arrive frequently from downtown Baltimore (one hour) and other Maryland towns, as well as Harpers Ferry, WV.

Taxi

Taxis queue outside Union Station's main entrance. A ride to downtown costs around $7, to Dupont Circle $10.

GETTING AROUND

The public-transportation system is a mix of Metro trains and buses. Visitors will find the Metro the most useful option.

The District Department of Transportation's goDCgo (www.godcgo.com) is a useful resource for biking, bus, Metro and parking information and route planning. It even has a carbon calculator that compares different modes of local travel.

Bicycle

DC is a cycling-savvy city with its own bike-share program. Lots of locals commute by bicycle.

Riders can take bikes free of charge on Metro trains, except during rush hour (7am to 10am and 4pm to 7pm Monday to Friday) and on holidays. Bikes are not permitted to use the center door of trains or the escalator.

All public buses are equipped with bike racks.

The Washington Area Bicyclists' Association (www. waba.org) has information on recommended trails, events, bike advocacy and more.

Here are some options for rental:

Capital Bikeshare (☑877-430-2453; www.capitalbike share.com; per 1/3 days $8/17) It has a network of 3700-plus bicycles scattered at 440-odd stations, including many that fringe the Mall. Kiosks issue passes (one day or three days) on the spot. Insert a credit card, get your ride code, then unlock a bike. The first 30 minutes are free; after that, rates rise fast if you don't dock the bike. There's also an option for a 'single trip' ($2), ie a one-off ride of under 30 minutes. Note helmets and locks are not provided.

Dockless bikeshare While Capital Bikeshare is the mainstay, heaps of dockless competitors entered the market in late 2017. Companies include Mobike (www.mobike.com), LimeBike (www.limebike.com), Ofo (www.ofo.com) and Spin (www.spin.pm). With these bikes, you can pick up and drop off anywhere legal (ie near existing racks, or on the area between sidewalks and curbs). A frame-mounted lock immobilizes the bicycle until riders scan a bar code or type in a PIN with their smartphone to activate it (done via the company's app, which you must download first). The average price per half-hour ride is $1.

Bike & Roll (Map p300; ☑202-842-2453; www.bike androlldc.com; 955 L'Enfant Plaza SW; tours adult/child from $44/34; ⊙9am-8pm, reduced hours spring & fall, closed early Dec–mid-Mar; MOrange, Silver, Blue, Yellow, Green Line to L'Enfant Plaza) To rent a bicycle for longer rides, with accoutrements such as helmets and locks, this company has an outpost at L'Enfant Plaza near the Mall, as well as branches at Union Station and Alexandria, VA.

Big Wheel Bikes (Map p302; ☑202-337-0254; www.big wheelbikes.com; 1034 33rd St NW; per 3hr/day $21/35; ⊙11am-7pm Tue-Fri, 10am-6pm Sat & Sun; ☐Circulator) A company with two-wheelers for longer rides, located in Georgetown near several great trails.

Boat

Water taxis operated by **Potomac Riverboat Co** (☑877-511-2628; www. potomacriverboatco.com; ⊙late Mar-Oct) toodle along the river between Georgetown (dock at 31st and K Sts, Washington Harbour), the Wharf (dock at Transit Pier, 950 Wharf St SW) and Old Town Alexandria (dock at corner of Cameron and Union Sts). The trip takes 25 minutes between each dock; one-way fares start at adult/child $12/8.40. In Alexandria you can transfer to another water taxi to reach the amusements at Maryland's National Harbor for around $8 more.

Bus

DC's public-bus system has two main fleets. Pay with exact change, or use a SmarTrip card.

The city has also launched a streetcar system, though

so far service is limited to one route.

Metrobus (www.wmata. com) Operates clean, efficient buses throughout the city and suburbs, typically from early morning until late evening. Fare is $2.

DC Circulator (www.dc circulator.com) Red Circulator buses run along handy local routes, including Union Station to/from the Mall (looping by all major museums and memorials), Union Station to/from Georgetown (via K St), Dupont Circle to/from Georgetown (via M St), and the White House area to/from Adams Morgan (via 14th St). Buses operate from roughly 7am to 9pm weekdays (midnight or so on weekends). Fare is $1.

Streetcar (www.dcstreetcar. com) The lone line zips along H St from Union Station to 15th St, then heads southeast along Benning Rd. It operates from 6am (8am on weekends) to midnight (2am Friday and Saturday). It's free as of research time.

Car & Motorcycle

DC has some of the nation's worst traffic congestion. Bottlenecks are in the suburbs, where the Capital Beltway (I-495) meets Maryland's I-270 and I-95, and Virginia's I-66 and I-95. Avoid the beltway during early-morning and late-afternoon rush hours (about 6am to 9am and 3pm to 6pm). Clogged rush-hour streets in DC include the main access arteries from the suburbs: Massachusetts, Wisconsin, Connecticut and Georgia Aves NW, among others.

Metro

DC's modern subway network is the Metrorail (www.

USEFUL BUS STATIONS

Cheap bus services to and from Washington, DC, abound. Most charge $25 to $30 for a one-way trip to NYC (it takes four to five hours). Many companies use Union Station as their hub; other pickup locations are scattered around town, but are always accessible by Metro. Tickets usually need to be bought online, but can sometimes be purchased on the bus itself if there are still seats available.

BestBus (Map p308; ☑202-332-2691; www.bestbus.com; cnr 20th St & Massachusetts Ave NW; ☎; Ⓜ Red Line to Dupont Circle) Several trips to/from NYC daily. The main bus stop is by Dupont Circle; there's another at Union Station.

BoltBus (Map p301; ☑877-265-8287; www.boltbus.com; 50 Massachusetts Ave NE; ☎; Ⓜ Red Line to Union Station) It goes to NYC multiple times each day, and to other East Coast cities. Lateness and spotty wi-fi can be issues. It uses Union Station as its terminal.

Greyhound (Map p301; ☑202-589-5141; www.greyhound.com; 50 Massachusetts Ave NE; ☎; Ⓜ Red Line to Union Station) Nationwide service. The terminal is at Union Station.

Megabus (Map p301; ☑877-462-6342; http://us.megabus.com; 50 Massachusetts Ave NE; ☎; Ⓜ Red Line to Union Station) Offers the most trips to NYC (around 15 to 20 per day), as well as other East Coast cities; arrives at/departs from Union Station. Buses run behind schedule fairly often.

Peter Pan Bus Lines (Map p301; ☑800-343-9999; www.peterpanbus.com; 50 Massachusetts Ave NE; ☎; Ⓜ Red Line to Union Station) Travels throughout the northeastern USA; has its terminal at Union Station.

Vamoose Bus (Map p318; ☑212-695-6766; www.vamoosebus.com; 1801 N Lynn St; $60) Service between NYC and Arlington, VA (the stop is near the Rosslyn Metro station).

Washington Deluxe (Map p308; ☑866-287-6932; www.washny.com; 1610 Connecticut Ave NW; ☎; Ⓜ Red Line to Dupont Circle) Good express service to/from NYC. It has stops at both Dupont Circle and Union Station.

wmata.com), commonly called Metro. It will get you to most sights, hotels and business districts, and to the Maryland and Virginia suburbs.

➡ There are six color-coded lines: Red, Orange, Blue, Green, Yellow and Silver.

➡ Trains start running at 5am Monday through Friday (from 7am on Saturday, 8am on Sunday); the last service is around 11:30pm Sunday through Thursday and 1am on Friday and Saturday.

➡ Trains run every 10 minutes or so, except during weekend track maintenance, when they slow down considerably.

➡ Fare cards are called SmarTrip cards. Machines inside all stations sell them. The plastic, rechargeable card costs $10, with $8 of that stored for fares. You then add value as needed.

➡ Fares cost $2 to $6, depending on distance traveled and time of day. Fares increase slightly during morning and evening rush hour.

➡ Use the card to enter *and* exit station turnstiles. Upon exit, the turnstile deducts the fare and opens the gate. If the value of the card is insufficient, you need to use an 'Addfare' machine to add money.

➡ SmarTrip cards are also usable on all local buses.

➡ Unlimited-ride Metro day passes cost $14.75, available at any station.

➡ All Metro stations have elevators, handy for travelers with strollers or mobility issues (otherwise you're relegated to escalators, which are very lengthy at some stations).

Taxi & Rideshare

Taxis queue at Union Station, the main hotels and sports venues, but it's not always easy to hail one on the street.

Ride-hailing companies Uber (www.uber.com), Lyft (www.lyft.com) and Via (www.ridewithvia.com) are popular in the District. Locals say they save time and money compared to taxis.

For those sticking with taxis, reliable companies include the following:

DC Yellow Cab ☑202-544-1212

Diamond Cab ☑202-387-6200

➡ Fares are meter-based. The meter starts at $3.50, then it's $2.16 per mile thereafter.

➡ There's a $2 surcharge for telephone dispatches.

TOURS

Tours are a great way to home in on DC's attractions. Jaunts by foot, van or bicycle are prime for exploring off-the-beaten path neighborhoods or delving into a particular topic of interest, such as monuments, haunted sites or breweries. Bus tours can be helpful if you're trying to cover a lot of ground in a short amount of time. Boat tours take in far-flung sights such as Mount Vernon in Virginia.

Bike & Roll (Map p300; ☑202-842-2453; www.bikeandrolldc.com; 955 L'Enfant Plaza SW; tours adult/child from $44/34; ☉9am-8pm, reduced hours spring & fall, closed early Dec–mid-Mar; MOrange, Silver, Blue, Yellow, Green Line to L'Enfant Plaza) This branch of the bike-rental company (from $16 per two hours) is the one closest to the Mall. In addition to bike rental, it also provides tours. Three-hour jaunts wheel by the main sights of Capitol Hill and the National Mall. The evening rides to the monuments are particularly good.

DC Brew Tours (Map p304;☑202-759-8687; www.citybrewtours.com/dc; 801 F St NW, Penn Quarter; tours $70-99; MRed, Yellow, Green Line to Gallery Pl-Chinatown) Visit three to four breweries by van. Routes vary but could include DC Brau, Atlas, Capital City and Port City, among others. Five-hour jaunts feature tastings of 15-plus beers and a light meal. The 3½-hour tour forgoes the meal and pares down the brewery tally. Depar-

ture is from outside the Reynolds Center. Tours go daily, at various times.

DC by Foot (Map p294; ☑202-370-1830; www.freetoursbyfoot.com/washington-dc-tours) Guides for this pay-what-you-want walking tour offer engaging stories and historical details on different jaunts covering the National Mall, Lincoln's assassination, Dupont Circle's ghosts and many more. Most takers pay around $10–$15 per person. Reserve in advance to guarantee a spot.

DC Metro Food Tours (☑202-851-2268; www.dcmetrofoodtours.com; per person $56-67) These walkabouts explore the culinary riches of various neighborhoods, stopping for multiple bites along the way. Offerings include Capitol Hill, U St, Little Ethiopia, Georgetown and Alexandria, VA. Most last from three to 3½ hours. Departure points vary.

Old Town Trolley Tours (Map p304;☑202-832-9800; www.trolleytours.com; 1001 E St NW, Penn Quarter; adult/child $40/30; MRed, Orange, Silver, Blue Line to Metro Center) This open-sided bus offers hop-on, hop-off exploring of some 25 major sights around the Mall, Arlington and Downtown. The company also offers a 'monuments by moonlight' tour and the DC Ducks tour, via an amphibious vehicle that plunges into the Potomac. Buy tickets at the **Washington Welcome Center** (1001 E St NW), at Union Station, or online.

Potomac Riverboat Co (☑877-511-2628; www.potomacriverboatco.com; ☉late Mar-Oct) It offers a monuments cruise (one way adult/child $16/10) between its Georgetown dock (Map p302; near 31st & K Sts NW) at 31st and K Sts, Washington Harbour, and its Alexandria dock at the corner of Cameron and Union Sts. You can disembark at either location to sightsee, then return via a later cruise. From Alexandria, it also offers a Mount Vernon trip (one way including Mount Vernon admission adult/child $31/18). Check the website for other themed tours. Potomac Riverboat Co also operates the water taxi that links Georgetown and Alexandria with the Wharf in DC's southwest waterfront area.

City Segway Tours (Map p296;☑202-626-0017; www.citysegwaytours.com/washington-dc; 502 23rd St NW; 3hr tours from $75) Popular way of seeing the major sites along the Mall and around the White House area.

Spirit of Mount Vernon (Map p300;☑866-302-2469; www.cruisetomountvernon.com; 6th & Water Sts SW, Pier 4; adult/child $50/45; ☉Mar-Oct, closed Mon; MGreen Line to Waterfront) The large, flashy *Spirit of Mount Vernon* boat departs for George Washington's estate from Pier 4, at the corner of 6th and Water Sts SW in southwest DC. The day-long tour includes site admission.

Directory A–Z

Customs Regulations

For a complete list of US customs regulations, go online to US Customs and Border Protection (www.cbp.gov).

Duty-free allowance per person is as follows:

➜ 1L of liquor (provided you are at least 21 years old)

➜ 100 cigars and 200 cigarettes (if you are at least 18 years)

➜ $200 worth of gifts and purchases ($800 if a returning US citizen)

If you arrive with $10,000 or more in US or foreign currency, it must be declared. There are heavy penalties for attempting to import illegal drugs. Note that fruit, vegetables and other food must be declared (whereupon you'll undergo a time-consuming search) or left in the bins in the arrival area.

Discount Cards

The **Explorer Pass** www.smartdestinations.com) lets you choose three, four or five attractions for discounted admission. You pick the sights from among 20 options, including the Newseum, Mount Vernon and the International Spy Museum. Prices start at adult/child $54/34 for three sites and go up to $84/54 for five sites. The pass saves a good 20% or so off door prices. Purchase it via the website.

Emergencies

Ambulance, fire, police ☑911

Etiquette

Smoking Don't smoke in restaurants or bars: DC is smoke free by law in those venues.

Dining People eat dinner early in Washington, often by 6pm.

On the Metro Stand to the right on the escalators; walk on the left.

Conversation It's OK to ask locals you've just met, 'What do you do for work?' Most people in DC have an intriguing job that they're happy to discuss.

Insurance

It's expensive to get sick, crash a car or have things stolen from you in the USA. Make sure you have adequate coverage before

Electricity

Type A
120V/60Hz

Type B
120V/60Hz

arriving. To insure yourself for items that may be stolen from your car, consult your homeowner's (or renter's) insurance policy or consider investing in travel insurance.

Worldwide travel insurance is available at www.lonelyplanet.com/travel-insurance. You can buy, extend and claim online anytime – even if you're already on the road.

Internet Access

→ Wi-fi is common in lodgings across the price spectrum. Lower-speed internet typically is free, but you sometimes have to pay for premium-speed service. Many properties also have an internet-connected computer for public use.

→ Many bars, cafes and museums – including most of the Smithsonian buildings – offer free wi-fi.

→ Outlets of the DC Public Library (www.dclibrary.org) offer free terminals for 15 minutes; to surf longer, you need to sign up for a free user's card.

→ For a list of wi-fi hot spots, visit Wi-Fi Free Spot (www.wififreespot.com).

Legal Matters

The blood-alcohol limit is 0.08%. Driving under the influence of alcohol or drugs is a serious offense, subject to stiff fines and even imprisonment.

Possession of illicit drugs, including cocaine, ecstasy, LSD, heroin and hashish, is a felony potentially punishable by lengthy jail sentences.

In November 2014 DC voted to legalize marijuana. The law lets residents and visitors have up to 2oz for personal use. Selling marijuana is prohibited, as is smoking in public, so it boils down to a home-grow, home-use policy and lots

of 'gift' giving. Marijuana remains illegal in parts of the city that are federal land, such as the National Mall and other National Park Service grounds. If you're caught in possession there, you could be arrested.

LGBT Travelers

DC is one of the most gay-friendly cities in the USA. It has an admirable track record of progressivism and a bit of a scene to boot. The rainbow stereotype here consists of well-dressed professionals and activists working in politics on LGBT issues such as gay marriage (legal in DC since 2010). The community concentrates in Dupont Circle, but U Street, Shaw, Capitol Hill and Logan Circle also have lots of gay-friendly businesses.

Capital Area Gay & Lesbian Chamber of Commerce (www.caglcc.org) Sponsors lots of networking events around town.

LGBT DC (https://washington.org/lgbtq) The DC tourism office's portal, with events, neighborhood breakdowns and a travel resource guide.

Metro Weekly (www.metroweekly.com) Free weekly news magazine. Aimed at a younger demographic than its rival, the *Washington Blade*.

Washington Blade (www.washingtonblade.com) Free weekly gay newspaper. Covers politics and has lots of business and nightlife listings.

Medical Services

Washington, DC, has no unexpected health dangers and excellent medical facilities.

Emergency Rooms

George Washington University Hospital (☏202-715-4000; www.gwhospital.com;

900 23rd St NW; ⊘24hr; ☏; Ⓜ Orange, Silver, Blue Lines to Foggy Bottom-GWU) Has a 24hr emergency department.

Pharmacies

The most prominent pharmacy chain is CVS, with locations all around the city. The following convenient branches are open 24 hours:

CVS Dupont Circle (☏202-785-1466; www.cvs.com; 6 Dupont Circle; ⊘24hr; Ⓜ Red Line to Dupont Circle)

CVS Thomas Circle (☏202-628-0720; 1199 Vermont Ave NW; ⊘24hr; Ⓜ McPherson Sq)

Money

The currency is the US dollar. Most locals do not carry large amounts of cash for everyday use, relying instead on credit and debit cards.

ATMs

→ ATMs are widely available at banks, airports and convenience stores

→ Most ATMs link into worldwide networks (Plus, Cirrus, Exchange etc).

→ ATMs typically charge a service fee of $3 or more per transaction, and your home bank may impose additional charges.

Credit Cards

Major credit cards are almost universally accepted. In fact, it's next to impossible to rent a car or make hotel or ticket reservations without one. Visa and MasterCard are the most widely accepted.

Money Changers

Although the airports have exchange bureaus, better rates can usually be obtained at banks in the city. **Travelex** (☏202-872-1428; www.travelex.com; 1800 K St NW;

⏰8am-6pm Mon-Fri; Ⓜ Orange, Silver, Blue Line to Farragut West) is another option.

Tipping

Tipping is not optional. Only withhold tips in cases of outrageously bad service.

Airport & hotel porters $2 per bag, minimum per cart $5

Bartenders 15% to 20% per round, minimum $1 per drink for standard drinks, $2 per specialty cocktail

Housekeeping staff $2 to $5 per night

Restaurant servers 18% to 20%, unless a gratuity is already charged on the bill

Taxi drivers 10% to 15%, rounded up to the next dollar

Parking valets $2 to $5 when you're handed back the keys

Opening Hours

Typical opening times in Washington, DC, are as follows:

Bars 5pm to 1am or 2am weekdays, 3am on weekends

Museums 10am to 5:30pm

Nightclubs 9pm to 1am or 2am weekdays, 3am or 4am on weekends

Offices & Government Agencies 9am to 5pm Monday to Friday

Restaurants Breakfast 7am or 8am to 11am; lunch 11am or 11:30am to 2:30pm; dinner 5pm or 6pm to 10pm Sunday to Thursday, to 11pm or midnight Friday and Saturday

Shops 10am to 7pm Monday to Saturday, noon to 6pm Sunday

Post

The US Postal Service (www.usps.com) is reliable and inexpensive. The postal rates for 1st-class mail with-

in the USA are 50¢ for letters up to 1oz (21¢ for each additional ounce) and 35¢ for standard-size postcards.

International airmail rates are $1.15 for a 1oz letter or postcard.

For an awesome selection of stamps for sale, go to the post-office branch in the **National Postal Museum** (Map p300; ☎202-633-5555; www.postalmuseum.si.edu; 2 Massachusetts Ave NE; ⏰10am-5:30pm; ♿; Ⓜ Red Line to Union Station) FREE.

Public Holidays

Banks, schools, offices and most shops close on these days.

New Year's Day January 1

Martin Luther King Jr Day Third Monday in January

Inauguration Day January 20, every four years

Presidents' Day Third Monday in February

Emancipation Day April 16

Memorial Day Last Monday in May

Independence Day July 4

Labor Day First Monday in September

Columbus Day Second Monday in October

Veterans Day November 11

Thanksgiving Day Fourth Thursday in November

Christmas Day December 25

Safe Travel

➡ While DC isn't dangerous, it does have typical big-city crime issues (mostly theft). Use common sense and be aware of your surroundings, especially around H St NE, Southeast DC and Anacostia.

➡ In the summer months DC boils. The humidity is outrageous, and you'll sweat buckets. Remember to stay hydrated.

➡ The Metro stops running at 11:30pm (1am on weekends). Allow more time for travel during weekends, as track maintenance work slows down trains.

Taxes & Refunds

A tax is levied on most goods and services. In DC it is 14.8% for lodgings, 10% in restaurants and bars, and 5.75% for other items. In

PRACTICALITIES

➡ **Newspapers** The daily *Washington Post* (www.washingtonpost.com) is among the nation's top newspapers. Its tabloid-format *Express* is free. The *Washington Times* (www.washingtontimes.com) is the *Post's* conservative daily competitor. *Washington City Paper* (www.washingtoncitypaper.com) is the free alternative weekly that scrutinizes DC politics and has great entertainment coverage. *Politico* (www.politico.com) is a free paper that covers DC's politics in depth.

➡ **TV** The main TV channels are Channel 4 (NBC), Channel 5 (Fox), Channel 7 (ABC) and Channel 9 (CBS).

➡ **Radio** National Public Radio (NPR) is headquartered in the District. Its programs can be found on WAMU-FM88.5.

➡ **Smoking** Washington, DC, is entirely smoke-free in restaurants, bars and workplaces.

general it's less in Virginia and Maryland. The tax typically is not included in the price, but added afterward when you pay.

Telephone

Phone numbers within the US consist of a three-digit area code followed by a seven-digit local number. In DC, you will always dial 10 numbers: ☑1 + the three-digit area code + the seven-digit number.

Cell Phones

If buying a US SIM card, you'll want to go with either AT&T or T-Mobile (or companies using their networks) as these carriers run on the GSM network, the standard used in most other countries. You may be able to preorder a card at home, or you can simply purchase one from the relevant carrier's store in Washington.

If purchasing a cheap US phone, you can also look into Verizon and Sprint, which use the CDMA network. Phones can be bought in telecom stores, drugstores, grocery stores and big retailers like Target.

If you plan on traveling outside Washington, make sure you are using AT&T or Verizon – these two carriers have the best coverage in more rural areas.

Phone Codes

US country code ☑1

DC area code ☑202

Making international calls Dial ☑011 + country code + area code + local number.

Calling other US area codes or Canada Dial ☑1 + three-digit area code + seven-digit local number.

Calling within DC Dial ☑1 + three-digit area code + seven-digit local number.

Directory assistance nationwide ☑411

Toll-free numbers ☑1+ 800 (or 888, 877, 866) + seven-digit number. Some toll-free numbers only work within the US.

Phone Cards

Private prepaid phone cards are available from convenience stores, grocery stores and pharmacies. AT&T sells a reliable card that is widely available.

Time

DC is in the Eastern Standard Time (EST) zone, five hours behind Greenwich Mean Time (London) and three hours ahead of Pacific Standard Time (Los Angeles). DC, like almost all of the USA, observes daylight saving time: clocks go forward one hour from the second Sunday in March to the first Sunday in November, when the clocks are turned back one hour.

Toilets

The Mall has 10 public bathrooms, including those at the Lincoln Memorial, Jefferson Memorial, Martin Luther King Jr Memorial and Washington Monument. You can also dash into any of the Smithsonian museums to use their facilities, though you'll have to go through the security line to enter the building.

Tourist Information

Destination DC (☑202-789-7000; www.washington.org) DC's official tourism site, with the mother lode of online information.

Smithsonian Visitor Center (Map p294;☑202-663-1000; www.si.edu/visit; 1000 Jefferson Dr SW; ☺8:30am-5:30pm; ☞; ☐Circulator, ⓂOrange, Silver, Blue Line to Smithso-

nian) Located in the castle, it is a great resource with a staffed information desk and everything you ever wanted to know about the museum programs.

NPS Ellipse Visitor Pavilion (Map p296;☑202-208-1631; www.nps.gov; ☺7:30am-4pm; ⓂOrange, Silver, Blue Line to Federal Triangle) Has a staffed information desk and sells snacks; located at the northeast corner of the Ellipse, south of the White House.

Travelers with Disabilities

DC is well equipped for travelers with disabilities:

➡ Most museums and major sights are wheelchair accessible, as are most large hotels and restaurants.

➡ All Metro trains and buses are accessible to people in wheelchairs. All Metro stations have elevators, and guide dogs are allowed on trains and buses.

➡ All DC transit companies offer travel discounts for disabled travelers.

➡ Hindrances to wheelchair users include buckled-brick sidewalks in the historic blocks of Georgetown and Capitol Hill, but sidewalks in most other parts of DC are in good shape.

➡ All Smithsonian museums have free wheelchair loans and can arrange special tours for hearing-impaired visitors. See www.si.edu/visit/visitorswith-disabilities for more.

➡ Hearing-impaired visitors should check out **Gallaudet University** (off Map p312; ☑202-651-5000; www.gallaudet.edu; 800 Florida Ave NE; ⓂRed Line to NoMa) in northeast DC, which hosts lectures and cultural events especially for the deaf.

➡ See also Lonely Planet's accessible travel resources guide: https://shop.lonelyplanet.com/

products/accessible-travel-online-resources-2017.

Visas

The Visa Waiver Program (VWP) allows nationals from some 38 countries (including most EU countries, Japan, Australia and New Zealand) to enter the US without a visa for up to 90 days.

VWP visitors require an e-passport (with electronic chip) and approval under the Electronic System For Travel Authorization at least three days before arrival. There is a $14 fee for processing and authorization (payable online). Once approved, the registration is valid for two years.

Those who need a visa – ie anyone staying longer than 90 days, or from a non-VWP country – should apply at the US consulate in their home country. Check with the US Department of State (www.travel.state.gov) for updates and details on entry requirements.

Volunteering

Anacostia Watershed Society (www.anacostiaws.org) Volunteers help restore wetlands, plant native plants and collect seeds. Check the events calendar for days/times.

Capital Area Food Bank (www.capitalareafoodbank.org) and **DC Central Kitchen** (www.dccentralkitchen.org) Opportunities to help prepare meals and sort and pack food donations.

Behind the Scenes

SEND US YOUR FEEDBACK

We love to hear from travelers – your comments keep us on our toes and help make our books better. Our well-traveled team reads every word on what you loved or loathed about this book. Although we cannot reply individually to your submissions, we always guarantee that your feedback goes straight to the appropriate authors, in time for the next edition. Each person who sends us information is thanked in the next edition – the most useful submissions are rewarded with a selection of digital PDF chapters.

Visit **lonelyplanet.com/contact** to submit your updates and suggestions or to ask for help. Our award-winning website also features inspirational travel stories, news and discussions.

Note: We may edit, reproduce and incorporate your comments in Lonely Planet products such as guidebooks, websites and digital products, so let us know if you don't want your comments reproduced or your name acknowledged. For a copy of our privacy policy visit lonelyplanet.com/privacy.

WRITER THANKS

Karla Zimmerman

Deep appreciation to all of the locals who spilled the beans on their favorite places. Special thanks to Kate Armstrong, Virginia Maxwell, Ryan Ver Berkmoes, Amy Schwenkmeyer and Bill Brockschmidt. Thanks most to Eric Markowitz, the world's best partner-for-life, who kindly indulges my Abe Lincoln fixation. You top my Best List.

Virginia Maxwell

Thanks to DC locals Barbara Balman and Bob Bresnahan for their convivial company and insider tips; to Trisha Ping for giving me the gig and supplying interesting leads; to DC expert Karla Zimmerman; and to traveling companions Eveline Zoutendijk, George Grundy and Ryan Ver Berkmoes. At home in Australia, thanks and much love to Peter Handsaker, who coped with apartment renovation chaos and didn't blame me for my absence (well, not too much).

ACKNOWLEDGEMENTS

Climate map data adapted from Peel MC, Finlayson BL & McMahon TA (2007) 'Updated World Map of the Köppen-Geiger Climate Classification', Hydrology and Earth System Sciences, 11, 163344.

Illustrations p64-5 & p80-1 by Javier Zarracina

Cover photograph: Statue of Thomas Jefferson, Jefferson Memorial, Holly Looney / AWL ©

THIS BOOK

This 7th edition of Lonely Planet's *Washington, DC* guidebook was researched and written by Karla Zimmerman and Virginia Maxwell, with contributions by Amy Balfour. The previous two editions were also written by Karla and Regis St Louis. This guidebook was produced by the following:

Destination Editor Trisha Ping

Senior Product Editors Kate Mathews, Vicky Smith

Product Editor Amanda Williamson

Senior Cartographers Mark Griffiths, Alison Lyall

Book Designer Virginia Moreno˙

Assisting Editors Jacqueline Danam, Emma Gibbs, Carly Hall, Victoria Harrison, Alison Morris, Rosie Nicholson, Charlotte Orr, Monique Perrin, Simon Williamson

Cover Researcher Nicholas Colicchia

Thanks to Steen Ballegaard, Imogen Bannister, James Hardy, PST, Alison Ridgway, Ross Taylor, Rob Vine, Brana Vladisavljevic, Sheila Wilson

See also separate subindexes for:

🍴 **EATING P287**

🍷 **DRINKING & NIGHTLIFE P288**

⭐ **ENTERTAINMENT P289**

🛍 **SHOPPING P289**

🏃 **SPORTS & ACTIVITIES P290**

🛏 **SLEEPING P290**

Index

Sights 000
Map Pages **000**
Photo Pages **000**

Washington, DC Maps

Sights

- Beach
- Bird Sanctuary
- Buddhist
- Castle/Palace
- Christian
- Confucian
- Hindu
- Islamic
- Jain
- Jewish
- Monument
- Museum/Gallery/Historic Building
- Ruin
- Shinto
- Sikh
- Taoist
- Winery/Vineyard
- Zoo/Wildlife Sanctuary
- Other Sight

Activities, Courses & Tours

- Bodysurfing
- Diving
- Canoeing/Kayaking
- Course/Tour
- Sento Hot Baths/Onsen
- Skiing
- Snorkeling
- Surfing
- Swimming/Pool
- Walking
- Windsurfing
- Other Activity

Sleeping

- Sleeping
- Camping

Eating

- Eating

Drinking & Nightlife

- Drinking & Nightlife
- Cafe

Entertainment

- Entertainment

Shopping

- Shopping

Information

- Bank
- Embassy/Consulate
- Hospital/Medical
- Internet
- Police
- Post Office
- Telephone
- Toilet
- Tourist Information
- Other Information

Geographic

- Beach
- Gate
- Hut/Shelter
- Lighthouse
- Lookout
- Mountain/Volcano
- Oasis
- Park
- Pass
- Picnic Area
- Waterfall

Population

- Capital (National)
- Capital (State/Province)
- City/Large Town
- Town/Village

Transport

- Airport
- BART station
- Border crossing
- Boston T station
- Bus
- Cable car/Funicular
- Cycling
- Ferry
- Metro/Muni station
- Monorail
- Parking
- Petrol station
- Subway/SkyTrain station
- Taxi
- Train station/Railway
- Tram
- Underground station
- Other Transport

Note: Not all symbols displayed above appear on the maps in this book

Routes

- Tollway
- Freeway
- Primary
- Secondary
- Tertiary
- Lane
- Unsealed road
- Road under construction
- Plaza/Mall
- Steps
- Tunnel
- Pedestrian overpass
- Walking Tour
- Walking Tour detour
- Path/Walking Trail

Boundaries

- International
- State/Province
- Disputed
- Regional/Suburb
- Marine Park
- Cliff
- Wall

Hydrography

- River, Creek
- Intermittent River
- Canal
- Water
- Dry/Salt/Intermittent Lake
- Reef

Areas

- Airport/Runway
- Beach/Desert
- Cemetery (Christian)
- Cemetery (Other)
- Glacier
- Mudflat
- Park/Forest
- Sight (Building)
- Sportsground
- Swamp/Mangrove

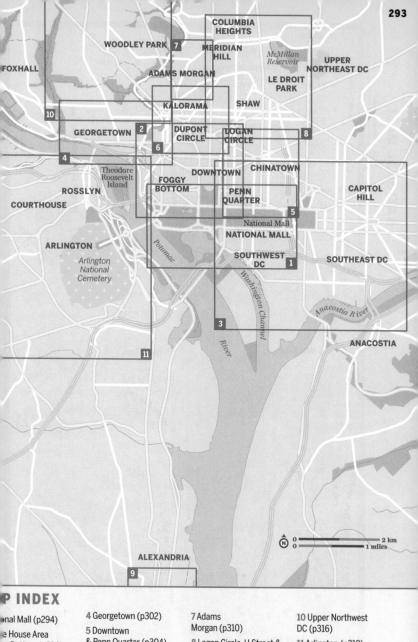

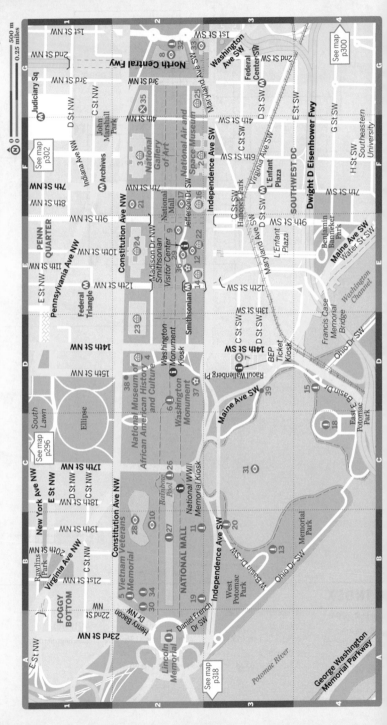

NATIONAL MALL

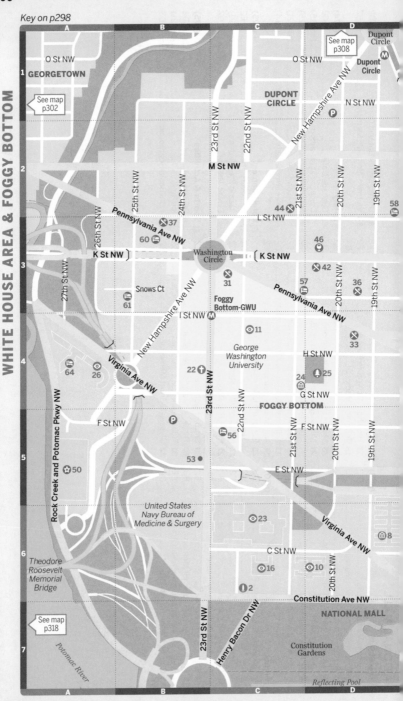

WHITE HOUSE AREA & FOGGY BOTTOM

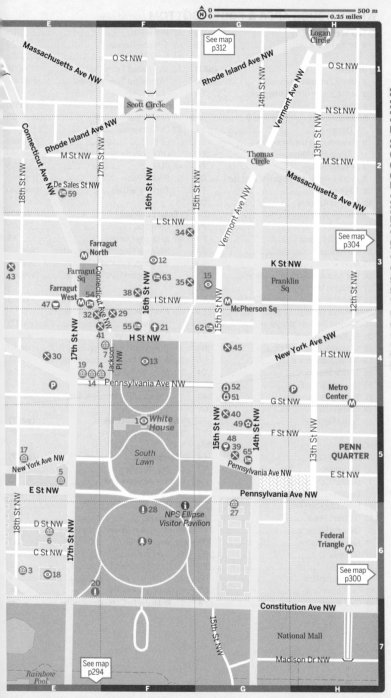

WHITE HOUSE AREA & FOGGY BOTTOM *Map on p296*

CAPITOL HILL & SOUTH DC *Map on p300*

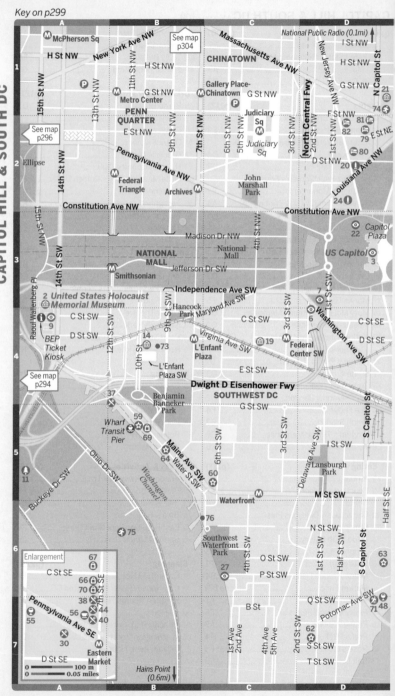

CAPITOL HILL & SOUTH DC

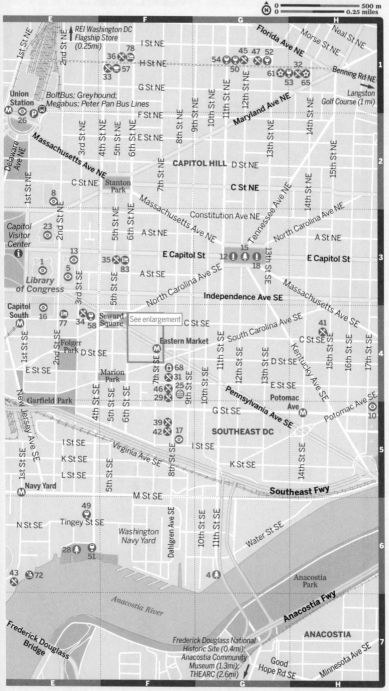

GEORGETOWN

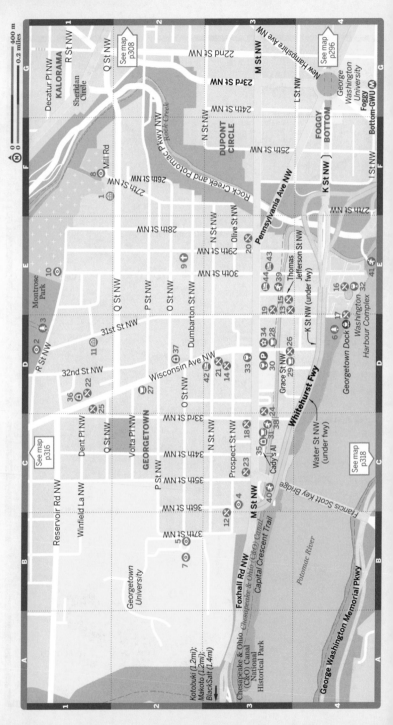

N 0 — 400 m
0 — 0.2 miles

See map p308

See map p296

See map p316

See map p318

KALORAMA

Decatur Pl NW

R St NW

Sheridan Circle

Q St NW

22nd St NW

New Hampshire Ave NW

M St NW

23rd St NW

24th St NW

N St NW

25th St NW

DUPONT CIRCLE

Mill Rd

27th St NW

26th St NW

Rock Creek and Potomac Pkwy NW

Rock Creek

28th St NW

29th St NW

Olive St NW

N St NW

30th St NW

Pennsylvania Ave NW

Thomas Jefferson St NW

K St NW

27th St NW

FOGGY BOTTOM

George Washington University

Foggy Bottom-GWU

L St NW

I St NW

Montrose Park

31st St NW

R St NW

Dumbarton St NW

K St NW (under fwy)

Georgetown Dock

Washington Harbour Complex

GEORGETOWN

Wisconsin Ave NW

32nd St NW

33rd St NW

Q St NW

Dent Pl NW

Volta Pl NW

P St NW

O St NW

N St NW

Grace St NW

Whitehurst Fwy

Water St NW (under fwy)

Reservoir Rd NW

Winfield La NW

34th St NW

35th St NW

36th St NW

37th St NW

Prospect St NW

Cady's Al

M St NW

Francis Scott Key Bridge

Foxhall Rd NW

Georgetown University

Chesapeake & Ohio (C&O) Canal
Capital Crescent Trail

Potomac River

George Washington Memorial Pkwy

Kotobuki (1.2mi);
Makoto (1.2mi);
BlackSalt (1.4mi)

Chesapeake & Ohio (C&O) Canal National Historical Park

DOWNTOWN & PENN QUARTER

0 0
N
0.25 miles
500 m

See map p312

See map p308

New York Ave Playground

New York Ave NW

New Jersey Ave NW

North Central Fwy

Vermont Ave NW

Thomas Circle

14th St NW

Green Ct NW

L St NW

14th St NW

Franklin Sq

H St NW

13th St NW

12th St NW

11th St NW

M St NW

N St NW

O St NW

9th St NW

8th St NW

7th St NW

6th St NW

Mt Vernon Sq/7th St Convention Center

Mt Vernon Sq

L St NW

7th St NW

New York Ave NW

L St NW

5th St NW

4th St NW

3rd St NW

K St NW

I St NW

H St NW

Massachusetts Ave NW

CHINATOWN

New York Ave NW

Massachusetts Ave NW

DOWNTOWN

K St NW

I St NW

H St NW

L St NW

I St NW

8th St NW

9th St NW

Blagden Al

DOWNTOWN

59

20

24

41

34

31

3
66
37
8

35

45

19

56

18

60

61

62

65

29

43
48
46
27
9

23

22

13

25

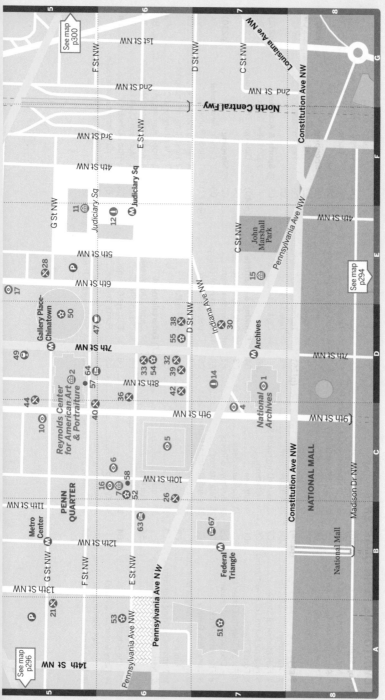

DOWNTOWN & PENN QUARTER Map on p304

DUPONT CIRCLE & KALORAMA *Map on p308*

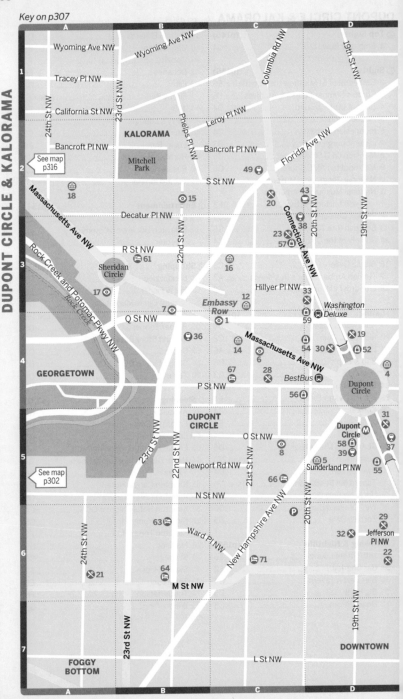

DUPONT CIRCLE & KALORAMA

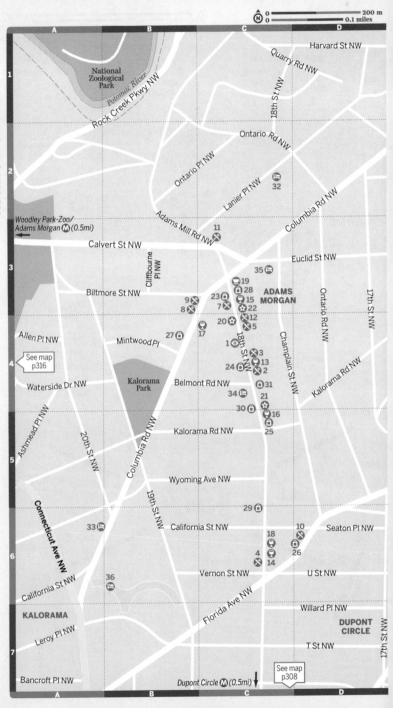

KALORAMA

ADAMS MORGAN

DUPONT CIRCLE

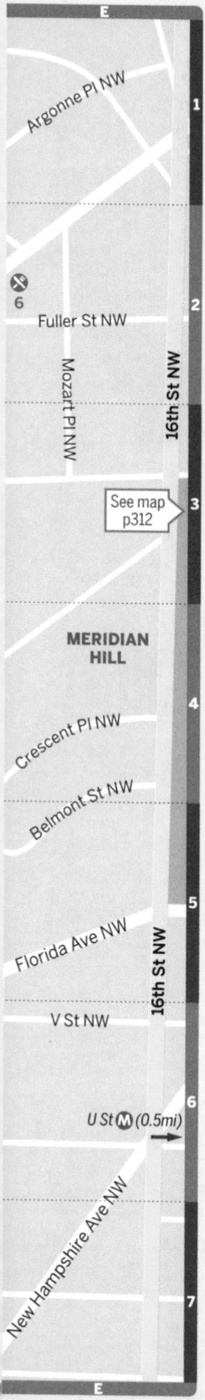

ADAMS MORGAN

See map
p312

Argonne Pl NW

Fuller St NW

Mozart Pl NW

16th St NW

MERIDIAN
HILL

Crescent Pl NW

Belmont St NW

Florida Ave NW

16th St NW

V St NW

U St Ⓜ (0.5mi)

New Hampshire Ave NW

LOGAN CIRCLE, U STREET & COLUMBIA HEIGHTS

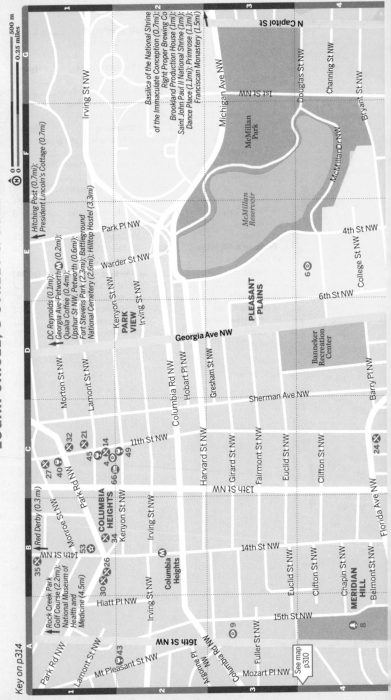

Key on p314

N

0   500 m
0   0.25 miles

Hitching Post (0.7mi);
President Lincoln's Cottage (0.7mi)

Basilica of the National Shrine
of the Immaculate Conception (0.7mi);
Right Proper Brewing Co
Brookland Production House (1mi);
Saint John Paul II National Shrine (1mi);
Dance Place (1.1mi); Primrose (1.1mi);
Franciscan Monastery (1.5mi)

N Capitol St

DC Reynolds (0.1mi);
Georgia Ave-Petworth Ⓜ (0.2mi);
Qualia Coffee (0.4mi);
Upshur St NW, Petworth (0.6mi);
Fort Stevens Park (2.3mi); Battleground
National Cemetery (2.6mi); Hilltop Hostel (3.3mi)

Rock Creek Park
Golf Course (2.2mi);
National Museum of
Health and
Medicine (4.5mi)

Red Derby (0.3mi)

See map
p310

Park Rd NW
Lamont St NW
Mt Pleasant St NW
Mozart Pl NW
Columbia Rd NW
Argonne Pl NW
16th St NW
Fuller St NW
15th St NW
Euclid St NW
Clifton St NW
Chapin St NW
Belmont St NW
Florida Ave NW
Irving St NW
Hiatt Pl NW
14th St NW
Monroe St NW
Park Rd NW
Morton St NW
Lamont St NW
Kenyon St NW
Irving St NW
11th St NW
Columbia Rd NW
Hobart Pl NW
Gresham St NW
Sherman Ave NW
13th St NW
Harvard St NW
Girard St NW
Fairmont St NW
Euclid St NW
Clifton St NW
Barry Pl NW
Warder St NW
Kenyon St NW
Irving St NW
Georgia Ave NW
6th St NW
College St NW
4th St NW
Park Pl NW
Michigan Ave NW
1st St NW
McMillan Dr NW
Douglas St NW
Channing St NW
Bryant St NW
Irving St NW

COLUMBIA
HEIGHTS

PARK
VIEW

PLEASANT
PLAINS

MERIDIAN
HILL

Banneker
Recreation
Center

McMillan Park

McMillan
Reservoir

Columbia
Heights Ⓜ

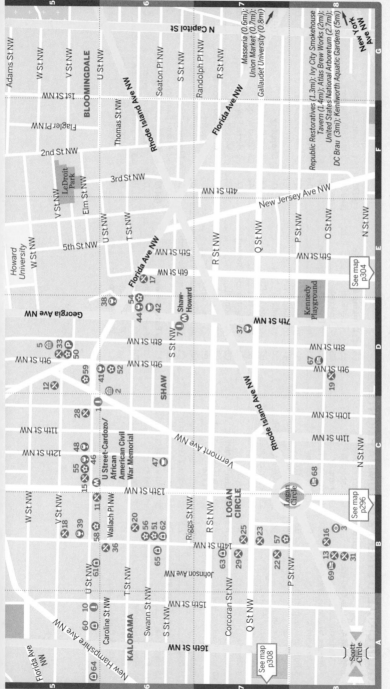

Republic Restoratives (1.3mi); Ivy City Smokehouse
Tavern (1.4mi); Atlas Brew Works (2mi);
United States National Arboretum (2.7mi);
DC Brau (3mi); Kenilworth Aquatic Gardens (5mi)

Masseria (0.6mi);
Union Market (0.7mi);
Gallaudet University (0.8mi)

New York
Ave NW

BLOOMINGDALE

Adams St NW
W St NW
V St NW
U St NW

1st St NW
Flagler Pl NW
2nd St NW
Thomas St NW

Seaton Pl NW
S St NW

Randolph Pl NW
R St NW

N Capitol St

Florida Ave NW

LeDroit
Park
V St NW
Elm St NW
3rd St NW
4th St NW

New Jersey Ave NW

Howard
University
W St NW
5th St NW
U St NW
T St NW
Florida Ave NW
6th St NW

R St NW
Q St NW
P St NW
O St NW
N St NW

5th St NW

Georgia Ave NW

See map
p304

Kennedy
Playground

38
54
44
42
17

7
Shaw–
Howard

37
7th St NW

8th St NW
9th St NW

Q St NW

33
5
50

59
12
41
52
2

SHAW

S St NW
8th St NW
9th St NW

19
67
9th St NW
8th St NW

10th St NW
11th St NW
N St NW

28
11th St NW
12th St NW

U Street–Cardozo/
African
American Civil
War Memorial

1
47

Rhode Island Ave NW

Vermont Ave NW

68
See map
p296

48
55
15
46

13th St NW

LOGAN
CIRCLE

Logan
Circle

Scott
Circle

18
39
11
58
36

Wallach Pl NW
20
56
51
62

Riggs St NW
R St NW

25
23
57
16
3

W St NW
V St NW

U St NW
61
65

T St NW
Johnson Ave NW

14th St NW

63
29
22
69
13
31

15th St NW
Corcoran St NW
S St NW
Q St NW

60
10
64

Caroline St NW
Swann St NW

KALORAMA

16th St NW

See map
p308

New Hampshire Ave NW

Florida Ave
NW

LOGAN CIRCLE, U STREET & COLUMBIA HEIGHTS

LOGAN CIRCLE, U STREET & COLUMBIA HEIGHTS Map on p312

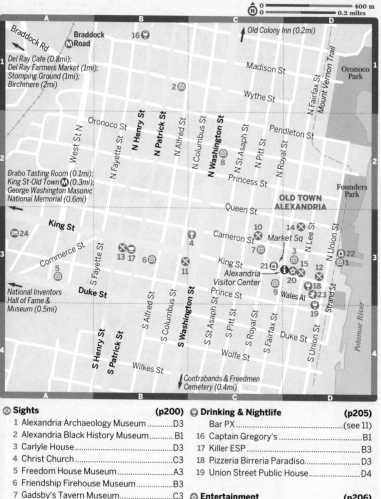

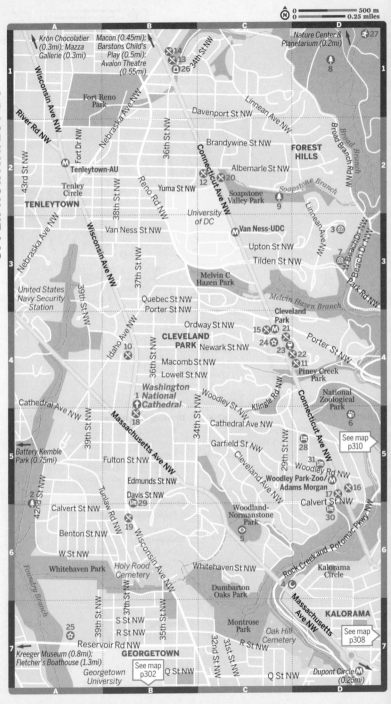

Krön Chocolatier (0.3mi); Mazza Gallerie (0.3mi)

Macon (0.45mi); Barstons Child's Play (0.5mi); Avalon Theatre (0.55mi)

Nature Center & Planetarium (0.2mi)

Wisconsin Ave NW

River Rd NW

Fort Reno Park

Nebraska Ave NW

Davenport St NW

Linnean Ave NW

FOREST HILLS

Broad Branch Rd NW

Broad Branch

Fort Dr NW

43rd St NW

Tenleytown-AU

TENLEYTOWN

Tenley Circle

Nebraska Ave NW

Wisconsin Ave NW

36th St NW

Reno Rd NW

Brandywine St NW

Connecticut Ave NW

Albemarle St NW

Yuma St NW

University of DC

Soapstone Valley Park

Soapstone Branch

Van Ness St NW

Van Ness-UDC

Upton St NW

Tilden St NW

M Beach Dr NW

Park Rd NW

38th St NW

37th St NW

United States Navy Security Station

39th St NW

Idaho Ave NW

Melvin C Hazen Park

Melvin Hazen Branch

Quebec St NW

Porter St NW

Ordway St NW

CLEVELAND PARK

Newark St NW

Macomb St NW

Lowell St NW

Cleveland Park

Porter St NW

Piney Creek Park

36th St NW

Washington National Cathedral

Cathedral Ave NW

Massachusetts Ave NW

Woodley St NW

Klingle Rd NW

Cleveland Ave NW

National Zoological Park

See map p310

Cathedral Ave NW

Garfield St NW

39th St NW

Battery Kemble Park (0.75mi)

42nd St NW

Fulton St NW

Edmunds St NW

Davis St NW

Calvert St NW

Tunlaw Rd NW

Benton St NW

W St NW

Whitehaven Park

Foundry Branch

Holy Rood Cemetery

Wisconsin Ave NW

Whitehaven St NW

Dumbarton Oaks Park

Woodland-Normanstone Park

29th St NW

Woodley Rd NW

Woodley Park-Zoo/ Adams Morgan

Calvert St NW

Kalorama Circle

Rock Creek and Potomac Pkwy

KALORAMA

Massachusetts Ave NW

See map p308

Kreeger Museum (0.8mi); Fletcher's Boathouse (1.3mi)

25

39th St NW

37th St NW

S St NW

R St NW

Reservoir Rd NW

GEORGETOWN

See map p302

Georgetown University

Montrose Park

Oak Hill Cemetery

35th St NW

32nd St NW

31st St NW

Q St NW

Q St NW

Dupont Circle (0.25mi)

UPPER NORTHWEST DC

24th St N

George Washington Memorial Pkwy

Lorcom La

Spout Run Pkwy

22nd St N

Custis Memorial Pkwy

N Quinn St

19

Vamoose Bus

N Key Blvd

18th St N

N Fort Myer Dr

Rosslyn

Lee Hwy

N Adams St

N Veitch St

N Troy St

N Rhodes St

Wilson Blvd

Clarendon Blvd

16th Rd N

ROSSLYN

N Key Blvd

N Curtis Rd

20

16th St N

N Meade St

N Fillmore St

COURTHOUSE

Court House

15th St N

9

N Highland St

Wilson Blvd

14th St N

N Courthouse Rd

N Troy St

Arlington Blvd

24

N Fairfax Dr

Marshall Dr

23

Washington & Old Dominion Trail (3.3mi)

Clarendon

21

CLARENDON

VIRGINIA

18

Wilson Blvd

10th St N

N Barton St

Jackson Ave

Sheridan Dr

N Irving St

9th St N

N Cleveland St

N Danville St

Fort Myer

McNair Rd

4

14 10

Buzz Bakeshop (0.4mi)

N Highland St

Washington Blvd

N Pershing Dr

Arlington Blvd

Meigs Dr

ARLINGTON

Mc Clellan Dr

N Kenmore St

N Ivy St

N Pershing Dr

2nd Rd N

N Filmore St

Wainwright Rd

Sheridan Ave

Wilson Dr

5

Roosevelt Dr

Grant Dr

1st St N

6

16

15

Columbia Gardens Cemetery

Arlington Blvd

Porter Dr

Clayton Dr

1st Rd S

S Wayne St

S Irving St

S Garfield St

2nd St S

Grant Dr

Southgate Rd

S Glebe Rd

6th St S

S Highland St

S Filmore St

S Barton St

8th S

Washington Blvd

Columbia Pike

7th St S

8th St S

22

12th St S

S Rolfe St

Army Navy Country Club

Columbia Pike

S Walter Reed Dr

Fort Ward Museum & Historic Site (3.3mi)

ARLINGTON

Our Story

A beat-up old car, a few dollars in the pocket and a sense of adventure. In 1972 that's all Tony and Maureen Wheeler needed for the trip of a lifetime – across Europe and Asia overland to Australia. It took several months, and at the end – broke but inspired – they sat at their kitchen table writing and stapling together their first travel guide, *Across Asia on the Cheap*. Within a week they'd sold 1500 copies. Lonely Planet was born.

Today, Lonely Planet has offices in Franklin, London, Melbourne, Oakland, Dublin, Beijing and Delhi, with more than 600 staff and writers. We share Tony's belief that 'a great guidebook should do three things: inform, educate and amuse'.

Our Writers

Karla Zimmerman

Adams Morgan, Capitol Hill & South DC, Downtown & Penn Quarter, Dupont Circle & Kalorama, Georgetown, Logan Circle, U Street & Columbia Heights Karla lives in Chicago, where she eats doughnuts, yells at the Cubs, and writes stuff for books, magazines, and websites when she's not doing the first two things. She has contributed to 40-plus guidebooks and travel anthologies covering destinations in Europe, Asia, Africa, North America, and the Caribbean – all of which are a long way from the early days, when she wrote about gravel for a construction magazine and got to trek to places like Fredonia, Kansas. To learn more, follow her @karlazimmerman on Instagram and Twitter. Karla also wrote the Plan, Understand and Survival Guide chapters.

Virginia Maxwell

Leesburg & Middleburg, National Mall, Northern Virginia, Shenandoah National Park, Upper Northwest DC, White House & Foggy Bottom Although based in Australia, Virginia spends at least half of her year updating Lonely Planet destination coverage across the globe. Though the Mediterranean is her major area of interest – she has covered Spain, Italy, Turkey, Syria, Lebanon, Israel, Egypt and Mo̶̶̶̶̶̶ ̶̶̶̶̶̶̶̶̶̶̶̶̶ ̶̶̶̶̶̶̶̶ ̶̶̶̶vers Finland, Armenia, the United States and Austra̶̶̶̶̶̶̶̶̶̶̶̶̶̶̶̶̶̶̶̶̶̶̶̶̶̶̶̶̶̶̶̶̶̶̶̶nia on Instagram and Twitter.

Contributing Writer

Amy Balfour (Annapolis, Baltimore, Harpers F̶̶̶

Published by Lonely Planet Global Limited
CRN 554153
7th edition – November 2018
ISBN 978 1 78657 181 6
© Lonely Planet 2018   Photographs © as indicated 2018
10 9 8 7 6 5 4 3 2 1
Printed in Singapore

Although the authors and Lonely Planet have taken all reasonable care in preparing this book, we make no warranty about the accuracy or completeness of its content and, to the maximum extent permitted, disclaim all liability arising from its use.